also by Tom Manoff

The Music Kit

MUSIC:
a living language

TOM MANOFF

W·W· Norton & Company
New York

Library of Congress Cataloging in Publication Data

Manoff, Tom.
    Music: a living language.

    1. Music—Analysis, appreciation. I. Title.
MT6.M267M9   780'.1'5   81-22346
ISBN 0-393-95194-4   AACR2

W. W. Norton & Company, Inc. 500 Fifth Avenue, New York, N. Y. 10110
W. W. Norton & Company Ltd. 37 Great Russell Street, London WC1B 3NU

1 2 3 4 5 6 7 8 9 0

In memory of my mother

. . . *and our ancient family line*
the wind's smoke, the sun's shadow

—MICHELANGELO

Acknowledgments

P. 133: Transcription of *Viderunt omnes* by Edward Roesner.

P. 165: Text for *Nuper rosarum flores* from *Norton Anthology of Western Music*, Vol. I, edited by Claude Palisca (New York: W. W. Norton, 1980).

P. 173: Translation of *Pase el agoa* by Lawrence Rosenwald from *Pleasure of the Royal Court* H-71326, © 1976. Nonesuch Records, A Division of Warner Communications Inc.

Pp. 185,186: Two excerpts from the musical *West Side Story* lyrics by Stephen Sondheim © 1957, 1959 by Leonard Bernstein and Stephen Sondheim. G. Schirmer Inc. Chappell and Co. Inc. Music Publishers.

P. 299: Translation of *Lied der Mignon* by Philip L. Miller in his *The Ring of Words: An Anthology of Song Texts* (New York: W.W. Norton, 1973).

P. 335: Translation of *Rastlose Liebe* from *The Book of the Hanging Gardens* by Steven Ledbetter, H-71320 © 1975. Nonesuch Records, A Division of Warner Communications Inc.

P. 409: Translation of *Dividido el corazón* reprinted from *Dark and Light in Spanish New Mexico: Alabados and Bailes* courtesy of New World Records.

Pp. 419-20: Discussion of *Appalachian Spring* with permission of Aaron Copland.

P. 422: Excerpt from Elliott Carter's notes from *Double Concerto* H-71314 © 1975. Nonesuch Records, A Division of Warner Communications Inc.

P. 440: *Banquet* from *For the Roses*, © 1972 Crazy Crow Music. Used by Permission. All rights reserved.

P. 440: *Judgment of the Moon and Stars* from *For the Roses*, © 1972 Crazy Crow Music. Used by permission. All rights reserved.

P. 441: Quote from *Shadows and Light*, © 1975 Crazy Crow Music. Used by permission. All rights reserved.

Pp. 442,443: *Amelia* from *Hejira*, © 1976 Crazy Crow Music. Used by permission. All rights reserved.

Contents

4 Music as a Universal Art, 95

5 Overview of Span I, 123

13 The Full Impact of Modernism: Overview of Span II, 345

14 American Music, 374

15 Toward a World Musical Language, 441

Appendices

Index, 513

Preface

Some years ago, as this book was beginning to take shape, a student said something to me I shall never forget. The scene was a typical college class-room; the occasion—"Music Appreciation." The music the class had just heard, and now the topic of discussion, was a traditional Anglo-Celtic ballad whose lineage is traced to Renaissance England and beyond to the dimly remembered culture of ancient Europe. Passed on along a human chain from singer to singer, it was rediscovered in the Appalachian moun-tains of the southern United States. Recorded by the great folksinger Jean Ritchie, it now reached across time and space into that room. The student, who was hearing it for the first time, seemed quite moved. In retrospect, perhaps I should not have intruded upon that moment, but as teachers are apt to do, I was trying to establish a connection that seemed tangible in words—a connection we could all write down in our books and carry away as proof of an hour well spent. Such is the style of our culture. When asked to comment, the student said simply, "There's nothing I can say about this song—I'm living it." In the silence that followed, some of us resonated with that tiny, awesome moment, while others shifted uncomfortably in their chairs, and still others, oblivious to it all, continued their secret ponderings of computer programs, misplayed basketball shots, and Friday night adven-tures. But it seemed to me that all that music can ever be had been revealed. There is nothing more than this, I thought. I still think so.

This book is meant to prepare the way for such moments, an attempt to deepen the meaning of such experiences through a living language of music.

I have many people to thank for their help with this project. My research assistants: Frank Reedmont, Cindy Jorgensen, Joshua Wallerstein,

Roberta Smythe, Jan Lundy, Karen Nestvold, Elvira James, Laura Giosh, and Mary McIntyre Bentley cheerfully executed their often tedious assignments with efficiency and enthusiasm. Morette Rider, Dean of the School of Music at the University of Oregon, earned my deep gratitude by allowing me to test my ideas in the classroom. For their participation in the recordings, I thank Meg Casell, Dinah Urell, and Jill Talve. Dr. Steven Dubovsky contributed generously to the ideas about human behavior that underlie the essential philosophy of this book. In addition, I am grateful to the following people for their time and expertise in various matters: Harold Schonberg, Ben Heller, Siegmund Levarie, Ernest McClain, Barry Brook, Alan Lomax, Neil Waltzer, and Jean Ritchie. Important additions to the manuscript were thoughtfully suggested by Allan Atlas, Timothy McGee, Robert Werner, and Clifford E. Watkins. Mr. and Mrs. William Riering provided warm hospitality during my extended trips to New York. I wish to thank Ray Morse, not only for teaching from the manuscript in its formative stages, but also for his invaluable advice and aid during the past few years. Ralph Bentley drew the diagrams and illustrations in record time. Don Hazeltine created the pictures for *Damnation of Faust*. Kathy Wilson of W. W. Norton was a life-saver during the hectic prepublication period. I also would like to thank Larry Lockwood, Ray Freedman, and Elizabeth Davis.

Finally, I could not have finished this book without the contributions of Robert Trotter, whose quiet, brilliant life's work greatly affected almost every page; Hinda Keller Farber, whose extraordinary ability to make all the details fit together was a godsend; Claire Brook, my editor at W. W. Norton, who has nurtured this book through good times and bad, with a firm and loving hand; and my wife Susan, for putting up with far more than was fair to ask.

Foreword

Remember the child who said, "The trouble with history is that nobody lives for more than two pages"? In many introductory music texts, facts march along in splendid isolation, confounding the student with their seeming irrelevance. What Tom Manoff has done in this exciting new book is to find patterns that connect. In a time when those connections often don't happen, it is marvelous to discover someone who succeeds in making them clear and gives them first priority. To help young, inquiring minds discover various connections between themselves and history seems worthwhile, but there is a necessary prior goal: that students become aware of the *idea* of connections, that connections do exist, and that seeking them can enhance life.

There is, in our time, an explosion of available information and sensation, generally considered to be unprecedented. Becoming an educated adult today is to face drowning. Raw sensations are cheap; abstract information is cheaper. Finding the pattern that connects one thing to another might indeed become a motto for teaching today. Pairs of urgently needed connections tumble out: between feeling and thought; between playfulness and seriousness—or as Auden put it, between "carnival and prayer"; between instruction and behavior; between behavior and attitudes; between heritage and change. . . . All the information in this text aims at such connections. It goes even deeper; because of its organization, its format, its choices of music and people and ideas to pay attention to, its prescribed activities, it can awaken the desire to be always on the alert for those connections. And despite what is new here, traditional material is presented so as to affirm the best virtues of that tradition.

Like many introductory texts in music listening, this one combines prose, graphic analogues, and recordings. The prose offers potentially useful information—actually less sheer bulk than most such texts, but selected with more concern for its relevance, from more angles than I've seen before. It offers selective details to serve as models for understanding experiences beyond those offered in the text. In choosing pairs of contemporaneous composers such as Berlioz and Mendelssohn, or Wagner and Brahms, the author takes advantage of an important instructional principle: use comparisons to make each one of the contrasted pair more vivid. Further, each pair comes from a common enough time-frame to make clear how any given period can bring forth different kinds of creativity.

When the presentation of an idea, of a relationship, defies the linear logic of prose, the author recognizes the difficulty and presents a vivid graphic analogue. Such analogues can burn themselves into memory with their dramatic imagery. Even more important, they can show at a glance the flux of connections, in a dance beyond words.

Both the prose and the graphic analogues, imaginative as they are, can become throwaways, false anchors, unless they bridge the gap between instructor and students, between the world of words and the world of musical sound-beyond-words. The recorded examples include several types chosen to accomplish these bridges. There is a breathtaking, global variety of complete pieces and excerpts, from many places and times, many aspects of the human spirit. Along with a single demonstration melody, variously treated, they serve specific purposes. For example, a sequence of ostinato pieces brings into relationship a piece by Stravinsky with examples from Bali, sub-Saharan Africa, and jazz; a sequence of chants relates American Indian, Vedic, Gregorian, and Hebridean pieces. Further, they exemplify constantly the search for connections, as they return again and again, becoming touchstones for various instructional aims.

Almost more than anything else, I am happy to find here a strong conviction, consistently expressed, in the validity of *all* musical styles. To some who study this text, it may seem an abdication of responsibility to hold such a position; I am convinced that many will be relieved finally to discover confirmation for their similar convictions—it is clearly an idea whose time has come. The fatal flaw in any alternative position is that it is likely to set up an adversarial pattern: "*My* music is good; *their* music is bad" (fill in either "Mozart" or "punk rock" in either half of that statement).

I am confident that anyone involved in a sustained study of this book, and the recorded musical examples offered with it, will experience a deep shift in awareness, so that details of experience and behavior outside the classroom can take on additional meaning, as mere raw material for the *real* agenda, finding the pattern that connects.

Prof. Robert Trotter
University of Oregon

Introduction

Listen Sequence 1 (Side 1, Pieces 1a, 1b, 1c, and 1d. See record box for an explanation of band format.)

There are four separate pieces in Sequence 1. Listen to all of them without pause. We shall be considering, in a general way, differences and similarities among these selections.

Listening Beyond Style

Sequence 1 is intended to demonstrate certain basic principles that affect your response to music. As you may have noticed, the sequence consists of a variety of musical styles. Style is easier to experience than to define. Most people don't need a definition to recognize familiar musical styles like "classical," "country," "jazz," or "rock." The style designation of these pieces appears in the diagram below. Musical style has a powerful affect on the listener. Sometimes, mere recognition is sufficient to trigger an immediate positive or negative response. To this extent, musical style may be thought of as the outer layer of musical experience. Your response to this outer layer is one reason the pieces in Sequence 1 seem different from one another.

But there is more to music than style. Consider these same pieces at a very basic level: *Each is music for the dance,* and because of this, each evokes a physical dance response. This fundamental characteristic transcends the differences between the selections. It connects them at a level that is *beyond style.*

Listening beyond style, then, will involve you at this deeper, more universal level of awareness than the outer layer alone can provide. When we strip music of that outer layer and expose the vibrant impulses that give it life, the interaction between music and style becomes clear. *Musical style is the characteristic manner in which a basic musical impulse is expressed.* Dance is but one of these impulses.

1

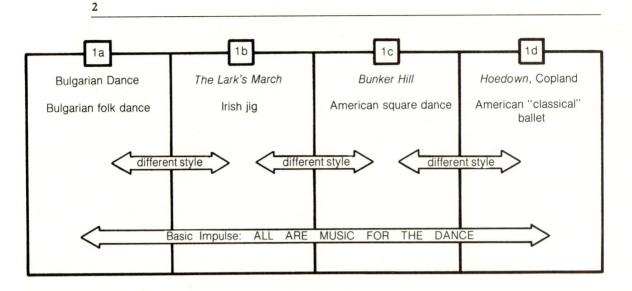

To explore further the concept suggested by the words "beyond style," examine the picture sequences on pages 500–511. This experience will not involve music, but will demonstrate an interplay between stylistic differences and basic impulses in a visual medium.

Listen   The following pieces are also in various styles. Once again, each piece involves the dance impulse. As you listen, focus on that quality which causes the body to "want to move." Some kind of movement (for example, tapping your foot with the music) will make the dance quality more vivid.

19   *Gigue* from *Partita in D minor for Violin*, J. S. Bach
13b *Ríu, ríu, chíu*, anon.
2b   *Danse* from *Four Etudes for Orchestra*, Igor Stravinsky
2d   *Super Blue*, Freddie Hubbard

MUSIC AND CULTURE

The pieces you have heard thus far reflect a variety of traditions, places, and times. Music is not an isolated art; *it grows from a culture*. When you listened to the Bulgarian Dance 1a , you experienced something of that country's culture. If a Bulgarian were to hear Freddie Hubbard's *Super Blue* 2d , he or she would be experiencing something of American culture. Today, in a world interconnected by electronic media, music is one channel through which people share cultural experience.

It is possible that the Bulgarian dance did not appeal to you. *Just as a culture affects musical style, it also conditions the listener*. Each of us inherits from our environment a *cultural filter*—a "feeling filter" which influences our perceptions. This filter causes us to accept, reject, and color our experience, and is at least partially responsible for our artistic values. One way a cultural filter may function is by blocking out the unfamiliar. Since the style of Bulgarian music is unfamiliar to many non-Bulgarian listeners, the music may not get through their cultural filters as a positive experience. (The opposite may also be true—an unfamiliar style can seem especially attractive because of its newness.) But what if you had a negative response to the style of *Bunker Hill* 1c or *Hoedown* 1d , both of which are American? Do cultural filters affect music from our own culture? The answer is yes. We live in a very complex and diversified society. It is, in fact a combination of many subcultures, with a variety of values and traditions. Consider a typical college class. The students come from a wide range of background and experience. *In such a diverse group it is natural for people to have acquired different cultural filters and to respond differently to the many musical styles that coexist in our society.*

Perhaps the idea of a cultural filter sounds too simple. But frequently musical response is just that simple. At one time or another, all of us have immediately dismissed a piece because of its style. Our response to style is often unthinking. But certainly there is more to music than automatic reactions: that is precisely what this book is about.

Before we go any further, it is important to understand that cultural filters are only part of what shapes musical response. Since these filters function in flexible ways, we cannot predict with any precision how they will work. After all, we are dealing with people, and human response to music is a nonquantifiable mystery. Each of us brings to that response a unique set of values and feelings. Music itself is absolute. What we say about it, how we describe it, how we react to it—these are flexible matters. And it is only in this spirit of flexibility that the concept of a cultural filter is useful. The ultimate value in recognizing one's own cultural filter may well be in one's conscious attempt to suspend it.

Among the negative aspects of modern musical culture is that music making is no longer expected of and practiced by everyone. The division between professional and amateur, and, even more important, the growth of mass-media resources, have deemphasized active participation in music by each member of society. This fact tends to obscure a basic truth—all of us are musical. Understanding music in a universal perspective cannot be accomplished without recognition and exposure to the everyday traditions of the world as a whole. For that reason, in the context of this book you will hear performances not only by highly trained professionals, but also by ordinary people. While these recordings may not be included in your future listening, they are indispensable for comprehending musical culture. Thus there is a "professional"-versus-"amateur" cultural filter which needs to be lowered at times in order to reach a deep understanding of why music exists.

GENRE

One of the strands that make up the fabric of musical culture is the continued existence of certain types of pieces. The French word *genre* may be used to identify these types.* The concept of genre cuts across stylistic barriers. For example, Bach's *Gigue* 19 and the Irish Jig 16 belong to the same genre. (In different languages, the same word may be *jig*, *giga*, or *gigue*.) Some genres with which you may be more familiar are symphony, blues, concerto, and ballad. Although pieces within the same genre may be in different musical styles, they usually share some basic quality.

Listen The following sequences are organized by genre. Rather than focusing on differences, listen for some shared musical qualities within each group.

Gigue

1b Irish Jig
19 *Gigue*, Bach
11c *Gigue*, Handel
20 *Gigue*, Schoenberg

Blues

35b *Stone Pony Blues*, Charles Patton
35c *Basin Street Blues*, Louis Armstrong
35d *Atherdoc Blues*, Heath Brothers
2d *Super Blue*, Freddie Hubbard

Lullaby

31a *Bressay Lullaby*, anon.
31b *One Grain of Sand*, anon.

THE IMPORTANCE OF STYLISTIC DETAIL

The basic impulses of music support an immense number of details which distinguish various styles. Such details help differentiate a Bach *Gigue* from an Irish Jig, or Hubbard's *Super Blue* from Patton's *Stone Pony Blues*. Among the distinguishing features in each of the examples are the instruments used and the way they are played. Such details are important. Style is as influential in music as it is in most areas of human experience. For exam-

*The meaning of *genre* in this book has been somewhat expanded beyond its traditional usage in relation to music. See Appendix IX for further explanation.

ple, what is the difference between a modern and a traditional house? What is the difference between **bold-face type** and *italics*? What is the difference between soul and country music? Stylistic detail! Through such details, we receive the basic message of any art.

THE HISTORICAL CONNECTION

Again, consider Sequence 1 . We have established that these pieces are in different styles. Nevertheless, you may have noticed that they have a strong resemblance to one another. In fact, there is a stylistic connection—a connection involving specific musical details—that runs through the sequence. The Bulgarian Dance 1a and the Irish Jig 1b are both from the European dance tradition and both tunes are of a similar type. The last three pieces are directly connected both culturally and historically. The square dance from Arkansas 1c is a direct descendant of the Irish dance tradition (for example, 1b). The *Hoedown* from the ballet *Rodeo* by Aaron Copland 1d is based on American country dance music. One of the stylistic details that connects these three pieces (as well as the Bulgarian Dance) is what might be called "country fiddlin'."

Listen Sequence 1 : Listen for "country fiddlin'" quality.

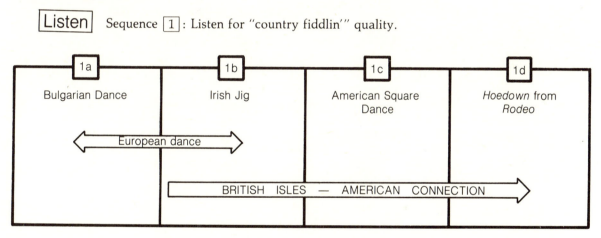

Music is bound up with history. Like all art, it is born of human experience. Many early American settlers came here from the British Isles. The musical traditions they brought with them became the basis of early American folk music. It is no surprise, then, to hear a similarity between Irish and American folk-dance music. And when a classical composer writes music based on American folk dance, it is possible to hear something of the original source "dancing" right along to Copland's portrayal of the American West.

THE INTERLOCKING STRANDS OF MUSICAL CULTURE

We can experience the music of Sequence 1 on many levels; for example, basic dance impulse, stylistic details, historical connections. These are all aspects of a larger concept, something we are all part of—musical culture. Musical culture results from the interaction of music with people, ideas, religion, geography, technology, language, and many other elements. Running through this diversity are powerful strands of continuity. We will use these strands as "musical lifelines" connecting all of us to the musics of the world. Approached from such a firm musical footing, the details of style and history will have both context and an enriching effect on the listening experience.

In the previous sequences, you listened to certain pieces more than once. For example, Bach's *Gigue* was part of a sequence demonstrating the universal dance impulse; you then heard it within the genre category *gigue*. Freddie Hubbard's *Super Blue* was also part of the dance impulse sequence, only later to be heard in the *blues* group. Those musical lifelines we referred to earlier crisscross in many places. They cut across stylistic barriers (for example, popular and classical); geographical borders (for example, British Isles and the United States); and the boundaries of chronological time (several listening sequences encompass thousands of years).

Obviously we cannot track all the interlocking strands of musical culture. No one can. But the ones we consider may be thought of as models for the larger network of the world's music. Our ultimate concern with any musical style is its connection to that larger network. If you understand this, you have, in a sense, already completed this course; all that remains are details of style, but what wonderful details they are!

MUSICAL STYLE The characteristic manner in which a basic impulse is expressed. A dance from Ireland and a dance from Bulgaria share a basic impulse. Their outward differences characterize their contrasting musical styles.

CULTURAL FILTER That part of a person's background and experience which affects his or her response to music (and other phenomena).

GENRE A type of musical piece; for example, gigue, symphony, lullaby, blues. Pieces that belong to the same genre may be in different musical styles.

1

Materials of Music – I

The Demonstration Melody

Throughout this chapter and the two that follow, you will be listening to a Demonstration Melody. It will be performed in various ways to demonstrate musical terms and concepts. The tune is deliberately simple and without distinction. To call it music may stretch your imagination, but manipulating this simple tune is preferable to an instructional massacre on a melody by Bach or Mozart, or *The Star-Spangled Banner*.

The success of this sequence depends largely on your willingness to internalize the Demonstration Melody. You can accomplish this by singing it. When you have completed this unit, you will be able to use the different versions of the Demonstration Melody as a sound resource for musical terms.

Listen | *Example 1,** the Demonstration Melody

Listen to the example several times. As you become familiar with it follow the visual representations along with the music. In the diagrams, each symbol (●) represents a single musical sound. (There are seventeen distinct sounds in the example.) As you listen, take a pen or pencil and point to each (●) in synchronization with each musical event. (You will tap seventeen times, in all.) Repeat, singing the example ("la, la" will do fine).

---

*The recorded material referred to as *Example 1, Example 2,* etc., will be found on the sound-sheets (soft vinyl discs) bound into this book.

Example 1, the Demonstration Melody—a Visual Representation

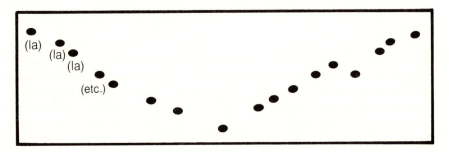

Although you may notice that the music as well as the dots goes "down and up," disregard this for the time being. Focus your attention on the flow of action from left to right.

Rhythm

One might assume that the initial discussion of the example will deal with the first musical sound. Not so. Instead, we turn our attention to the moment before the first sound. In a very real sense, music begins with silence. Like a beam of light surrounded by darkness, musical sound is surrounded by silence. Thus, we may reconsider our example as a movement from silence to action, returning to silence.

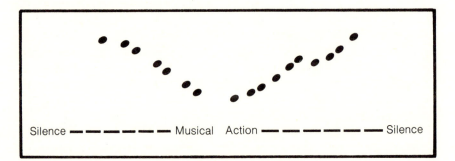

In this context (silence—musical action—silence) we become aware of the most basic element in music—rhythm. *Rhythm is action in time.* This definition is not limited to musical action, but applies to everything around us. Rainfall, walking, and breathing are all actions in time. Anything that moves, changes, or sounds has rhythm. While action in time describes in a general way the basic similarity between musical rhythm and other rhythms, we need to "fine-tune" this definition to grasp the traditional meaning of rhythm in music. Before, you pointed to each symbol (●) at exactly the same moment the corresponding musical sound occurred. Now, sing the Demonstration Melody while tapping on a desk with each musical sound. Each time you get to the end, begin again. After several repeats, stop singing, but *keep the tapping going*. Although the music has stopped, the rhythm of the Demonstration Melody is still sounding now, isolated from the actual music. What you hear is certainly action in time. But it is more. There is a definite pattern to this sound. You can sense how these taps relate to the time through which they flow and to the silence which surrounds them. *You are tapping out the rhythm of the Demonstration Melody.* You hear repeated patterns of long and short events; the action flows to a momentary silence, then continues its motion, returning once again to silence. There are, in fact, many details that cause this perception of unity. Even without identifying these details, you can sense that these events are organized in relation to time and silence. This is musical rhythm.

RHYTHM   (a general definition) Rhythm is action in time. Everything that moves or sounds has rhythm. We are continuously experiencing such "life rhythms" as walking, breathing, and, on a longer scale, the cycles of night and day, the changing seasons.

RHYTHM   (a musical definition) Music is also action in time. But in describing music we use rhythm in a more specialized sense. In music, rhythm describes how musical events are perceived in relation to time, silence, and each other.

SOME ASPECTS OF RHYTHMIC ORGANIZATION

Tapping out the rhythm of the Demonstration Melody, you hear repeated patterns of long and short sounds. These patterns are represented below. To experience this rhythmic organization, speak while tapping, using the appropriate word, "long" or "short," as indicated below. (L is long; s is short.)

L   s L   s L   s L   L   s s L   s s L   s s L

The word *duration* refers to the length of rhythmic events. Using this term to describe the beginning of the Demonstration Melody, we say "the first sound has a longer duration than the second." As you can hear and see in the diagram above, the rhythm is organized by two repeated patterns. These patterns are called *rhythmic motives*. They lend a sense of unity to music in which they are found.

> DURATION   The length of a rhythmic event. A phone ring has a longer dura-
> tion than the sound of a falling raindrop.
>
> RHYTHMIC MOTIVE   A repeated rhythmic pattern.

PULSE, BEAT, AND PERIODICITY

When you tap your foot in time with a marching band, you are recreating the *basic pulse* or *beat* of the music. This pulse is said to be *periodic*, since it repeats in a steady, evenly spaced manner. Rhythms that do not repeat in this predictable manner are said to be *aperiodic*. When represented visually, the relationship between a periodic pulse and an aperiodic one is quite obvious. In the diagrams below, the horizontal plane of the grid represents time. Each box is therefore a small unit of time. The symbol (●) represents a pulse.

Periodic

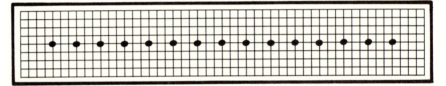

Aperiodic

Periodic rhythm can have a powerful effect on the human body. If you find yourself involuntarily tapping your foot to a march, or hypnotized by a ticking clock or a dripping faucet, you are experiencing the effects of periodicity. This kind of response is not limited to sound; it may reach us through other senses as well. For example, stare at the diagrams above, first at one, then at the other. You will probably find the perfectly symmetrical pattern of the first diagram more "hypnotic" than the second. We have circuits in our nervous system that respond readily to periodic actions, sounds, and visual patterns. This response occurs on an unconscious level and is one of the reasons that music has such profound effects on creator, performer, and audience.

Most of the traditional music we hear is based on a *periodic* pulse. Marching band and dance music are obvious examples. The Demonstration Melody also illustrates this common type of rhythmic organization. In the following example, the periodic pulse is emphasized.

Listen | *Example 2,* Demonstration Melody with basic pulse emphasized

Listen | *Examples 16a and 16b* are both periodic pulses. There is, however, one difference between them. What is it?

TEMPO

Both pulses in the example above are periodic; what differentiates them is their tempos. *Tempo is the rate of musical action.* We can compare these rhythms as follows: "The tempo of the second pulse is faster than the tempo of the first." On the graph, the relationship between them is easily discernible:

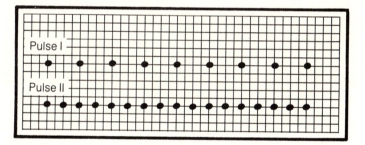

BEAT   The basic regular pulse underlying music. When you tap your foot to a marching band or a popular dance, you are tapping out the beat or *basic pulse.*

PERIODIC RHYTHM   A rhythm which is repeated in an even and regular manner. An *aperiodic* rhythm repeats at random, or not at all. The beat of a marching band and walking are both periodic rhythms. The random sound of typing is an aperiodic rhythm.

TEMPO   The speed of the basic pulse. Tempo describes how fast or slowly music moves through time. Composers often indicate the tempo of a piece with *tempo markings.* A list of these is found in Appendix III.

METER

The Demonstration Melody with its basic pulse reveals another aspect of rhythmic organization. The basic pulse is heard as a repeating group of three beats; the first beat in each group is slightly accented. In the following diagram the symbol (>) is used to indicate these accents.

> ● ● ● > ● ● ● > ● ● ●

This organization of basic pulses into a repeated pattern is *meter*. We can describe this meter as *"in three."* For visual clarity, groups of beats are enclosed within *barlines* drawn vertically after every group. We call each enclosed group of beats a *measure* (or *bar*).

barline ➤ | ● ● ● | ● ● ● |
◄ measure ►

Traditionally, meters are counted verbally. Count this meter and at the same time tap the basic pulse.

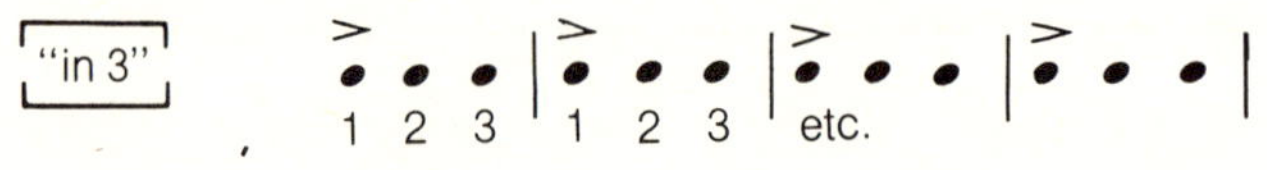

"in 3"   > ● ● ● | > ● ● ● | > ● ● ● | > ● ● ● |
         1 2 3   1 2 3   etc.

Three is not the only metrical grouping. Repeat counting and tapping with these other meters:

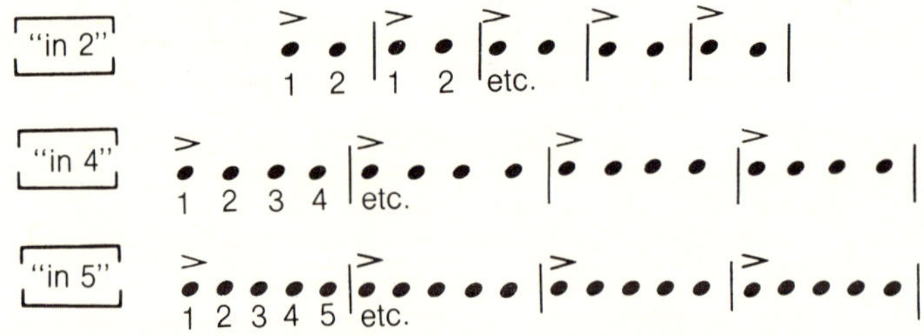

"in 2"   > ● ● | > ● ● | > ● ● | > ● ● | > ● ● |
         1 2   1 2   etc.

"in 4"   > ● ● ● ● | > ● ● ● ● | > ● ● ● ● | > ● ● ● ● |
         1 2 3 4   etc.

"in 5"   > ● ● ● ● ● | > ● ● ● ● ● | > ● ● ● ● ● | > ● ● ● ● ● |
         1 2 3 4 5   etc.

When tapping meters larger than three, the meter may be divided into sub-groups of 2 or 3. For example:

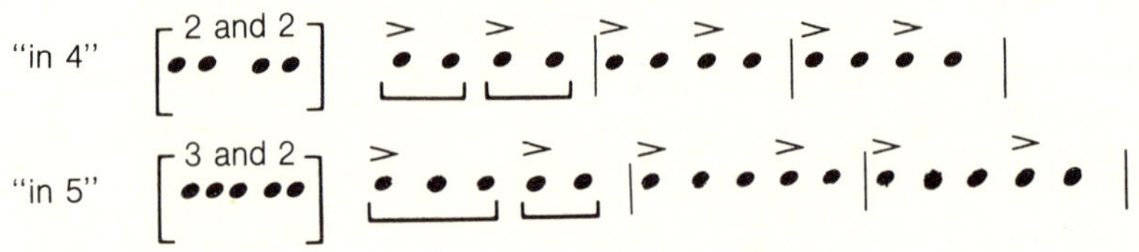

"in 4"   [2 and 2 / ● ● ● ●]   > ● ● ● ● | > ● ● ● ● | > ● ● ● ● |

"in 5"   [3 and 2 / ● ● ● ● ●]   > ● ● ● ● ● | > ● ● ● ● ● | > ● ● ● ● ● |

Listen *Examples 3 and 4.* In these examples the Demonstration Melody has been altered to sound "in four" and "in five."

One of the basic principles of rhythm is that it is perceived simultaneously at faster and slower levels. You can prove this easily by tapping out meters in which groups of twos, threes, or both are synchronized in a "layered" structure. Tap out groups of six using a fast pulse. Use the right hand.

Now add this slower rhythm with the left hand.

There are two pulses in this meter. The fast pulse is "in six." The slower pulse is "in two." Thus it can be counted either in a fast six or a slow two.

The following meters show different combinations of faster and slower synchronized pulses:

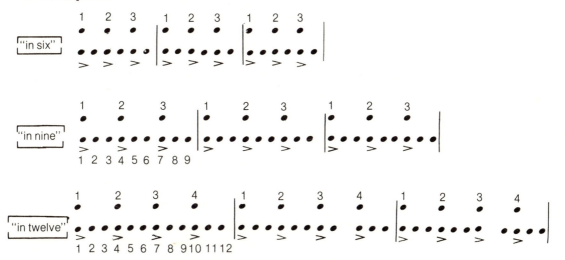

TIME SIGNATURES

Meter is represented in notation by time signatures, which indicate the number of pulses (beats) in a measure and the relative duration of each pulse. For examples and further explanation of time signatures, see Appendix IV.

SYNCOPATION

Once a basic pulse is established, it provides a coordinated rhythmic environment in which more complex rhythmic patterns can exist. One example of rhythmic complexity is *syncopation*, which will be demonstrated before it is defined.

Tap this example:

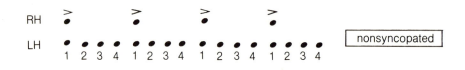

What follows is a slightly altered version of the example above. You will notice that the right-hand tap now falls between 4 and 1. Keep the left hand steady, since it is the basic pulse.

Thus, one type of syncopation is an accented rhythm "off the beat." The example below demonstrates another type of syncopation. Tap the basic pulse in a fairly fast tempo.

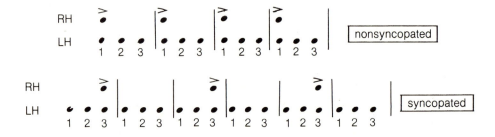

In this type of syncopation, one of the usually weak beats of a metrical group is emphasized. Since we are accustomed to a pattern of strong-weak-weak, an accent on the third beat of the measure feels syncopated.

Listen | *Example 5.* In this example the Demonstration Melody has been syncopated.

Forward Potential

The body responds to meter with a readiness to move. To demonstrate, count this meter evenly:

```
  >        >        >        >
1  2  3  1  2  3  1  2  3  1  2  3
```

In addition to counting, sway left, then right on "1."

```
>        >        >        >        >        >
1 2  3  1  2  3  1  2  3  1  2  3  1  2  3  1  2  3    [keep going]
L     R     L     R     L     R
```

Continue this activity for a while, then *stop abruptly on "3."*

```
>        >        >        >        >        >        >
1 2 3  1 2 3  1 2 3  1 2 3  1 2 3  1 2 3  1 2 3    Stop!
L      R      L      R      L      R      L
```

Consider what your body wants to do at this moment. You probably feel a need for more motion. The term *forward potential* describes the desire for continued rhythmic action. One need not move at all to experience this sensation. Repeat the entire exercise (counting, moving, abruptly stopping) in your imagination. This "action in the mind" demonstrates that one's response to forward potential may be as much a matter of perception as a physical impulse. (It also demonstrates, by the way, how the mind recreates the rhythmic sensations of motion.)

The Rhythmic Bond

Music often causes a rhythmic connection between musicians and audiences. Consider a marching band at a sports event. Not only do the performers march in time, but the audience, with their tapping feet, also participate in this synchronized movement. We can speak of this rhythmic coordination as a *rhythmic bond*. We have only to experience the incredibly powerful interaction between performers and audience at a rock concert to understand just how forceful a rhythmic bond can be. The same phenomenon, though in a more subdued style, can be found at a concert of symphonic music. Audiences may seem to be still, but a more careful look will reveal that many types of synchronized movements bond the members of the audience with the performers on the stage.

Phrase and Form

Both music and poetry begin with rhythm. Musical (or poetic) motion toward a moment of rest is a *phrase*. The moment of rest is a *cadence*.

Demonstration Melody

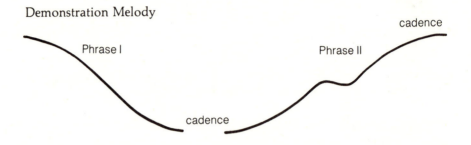

The Demonstration Melody has two phrases. The first cadence seems more like a pause than a rest; we feel that the action will begin again. This type of momentary pause is a *semicadence*. The second cadence returns us to silence. We sense it to be final, almost invisible; it is thus called a *full cadence*. When considering the Demonstration Melody as two phrases, we are describing one aspect of its *form*—the broad shape or organization of the music. All music has form.

Form, like rhythm, is perceived simultaneously at short- and long-range levels of awareness. For example, the Demonstration Melody flows in metrical groupings of three. This short-range detail supports the individual rhythmic motives, which, in turn, become the longer phrases. The following diagram illustrates short- and long-range musical design.

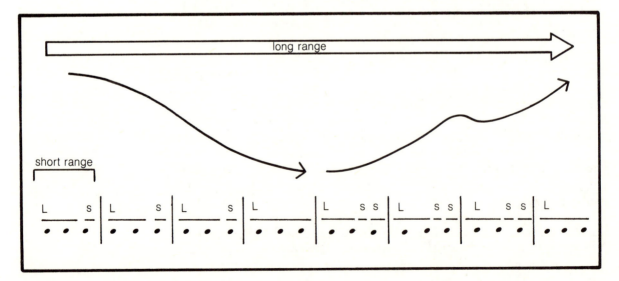

The form of a painting begins to take shape as the artist's brush touches the canvas. Musical form begins with rhythm: its canvas is silence; its space is time.

Rhythm Gives Life to Form

Musical form may grow from *life rhythms*—the ordinary motions and activities of human life. The rocking motion of a mother holding a child becomes the gentle meter, usually "in three," of a lullaby (*Bressay Lullaby* 31a , for example). The repeated rhythms of physical labor create the powerful meter of a work song. A game in which each child takes turn being leader translates musically into soloist and group (African Game Song 2a). An ancient tale (which is, in fact, a very long life rhythm) becomes a song or chant. Rhythm is a basic element from which form grows.

METER   The organization of the basic pulse into regularly repeated groups.

MEASURE (BAR)   The notated group of beats that organizes rhythm into meter. Measures are indicated by vertical lines—*barlines*—drawn through the staff.

SYNCOPATION   A rhythm which is accented "off" the beat. The effect of syncopation is a result of its contrast to a periodic pulse or established meter.

FORWARD POTENTIAL   The expectation of continued rhythmic activity that may be caused by a musical pattern.

FORM   The shape or outline of a piece of music. We perceive form as the growth of short-range detail into long-range design.

PHRASE   Musical motion toward a moment of rest.

CADENCE   The moment of rest at the end of a phrase. Two types of cadences are *full cadence* and *semicadence*, determined by their relative degree of finality.

RHYTHMIC BOND   A rhythmic connection between performer and audience. The rhythmic bond may be considered as a type of synchronized rhythmic environment in which music is created and perceived.

THE NOTATION OF RHYTHM

You don't have to read music in order to use this book. However, viewing notation in a nonspecific way can be helpful in the acquisition of information and listening skills. If you wish to explore notation at a more detailed level, now or at a later time, it is presented in Appendix IV.

NOTES CONTROL SPACE

On the grid below, rhythm is represented moving through time from left to right. Each box on the graph corresponds to a unit of time. Longer notes, since they take more time, control more space (i.e., boxes) than shorter notes. Consider the three notes on the grid. Don't be concerned with exactly how many boxes each note controls. Gauge the space in a general way.

When these notes are written one after the other their relative spacing reflects their duration.

Relatively long notes cannot be bunched together, because the space after each note is already "occupied."

Relatively short notes, on the other hand, are spaced closer together:

When a slow rhythm is notated together with a fast rhythm, their relationship is signaled by the *spacing*.

RESTS

Musical notation provides symbols called *rests* to indicate silence. Rests, like notes, control space in proportion to their duration.

SCORE

A *score* is notated music for more than one instrument. To demonstrate the way a score is organized, consider some imaginary music for two flutes and a trumpet. Each instrument is notated on its own group of five lines called a *staff*. (For the moment, disregard the symbol at the beginning of each staff.)

If they all played one note *at the same time*, it would be notated this way:

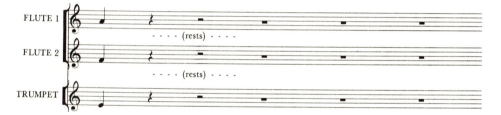

If they played one note *one after the other*, it would be notated:

If they all played the *same rhythm* at the same time it would be notated:

An important element in the organization of a score is the barline, which identifies the measures.

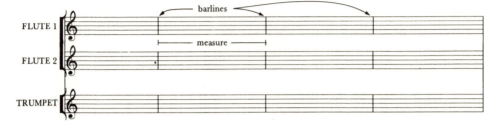

As an example of the practicality of a score, consider the following situation: The trumpet plays a wrong note (it's circled in the following diagram). The conductor can then say, "You've played a wrong note at the beginning of measure 3."

Now we will examine some music and describe its rhythmic structure in general terms. Questions are provided to help you conceptualize the rhythmic features of each example.

Answer flute 1, flute 2, or trumpet.

Which instruments play the fast
rhythm in measure 1?

_____

Which instrument plays the fewest
notes?

_____

Which instrument plays the slowest
notes?

_____

Cross out the wrong word(s).

Each instrument plays (the same, a different) rhythm.

Compared with measure 1, the rhythms of measures 3, 4, and 5 are
(faster, slower).

The measure without musical sound is measure (2, 3).

Which statement describes this rhythmic structure? (Circle a or b.)

(a) The instruments play the same rhythm.

(b) The instruments enter one after the other.

RHYTHMIC TEXTURE

The examples notated on pages 20–21 illustrate various types of *rhythmic
texture*, the simultaneous combination of various rhythms. There are many
types of rhythmic texture: some are relatively simple, others are more com-

plex. Often complex rhythmic textures create a certain tension that seeks resolution in a simpler texture. In other words, a complex rhythmic texture produces forward potential toward a more relaxed state. The following diagram and listening example demonstrate this phenomenon.

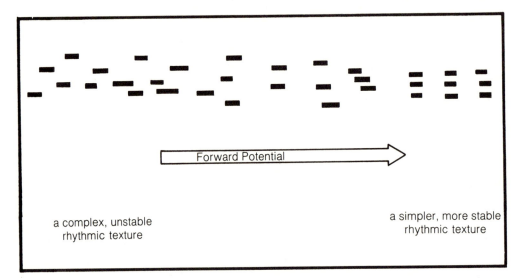

Forward Potential

a complex, unstable
rhythmic texture

a simpler, more stable
rhythmic texture

Listen   *Example 17. A complex rhythmic structure moving toward a less complex, more relaxed one.*

Additional Listening   Excerpt from *Momente*, by Stockhausen 24f . This piece involves various types of rhythmic textures which produce areas of tension and relaxation.

RHYTHMIC TEXTURE   The simultaneous combination of various rhythmic elements.

SCORE   A notational device showing music for more than one instrument.

A NOTE ON QUESTION FORMAT

Some of the questions in this book appear in a format that needs explanation. Once you become familiar with the style of these questions, you may find them especially useful for review. Consider the following as a model:

1. Concerning the term *cultural filter*: find any false statements and correct them by changing the word(s) in italics. More than one statement may be false; all the statements may be true.

   (a) It is a *personal* response.

   (b) It *does not* affect how we respond to musical style.

   (c) It is created, in part, by one's *cultural background*.

   (d) It is something that *can* be measured in an exact, scientific manner.

Corrected version:

   (a) It is a *personal* response.

   (b) It *does* affect how we respond to musical style.

   (c) It is created, in part, by one's *cultural background*.

   (d) It is something that *cannot* be measured in an exact, scientific manner.

The corrected version now serves as a concise summary of the topic, and in some cases expands the material to relate to other sections. You can review a chapter by reading through the corrected questions. This format also requires you to consider each answer carefully, deepening your understanding and control of the material. Finally, these directions ("Find any false statements . . .") will not appear with each question, but only at the beginning of each series using this format.

QUESTIONS

Find any false statement(s) and correct them by changing the word(s) in italics. More than one statement may be false; all the statements may be true.

1. Concerning musical style:

   (a) It describes the *"outer layer"* of music.

   (b) It grows from and reflects a particular *culture*.

   (c) Different musical styles are *never* connected.

   (d) The perception of musical style is usually affected by one's *cultural filter*.

2. Considering Sequence $\boxed{1}$ (see pages 1–2):

   (a) *All* the pieces are connected through dance.

   (b) The sequence demonstrates that connections *do exist* between "popular" and "serious" musical traditions.

   (c) Although pieces $\boxed{1b}$, $\boxed{1c}$, and $\boxed{1d}$ are in different musical styles, certain stylistic connections *can be* sensed in all three.

   (d) Pieces $\boxed{1b}$, $\boxed{1c}$, and $\boxed{1d}$ demonstrate the *historical connection* between music of the British Isles and of the United States.

3. Concerning genre:

   (a) It describes a *type* of piece.

   (b) Pieces of the same genre are *never* in different styles.

   (c) The Irish Jig is in a *different* style from Bach's *Gigue*.

   (d) Genres are an aspect of *continuity* in musical culture.

4. Concerning musical culture:

   (a) It encompasses great *diversity*.

   (b) It *connects* each of us to the musics of the world.

   (c) It is *deeply* involved with history.

   (d) *Unrelated* strands make up the fabric of musical culture.

5. Concerning rhythm (in the broad sense):

   (a) It is *action in time*.

   (b) It is *movement*.

   (c) We experience it at *multiple* levels, from short range to long range.

   (d) It has a *minimal* effect on the human senses.

6. Concerning musical rhythm:

   (a) It is *action in time*.

   (b) It describes, among other things, how musical events are related in *time*.

   (c) It has *no relationship* to the broader definition of rhythm.

   (d) It is one aspect of *musical organization*.

7. Concerning periodicity:

   (a) It *is not* related to repetition.

   (b) Basic pulses are usually *aperiodic*.

   (c) It *is* the only type of musical rhythm.

   (d) It *does* occur in both musical and nonmusical contexts.

8. Concerning the rhythm of the Demonstration Melody:

   (a) The melody has *one* rhythmic motive.

   (b) It illustrates that repetition *is often* an important part of rhythmic organization.

   (c) We respond to its *periodicity*.

   (d) It is synchronized with a *basic pulse*.

9. Concerning meter:

   (a) It is rooted in a *body response* to strong and weak beats.

   (b) It *is not* related to repetition.

   (c) In notation, meter is organized with the aid of *barlines*.

   (d) Meter is *never* perceived at simultaneously fast and slow levels.

10. Concerning syncopation:

   (a) It is perceived in relationship to a *periodic* pulse.

   (b) It *may* occur "in between the beats."

   (c) It *may* occur as an accent on a normally weak beat.

   (d) It is an aspect of *rhythmic organization*.

11. Concerning forward potential:

   (a) It describes a *human perception*.

   (b) It *may be* created by meter.

   (c) Different meters produce *the same* amount of forward potential.

   (d) If the music stops abruptly, the forward potential at that moment is likely to be *lower* than at the normal ending of the piece.

12. Concerning a phrase:

   (a) It *begins* with a cadence.

   (b) It is *musical motion* to a moment of rest.

   (c) It creates *some amount* of forward potential.

   (d) In general, the forward potential at the middle of a phrase is *greater* than at the end.

13. Concerning form:

   (a) It is the *outline* of a piece.

   (b) One characteristic of form may be the *number of phrases*.

   (c) It begins with *rhythm*.

   (d) *Some* music has form.

14. Concerning the idea "rhythm gives life to form":

   (a) *Rhythmic movement* is a basic human activity from which form may grow.

   (b) *Rhythmic perception* is a basic human awareness through which form may be experienced.

   (c) Certain *life rhythms* may create musical form.

   (d) There *is no* relationship between form in music and form in poetry.

2

Materials of Music – II

Rhythm is but one essential characteristic of music. We will now consider an important element missing from the previous analysis of the Demonstration Melody—pitch. *Pitch* describes the relative "highness" or "lowness" of sound. Specifically, the Demonstration Melody seems to proceed down and then up.

Pitch is a physical property of all sound. Sound is created by vibration. For example, when you pluck a string, it vibrates. This causes the air around the string to vibrate sympathetically. These vibrations in the air (sound waves) carry the sound of the plucked string to your ear. Look at the illustration of a plucked string on page 71 (frame A). Notice that the string vibrates back and forth. Sound waves behave in a similar way. The faster they vibrate back and forth, the higher the pitch. As a general rule, small objects produce higher pitches than large ones. If you blow into two bottles of different size, the sound produced from the smaller will be higher in pitch than that of the larger. A guitar is an excellent medium for demonstrating additional factors affecting pitch, such as string length and tension. When the sound produced by a full-length string is compared to that of a shortened string (this is accomplished by stopping the string with the left hand somewhere on the neck), the shorter one is higher in pitch. The full-length string can be made to produce a higher pitch by increasing its tension (this is accomplished by turning the tuning key to tighten the string). A tighter string vibrates more rapidly than a loose one. (As jump-rope enthusiasts know quite well, a rope turns faster when either tightened or shortened.)

Pitch can be measured in various ways. Electronic technology measures it in terms of *frequency*, the number of back-and-forth vibrations (cycles) per second. The term *hertz* (Hz) is used to identify this number. Thus, any pitch can be quantified by number. The human ear responds to frequencies as high as 20,000 Hz and as low as 20 Hz. These statistics are very familiar to stereo enthusiasts, since their equipment has certain limits of sound reproduction. When you read that a tape deck can reproduce from 20 Hz to 18,000 Hz, this describes its range for the reproduction of pitch. Exact measurement of pitch is quite useful in various ways, as we shall soon discover.

Pitch is represented visually on our diagrams in the vertical dimension. The relative pitch of each musical event is reflected in its low-to-high placement on the grid.

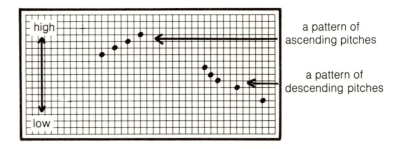

a pattern of ascending pitches

a pattern of descending pitches

We now consider three basic pitch-types: *indefinite*, *steady*, and *sliding*. *Indefinite* pitches are easily demonstrated. Take a book (this one if you wish) and drop it on the floor. Then, drop a pencil on the same spot. The impact of the book makes a lower-pitched sound than that of the pencil. Although indefinite in *precise* terms of pitch, both sounds can still be identified in general categories of high or low. Now, play two keys on a piano, one near the extreme left of the keyboard, the other near the extreme right. These are *steady* pitches. Not only do we hear the first as "lower" than the second, but the pitches are very clear. Play a key in the middle of the keyboard and sing it (on "la"). The clarity of a steady pitch makes it easy to hear and reproduce with relative exactness. (Try to sing the pitch of that falling book!) If a guitar is available, you can use it to demonstrate the difference between a *steady* pitch and a *sliding* pitch. To produce a steady pitch, pluck any string with the right hand. Now place a finger of the left hand in one of the frets (the boxes on the neck of the guitar). With the finger pressed firmly down, pluck the string with the right hand. Immediately after you pluck the string, slide the finger on the fret toward the right hand. The resulting sound is a sliding pitch moving from low to high. A common sliding pitch we hear in daily life is the warning sound of a siren; another is crying.

PITCH   The relative highness or lowness of a sound. Technically, pitch is
measured as the number of cyclic vibrations per second. A flute plays
higher-pitched sounds than a tuba. Adults speak in lower-pitched voices
than children.

INDEFINITE PITCH   A pitch whose relative highness or lowness is not exact.
For example, thunder has a more indefinite pitch than a telephone ring.

STEADY PITCH   A pitch whose relative highness or lowness is exact; for
example, a telephone ring or a plucked string.

SLIDING PITCH   A pitch which is continuously changing. The sound of a
siren and a wailing voice are two examples.

PITCH NAMES

To name musical pitches we use the first seven letters of the alphabet—A
through G, arranged from low to high:

After G, the sequence begins once again. (This repetition is explained in a
later section.) This organization may be seen and heard on a piano keyboard:

In music notation, pitch is represented on a staff—five parallel lines.
Pitches, represented by notes, are placed either on lines or on spaces.

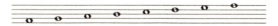

Pitches that sound beyond the five lines of the staff are notated with *ledger
lines*.

The exact pitch identity of each line or space is determined by a *clef*. Two commonly used clefs are the *treble* (𝄞) and the *bass* (𝄢). The treble clef identifies the second line from the bottom as G.

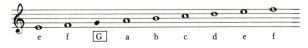

The bass clef identifies the second line from the top as F.

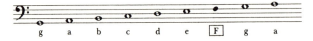

The treble clef is used for higher pitches, the bass for lower:

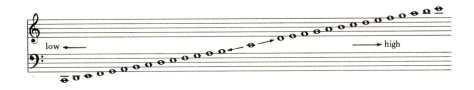

ACCIDENTALS

You may notice that the letters do not identify all the notes on the keyboard. Traditionally, our musical system has twelve basic pitches. On the piano, seven of these are white keys; the other five are black keys. In naming the black keys, we use symbols called *accidentals*. Notice in the diagram below that the black-key tones bear the name of either the lower or higher white key plus a *sharp* (♯) or *flat* (♭). *Sharps* and *flats* are accidentals.

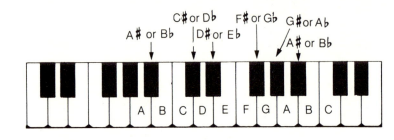

Accidentals in Notation

You may also encounter other accidentals: ✕ , ♭♭ , and ♮ . These are explained in Appendix V.

DYNAMICS

Dynamics describes the relative loudness and softness of music. Sudden or gradual changes in dynamics constitute one of the basic means of musical communication. Composers indicate dynamics by traditional *dynamic markings*. It is not vital to learn all of them, but familiarity with the basic ones will be quite useful. (A more complete list appears in Appendix III.)

Italian term	Abbreviation	Translation
fortissimo	ff	very loud
forte	f	loud
mezzo forte	mf	somewhat loud
mezzo piano	mp	somewhat soft
piano	p	soft
pianissimo	pp	very soft
crescendo	cresc.	getting louder
decrescendo (diminuendo)	decresc. (dim.)	getting softer

CLEF   In notation, a symbol at the beginning of each staff indicating the pitch identity of the lines and spaces. The *treble* clef ( ) is used for higher pitches, the *bass* ( ) for lower ones.

DYNAMICS   The relative loudness of music.

ACCIDENTALS   Symbols that indicate a note is to be raised or lowered. Two common accidentals are the *sharp* (♯), which raises the pitch, and the *flat* (♭), which lowers it.

Timbre–Tone

Listen   *Example 24.* The Demonstration Melody is played first by a *violin* and then by a *flute*.

In these two versions of the Demonstration Melody, both rhythm and pitch are the same. What is different is the *timbre* (pronounced tám-bur). Timbre describes the characteristic quality of a sound source. For example, the human voice has a different timbre from the saxophone. One person's voice has a different timbre from another's, and the violin has a different timbre from the flute. Humans have found certain timbres to be particularly pleasing, especially the rich ones of some voices and instruments. Timbre is an essential element in the musical experience. For example, consider the steady pitch of a test-pattern sound (heard on television and radio after those famous words, "This is a test"). It has a steady pitch, but is it musical? Some would say yes (especially electronic composers), while others would disagree; but most would concur that if the same pitch were played on a flute, the result would be closer to what is traditionally considered musical. While the answer to this interesting question is a matter of personal taste, there is no doubt that timbre, like pitch, is a basic quality of musical sound. The musical combination of timbre and pitch is called a *tone*. In common usage, it is synonymous with "note" and "pitch."

INSTRUMENTAL TIMBRE

There are various methods for producing a musical tone. Both flute and clarinet, for example, employ a column of air; but they don't sound very much alike. In each one, the air is made to vibrate in a different way. Furthermore, the column of air is enclosed by different materials fashioned into different shapes. To make another comparison, both guitar and violin use a stretched string. Again, differences in construction and method of causing the string to vibrate result in different timbres. Thus, timbre is created by several interacting factors of instrumental design.

Most instruments belong to a family group, related by a common method of tone production. Instruments within the same family have recognizably similar characteristics of timbre. For example, violins, violas, cellos, and basses all belong to the string family. What differentiates the individual string instruments is how high or low they are able to play.

PITCH RANGE

Musical sound exists within the boundaries of pitch, determined by the limits of our perception and the capability of instruments or voices. This gamut of available pitch for any one instrument is its *pitch range*.

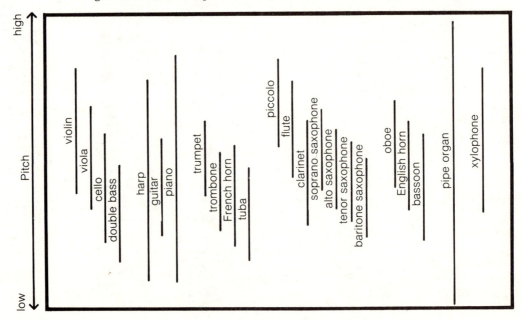

Instrumental Groups		Examples
Strings	The sound is produced by a stretched string which is bowed, plucked, or sometimes struck.	violin, viola, cello, double bass, guitar, mandolin, harp

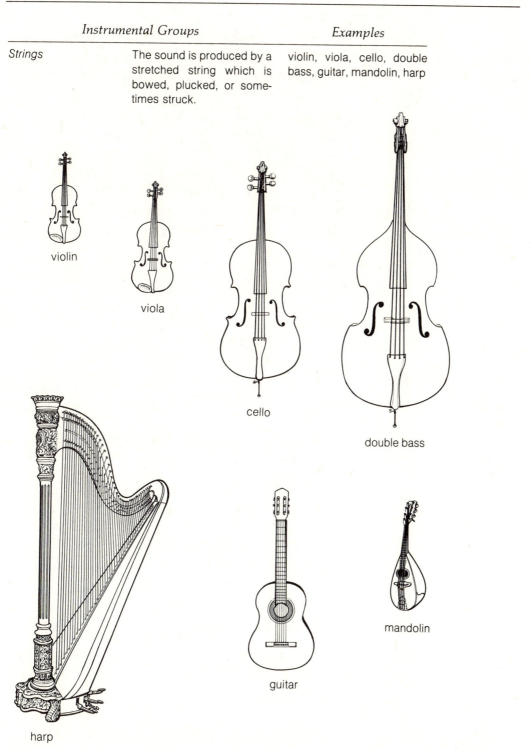

violin

viola

cello

double bass

harp

guitar

mandolin

Instrumental Groups		*Examples*

Woodwinds — So named because at one time all were made of wood. Today some are made from metal. The sound is produced by a column of air with the player blowing: 1) across an open hole (flute); or 2) on a single *reed* (clarinet)—a reed is a small piece of wood which vibrates easily; or 3) on a double reed (oboe).

piccolo, flute, clarinet, saxophone, oboe, English horn, bassoon

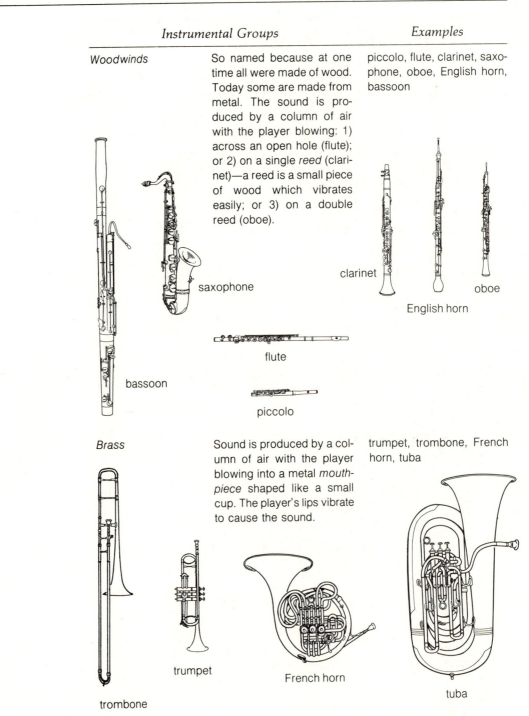

saxophone

clarinet

oboe

English horn

flute

bassoon

piccolo

Brass — Sound is produced by a column of air with the player blowing into a metal *mouthpiece* shaped like a small cup. The player's lips vibrate to cause the sound.

trumpet, trombone, French horn, tuba

trumpet

French horn

tuba

trombone

Instrumental Groups		*Examples*

Keyboard — The player causes the sound by depressing keys, which activate a variety of sound sources. For example, the piano key causes a felt hammer to strike a string. It thus has characteristics of both the percussion and string families. The organ produces its sound by means of a column of air (like the brass and woodwinds).

piano, organ, harpsichord

organ

harpsichord

Electric instruments — Electric instruments produce sound through electronic circuits. In some cases, like the electric guitar, an existing *acoustic* (nonelectronic) instrument is combined with electronic alteration and amplification, while others depend totally on electronics for sound production.

electric bass, electric guitar, electric organ, synthesizer

Hybrid instruments combining various means of sound production

electric guitar

electric bass

Instrumental Groups		*Examples*
Percussion	Sound is produced by *striking*: 1) a stretched membrane (drum); or 2) a solid substance like wood, metal, or stone (xylophone).	drum, chimes, xylophone, timpani, wood blocks

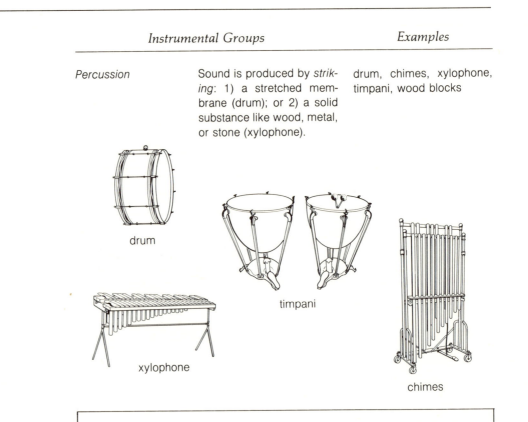

drum

timpani

xylophone

chimes

TIMBRE   The characteristic quality of a sound source. A flute has a different timbre from a guitar. Timbre is often described with words like "rich," "thin," "shrill," "mellow," etc.

TONE   A combination of timbre and pitch producing a sound perceived as musical. "Tone," "note," and "pitch" are often used interchangeably.

INSTRUMENTAL GROUPS (OR FAMILIES)   Instruments are classified in groups according to the manner in which they produce tones.

PITCH RANGE   The possible pitches an instrument or voice may produce.

Melody and Harmony

At a basic level, a writer creates with words, a sculptor with clay or stone, a composer with tones. Suppose for a moment that you are a composer seated at the piano. In front of you are your two hands and eighty-eight keys which create tones. You have an immediate choice. Play tones one after another—this is the world of *melody*. Play tones simultaneously—this is the world of *harmony*.

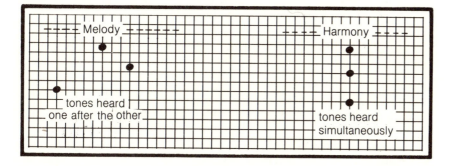

Melody and harmony are profoundly related. Before we can discuss either, certain basic information is necessary.

INTERVAL

An interval is the relationship between two tones. These can be heard one after another as a *melodic interval,* or simultaneously as a *harmonic interval.*

A melodic interval: The tones are heard one after the other.

A harmonic interval: The tones are heard simultaneously.

An interval may be large (wide) or small (close) depending on the proximity of the tones.

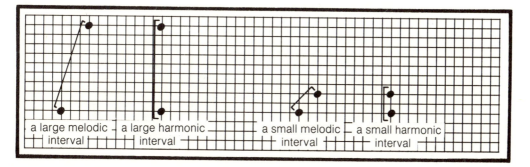

a large melodic interval · a large harmonic interval · a small melodic interval · a small harmonic interval

CONSONANT AND DISSONANT INTERVALS

Each interval has its own particular quality. An interval which sounds "at rest" and "relaxed" is said to be *consonant*. By contrast, an interval which sounds "in motion" and "tense" is said to be *dissonant*.

Listen | *Example 18a.* Follow the visual representation below:

Dissonant intervals often generate forward potential. Their tense quality creates a need for movement toward consonant intervals. When this occurs, the dissonant interval is said to *resolve* (move) to the consonant one. A sound that is "in motion" has sought out and resolved to a sound "at rest."

CHORD

When more than two tones sound simultaneously, the result is a *chord*. Another way to consider a chord is as a combination of intervals:

Like intervals, chords may be *consonant* or *dissonant*. A dissonant chord may tend to move toward a consonant chord. When chords sound in succession, the result is a *progression*.

Listen | *Example 18b*

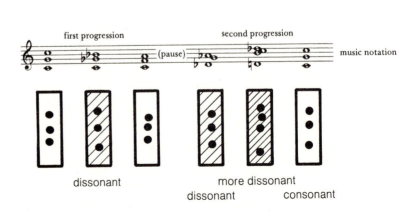

In the first progression, the second chord is dissonant and resolves to the third chord. In the second progression, the first chord is dissonant. It does not resolve. The second chord is even more dissonant. The tension of the first two chords is resolved in the third.

MELODY (MELODIC)   A related succession of tones heard one after the other.

HARMONY (HARMONIC)   The result of simultaneously sounding tones. Chords and harmonic intervals are part of harmony, since each involves more than one tone sounding at the same time.

INTERVAL   A pitch relationship between two tones. *Melodic interval*: the tones sound one after the other. *Harmonic interval*: the tones sound simultaneously.

CHORD   The simultaneous sounding of three or more tones. Chords are made up of intervals. In this book, they are represented in the following manner:

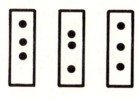

PROGRESSION   A chain of related chords, heard as a unified musical action. Like a melody, a progression may also move to a cadence.

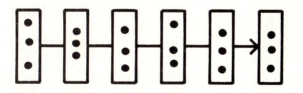

DISSONANT AND CONSONANT   Relative terms that describe harmonic sound as either "tense" (dissonant) or "relaxed" (consonant). Dissonant harmony tends to resolve to consonant harmony. In this book chords may be shaded in proportion to their dissonance.

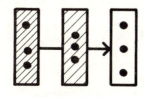

Melody and Scale

When different tones sound one after the other, a melody is created. It takes but a few tones to move the senses with melodic patterns. Listening to the chants in Sequence 7 we hear ancient melodic patterns based on very few pitches.

Listen | Sequence 7

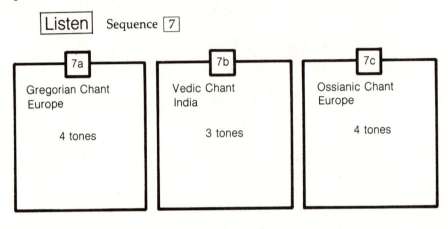

7a	7b	7c
Gregorian Chant Europe	Vedic Chant India	Ossianic Chant Europe
4 tones	3 tones	4 tones

Listen | *Agnus Dei* 8 . This melody is created with six tones.

As you have heard, a melody often uses the same tones over and over. When these tones are arranged in a theoretical model, traditionally from low to high, the result is a *scale*.

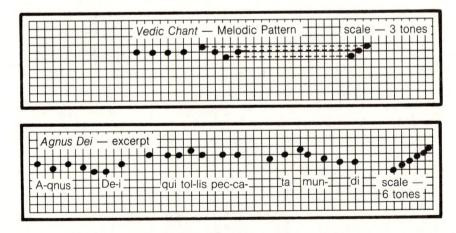

There are many types of scales. Some melodies, especially very ancient ones, are based on two- or three-tone scales. Most of our traditional melodies are based on a seven-tone scale. The number of tones does not constitute the only possible difference between scale-types. Since scales are a succession of tones, they are made up of various *melodic intervals*. Differences in the size of these intervals have an effect on the character of the scale.

Two Four-Tone Scales Containing Different Intervals

A scale is like a pitch vocabulary for music. Just as a word vocabulary provides words for making sentences, a scale provides tones for creating music. Anyone who has studied a musical instrument in a traditional manner knows all about scales; they are used as technical learning patterns which help initiate the musician into musical craft. In the repetitive act of playing scales, the student not only acquires technical skills, but also absorbs the tonal patterns of a particular musical tradition. In this way, scales both reflect and perpetuate musical style.

HALF STEPS AND WHOLE STEPS

Half steps and whole steps are relatively small intervals used in our musical system. The half step is the smallest interval of that system.

Examples of Half Steps

The whole step is the next smallest interval (comprised of two half steps).

Examples of Whole Steps

MAJOR AND MINOR SCALES

The two most widely used scales in our musical culture are the *major* and the *minor*. Both are constructed of half steps (2) and whole steps (5). The following major and minor scales both begin on C. If a piano is available, play each scale by following the keyboard diagram.

Major Scale

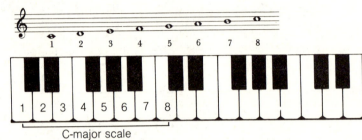

C-major scale

Minor Scale*

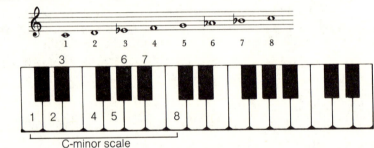

C-minor scale

Melodies based on the major and minor scales have been important in Western music. These two scales have provided the main pitch vocabulary for many of the familiar traditional melodies of our culture. This is a primary reason that you may feel comfortable with their sound. For contrast, consider some melodies based on another scale type.

Listen   Sequence 5 . Melodies 5a , 5b , and 5c use some scale patterns found in the Mideastern-Mediterranean region.

THE CHROMATIC SCALE

The *chromatic scale* is comprised entirely of half steps:

*There are several types of minor scales, of which this is one. See Appendix VI.

Few melodies are based exclusively on the chromatic scale. Rather, chromatic passages are often used to enhance melodies based on the major and minor scales. This can be heard by comparing the original Demonstration Melody (which uses the major scale) with a chromatic variation of that melody.

| Listen | Compare the original Demonstration Melody, *Example 7a*, with its chromatic enhancement, *Example 7b*.

You may notice that chromatic passages produce what some have described as a "sliding" feeling. *Chromatic harmony*—harmony based on tones of the chromatic scale—may also produce this "sliding" effect. The term traditionally used to describe music relatively free of chromatic melody or harmony is *diatonic*.

| Listen | *Example 20c* demonstrates chromatic harmony.

CHURCH MODES

An ancient group of scales called *modes** is quite important in the history of Western music. As you will discover in subsequent chapters, the music of the Christian Church played a vital role in the development of Western music. The melodies of the Church were based on these modes. Melodies that use them are described as *modal*. If a piano is available, play through the following examples of the modes to hear their unique quality (follow the diagrams).

Dorian Mode

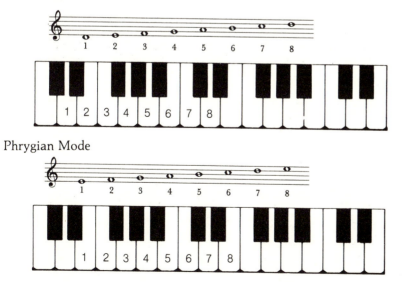

Phrygian Mode

*Theorists often distinguish between *scale* and *mode*. The interested reader should consult a music dictionary.

Lydian Mode

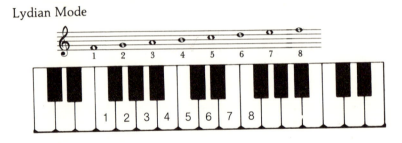

Mixolydian Mode

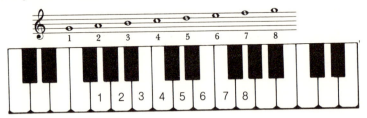

Harmony based on tones of the church modes is described as *modal harmony*. In later chapters, the importance of modal melody and harmony in the development of the Western musical tradition will be discussed.

Melodic Shape

As you have already experienced, an essential quality of melody is the up-and-down patterns created by successive tones. Because of these patterns, melodies both sound and look (when they are notated) as if they have a shape. *Melodic shape* or *contour* describes this basic aspect of melodic design. Melodic shape may be represented by drawing a line through the noteheads.

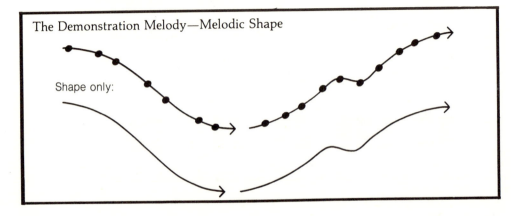

The Demonstration Melody—Melodic Shape

Shape only:

Melodic shape is created by various combinations of intervals. Consider a few of the intervals that make up the Demonstration Melody:

As it happens, the Demonstration Melody proceeds down and up the scale. Its melodic intervals mirror the scale's sequential pitch organization. Describing such a melody (or excerpt), one might say, "It proceeds stepwise." In contrast, the opening of the fourth movement of Mozart's *Symphony No. 40* proceeds by dramatic leaping intervals:

Relatively wide intervals in succession

Melodic shape has sometimes been used for very graphic purposes. For example, Heinrich Schütz (1585–1672), in his *Psalm 116*, sets the German word for hell (*Höllen*) to this dramatic melodic shape:

This rapidly descending line, which is a sudden, new melodic experience in the composition, is an example of how shape may be used for expressive means. A more gentle example is a wordless song from Lapland. In this melody sung on a repeated syllable, the performer is expressing the shape and rhythm of the mountains:

Excerpt from a Lapp Song about Mountains

Both these examples, in which melodic shape is used in such a direct, symbolic manner, are exceptions. Such literal imagery is not usually suggested by most melodies.

MELODIC SHAPE AND SCALE

One of the distinguishing characteristics of a musical tradition is its use of particular scales. A particular melodic shape, on the other hand, may be found in various musical tradition. This is apparent in the following versions of the Demonstration Melody:

Listen   *Examples 6a, b, and c.* In this example, you will recognize that the shape of the Demonstration Melody remains the same. However, its character will change, because it is being played in different scales. Although only an exercise, the Demonstration Melody, played in a scale typical of the Mideastern-Mediterranean area, may evoke something of that region.

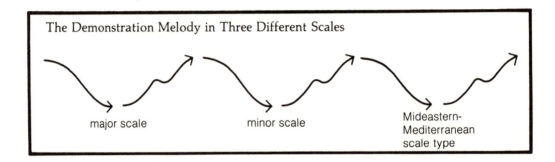

The Demonstration Melody in Three Different Scales

major scale   minor scale   Mideastern-Mediterranean scale type

Form, Shape, and Song

Melodic shape often influences how we respond to form. Again, consider the Demonstration Melody:

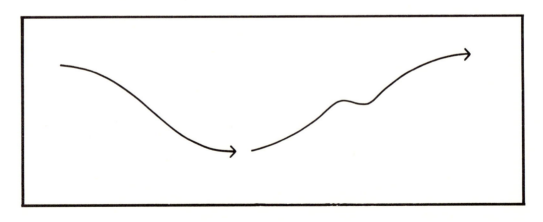

The melody flows through time in two phrases. The phrases have additional meaning through their relationship to each other as shapes. The contour of the second phrase grows from the first like a reflection. The two phrases balance each other, not only in duration but also in shape.

The melodic shape of a song is intertwined with the flow and meaning of the words. Consider the poetry of this song:

> I will give my love an apple without ere a core,
> I will give my love a house without ere a door.
> I will give my love a palace wherein she may be,
> And she may unlock it without any key.
>
> My head is the apple without ere a core,
> My mind is the house without ere a door.
> My heart is the palace wherein she may be,
> And she may unlock it without any key.

Speaking this poetry, one immediately senses an intriguing balance between word, rhythm, phrase, rhyme, and meaning. Without specifically analyzing these details, we know that the poetry flows in a unity in which "all the pieces fit." The melody of the song, including its melodic shape, will also fit into this perfectly balanced plan.

Listen *I Will Give My Love an Apple* 6a . Follow the melodic shape as you listen.

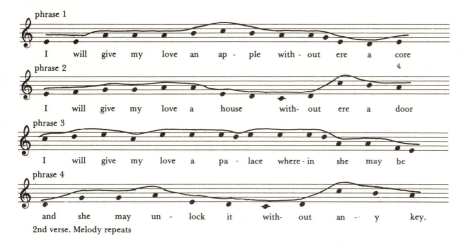

The form of this melody is made up of four related phrases. They are related to each other in a way both ear and eye can appreciate. Each phrase begins in very much the same way. However, slight changes thereafter create beautiful internal balances of melodic shape. For example, the middle to end of the second phrase reflects that part of the first seen right above it. The endings of phrases two and four both balance each other through similar shapes. Of the four phrases, the third seems most different, since its melodic shape "flattens out"—that is, it stays around one tone—for most of its duration. This tone, by the way, is the highest pitch of the song. Thus, the third phrase is a gentle climax of the melody, while the last phrase brings the form to a balanced close. The entire four-phrase structure is repeated in the second verse. Songs in which the same melody is repeated with new verses are in *strophic form*.

Strophic Form

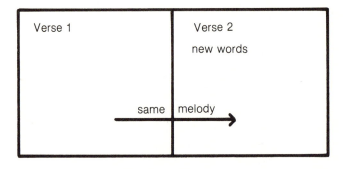

Traditionally, letters are used to represent patterns of musical form. The four phrases of this song can be represented with A . Since the second verse is identical to the first, the form of this song is A A . A song with five verses, each with the same music, is represented as A A A A A . A later version of this song adds something new to the form.

Listen   *The Riddle* 6c . Follow the diagram:

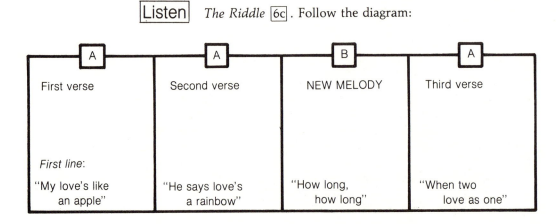

Halfway through *The Riddle* something new happens: We call this B . The form of the complete song may be represented thus: A A B A .

A question often asked about the analysis of a melody (like the one above) is, "Did the person who composed this song really think about all these details?" The answer is often no. The question is a good one, for it shows an innate understanding of the natural unity of musical experience. Although composers sometimes work out the details of melodic construction, this process is mere fine-tuning of their natural inspiration. Melody is the life-blood of music and is universal to all musical traditions. Although we can analyze logical melodic patterns, even in a spontaneous creation like *I Will Give My Love an Apple*, melody essentially exists as a natural expression of human musicality. This observation is supported by the fact that no one has ever found a way to teach a young composer to write a good melody: it seems to be a gift.

Melody and Motive

You have already encountered the word *motive* in the discussion of *rhythmic motives* (page 9). Now this idea will be expanded to include repeated patterns of both rhythm and pitch. A motive is the basic musical idea from which melodies, even entire pieces, may grow. A technique which demonstrates this idea is *ostinato*, the continual repetition of a single motive as the structuring principle of a musical form.

Listen   Sequence 2 . Each piece is created by the ostinato technique.

To examine the process further, consider the first phrase of the Demonstration Melody. It grows from a motive of two tones. Sing it slowly, pausing at the first cadence.

The two-note motive is heard in measure 1. Measures 2 and 3 repeat the idea, beginning on a different pitch. This type of repetition is called a *sequence*. A melody which uses motive repeated in sequence is said to be *sequential*. The second phrase sounds a new three-note motive. Reflecting the design of the first phrase, the new motive is followed by two sequences.

Listen *Example 7b.* You may recognize this example as an altered version of the Demonstration Melody. Like the original, it has two phrases, each with its own motive.

Listen *Example 7c.* This example is also derived from the Demonstration Melody.

Listen *Example 7d.* This example grows from one motive only.

VARIATION

The term *variation* describes the relationship among the melodies just heard (*Examples 7a, b, c, d*). The original Demonstration Melody (*Example 7a*) was followed by three variations. Some compositions follow this procedure for musical design, in which case their form is described as *theme and variations*. (This will be expanded upon in Chapter 9.)

DESCRIBING MELODY

Various overlapping terms are used to describe a melody. The word *tune*, for example, is often applied to a melody that is catchy and dancelike. A *theme* is an important melody in a long piece like a symphony. Short parts of melody are often called *motives* or *figures*. A longer melodic span is called a *phrase*. There are no exact rules concerning these applications; their usage depends upon both source and situation.

What one calls the various parts of a melody is less important than understanding the basic principle that creates the need for such terms: *a melody may be perceived simultaneously at both short- and long-range levels of awareness.* Terms such as *motive, figure, fragment,* as well as *phrase,* all describe a span, perceived as a unit of melodic growth. The opening theme of Mozart's *Symphony No. 40* demonstrates this vital understanding. The very shortest melodic idea is a brief stepwise motive of three notes. This motive is the heart of the melody. For our purposes, this motive may be spoken or sung with "da-da-dum."

 The "da-da-dum" motive (first three notes only):

Examine the notation of the melody for all the places where the short motive is found [in the brackets]:

That short motive ("da-da-dum") repeats rather effortlessly and quickly begins to expand, the original three-note motive growing into four notes with the addition of a new melodic shape. In contrast to the stepwise motion of the motive, the melody now leaps upward. The new wide interval will be very apparent if you sing this opening span on "da-da-dum." (Notice the change to "da-da-dum-da.")

 *Example 21a*, complete

But "da-da-dum" is not the only impulse that flows through the melody. At a slightly longer level of awareness, we perceive another pattern repeating and growing, namely—"da-da-dum da-da-dum da-da-dum-da." This longer span is developed as a unit in the same way that the shorter motive was.

Listen *Example 21b*

At a slightly longer level of awareness, another musical span may be sensed as a repeating and growing pattern:

All these interlocking impulses create an ever longer musical span—the first phrase.

The phrase then becomes one span in the overall form of the movement.

Another melody that grows from short and long patterns is *Ponta de areia*, from Wayne Shorter's album *Native Dancer*. In this melody you will hear a basic motive of two parts that results in a lilting meter of 4 beats plus 5 beats.

Motive

4 + 5

This motive repeats, creating a longer unit of form.

4 + 5

This span grows into the longer form of the melody. Its motion is of the 4 + 5 meter grouping and the alternation of semi and full cadences.

 Listen | *Ponta de areia* 23 by M. Nascimento

DEVELOPMENT

The term that describes the way the short motive of a theme grows into a longer span is *development*. This process, which is not confined solely to melodic design, but can affect all aspects of composition, is basic to much of the music in Western culture, as well as many other traditions.

MELODY AND MOTIVE—SUMMARY

1. A melody may grow from one or more short impulses traditionally called *motives*.
2. These motives may repeat and grow in a process we call *musical development*. A motive, then, is a *unit of growth*.
3. Shorter units of growth (motives, for example) join to create longer spans (phrases, for example), which create even longer spans (sections of a piece or a complete piece, for example). The most important principle of this process is the following: *the life of a melody may be perceived simultaneously at short- to long-range levels of awareness.*

It must be pointed out that all melodies do not fall neatly into such a plan. There are melodies that have no apparent development. Consider the analysis above as one possible but very important type of melodic organization. Finally, the entire process described above applies not only to melody alone, but to music in general.

SCALE   A pitch vocabulary for music. Traditionally it is arranged in an ascending or descending order. The individual tones of a scale are called *steps* or *scale degrees*. Two widely used scales are the major and the minor.

CHURCH MODES, MODAL   A group of scales associated with early Christian music. A melody or harmony based on a mode is described as *modal*. Modal music has a continuous history into the present time.

CHROMATIC SCALE   A scale made up of half steps. Melody or harmony based on this scale is described as *chromatic*.

DIATONIC MUSIC   Music with little or no chromaticism.

(continued on next page)

MELODIC SHAPE   The pitch contour of a melody. Melodic shape may be represented visually by a line drawn through the noteheads.

MOTIVE   A musical idea, often used as a basis for development. A motive may have a distinctive rhythm, melodic shape, or both.

OSTINATO   A repeated rhythmic or melodic motive which forms the basis for a musical piece.

SEQUENCE   The repetition of a motive beginning on a new pitch. Sequences may be found in many melodies, which are thus called *sequential*.

VARIATION   Repeating a melody or section basically intact, but with changes in musical details.

DEVELOPMENT   The process by which a short musical idea is transformed into a longer span.

THEME   A basic melody in a musical work. For example, one might speak of the main theme from Mozart's *Symphony No. 40*.

STROPHIC FORM   A song design in which the words change, but the melody is repeated. One such form may be represented as ⟨ A | A | A | A | A ⟩ , etc. Another strophic form—verse and chorus—would be ⟨ A | B | A | B | A | B ⟩ , etc.

Texture–Monophonic and Polyphonic

Melody and harmony are available resources for creating *musical texture*. Texture is the result of combining musical elements. A melody alone, for example, is one of the simplest textures. This texture is *monophonic*. When harmony is added to a melody, the resulting texture is *homophonic*.

⟨Listen⟩   *Examples 8a and 8b.* In both these examples, the Demonstration Melody is accompanied by one chord. The textures of both examples are homophonic.

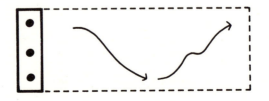

Listen *Example 9.* The Demonstration Melody (in the minor scale) is accompanied by repeated chords in a faster rhythm than the melody. The texture is homophonic. The example begins with the accompaniment.

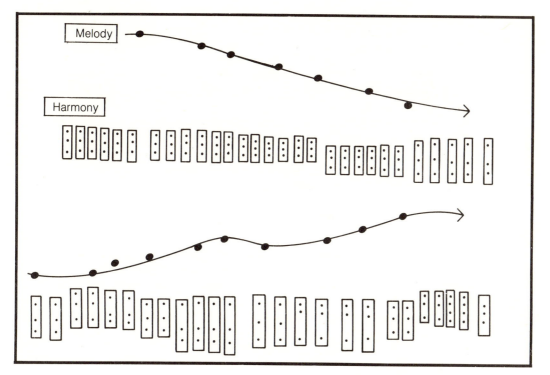

Listen *Example 10a.* Another texture resulting from a somewhat different use of melody and harmony is heard in *Example 10a,* in which each tone of the Demonstration Melody is heard with its own chord. In fact, the melody is the highest tone of each chord.

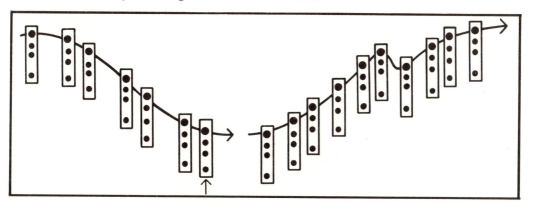

This type of *harmonization* (adding harmony to a melody) is a traditional texture of choral singing. It is especially suited for hymns, since all the voices sing each word at the same time, making the text quite clear. Because of this tradition, this texture has been called *familiar style*.

Listen   In *Example 10b* you will hear the Demonstration Melody in a texture similar to that of *Example 10a*; however, the chords are considerably more dissonant than in the previous example.

Each of the textures considered in this section has featured a melody harmonized with chords. Melody was the main component of each example. If you were to take away that melody, what remains would sound bare and incomplete. On the other hand, taking away the harmony still leaves an essential musical element intact. Thus, all these textures can be described as having a melody as the primary element, while the harmony plays a supporting role. The relationship of *primary* melody to *supporting* harmony is an essential characteristic of a homophonic texture.

FOREGROUND AND BACKGROUND

The term *background* may be used to describe the harmony in a homophonic texture, implying that the melody is in the *foreground*. This balance between background and foreground material is essential in a homophonic texture. There are times when a composer or performer places certain material "up front" to clarify musical meaning. Timbre may play an important role in creating a foreground–background relationship, by helping to single out the melody, while unifying the sound of the background harmony. This is apparent in the next piece.

Listen   *Walk Around* 3a . In this piece, the background is created by repeated *chords*, sung in an ostinato rhythm to the words "walk around."

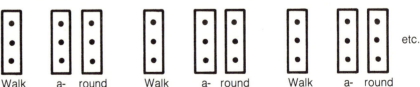

Walk   a- round   Walk   a- round   Walk   a- round   etc.

The rich vocal harmony and the repeated rhythmic motive provide a solid background for the more complex solo melody.

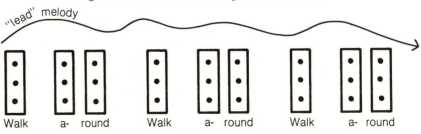

Walk   a- round   Walk   a- round   Walk   a- round

Polyphonic Texture

When several independent melodies sound simultaneously, the result is a *polyphonic texture*, or *polyphony*. The following example demonstrates what might be called "polyphonic in the extreme," since the melodies were never meant to go together.

Listen | *Example 11a*. In this example the Demonstration Melody is heard simultaneously with the well-known *Twinkle, Twinkle, Little Star*.

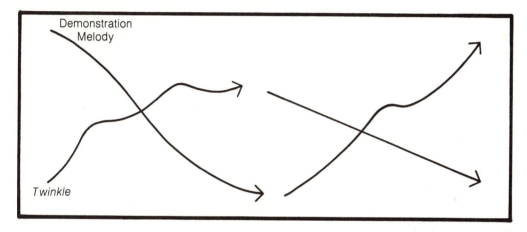

As you may have noticed, this polyphonic texture sounds a bit odd; these melodies are so independent that they don't really fit together. Obviously, the simultaneous sounding of several melodies has to be well planned. The creator of a polyphonic texture must consider the resulting intervals or chords carefully. In the next example, the Demonstration Melody is played with another tune, but in contrast to the previous example, the total effect has been more carefully planned.

Listen | *Example 11b*. The Demonstration Melody sounds with another tune. The resulting combination is an example of a traditional polyphonic texture in which the independent melodies fit together.

THE ART OF COUNTERPOINT

To create a successful polyphonic texture, a composer is obliged to follow certain principles and traditions which, taken together, constitute the *art of counterpoint*. *Counterpoint* describes the procedures with which composers create polyphonic textures. A related term—*contrapuntal*—is also used to identify polyphonic pieces. Thus, a texture of simultaneously sounding melodies may be described as *polyphonic* or *contrapuntal*.

MELODIC SHAPE IN POLYPHONY

A polyphonic texture is in some ways like the inner workings of a clock. Imagine, for a moment, the contrasting movement and speed of the various mechanical wheels as they turn in synchronized motion. The word *motion* is often used to describe the "inner workings" of polyphony, especially the relationship between melodies that move simultaneously in harmonic synchronization. This motion may be *parallel, contrary,* or *oblique.* Represented as melodic shapes, these contrapuntal relationships look like this:

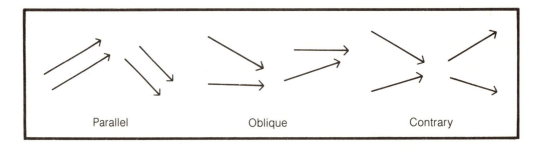

Parallel   Oblique   Contrary

Listen *Example 12.* This example demonstrates two types of contrapuntal motion—*oblique* and *parallel.* You will hear two voices (or lines): the Demonstration Melody is one. The first phrase of the example illustrates oblique motion, after which there is a slight pause. The second phrase proceeds in parallel motion. Look at the melodic shapes before you listen. Also, notice that the example does not begin with the Demonstration Melody, but with the counterpoint.

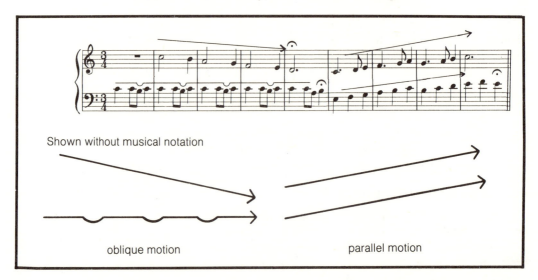

Shown without musical notation

oblique motion   parallel motion

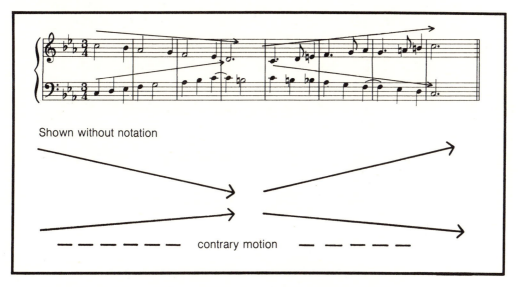

Listen | *Example 13*. This two-voice contrapuntal example illus-
trates contrary motion. The Demonstration Melody sounds in the
minor scale.

Before listening to the next example, consider again the inner movement of the clock: many wheels move in similar and contrasting motion
(some turn clockwise, others counterclockwise). This image is a good analogy for the various directions the melodies pursue in a polyphonic texture.
Take the image one step further. The wheels turn not only in different directions, but at different speeds. A large wheel may be meshed with a smaller
one. As they turn, one sees a rhythmic relationship between fast and slow
motions. Look at the diagram below and imagine it in action: the large
wheel turns slowly while the smaller one turns faster; the third wheel of
even smaller size turns faster still.

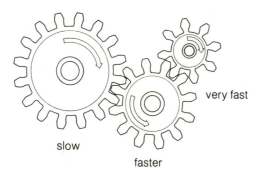

With this image in mind, consider the next example.

Listen   *Examples 14a and b.* In this example, the Demonstration Melody is first heard alone and then with a counterpoint in faster rhythm.

Listen   *Examples 14a, b, c.* A third voice has been added to the two-part texture you have just heard (*Example 14b*). *Example 14c* begins with three patterns of rhythmic motion, ranging from slow to fast. Listen to *14a, b,* and *c* a few times. This gives you an opportunity to hear a three-part polyphonic texture built up one part at a time.

DISSONANT POLYPHONY

Polyphonic textures are often encountered in a more dissonant harmonic style than the ones you have just heard. In fact, during the twentieth century, polyphony has been one of the basic organizational techniques in the creation of more dissonant harmonic styles. In the following example, the Demonstration Melody is heard in a dissonant polyphonic texture. Notice, however, that the dissonance is *resolved* at the two cadences.

Listen   *Example 15.* The Demonstration Melody in a dissonant, polyphonic texture.

The Interplay between Linear and Harmonic Organization

Polyphony makes possible a perceptual interplay between simultaneous sounding melodies and the harmony they produce. We may summarize the basic principles of this interaction as follows:

1. Whenever different melodies are combined, some type of harmony results.
2. Therefore, polyphony involves two ways of listening:
   melodic (linear)—a response to the melodic aspects of each individual part:

harmonic (vertical)—a response to the harmony that the melodies generate.

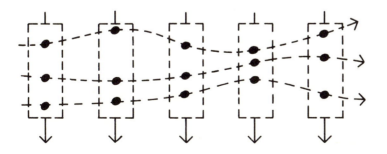

These exist simultaneously:

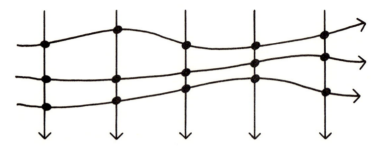

3. Different polyphonic textures may emphasize either the linear or the harmonic aspect. There are textures in which the linear aspect is so strong that the chords are hard to hear. Other textures tend to emphasize the harmony, in which case the chords are easy to hear.

Listen *Northfield*, by Jeremiah Ingalls 32a

This short choral piece by an early American composer illustrates an alternation between homophonic and polyphonic textures. The majority of the words are set in *familiar style*, a type of homophonic texture which facilitates easy comprehension of the words (see page 56). One line of the text, however, is set contrapuntally. Appropriately, on the words "fly swifter round ye wheel of time," each part enters *imitating* the one before. The texture is indicated in a small box with a dot under m, h, or p (for monophonic, homophonic, or polyphonic).

Northfield, by Jeremiah Ingalls

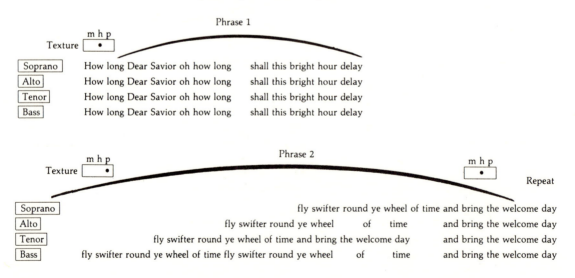

Texture–A Continuum

Some textures, like the two just heard in *Northfield*, are clearly identifiable. But in other pieces, there is often ambiguity. It is useful to consider texture on a continuum so that its flexible nature can be understood.

monophonic	homophonic	polyphonic
single melody	a main melody with some type of secondary accompaniment	several independent melodies

growing complexity and linear organization

This plan allows for the representation of different degrees of textural complexity. For example:

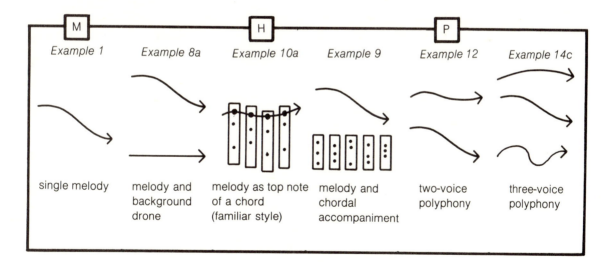

M		H		P	
Example 1	Example 8a	Example 10a	Example 9	Example 12	Example 14c
single melody	melody and background drone	melody as top note of a chord (familiar style)	melody and chordal accompaniment	two-voice polyphony	three-voice polyphony

It is not uncommon to encounter *mixed textures* within a single work. For example, a single melody accompanied by a drone is not really what most experts mean when they refer to homophonic texture, since it leans more toward monophonic, but not all the way. The *Trauermusik* by Paul Hindemith [3c] is a good example of mixed texture. It opens with an instrumental chorale, the melody in the top voice:

Clearly Homophonic Texture

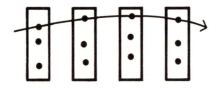

But at certain moments in this piece, we hear considerable melodic activity in the other parts. Although our basic response is to the chordal or homophonic organization, there is enough counterpoint to push the texture a little toward the polyphonic side of the continuum. Calling it either homophonic or polyphonic seems to miss the point. Perhaps "homophonic with some polyphonic tendencies" might be more accurate. This mixed texture can be easily positioned on the continuum thus:

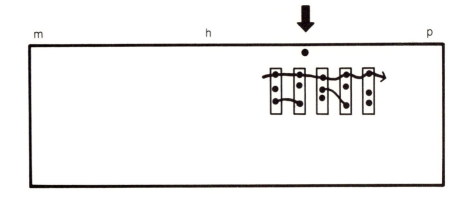

TEXTURE   The result of the combination of musical elements. In this book, texture is shown on a continuum ranging from simple to complex.

MONOPHONIC   The simplest musical texture consisting of a single melody.

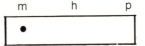

HOMOPHONIC   A texture made up of a melody with a harmonic background.

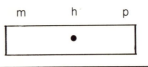

FAMILIAR STYLE   A homophonic choral texture in which all the voices sing the same words at the same time.

FOREGROUND–BACKGROUND   The relationship between an emphasized musical element that sounds "up front" and a supporting musical element.

POLYPHONIC (POLYPHONY)   A musical texture in which several melodies are combined.

COUNTERPOINT (CONTRAPUNTAL)   The technique of creating polyphony. The term *contrapuntal* is often used in place of *polyphonic*. For example, the combination of several melodies can be described either as polyphonic or contrapuntal in texture.

IMITATION   A contrapuntal practice in which a motive is repeated by different voices one after the other.

CONTRAPUNTAL MOTION   Relationship between melodies in a polyphonic texture. Three types of contrapuntal motion are *parallel, oblique,* and *contrary.* Represented visually, these polyphonic textures appear as:

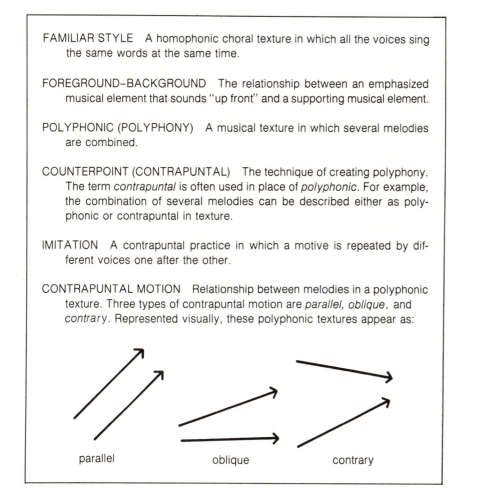

parallel   oblique   contrary

QUESTIONS

Find any false statement(s) and correct them by changing the word(s) in italics. More than one statement may be false; all the statements may be true.

1. Concerning pitch:

   (a) It describes the relative *highness or lowness* of musical sound.

   (b) It is caused by some type of *vibration.*

   (c) Smaller vibrating objects produce *lower* pitches than larger objects.

   (d) When you loosen a guitar string, its pitch goes *up.*

2. Concerning pitch types:

   (a) Most noise is of *indefinite* pitch.

   (b) The sound of a piano is characterized by *sliding* pitches.

   (c) A siren has a *steady* pitch.

   (d) Indefinite pitches *may be* sensed as high or low.

3. Concerning timbre and tone:

   (a) *Tone* is the characteristic quality of a sound source.

   (b) Tone is the musical combination of *timbre and pitch*.

   (c) A flute has a different *timbre* than a guitar.

   (d) *Pitch, rhythm, and tone* are terms which are commonly used interchangeably.

4. Concerning instruments:

   (a) They are classified according to the *way they produce* tone.

   (b) They are grouped into *families*.

   (c) The difference in the character of sound between one instrument and another is described as *tone*.

   (d) Tha material from which an instrument is created *does not* affect its timbre.

5. Concerning melody and harmony:

   (a) In a melody, one tone *follows* another.

   (b) A melody is made up of *harmonic* intervals.

   (c) *Both* melody and harmony are created with tones.

   (d) When two tones sound together, they produce a *melodic* interval.

6. Concerning harmony:

   (a) Harmony involves the *simultaneous* sounding of tones.

   (b) A *chord* produces harmony.

   (c) *Intervals and chords* may be consonant or dissonant.

   (d) An *interval* produces harmony.

7. Concerning consonant and dissonant harmony:

   (a) Each is *relative* to the other.

   (b) Dissonant harmony may *resolve* to consonant harmony.

   (c) Dissonant harmony creates *less* forward potential than consonant harmony.

   (d) Consonant or dissonant harmony can be created by *polyphony*.

8. Concerning a progression:

   (a) It is a chain of *chords* heard as one flow of musical action.

   (b) It may involve *consonant and dissonant* chords.

   (c) A progression may create *forward potential*.

   (d) A progression is mainly a *melodic* consideration.

9. Concerning melody and scale:

   (a) A scale provides a *pitch vocabulary* for melody.

   (b) Many melodies may use the *same* scale.

   (c) Major and minor are the *least familiar* scales in our culture.

   (d) Some *ancient* melodies use a scale of only three or four tones.

10. Concerning melodic shape:

    (a) Melodic shape is a *universal* element in the music of the world.

    (b) Another term for it is *melodic contour*.

    (c) Melodic shape is *always* used to represent a visual idea.

    (d) Melodic shape may be a short-range element that helps to create *long-range form*.

11. Concerning melody and motive:

    (a) A melody may *grow* from a motive.

    (b) A melody *never* has more than one motive.

    (c) The original Demonstration Melody is based on *two* motives.

    (d) Changes in a motive as it moves through a piece can be described as a motivic *progression*.

12. Concerning a motive:

    (a) It is a relatively short *musical span*.

    (b) When it repeats starting on another tone it is called a *cadence*.

    (c) It is a *longer* musical span than a phrase.

    (d) It *may* play a role in the perception of form.

13. Concerning strophic form:

    (a) It applies to *vocal* music.

    (b) In a strophic form the words change while the music *repeats*.

    (c) Verse–chorus—a common strophic plan—is represented by $\boxed{A}\,\boxed{A}\,\boxed{A}\,\boxed{A}\,\boxed{A}$ etc.

    (d) "The Riddle Song" $\boxed{\text{6b}}$ has a strophic design. Its form is $\boxed{A}\,\boxed{B}$.

14. Concerning the theme from Mozart's *Symphony No. 40*:

    (a) The shortest unit of growth is a motive of *four* notes.

    (b) The heart of this melody includes a *stepwise* interval.

    (c) The melody grows out of a distinctive *three-note* impulse.

    (d) The first development of the original three-note motive may be spoken "*da-da-dum-da*."

15. Concerning a monophonic texture:

    (a) It is the most *complex* musical texture.

    (b) It emphasizes the *harmonic* aspect of organization.

    (c) It is a *single* melody.

    (d) It is *less* complex than a homophonic texture.

16. Concerning a homophonic texture:

    (a) It falls *between* monophonic and polyphonic on the texture continuum.

    (b) It *rarely* involves a foreground–background relationship.

    (c) It includes a melody *and* harmony.

    (d) One type of homophonic texture especially suited for choral pieces is familiar style, in which each voice sings in *different rhythms*.

17. Concerning a polyphonic texture:

    (a) It combines *independent* melodic lines.

    (b) It creates an interplay between *linear* and *melodic* organization.

    (c) It may also be spoken of as a *contrapuntal* texture.

    (d) It is the *most* complex of musical textures.

18. Concerning a polyphonic texture:

    (a) Diversity is often created by *faster and slower* rhythms sounding at the same time.

    (b) Diversity is often created by a combination of *various* melodic shapes.

    (c) Polyphonic textures *have no* harmony.

    (d) Polyphonic textures may be consonant *or* dissonant.

19. Concerning imitation between voices:

    (a) It may occur in a *monophonic* texture.

    (b) It is a type of *repetition*.

    (c) It may occur in *vocal and instrumental* works.

    (d) In a choral piece, imitation often involves the singing of the *same* words.

3
Materials
of Music–III

The musician has access to one of life's most ecstatic sensations—artistic freedom. But this freedom exists within certain universal norms. As used in this context, a norm is a natural phenomenon which affects our existence. Gravity is a good example; we are born into a world in which gravity exists, and we live within its natural boundaries. Music also has norms, one of which you have already encountered—rhythmic periodicity. In this section, we will discuss another—the *harmonic series*, a basic principle of physics. A technical explanation of the harmonic series appears on pages 495–6. For the moment, it is only necessary to understand that the harmonic series is a force of nature on which the existence and perception of musical sound is based.

The Magic of the String

The word *tone*, which we can use to describe the very essence of musical sound, comes from the Greek *tonos* meaning rope, cord, tension, exertion of force. As we shall discover in later pages, the etymology of the word reflects an experience that was sacred and magical throughout the ancient world. In the illustration on page 71, we see the same string vibrating in different ways as a result of being touched along its length at exactly the right places. As you will hear, each touch produces a different tone. We are interested in the relationship between the tones and the exact place the string must be touched to produce them.

The Magic of the String

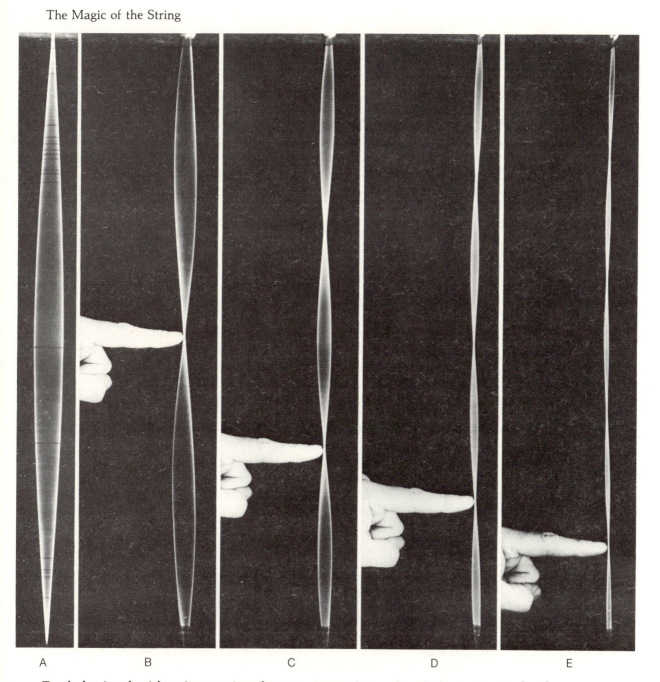

A   B   C   D   E

Touched at just the right points, a string vibrates in sections that produce the harmonic series; heard (on piano) as recorded *Example 19b*.

FROM *SOUNDS OF MUSIC*, CHARLES TAYLOR, BBC LONDON

Listen *Example 19b.* Heard in order are the tones produced by dividing the string as shown above, constituting the first five tones of the harmonic series.

THE OCTAVE

Listen The sound of this sequence is heard as *Example 19a.* We pluck the string. It produces a steady tone. We pluck the string while touching it at its midway point. It produces a higher tone. We compare these tones as an interval by playing them one after another.

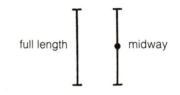

What we experience is a remarkable sensation. While the tones are definitely different—one is high and one is low—they are so consonant that they seem to form a unity—so much so, that one may easily hear them as being the same. The ancient Greeks called this interval the *diapason*, meaning "through the whole." We call it an *octave*. (This terminology is explained later.) *What we hear in the octave interval is a sensation of two tones that sound both different and the same.* If this seems to you like a riddle, you're right. In fact, this relationship has been called a "cosmic riddle." The answer is both simple and complex, depending on how detailed one chooses to be. But we can accurately say that the octave sensation is related to a symmetrical pattern found in nature. This is apparent when we examine how the string is divided to produce the octave—exactly in half. The shorter length of the string produces the higher tone of the octave. If the whole string were 12 units long, the octave would be produced by a portion 6 units long.

Although one is obviously higher than the other, both these tones have that amazing quality of sounding practically the same. It is no wonder then that they both bear the same pitch designation. (Pitches are named with letter names; see page 29.) So, if the string 12 units long is an A, its octave, produced by dividing the string in half, is also an A. This relationship is seen and heard on the piano by playing two A-keys.

73

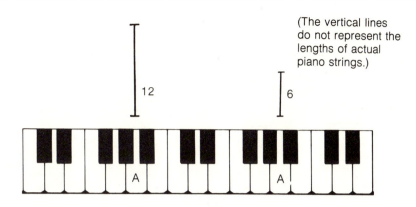

(The vertical lines
do not represent the
lengths of actual
piano strings.)

The creation of additional A's continues by dividing or multiplying the string length by two. In fact, the tone A exists at higher and lower levels throughout the pitch range.

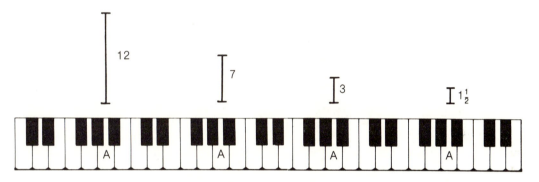

The implications of this relationship go to the very core of that norm that holds musical sound together. For example, a melody can exist simultaneously at higher or lower levels. Suppose a melody begins with three pitches—A, B, and C. On the piano:

We can play them simultaneously on any level:

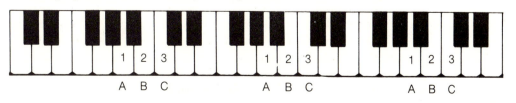

OCTAVE AND SCALE

Consider, for a moment, how the pattern of days we call a *week* organizes time. The first thing we notice is a repeating pattern of days:

M T W Th F Sa S M T W Th F Sa S M T

The week is a cyclical pattern—it repeats every seven days. It really has no beginning and no end until we choose those boundaries. Even then, the sequence of days will keep repeating. As weeks can organize time, the octave organizes tonal space, and the tones within the octave simply keep repeating as a scale.

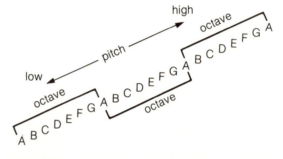

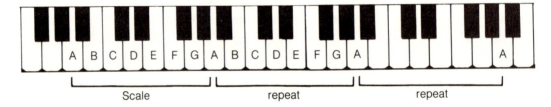

Tonality

Tonality is a force that affects music in much the same way that gravity affects objects—drawing them toward a center of attraction. In music, this center of attraction is a tone to which other tones gravitate. It is called the *tonic*, and its "magnetic power" can be easily sensed in the following example: Sing the Demonstration Melody up until the last tone. Do not sing the final tone.

You most likely have a feeling of musical frustration—a desire to sing or hear that final tone. That tone is the tonic. Without it, we have an unstable feeling that can be satisfied only by "coming home."

TONALITY AND HARMONY
Again, look at the illustrations on page 71. The various tones derived from one string would form a chord if sounded simultaneously.

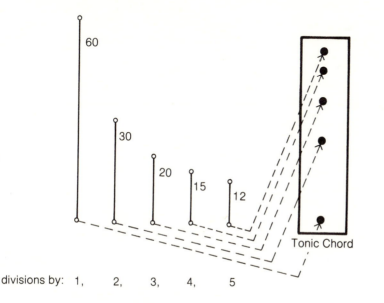

divisions by: 1, 2, 3, 4, 5

This symmetrical division of the string has generated a *tonic chord*. There are many implications to be drawn from this "natural harmony"; one is of immediate importance to this discussion.

Tonality often affects a harmonic progression. Just as the single tones of a melody may be attracted toward the tonic, the chords in a progression may be attracted toward the tonic chord:

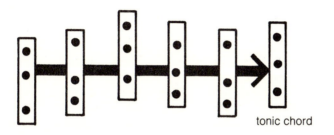

tonic chord

76

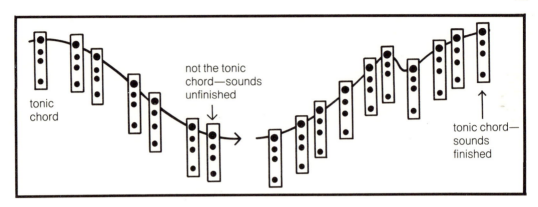

[Listen] *Example 10a.* Listen to the Demonstration Melody in a homophonic texture.

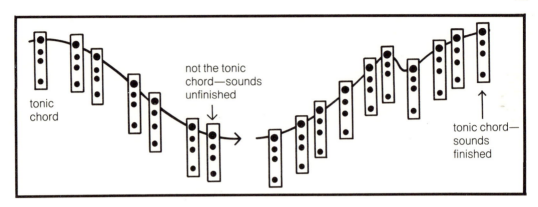

[Listen] *Example 10b.* In this more dissonant chorale version of the Demonstration Melody, tonality is the principle that brings order to the experience. The dissonant chords are heard in relation to their ultimate arrival at the tonic chord.

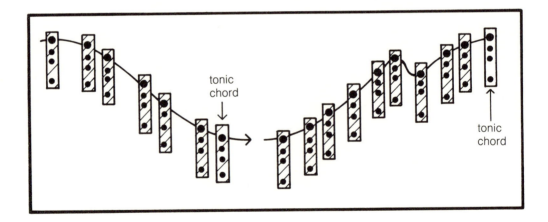

[Listen] *Examples 14b and c.* In both of these polyphonic versions of the Demonstration Melody, tonality is the most important organizing principle. All the intervals, chords, melodic shapes, and rhythmic textures are held together by the pull of the tonic. Each melody begins as a member of the tonic chord and after its journey returns to the tonic chord.

Imagine, for a moment, the following: visualize a juggler tossing a single ball into the air and gently catching it each time it descends. Now jugglers don't just throw balls into the air, even one at a time. To them, a toss into space is a moment of art. The single ball moves at various speeds and to various heights. The succession of tosses might create a simple but beautiful pattern of inevitability, for the ball always returns. As the juggler tosses the single ball, so the musician may sing a simple tonal song (a chant perhaps). The tones create patterns and shapes of another inevitable plan, for those tones will eventually return to the tonic. When the juggler uses several balls at the same time, the resulting patterns are more complex. But like the movement of the single ball, this complexity can only exist within the ordering world of gravity. And, like the simpler pattern of a single melody, the complex patterns of tonal polyphony can only exist within the ordering world of tonality.

| Listen | The following are two examples of polyphony:

Bach, *Fugue* [17]
Stravinsky, *Danse* [2b]

TONALITY AND KEY
The tonic is also called the *tonal center* of a piece. *Example 1*, in which the Demonstration Melody uses C as the tonic, can be described as "having C as the tonal center." Another way to describe the tonal center is with the words "in the key of." If the tonic is D, for example, the piece is "in the key of D." The Demonstration Melody has been presented in various keys. *Example 1* is in C; *Example 10a* is in G. We can also identify what scale the piece uses. If a piece uses notes from the major scale starting on A, for example, it is in A major. If the composition uses the minor scale which begins on F♯ (F-sharp), it is said to be "in the key of F♯ minor." Traditionally, if neither major nor minor appears after the pitch name, we assume the piece to be in the major.

TONALITY AND FORM
Many pieces sound continuously in one tonality. *I Will Give My Love an Apple* is a good example.

| Listen | *I Will Give My Love an Apple* [6a]

We hear the entire melody in a secure tonal environment. Each tone is given meaning and direction by the pull of the tonal center. In this piece, the forward potential created by the tonic is a gentle presence, continually leading the tones back home.

Listen   *The Riddle* 6c

In this song, as you may recall, the verse A appears twice and is followed by a new section B . The B section *is in a new key.* We use the word *modulation* to describe the movement from one key to another. Listen through the B section, stopping at the words "There ain't no tomorrow."

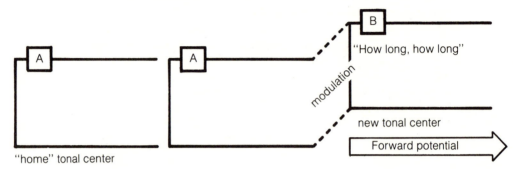

"home" tonal center

We have heard two tonal centers. The first one is home base; when the music modulated to the new key, we were taken on a "journey" into a new tonal region. At this moment, we feel a good deal of forward potential toward the home key. Now go back and listen to the entire piece, taking special notice of the departure from and return to the home key.

Complete Form

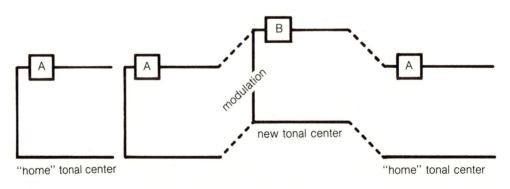

In *The Riddle,* we have experienced the juxtaposition of tonal centers shaping our response to form.

HARMONIC SERIES, TONALITY—SUMMARY

So far, this chapter has been concerned with important aspects of musical organization determined or influenced by the harmonic series. This section may be summarized as follows:

1. The harmonic series is a universal principle of nature (a norm).
2. When the harmonic series is demonstrated on a string, we see that it is related to symmetrical proportion.
3. The harmonic series allows for the very existence of music through the organization of tonal space into repeating octaves.
4. The harmonic series is responsible for tonality, an important factor in the organization of many musical works.

Additional information on the harmonic series is found in Appendix VIII.

HARMONIC SERIES A universal principle of nature, organizing the existence and perception of music.

TONALITY The attraction of musical sound toward a central tone. Music that is affected by tonality is described as *tonal*.

TONIC, TONIC CHORD The pitch or chord to which tones are drawn.

MODULATION A shift from one tonal center to another.

OCTAVE The interval at which the same tone sounds in a higher or lower pitch range.

The Major-Minor Tonal System

The tonal design of *The Riddle* is made possible by the *major-minor tonal system*. It is quite likely that the majority of music with which you are familiar uses this system, or has been deeply influenced by it in some manner. A basic part of our traditional musical language, the major–minor tonal system has become an important influence on many musical styles throughout the world. In later sections we will consider its development and far-reaching effects; for now, the following characteristics will suffice.

1. *The use of major and minor scales.* Although they are *not the only scales* that are used within our tradition, the major and minor scales are among its basic musical materials. Another important scale within the major–minor tonal system is the chromatic scale, often used to enhance a major or minor melody.

2. *The presence of a strong tonal center.* A strong tonal center (home-base or tonic key) is basic to music within the major–minor tonal system. Tonal music has always existed throughout the world as a universal expression of the harmonic series (see page 495–6). But the way this natural tendency developed in the music of the West had certain unique characteristics. One of these is tonal contrast—the establishment of the home key, the modulation to a new key (or keys), and the eventual return home.

3. *Use of major–minor chord progressions.* One way to support tonal contrast is through the use of chord progressions by which we *leave* and eventually *return* to the tonic chord.

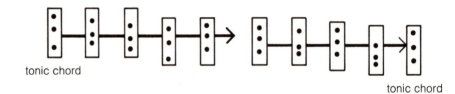

tonic chord

tonic chord

The diagram above represents a simple version of this process. Other progressions may travel through many different chords and key centers, return, leave again—the possibilities are endless. But the final outcome is certain. The progression eventually "comes home" to the tonic chord.

4. *A strong sense of forward potential.* All the musical practices of the major–minor tonal system help create a heightened sense of forward potential. Major and minor scales, harmonic progressions, chromatic elements, and tonal contrast, all generate *goal-directed* musical structures. In works of the major–minor tonal tradition, music "seems to go somewhere."

MODAL HARMONY

Perhaps one way to emphasize the forward-moving quality of the major–minor system is to compare it with another tradition. The following pieces compare the effect of *modal harmony* based on the ancient church modes (see page 43) with that of the major–minor tonal system. Both selections contain chord progressions. But the *modal* progression has less forward potential than the major–minor one. The chords are still related—that is the definition of a progression—but they sound less goal-directed. On the other hand, the major–minor progression moves through time with a much greater forward potential.

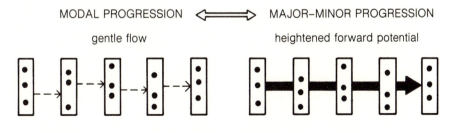

MODAL PROGRESSION   ⟸⟹   MAJOR–MINOR PROGRESSION

gentle flow   heightened forward potential

Listen   Compare *Examples 20a and 20b*. Then compare the harmony of Gibbons, *I Am the Resurrection* [12], with that of the *Kyrie* from Bach, *B-minor Mass* [18] and Bonoff, *Isn't It Always Love* [22].

CULTURAL CONDITIONING AND THE MAJOR-MINOR TRADITION

The two kinds of harmonic progressions you have just heard illustrate the degree to which the major–minor system has entered the musical consciousness of our culture. We are so accustomed to its strong forward potential that music outside this tradition may "seem to go nowhere" or at least to go there a bit slower than we would wish. This is a good example of how music is heard through a cultural filter. In this case, some people will hear ancient modal music through a "major–minor filter" that affects their response.

THE MAJOR–MINOR TONAL SYSTEM   An important musical tradition characterized by a strong emphasis on tonality, affecting melody, harmony, rhythm, and form. The major–minor tonal system has had an enormous influence on the musical traditions of the world.

MODAL HARMONY   A type of harmony created from the ancient church modes. Modal progressions often lack strong forward potential.

Basic Principles of Form

Form has already been touched on in previous sections. Now, we seek a deeper understanding of this fundamental aspect of musical organization. To review the basic information presented so far:

1. All music has form.
2. Form describes the outline or shape of a piece.

3. Form begins with rhythm.
4. Form may be influenced by life rhythms; for example, lullabies, work songs, game songs, etc.
5. Form is shaped by musical detail, such as phrase, cadence, melodic shape, motive, and tonality.
6. We respond to form at both short- and long-range levels of awareness.

Examine again the picture sequences (pages 500–11) based on three visual forms: mother and child, circle, and mountain-tower shape. These forms are specific configurations in a geometric sense. But their origins, significance, and affects are not limited to mere visual imagery. These shapes, after all, reflect a deeper universal reality: The mother and child shape may evoke a wide range of natural feelings; the circle touches our perception of periodicity, balance, and proportion; the powerful religious connotations of the mountain-tower shape are reinforced by an inner response to its pointed contour, which seems to reach toward the heavens. Examination of these forms suggests a basic principle: *Our perception of form is partially determined by innate, universal responses*. In the following section, we examine some of those responses that influence the creation and perception of musical form:

1. Repetition
2. Contrast
3. Unity and Variety
4. Balance and
   Proportion

For the most part, the examples we will use have already been heard, and in some cases the form has already been discussed. Also, some pieces will appear several times. There is a reason for this repetition of material. Form is a multifaceted phenomenon. It will be useful to examine it from different yet overlapping viewpoints, using familiar examples. It is not necessary to listen again to pieces you already know. In most cases, the diagrams provided will be enough to demonstrate the concept. If you encounter a piece you haven't heard, or if you would find it useful to hear it again, do so at your own discretion.

REPETITION

In a fundamental sense, musical form is created through the repetition of musical events. Various types of repetition help build musical structure at both short- and long-range levels.

Examples:

A single musical event

●

becomes a pulse through repetition.

● ● ● ● ● ● ●

Groups of pulses are repeated to create meter:

● ● ● |● ● ● |● ● ● |● ● ● |

Pulses and meter support longer phrases which may also be repeated.

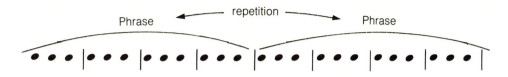

Repeated phrases create longer spans which may also be repeated.

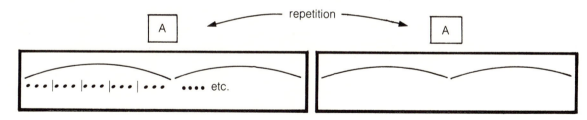

Motives may be repeated in various ways to create melodies and phrases.

Demonstration Melody

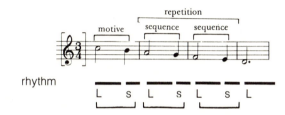

Ostinato form is created through extended repetition of a motive.

West African Game Song [2c]

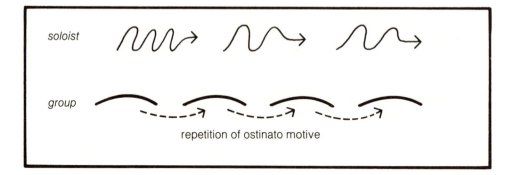

Strophic form is created by the repetition of the same melody for each verse.

I Gave My Love a Cherry [6b]

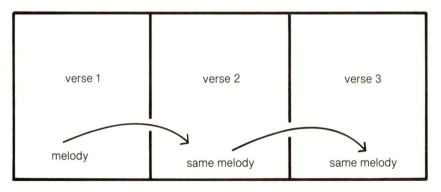

Polyphonic imitation is created through the repetition of a motive in different voices.

Northfield (excerpt) [32a]

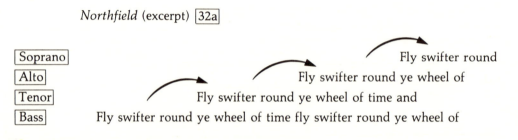

A common type of polyphony based in repetition is the *round* (for example, *Frère Jacques* or *Row, row, row your boat*). This kind of piece is created through *exact repetition* of a melody in different voices, at different times. When the end of the melody is reached, each singer begins the tune again. If the melody is not repeated, the result is called a *canon*.

 Example 23, canon

CONTRAST

One natural affinity for repetition is balanced by a delight in contrast. Contrast creates diversity, which often plays an important part in both short- and long-range design.

Examples:

Demonstration Melody

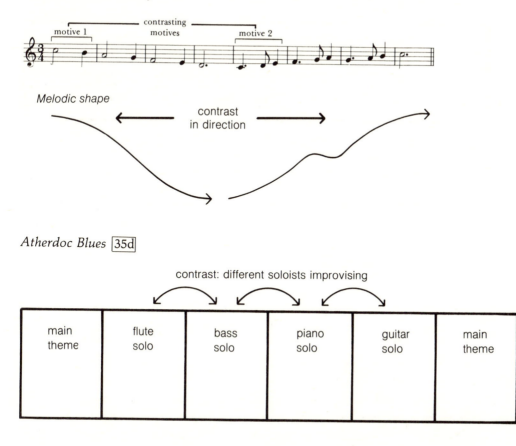

Atherdoc Blues 35d

contrast: different soloists improvising

main theme	flute solo	bass solo	piano solo	guitar solo	main theme

The Riddle 6c

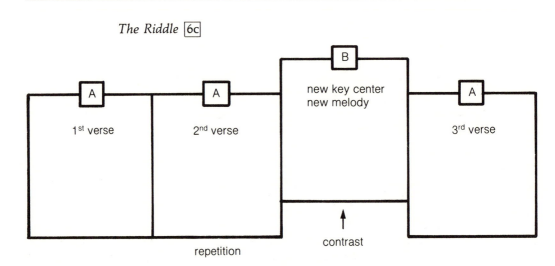

repetition   contrast

Northfield 32a : Contrast in Texture

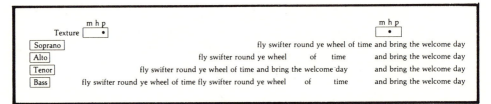

UNITY AND VARIETY

Repetition and contrast are elements in the balance between *unity and variety*—a basic and fascinating aspect of musical organization. This principle represents a balance between *order* and *freedom* in musical form.

Examples:

Atherdoc Blues 35d

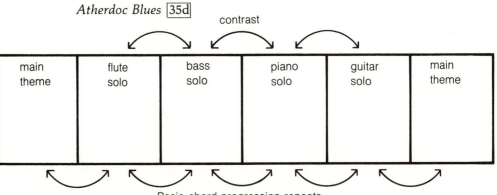

West African Game Song 2c : Soloist and Group

The group repeats the ostinato motive, bringing unity to the piece. The soloist has more freedom to create contrast and thus provides variety.

Soloist

Group

unity through repetition of group ostinato

The interplay between soloist and group demonstrates the principle of unity and variety. Traditionally, the group supplies the basic foundation (through repeated patterns, chord progressions, for example) while the soloist is free to create variety (sometimes through improvisation). This balance is apparent in some of the other selections featuring soloist and group: *Atherdoc Blues* 35d , *Super Blue* 2d , *Gigue* by Handel 11c , *Trauermusik* by Hindemith 3c .

BALANCE AND PROPORTION
In all arts, a sense of balance and proportion is basic to form. Music is no exception. Although these qualities may be difficult to quantify, their presence (or absence) in musical form is often a critical factor.

Examples:

Atherdoc Blues 35d

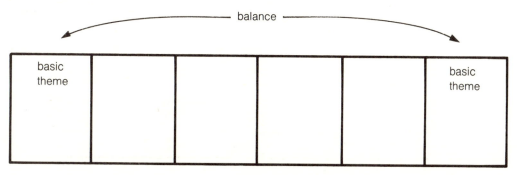

The piece opens with a statement of the basic "blues" melody. After the various soloists play their improvisations, that same melody returns to balance out the form.

I Will Give My Love an Apple 6a

The phrases of this song have melodic shapes which complement each other, creating a well-balanced four-phrase design. Repetition, reflection of the melodic shape, and the presence of a melodic peak are determining factors in the proportions of the form.

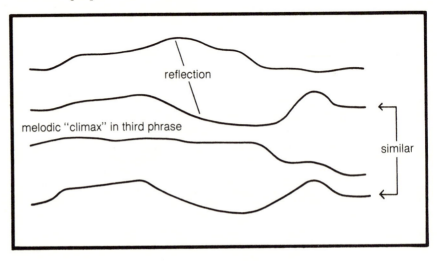

The Riddle 6c

The imbalance created by the new tonality of the B section is resolved by the return to the home key.

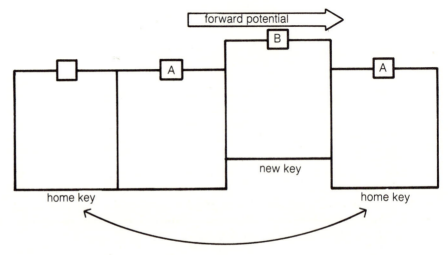

| Listen | *Trauermusik*, by Hindemith | 3c |

Balance and proportion are evident not only in obvious symmetrical patterns (for example, *exact* repetition of sections and melodies, phrases of *equal* length, etc.), but also in more flexible musical designs. One example is a gradual buildup to a climax, followed by subsiding action. This goal is accomplished in Hindemith's *Trauermusik* through dynamics and melodic shape, among other techniques.

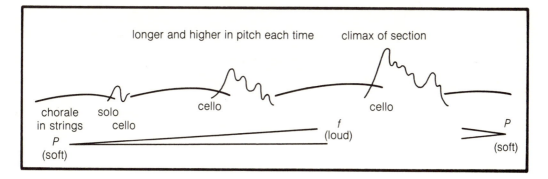

SUMMARY

Repetition, contrast, unity and variety, balance and proportion help shape musical form (and the form of other arts as well). Perception of these characteristics occurs at both short- and long-range levels. These perceptions begin as spontaneous, universal responses and affect form in all musical styles.

Describing Form

Although all musical form is affected by the same universal perceptions, each culture and tradition further shapes those responses. The interaction between universal patterns and cultural influences has resulted in many musical forms. Some have names, others do not; some lend themselves to description, others do not. The possibilities of musical organization are infinite. Thus, the following survey should not be considered either comprehensive or even representative of the many forms found in music. It is, rather, an introduction to some of the more traditional types.

PHRASE-GROUPS

A phrase-group contains a number of related phrases. It may have as few as two (the Demonstration Melody, for example); it might have three (*Silent Night*); it often has four (*I Will Give My Love an Apple*), and sometimes more. The essential feature of all phrase groups is that *the phrases are perceived as parts of a unified musical flow.*

Individual phrases of the group are delineated by cadences, which help control the interplay of action and rest. Phrases, like longer musical spans, may be *clearly separated* by a break in rhythmic action.

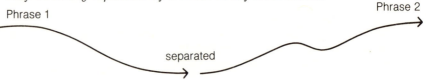

They may be *joined* one to the next without any clear break.

When more than one sound source is used, phrases may be *overlapping*; the new one enters just before the previous one is finished.

An example of overlapping phrase design may be heard in *One Hand, One Heart* from Leonard Bernstein's *West Side Story* 29a .

PHRASE DESIGN

Phrases *may* be labeled with letter names to show repetition and contrast.

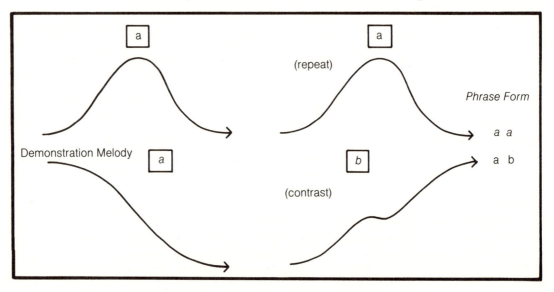

Should additional material be used, more letters may be added as the form requires.

SECTIONAL FORMS: BINARY AND TERNARY

Many forms are heard in clear sections. One traditional *sectional form* that has already been presented is *two-part (binary)*.

Bach, *Gigue* 19

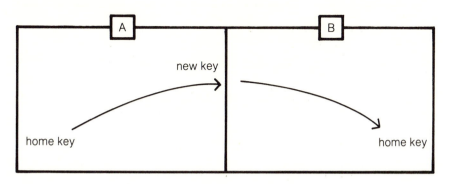

The A section of this two-part form features a melody moving away from the home key. The cadence at the end of A, which clearly closes the section, is in a new key. After a definite pause, section B begins and the melody, built on the *same* motive, returns to the tonic.

Another common binary form is the verse–chorus design found in many traditional songs.

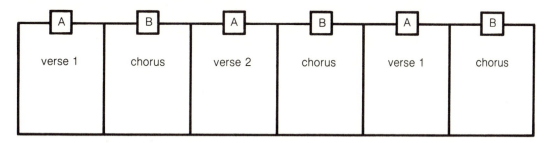

Notice that the repeats of A B do not change the basic designation of the form as *binary* (two-part). Since this design also uses words which change while the melody remains constant, this form is also called *strophic*.

Another common sectional form is a *three-part* or *ternary* design A B A. As an example, consider the *Branle* dance group 11b :

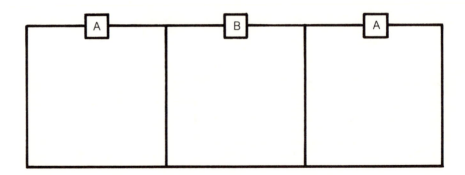

CONTINUOUS FORM

Some forms are *continuous*, since they do not contain any clearly set-off sections. Characteristic of continuous form is its unceasing rhythmic activity. Among the continuous forms you have already heard are African Game Song 2c , Stravinsky's *Danse* 2b , and the Bach *Fugue in G minor* 17 .

Stravinsky, *Danse*

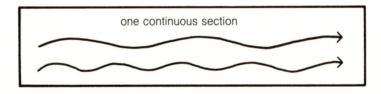

one continuous section

INTRODUCTION AND CODA

Some forms have an *introduction*—a short section which often sets the mood for the main material of the piece. The counterpart to an introduction is a *coda*—a section which sums up or ends the work. An introduction and/or coda may be used to expand traditional designs. For example:

A Three-Part Form with Introduction and Coda

| Introduction | A | B | A | Coda |

A Two-Part Form with Coda

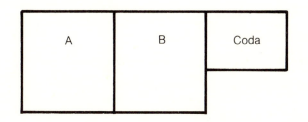

SECTIONAL FORM   A musical form containing distinct parts.

CONTINUOUS FORM   A form in which the musical action continues without interruption.

INTRODUCTION   An opening section preceding the main formal design of the piece.

CODA   A concluding section following the main formal design of the piece.

BINARY   A two-part musical form (*AB*).

TERNARY   A three-part musical form (*ABA*).

QUESTIONS

Find any false statement(s) and correct them by changing the word(s) in italics. More than one statement may be false; all the statements may be true.

1. The harmonic series

   (a) is a phenomenon that *changes* from culture to culture.

   (b) may be described in the *technical language of physics*.

   (c) is related to *symmetrical proportion*.

   (d) is *fundamental* to the existence of music.

2. The octave

   (a) is created by the *harmonic series*.

   (b) is an *interval*.

   (c) is created by dividing the string (on page 71) in *three* parts.

   (d) contains two pitches of *different names*.

3. Tonality

    (a) is related to the *harmonic series*.

    (b) may affect melody, *but not* harmony.

    (c) is important to the perception of *modulation*.

    (d) *may be* important to the perception of form.

4. Concerning *The Riddle* 6c

    (a) Tonality plays an *important* role in the perception of its form.

    (b) The section which is not in the tonic key *is* A .

    (c) After section A , the song *sequences* to a new key.

    (d) The final A section of the song *is not* in the original key.

5. Concerning the following diagram:

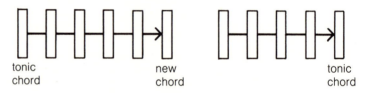

tonic chord   new chord   tonic chord

    (a) It represents a *progression*.

    (b) It *is not* under the influence of tonality.

    (c) The chords are perceived as a *nonrelated* group.

    (d) It probably has *a small* amount of forward potential.

6. Concerning the major–minor tonal system:

    (a) *Tonality* is a basic feature.

    (b) It generates a *strong* sense of forward potential.

    (c) Our familiarity with it *may* affect our perception of music from other traditions.

    (d) It *has not* affected other musical traditions.

7. Concerning modal progressions:

    (a) They are created with tones from *modal* scales.

    (b) They often have *more* forward potential than major–minor progressions.

    (c) They are *often* heard through a major–minor cultural filter.

4

Music as a Universal Art

The Art of Music: A Universal Perspective

The preceding pages have been primarily concerned with technical aspects of musical language. The terms and concepts you have acquired enable us to discuss some of the details of musical style. But as suggested at the beginning of this book, all stylistic detail grows out of a more universal context. It is something of this broader perspective we now seek. The discussions that follow deal with such elusive questions as: What is music? Where does it come from? What are its universal qualities? Are some musical styles better than others? These questions may seem naive; so be it. The "answers" (and there are no precise answers to these questions) inhabit a special realm of wisdom and feeling.

Music as a Heightened Experience

"When music sounds, all that I was, I am."—from the poem "Music," by Walter de la Mare (1873–1956)

"singing, he remains . . . wonder . . . wonder . . . wonder"—Vedic Chant (1000 B.C.?)

Throughout human history, music has been a medium for heightened experience. Something special happens when music begins. At a funeral, a football game, a country wedding, sung by a monk, a minstrel, or a stone-deaf Beethoven, music carries the human spirit through the widest range of experience. Many moments of your life will be enhanced because of music.

Throughout history, music and dance have been a cohesive activity in family and community life. To a great extent, modern culture has diffused this universal strand, replacing it with more passive media such as recordings and television.

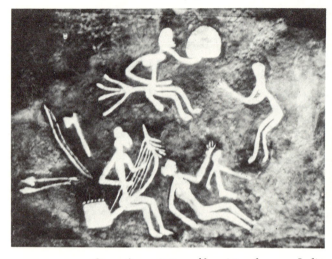

Stone Age painting of harpist and group, India.

FROM *STONE AGE PAINTING IN INDIA*, BY ROBERT R. R. BROOKS
AND VISHU S. WAKANKAR (YALE UNIVERSITY PRESS, 1976)

Family making music depicted in a painting by Girolamo Forni, sixteenth century, Italy.

COURTESY THE METROPOLITAN MUSEUM OF ART. THE CROSBY BROWN
COLLECTION OF MUSICAL INSTRUMENTS, 1889

In this respect, you are connected to all humankind. *Music as a world art exists because it is one of the primary heightened experiences of human culture.* The very existence of music depends upon its role as a means to higher experience. Understanding this is far more useful than trying to determine exactly how and why music began. Its origins will always elude the search for exact, quantifiable explanation. Music begins whenever and wherever one chooses to sense the imprint of humankind. The frustration of trying to explain music in words reveals it to be a medium for expressing the inexpressible.

Music is Motion

The connection between music and dance brings to life an essential concept: *all music is motion.* Since another word for motion is rhythm, this discussion is a further exploration of that basic musical element. In order to make music, something has to move—the voice, the hands, the breath. In fact, this musical motion may even be sensed before music sounds. (You may remember the demonstration on page 15 in which you could experience the forward potential of a meter in your imagination.) Like a dancer who visualizes a dance before it happens, a composer imagines the "motion" of music before it begins.

To grasp the unity between music and dance, it is essential to relinquish certain assumptions about both. For a moment, forget that dance exists only as a deliberate and conscious activity. Many types of motion can be considered dance. When a child improvises a little song with coordinated movements—a step here, a sway there—is this not a dance? When a marching band performs its complex step-patterns, isn't this also a dance? Consider this account of Beethoven composing a section of his *Missa solemnis*: "In the living room, behind a locked door, we heard the master singing parts of the fugue in the Credo—singing, howling, stamping."* There is, in fact, a sort of demonic dance quality in much of Beethoven's music, which may well have been the result of his physical involvement with sound. Johann Sebastian Bach, considered among the most intellectual of composers, was described by a contemporary as having "rhythm in every part of his body."** The "stuffy" image of the great composers, somehow glued to their chairs, unable to move freely from the neck down, is a sad misconception. Movement is an essential skill for the musician. The very performance of music is a kind of dance. And when composers hear complex musical patterns in their heads, these are not only intellectual puzzles, but living reflections of the body's ability to coordinate motion in a powerful environment of music, rhythm, and meaning.

The Ancient Unity

An interesting discussion that occurred in a college classroom recently illuminates an important understanding about music's historic meaning. A song was being examined from a structural point of view—poetic balance of the text, melodic shape, etc. One student seemed bewildered by the analysis and finally asked, "Are melody and words different parts? I really don't understand how they can be considered separate." Although this question may seem unsophisticated, actually the opposite is true. The student's sense of the unity between melody and text is an important perception, historically accurate and still relevant to music's meaning. *In its original and purest form, song was a spontaneous unity of melody and word.* Poetry, as we know it, is a relatively late offspring of song. Song is the mother art.

DANCE AND DRAMA AS PART OF THE ANCIENT UNITY
But we haven't gone far enough if we limit our discussion of the ancient unity to melody and words. If you are a fan of popular dance, you may have experienced this phenomenon in its more complete form. Certain contemporary traditions of popular dance (the television program "Soul Train"

*Quoted in Thayer, *Life of Beethoven*, rev. and ed. by E. Forbes (Princeton, 1967), II, p. 851.

**Letter from Johann Matthias Gesner in Hans David and Arthur Mendel, *The Bach Reader* (New York, 1966), p. 231.

98

Right: Participants on the television show "Soul Train" often perform in a unified flow of dancing, singing, and acting.

Below left: Characters in motion from the Roman drama *Phormio* by Terence (c. 190–145 B.C.). Roman drama continued the Greek tradition.

Below right: A scene from *Oedipus Rex* by Sophocles (496–406 B.C.), perhaps the most famous Greek drama. In this modern production at the Stratford Shakespeare Festival, Oedipus addresses the chorus. In classical Greek times, the chorus would have been in dancing formation.

Oedipus Rex, Max Rheinhardt's production at Covent Garden, 1912.

is a good example) illustrate a remarkable union of music, motion, and verse. First of all, they include complex dance patterns representing a highly refined "state-of-the-art" tradition. But there is more than movement involved. Often the dancers sing while dancing. Yet even more is going on. In a real sense, the dance becomes a drama as the performers express and enhance the meaning of the words through movements and gestures. We think of the performers as dancers, but are they not also singers and actors? This brings us to the heart of the matter: although one element may be emphasized more than another, the ancient unity is experienced as a synchronized flow of music (or song), dance, and drama.

"SOUL TRAIN" AND GREEK DRAMA

It may well be that the modern-day Greek scholar has something to learn from the "Soul Train" dancers, for one obstacle to recreating classical Greek theater lies in the difficulty of recapturing this unity of expression. "The rhythm of Greek verse was one and the same in poetry and music. In the chorus, which was actually danced, the rhythms of the verse also constituted that of the dance."*

Song

Like the impulse to dance, the impulse to sing provides a basic source of music. A song, especially a good one, is much more than a tune with words. It is a neatly contained dramatic world in which a wide range of human experience may be recreated. Since it is produced through the body in tone, rhythm, and words, song has an especially human quality. More than any other musical type, it has been a primary medium for encoding and preserving a culture's most sacred traditions.

SONG—A SOURCE OF MELODY

Since song was part of the ancient unity, it was from this multifaceted mode of expression that melody was born. Thus, the roots of melody are intertwined with the singing-moving-acting unity of human experience. And the expressive component became melody's special domain in what later would be the separate art of music. Trace melody back into the slow dawn of humanity and you find not just the voice, but the whole body—singing, dancing, and acting. This is Beethoven's song as he composed the Credo (described on page 97)—basic primal-universal. The "singing" cello melody in Hindemith's *Trauermusik* is rooted in the universal gesture of mourning. The spirited melody of Bach's *Gigue* springs from the impulse to dance and

*Thrasybulos Georgiades, *Greek Music, Verse and Dance*, trans. by E. Benedikt and M. L. Martinez (New York, 1956), p. 16.

sing joyously. The chant melodies of Sequence 7 are sacred songs whose meditative rhythms and simple melodic structures have been a central element of worship for thousands of years.

The Flexible Interplay of Components in the Ancient Unity

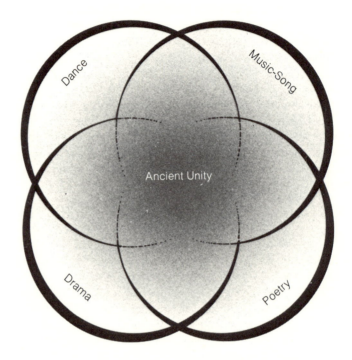

THE IMPORTANCE OF THE ANCIENT UNITY

The ancient unity is not some obscure concept that has no relationship to you. All of us have an ability to synchronize singing, dancing, and acting in a fluid, spontaneous manner. Although this ability may never have been developed, or may have simply gone into hiding, it is still a part of our natural human makeup. For many people, going out on the dance floor revitalizes this impulse. For others, a rock concert may set off the dancing-singing response. You need not actually participate in the ancient unity in order to respond to its presence. The latent impulse to sing-dance-act is vital to listening. For example, your body's natural impulse to dance is one reason the music of a gigue sounds so catchy. By the same token, it is your body's natural impulse to sing-dance-act that responds to these qualities (however obscure) in all types of music, from opera and symphonies to hit tunes and jazz improvisations. Although this concept does fit neatly into traditional definitions, its importance should not be minimized. Music is a body-based art. The ancient unity is perhaps the oldest and purest body-state in which music (as well as dance and drama) is given life.

Universal Norms Affecting All Music: A Summary

Music exists within the laws of nature, and these laws provide both possibilities and limits for musical expression. Much the same way that dance exists within the capabilities of the human body and the force of gravity, music sounds within certain natural boundaries. *The following norms can be considered as universal patterns which affect the creation and perception of music.* These are not the only principles that affect music. In fact, there are musical styles that bypass some of these norms (tonality, for example). Yet, when considered in a universal setting, the following norms emerge as a fundamental basis for human musicality.

Principle	*Review (if necessary)*
rhythmic periodicity	pulse, beat, periodicity (pages 9–11) related topics: meter, syncopation
the relationship of musical rhythms to life rhythms	"Rhythm Gives Life to Form" (page 17)
a rhythmic bond between performer and audience	"The Rhythmic Bond" (page 15)
harmonic series	"The Magic of the String" (pages 70–71) "Harmonic Series" (App. VIII)
tonality	basic explanation (pages 74, 79) "Tonality and Form" (pages 77–78)
an affinity for repetition	under "Basic Principles of Form" (pages 82–84) related topics: meter (pages 12–13), periodicity (pages 10, 11)
an affinity for contrast	under "Basic Principles of Form" (pages 85–86)

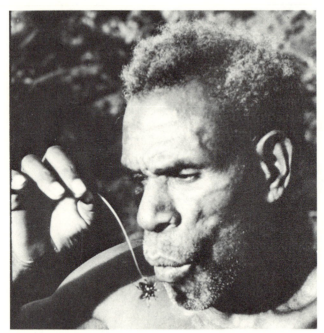

USED WITH PERMISSION OF ROBERT MACLENNAN, M.D.

The harmonic series is a universal norm of musical culture. In this picture of music making from New Guinea, we see a man with a live beetle. The vibrations of the wings produce tones of the harmonic series which are emphasized by the shape of the lips and mouth cavity.

a response to unity and variety	under "Basic Principles of Form" (pages 86–87) soloist and group (page 87)
a sense of balance and proportion	under "Basic Principles of Form" (pages 87–89)
a response to the expressive qualities of melody	melody (page 99) "The Ancient Unity" (page 97)
the impulse to dance, sing, and act	"The Ancient Unity" (pages 97–99)

THE REPETITION OF BASIC FORMS

At the short-range level, repetition helps to organize the immediate structure of music. For example, once a meter "gets going," it is our affinity for repetition that prolongs its existence; ostinato form grows from a human satisfaction with the continual repetition of a melody or rhythm. The examples are many, the principle is clear: Repetition is basic to music.

In the long range, repetition is also basic to artistic tradition. Consider again the picture sequences on pages 500–11. *In each sequence, a basic form has been repeated.* In a general sense, this kind of repetition may occur from person to person, from generation to generation, and from culture to culture. In music, for example, genres are repeated in various styles, times, and places (the gigue, for example). The history of artistic expression may be seen as a cultural chain; the continuous repetition of traditional forms and patterns are its links.

THE FLEXIBLE INTERPLAY OF BASIC FORMS

Obviously, all art cannot be described as *only* the repetition of basic forms and patterns. The recurrence of these models is part of a much larger, complex process by which the creative artist accepts, rejects, alters, and combines the materials at hand. The picture sequences on pages 500–10 hint at the complexity. Several pictures reveal the *interplay* of forms C10, C11: tower *and* circle; A3, A4: mother/child *and* circle.

The same kind of interplay takes place in music, as well. To demonstrate this point, we will use the three songs of Sequence 6 . These songs are all derived from one basic model. One element of that model is a four-line musical form, which is repeated with each verse. The replication of this structure in 6a and 6b is clarified below:

I Will Give My Love an Apple 6a   *I Gave My Love a Cherry* 6b

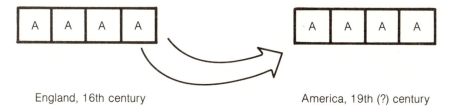

England, 16th century   America, 19th (?) century

A later version of this song, *The Riddle,* combines the older form with another design: A B A .

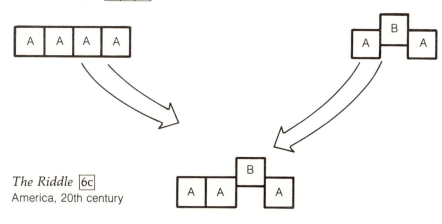

The Riddle 6c
America, 20th century

This example, although easy to analyze, is symbolic of the broader, often hidden process by which composers enhance and combine traditional models.

Having acknowledged the importance of repeating models in musical culture, we must deal with the notion of originality. Certainly, the creativity of the individual plays a vital role in artistic expression. But this need not obscure the continuous traditions which allow such originality to have meaning and context. Similarly, each of the pictures in the sequences on pages 500–10 has original features. Yet each is derived from an already existing basic pattern.

MUSIC ACROSS DISTANCE AND TIME

Forms, techniques, instruments, individual pieces, melodies, songs, styles—the whole complex of musical art flows along a cultural chain and enters into tradition. This happens on the short-range level (for example, you teach your neighbor a song) or over a much longer span of time or distance (your neighbors move to another country, and their children continue to sing that song). This dynamic process is suggested in Sequences 1, 6, and 32. The connection between a musical tradition and the people who make it is one characteristic of a *living language* of music.

A Living Language of Music

Living language of music is a broad term describing the continuous interplay between music and culture. The term may be applied to any musical style provided some of the following characteristics are present:

1. Various musical techniques are internalized by musicians, usually at a young age. Most great composers have been born into a stylistically secure musical world. Early in life, they have absorbed the basic techniques of their musical language. Although their musical style may undergo change as they mature, their language was rooted in a strong, vibrant tradition.

2. The elements of a living language are usually related to the world beyond music. The symbolic connection of music to ideas, feelings, values, etc., directly or indirectly, is a flexible and vital aspect of most musical traditions.

3. There is common ground, at some point, among composers, performers, and audiences. While such concurrence may not happen all at once, a living musical language, by definition, involves interaction within a culture.

4. A living language is often the basis of a tradition. For the most part, successful musical styles continue and evolve from earlier practices.

Even the most "radical" composer may later seem "traditional" when considered in retrospect.

5. Accomplished musicians in a living language are usually able to demonstrate a spontaneous control over that language through improvisation. Great composers such as Bach, Mozart, Beethoven, Bartók—all could sit down at the keyboard and improvise a piece in their style. This physical control illustrates the instinctive, natural character of a living language. There are exceptions to this idea, especially in the twentieth century, but for most of music's history, it applies at the highest levels of musical creativity.

Responding to a Musical Style

How does one learn to respond to a musical style? In this section, the word *cue* will be used to describe anything that elicits a response. For example, a melody in an unfamiliar Mideastern-Mediterranean scale-type is a cue to most Western ears that the music is "strange and exotic." If you are a fan of popular dance, it is likely that you have heard many pieces that start with a "good beat." This is a cue that gets your body moving. In the American hymn tradition, there is a certain chord progression known as the "Amen cadence," because it is often used at the end of a hymn on the word "Amen." Thus, these chords, even without the words, may act as a cue for this particular religious image. The rich polyphony in a work by Bach, a composer noted for his contrapuntal skill, may suggest another cue: that the piece is concerned with "complex" and "logical" musical structure. These are by no means absolutes, but are general responses that often occur. They illustrate the way musical cues trigger certain cultural reactions. To a great extent, our cultural filters determine how these cues will affect us. Since we come from a variety of backgrounds, *the same cue can elicit different responses from difference people*.

How do we learn our living language? To begin with, *each living language has its own set of cues*. Some of these are obvious, but most are subtle and hidden. These cues originate in musical practices: for example, a chord progression, a manner of singing, a type of rhythm, a way of combining timbres and melodies. Interacting with these musical phenomena are the broader cultural responses, such as feelings, ideas, body image, etc. The result of the interaction—the cues—are internalized through habit and create the basis of the living language, a common ground for composer, performer, and audience. All this happens *within* a particular culture or group. It may be as large as the population of a country or as small as that of an isolated community.

Here are some observations on the process described above:

1. How a person learns to respond to style is subtle, hidden, and difficult to describe in exact terms, reflecting the complex nature of music and art.
2. By and large, people outside a cultural group cannot respond to the meaning of its living language at the fullest level.
3. It is commonplace for a person outside the cultural group to misinterpret cues, by applying another set of responses.

"GOOD" AND "BAD" MUSIC WITHIN A STYLE

Suppose you had grown up on an isolated island. All the subtleties of the living language would be quite clear to you. Within your cultural group there would be widespread understanding of the basic cues of a common musical style. In this stylistically *secure* environment, it would be fairly easy to respond to music as "good" or "bad." You would most likely be able to recognize musicians with special talent and skill. Within this small group, "I know what I like" is an important and valid yardstick for evaluating music.

"GOOD" AND "BAD" MUSIC IN A MORE COMPLEX STYLISTIC WORLD

Suppose your little island was absorbed into a larger society, and was thus subjected to many new influences, including new musical styles. Here "good" and "bad" lose their simplicity as evaluative responses. Some people might find the new musical styles different and exciting. Others might feel that their familiar traditions are threatened. And what if there were friction within the new social structure? Would it be possible to divorce musical response from its social implications? From our hypothetical situation, we can extract certain principles basic to this complex interaction:

1. The smaller the group, the more likely a uniform response of "good" and "bad."
2. The larger and more diverse the group, the less chance there is of a uniform response.

These principles are particularly relevant in our society, a vast network of peoples and traditions. Our musical environment is saturated with musical cues, each a legitimate expression of some group's living language. *Taken all together*, they result in stylistic chaos. It is impossible for an individual with a single set of cues to evaluate all existing musical styles.

COMPLEXITY IN MUSICAL STYLES

Complexity and virtuosity are qualities that can be found in many musical styles. In and of themselves, they have no particular artistic value. A piece need not be complex to be good. For example, some of the most moving moments in the works of Mozart have a poignant simplicity. And while virtuosity can be exciting, it may also produce a sense of boredom and artificiality. Since different traditions have evolved different types of complexity, a person from one group or culture may have considerable difficulty in responding to complexity in an unfamiliar musical style.

THE INFLUENCES ON A MUSICAL STYLE

A common misconception about music is the belief in the existence of a "pure" style. Except for very special circumstances (perhaps that of a lost tribe, isolated for thousands of years from the rest of the world) *most musical styles reflect many influences*. Music is always changing, blending old practices with the new. One of the most important reasons for the rapid development of Western classical music (which we will discuss shortly) was the rich cross-fertilization among various styles: French music blended with Italian; English music with both Italian and French; etc. Examples of this kind of interacting are endless; many can be documented, but many are hidden within the dynamic development of living musical languages.

The Western Notated Tradition

Much of this book is concerned with "classical" music, a tradition that developed in Europe from about 1000 A.D., and later in America. Various labels, none of them completely satisfactory, have been applied to this tradition, among them "serious," "learned," "cultivated," and "art music." In general, the word "classical" is most widely used.

In this book, we will often use the term *notated tradition*, since it more accurately reflects one of its important distinguishing features (at least up to the twentieth century). From time to time, the aforementioned labels may also be used when they evoke an essential quality or idea relevant to our study. Following are some generalizations about the notated tradition, which will provide a basis for future discussions:

1. The development of this tradition parallels that of Western civilization since the Middle Ages. One of the traits that separated this civilization from other world cultures was its capacity for comparatively rapid change. Western culture may be thought of as a "mega-culture" made up of changing subcultures. In terms of chronology, these subcultures correspond to historical eras,* as diagrammed:

*There are considerable differences among historians concerning the names, dates, and very existence of these periods.

Historical Eras

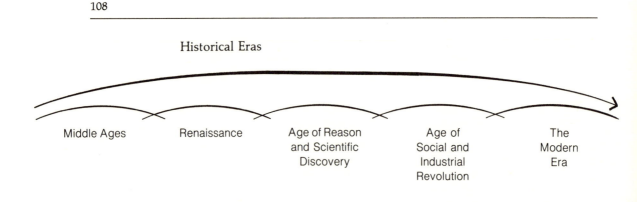

Middle Ages · Renaissance · Age of Reason and Scientific Discovery · Age of Social and Industrial Revolution · The Modern Era

2. As we have observed, musical styles grow out of particular cultures. Therefore, it is not surprising to find that Western notated music reflects the changes in the society from which it comes. Arranged chronologically, these historical style periods are shown on the following diagram. You will notice that they do not strictly correspond to the historical periods shown above, indicating the flexibility of these categorizations.

The Western Notated Musical Tradition

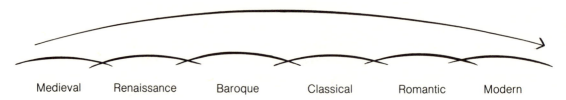

Medieval · Renaissance · Baroque · Classical · Romantic · Modern

The Folk-Popular Tradition

Folk and *popular* are related terms that have been used to describe somewhat different traditions. Scholars have usually applied the term *folk* to the everyday music of nonprofessional musicians, often in a rural setting (for example, African Game Song 2c). *Popular music*, on the other hand, has been the phrase used to identify music enjoyed by the masses, but created by professional musicians, and often in an urban setting. These categories had some validity in the past, but revolutionary changes in the world musical culture have made the terms less useful when applied to our time. Nearly every rural outpost of human society is now connected through radio, records, or television, into a larger musical network. For example, children in Hong Kong, who thirty years ago would have learned their everyday music from the oral tradition of their parents, now sing songs they hear on "Sesame Street," while their older brothers and sisters sing the latest hit tune of The Jackson Five, The Rolling Stones, or Earth, Wind, Fire. Folk-music traditions which had undergone gradual change in the past are now transformed overnight as they interact with mass-media music from the West. A broad tradition of "popular" music, listened to and then sung by the "folk," is reaching every corner of the earth. At this moment in history, it will be more useful to focus on the common features of the folk-popular tradition, rather than on the differences.

General Characteristics of the Folk-Popular Tradition

1. The music is created for the public at large.
2. These traditions have remained close to the basic musical impulses: song, dance, and drama.
3. Spontaneous impact is favored over abstract or intellectualized qualities.
4. Although notation is sometimes utilized, it is not usually central to the musical practices.

There are, of course, many exceptions to these generalizations. Such categorization becomes especially meaningless when dealing with high-quality music created by great artists, such as Duke Ellington, Stevie Wonder, or Joni Mitchell. We will deal with this problem in the last chapters of this book.

Listening Beyond Style: A Summary

Listening beyond style begins with these ideas:

1. Style is the "outer" layer of basic musical impulse.
2. There is a general tendency to respond more to style than to universal patterns.
3. Many musical styles may express similar basic patterns.
4. We acquire certain "cultural filters" through habit. These help to shape our responses, both positive and negative.
5. All musical styles have the potential to be rewarding for the listener.
6. In the final analysis, response to style is a matter of personal taste and not a matter of "right" or "wrong."
7. All widely accepted musical styles have value, since they represent the expression of a cultural group.
8. Listening to music of various styles can have two beneficial effects: (a) expanding your musical horizon; (b) deepening your awareness of the styles you already know and like.

Certain procedures help to create an environment which encourages a response beyond style. The most basic of these is comparative listening. Only through such experience can one acquire the *skill* of bypassing "surface" response. However, this is not the only way to approach music and is not meant to take the place of more usual listening habits. But used consciously and in depth, as in this book, comparative listening can expand your understanding of any music on both a technical and spiritual level.

SOME PROCEDURES FOR LISTENING BEYOND STYLE

When you listen comparatively, as in Sequences ☐1☐ – ☐7☐ which follow, use these guidelines:

1. Trace a tradition through time and across stylistic barriers.
2. Listen to a group of pieces drawn from a basic impulse (dance, or sacred music, for example).
3. Compare pieces in different styles, but from a specific genre (sea chanteys, gigues, for example).
4. Compare pieces that have a similar structural element (ostinato, leader and group, homophonic texture, for example).

Sequence ☐1☐ : *Dance*

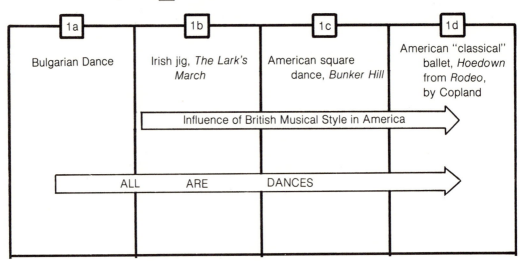

Important Ideas

Ancient unity—music and dance, song.
The special qualities of the dance genre.
Music is motion, rhythm.
Music "moves" through time.

1b, 1c, and 1d illustrate the stylistic connections between British folk music and various American styles. Copland's ballet music evokes this heritage. One may hear similar melodies, rhythms, and "country fiddlin'" in each of these pieces. Both 1b and 1c are songs and could be sung while people dance.

Sequence 2 *: Ostinato*

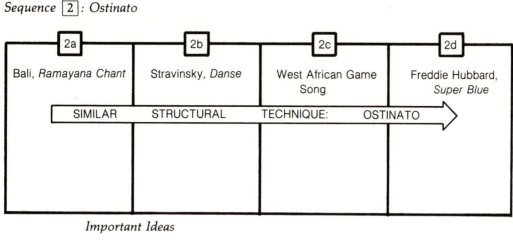

Important Ideas

Repetition.
Unity and variety.
Soloist and group (1a, 1c, 1d).

Sequence 3 *: Melody and Harmony*

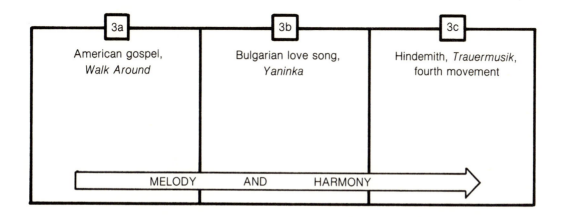

Yaninka

Yaninka, my dear girl,
Why are your eyes so sad?
Your eyes are olive-black, Yana.

Was your father deeply in debt
That he sold the house
And the garden behind the little door,
The garden with the green pine tree?

There we used to stand together, Yana,
And pass the time so sweetly.

Important Ideas

This sequence is not organized by direct stylistic connection, but is a comparison of similar musical structures:

1. Homophonic texture (3c is slightly more polyphonic).
2. Foreground–background (3b is somewhat different).
3. Soloist-group (with soloist showing more freedom, variety).
4. All of the above are reinforced through the use of timbre.

Sequence 4 *: Sea Chanteys (and a Sailor's Jig)*

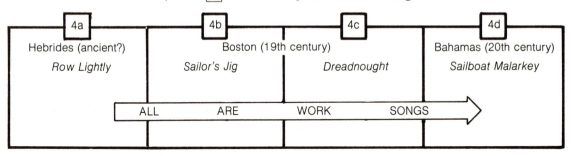

Important Ideas

Music "moves" through time.
Music is motion, rhythm.
Rhythm gives life to form.
Leader and group.
All musical styles are a blend of other styles.

The final selection from the Bahamas reflects a blending of traditions—that of the British-American sea chantey and the Afro-American melodic style.

This sequence demonstrates how *rhythm gives life to form*. The life-rhythms of the rowing, pulling, turning motions of the sailors become the basis for these songs. The *group* is spurred on by a *leader*, who sings out the verses.

Sequence 5 : *Mediterranean Styles*

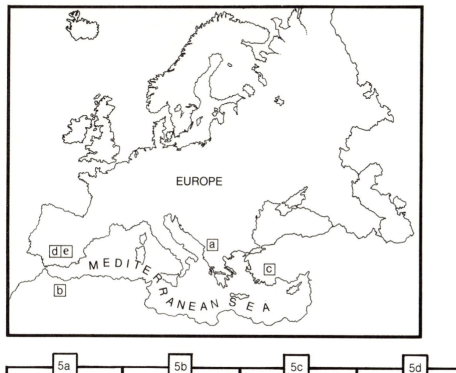

5a	5b	5c	5d	5e
Greece, *El Rey de Francia tres hijas tenía*	Morocco, *To Whom That Inscription*	Turkey, *Misket*, a dance	Spain, *Bulerías*, a flamenco dance	Spain, excerpt from Joaquin Rodrigo, *Guitar Concerto*, second movement
	VARIOUS STYLISTIC CONNECTIONS →			
The first selection is a ballad brought to Salonika by Jews fleeing the Spanish Inquisition in 1492.	The singer improvises words and music accompanied by an *ud*, a guitar like instrument.			

Important Ideas

Musical style is affected by geographical considerations.
Music "moves" across distance.

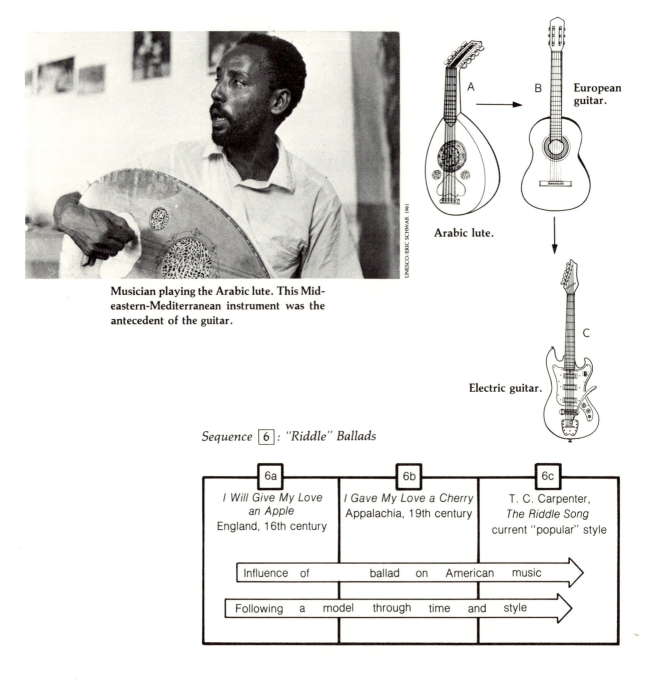

Musician playing the Arabic lute. This Mideastern-Mediterranean instrument was the
antecedent of the guitar.

UNESCO/ERIC SCHWAB, 1961

A → B   European
guitar.

Arabic lute.

C

Electric guitar.

Sequence 6 : *"Riddle" Ballads*

6a	6b	6c
I Will Give My Love an Apple England, 16th century	*I Gave My Love a Cherry* Appalachia, 19th century	T. C. Carpenter, *The Riddle Song* current "popular" style

Influence of   ballad   on   American   music →

Following   a   model   through   time   and   style →

TEXTS

I Will Give My Love an Apple

I will give my love an apple without ere a core,
I will give my love a house without ere a door.
I will give my love a palace wherein she may be,
And she may unlock it without any key.

My head is the apple without ere a core,
My mind is the house without ere a door.
My heart is the palace wherein she may be,
And she may unlock it without any key.

I Gave My Love a Cherry

I gave my love a cherry that had no stone,
I gave my love a chicken that had no bone,
I gave my love a thimble that had no end,
I gave my love a baby with no cryin'.

How can there be a cherry that has no stone?
How can there be a chicken that has no bone?
How can there be a thimble without an end?
How can there be a baby with no crying?

A cherry when it's a bloomin', it has no stone,
A chicken when it's a pippin, it has no bone,
A thimble when it's a rollin', it has no end,
And a baby when it's a sleepin', there's no cryin'.

The Riddle

My love's like an apple without any core
He lives in a house without any door
He's gentle as a baby, he cries when he sings
I'd always be his lady if he'd only let me in.

He says love's a rainbow, seek it and it's gone,
He says love's a flower, touch it, turn it to stone,
He says he wants a baby but he'll never wear no ring,
I'd always be his lady, if he'd only let me in.

How long, how long can he sing this same song
  like riddles without any end?
To me, they are nothing but circles of sorrow
  and if they don't end in love, then there ain't no tomorrow.

When two love as one neither loves alone
And they don't live in a house, they live in a home.
And when two love a baby, one world will sing,
I'd always be his lady, if he'd only let me in.

This sequence, like the picture sequences (circles, tower-mountains, mother and child) demonstrates how a basic pattern may be expressed in different styles. Here we have a story, based on a dramatic technique of riddle and answer. Another pattern that forms each song is the four-phrase group. Also, the melodic shapes of each melody, while not exactly alike, are somewhat similar. Thus, the details of style change, but a basic pattern is evident.

This sequence also suggests the universal principle that artistic creation is rarely, if ever, completely original. Usually it is based on preexisting patterns, techniques, and traditions.

These songs may also be called *ballads*, indicating that they tell a story and are in strophic verse form. Ballads have two components—a melody and a story. Each part may vary as the song is passed on. Often, melody and story may split up, each component reappearing in other songs. Certain story-types may be traced around the world. Consider, for example, the Appalachian *There Lived an Old Lord* 31f . The same story model, the king whose three daughters are courted, is heard in *El Rey de Francia tres hijas tenía*, of Spanish origin, recorded in twentieth-century Greece (passed on orally for five centuries).

Sequence 7 : Chant, the Sacred Language

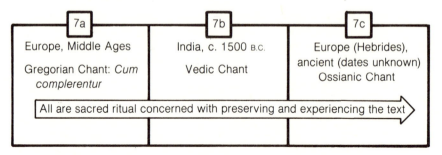

7a	7b	7c
Europe, Middle Ages Gregorian Chant: *Cum complerentur*	India, c. 1500 B.C. Vedic Chant	Europe (Hebrides), ancient (dates unknown) Ossianic Chant

All are sacred ritual concerned with preserving and experiencing the text

TEXTS

Gregorian Chant (translation)

When the days of Pentecost were over, all were assembled together; and suddenly, from the sky came a noise like a furious spirit, which filled the dwelling.

Vedic Chant (translation)

. . . This food made of individuality, crossing beyond this vital bread made of individuality, crossing beyond this mind made of individuality, crossing beyond this knowledge made of individuality, crossing beyond this joy made of individuality, crossing beyond these worlds as desired in food, desired in shape, moving about this chant, singing, he remains

> wonder, wonder, wonder
> I the food, I the food, I the food
> I food eater, I food eater, I food eater,
> I their uniter, I their uniter, I their uniter.

I am the firstborn of absolute truth.

Ossianic Chant

The text retells a legend concerning mythical warriors in the sky.

Important Ideas

Ancient unity—melody and word (prose, poetry).
Music "moves" through time.
Music as heightened experience.

Monks of the Thupten Choling Monastery chanting in a solemn religious ceremony.

Chant, the Sacred Language

The basic characteristics of chant may be described as follows:

Chant is sung as part of the heightened experience of religious ritual. It is misleading to consider chant in musical terms only. Its purpose has been the practice and preservation of religious belief. We do not expect chant to affect us like music intended to entertain. It was never meant to be recorded or performed in concert, but was part of the personal experience of the chanter. One might be tempted to say that a continually repeated pattern of only three of four tones is boring, and not really music at all. But the continual repetition is well-suited to the purposes of chant—in that focused, hypnotic environment, whether it be in India in 1500 B.C. or fourteenth-century Europe, the singer loses the sense of this world and enters the universal world of God.

Chant exists in a region of perception between speech and song. The hypnotic rhythms and simple melodic patterns of chant are meant to internalize the sacred word inside the body of the singer. It is an act both of worship and of cultural preservation. The simple melodic structures used for the Vedic chant 7b or the Gregorian *Cum complerentur* 7a are not really melodies in the fullest sense. They are more a kind of sacred speech. Other chants, like the Gregorian *Agnus Dei* 8 , are full-fledged melodies, more song than chant. What is chant, then? Is it speech or song? There are many types of chants: some are closer to speech, others to song. The identities often overlap. Considered as a continuum, a useful image emerges:

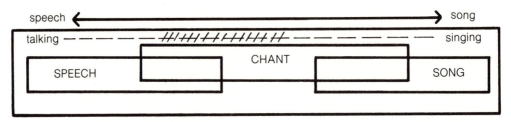

This flexible approach facilitates the understanding that some chants are midway between speech and song. The Vedic chant uses only three tones; its melodic shape is very gentle—in fact, it is not all that different from certain speech patterns. In contrast, the Gregorian *Agnus Dei* 8 can be heard as a real song. It uses six tones and has a sweeping melodic shape. (You may wish to place the other chants on the diagram in appropriate positions.)

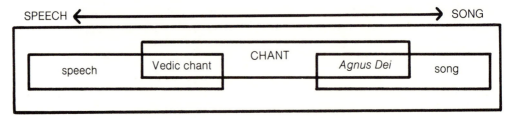

The determining element in this continuum is melody. In some chants melody seems to have a full life; these are easily perceived as song. In others, melody is more subservient to the recitation of the text; these can be accurately described as a musical form of *sacred speech*.

The chant tradition is an oral one and represents a mode of sacred communication from the past. It is difficult for us to comprehend a time when the important words of humankind were preserved only in sound and not in writing. But long before the written word was known, people recorded the stories, wisdom, knowledge, in short, the sacred information of their religion and culture, in chants and songs. For the most part unknown in our society, this tradition is still quite real in others. For example, even if the written texts of the Veda were destroyed, any one of many priests could chant it in its entirety and duplicate it exactly. There are ten-year-old boys in Egypt who can chant the entire Koran from memory. These examples are living proof of the power and purpose of chant in oral culture. The phenomenon is not exclusive to Eastern cultures. Throughout European history, illiterate folk entered religious orders. Some learned to read, others did not. The essential rites of Christianity could be taught in chant, whose basic nature is rooted in sound, not sight.

GREGORIAN CHANT

Of particular interest to us is the religious chant of early Christendom. This practice, with roots in an ancient past, became one of the main sources of the Western notated tradition. While it shares many basic characteristics with the chant traditions of the world, it developed new and important differences that would eventually be crucial for the music of Europe.

At its beginnings, Christianity was an Eastern religion. Jerusalem, the holy city for Christians (as it is for Jews and Moslems), lies beyond the eastern shores of the Mediterranean in Asia Minor. It was in this region that Christianity developed. The first music of the new religion was adapted from the older Hebrew service. Thus, some of the oldest Gregorian chants can be traced to the ancient Judaic chant formulas. The age of these archaic melodic patterns is unknown. It is likely that they reach back thousands of years into the religious history of that area. But these were to be only a part of the Gregorian tradition. As Christianity spread westward toward Europe, it absorbed a variety of musical traditions. Byzantium (present-day Turkey), Syria, Milan, Spain, and Ireland are a few of the early centers of Christianity, each of which developed its own musical liturgy, partly inherited from other Christian centers, often interacting with local musical traditions.

It was an ancient belief that for a religious ritual to be valid, it must be performed correctly. An error of detail was analogous to a misrepresentation of the cosmos. The concern for accuracy became an important issue for the Church authorities in Rome. Music, like Christianity itself, had embraced a wide variety of practices. It was to be expected that the Church would seek some standardization. Throughout the history of Christian music, in fact, there has been a continuing interplay between the diversity created by local musicians and the standardization of ritual decreed by central authorities.

One of the first great efforts to standardize the ritual was made around 600 A.D. under the leadership of Pope Gregory I. Sometime later, the complete body of Roman Catholic chant became identified with his name. The chant liturgy was remarkable in many respects. Its melodies reflected a rich heritage, drawn from the many cultures where Christianity had taken hold. Throughout the Middle Ages, the tradition continued to grow with the addition of new chants, some composed specifically for the liturgy, others adopted from the popular-folk traditions. The process worked in reverse as well: church melodies found their way back into the everyday music of the people. Chant was, then, a living language which reflected the social and religious life of the time.

GREGORIAN CHANT: SUMMARY OF CHARACTERISTICS

1. It is the European branch of the world chant tradition.
2. As we know them today, most chants have no meter.* Their rhythms are flexible and flow with a gentle pulse supporting the text. (They may well have been sung in meter during the Middle Ages.)
3. Its texture is monophonic.
4. Its melodic shapes are smooth and gentle, with many stepwise intervals.
5. The general feeling of chant is one of universality, not individuality.
6. Although it was eventually notated, the source and performance of Gregorian chant was part of the oral tradition.

QUESTIONS

Find any false statement(s) and correct them by changing the word(s) in italics. More than one statement may be false; all the statements may be true.

1. The idea that music is a "heightened experience"

   (a) applies to *some* musical cultures and styles.

   (b) *separates* music, dance, and drama.

   (c) helps explain the *origins* of music.

   (d) explains why music is *important* in worship.

2. The unity of word and melody

   (a) is an *ancient* reality.

*However, some may have been sung with meter during the Middle Ages.

(b) is the *main element* of the art of song.

(c) is the basis of *chant*.

(d) *does not* affect a historical understanding of poetry.

3. Concerning "Soul Train" and Greek drama:

   (a) *Both* illustrate the unity of song, dance, drama, and poetry.

   (b) They are perceived through *different* cultural filters in our society.

   (c) They illustrate that art from two apparently different stylistic worlds may have something important *in common*.

   (d) The comparison indicates that the interplay of dance, song, and drama is *no longer* found in our culture.

4. Concerning the simultaneous interplay of music, dance, and drama by one performer:

   (a) It demonstrates that an essential part of music is *motion*.

   (b) It demonstrates that *rhythm* is one of the fundamental elements of music.

   (c) It is *not found* in current "classical" musical styles.

   (d) It is basic to many singing styles of today's *popular music*.

5. Concerning song:

   (a) It has roots in *human experience*.

   (b) It is a main source of *melody*.

   (c) It is a *universal* element.

   (d) There *is no* relationship between song and purely instrumental melody.

6. Concerning the description of Beethoven on page 97:

   (a) It supports the idea that music and dance are deeply *related*.

   (b) It supports the idea that an essential part of music is *rhythm and motion*.

   (c) It suggests that Beethoven's music had *little* to do with his physical being.

(d) It suggests that the way Beethoven *moved* when he composed the Credo evokes a particular quality that one may sense in his music.

7. Which of the following natural patterns are universal?

(a) *periodic rhythm*

(b) *repetition*

(c) *contrast*

(d) *the modal scale*

8. Concerning music as a universal art:

(a) Music is *rarely* related to tis cultural context.

(b) *Very few* musical styles have qualities that can be called complex.

(c) Musical traditions *may endure* across long spans of time.

(d) Musical traditions *may be transmitted* across great distances.

9. Concerning how one learns to respond to style:

(a) *Habit* plays a role.

(b) *Tradition* plays a role.

(c) *Individual taste* plays a role.

(d) Cues, relating music to life, are *not important*.

5

Overview
of Span I

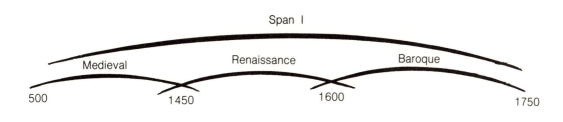

Span I

Medieval   Renaissance   Baroque

500   1450   1600   1750

From Medieval through Baroque

We will now take a rather long-range view of music history—from the *Middle Ages* through the *Renaissance*—ending in the *Baroque* (see dates above). By considering this span of time as a whole—hereafter referred to as Span I—we are able to discern some of the early developments in the Western notated tradition. By making generalizations about a complex topic, a comprehensive understanding may emerge, allowing details to have meaning in a larger context.

THE IDEA OF EVOLUTION IN MUSICAL STYLES

The following discussion involves the *evolution* of musical styles. Contrary to the prevailing connotations of this term, evolution, as used here, does not mean that "things get better." Instead, we will acknowledge long-range changes in musical styles as a matter of historical interest, and also to deepen the listening experience. Since we are listening with a modern cultural filter, it may seem that the styles become more modern as we move from the Medieval toward the Baroque. In following chapters, we will balance out this long-range consideration by dealing with the music of these eras on their own terms and within the context of their own times.

DANCE, SONG, CHANT, AND DRAMA IN MEDIEVAL EUROPE

Separately and in various combinations, dance, song, drama, and sacred chant carried the world music tradition into Medieval Europe where they were interwoven with the artistic and religious fabric of society. All were essentially oral traditions, internalized through the rhythms of everyday life. Music accompanied many celebrations, such as the harvest, midsummer's eve, weddings, and funerals. People danced and sang as part of traditions whose origins are lost in an ancient past. Songs and dances might be accompanied with various instruments that had reached Europe from Asia or the Arab world. At some festivals, ritual dramas were performed with chants and spells from the pre-Christian era. There were traveling professional musicians who also danced, juggled, told stories or riddles, and sang epics about the latest exploits of kings. In the church, the musical environment was severely controlled. Dance and secular song were forbidden. Gregorian chant was the single musical voice of the faith. In continuing conflict with old traditions, Church authorities tried again and again to eradicate powerful remnants of a pre-Christian past. A more successful approach was the adaptation of some of these practices (songs and festivals, for example) to Christian themes. But many old traditions survived to enrich the European musical heritage. From this musical mosaic, a new practice gradually emerged featuring an innovative technique of composition and musical perception—notated polyphony.

Notated Polyphony

The complex interaction of events we call history defies description in absolute terms. Isolating any moment in this chain reveals an interplay of countless actions, ideas, traditions, and natural phenomena, all channeled through the flexible genius of humanity. And yet, looking back on this often hidden process, it is possible to isolate moments symbolic of great change, moments that can be considered models of some larger development in the history of culture. In the following discussion we will examine one such model which reflects a vital change in the conception and awareness of musical art. Evolving in gradual stages throughout the Middle Ages, notated polyphony represented a distinct crossroad in the musical language of the world. In the long-range development of musical culture, this turning point was to be equally important to musicians of such diverse styles as Bach, Duke Ellington, Beethoven, Stevie Wonder, Mozart, and the Beatles.

Listen   *Viderunt omnes* 9, by Leonin (twelfth century)
This piece is an *organum* (plural *organa*), the earliest notated polyphonic genre, which used chant as its basic musical structure (see score
below). Because the *pitches* of the chant remained unchanged, it was
called the *cantus firmus* (fixed song). At first, we hear a part of the
chant alone, in its original version. But when the second voice enters,
the *rhythm* of the chant is changed considerably—drawn out into long,
sustained tones, above which the new, much faster melody is added.

Viderunt omnes, chant

Leonin, *Viderunt omnes*, beginning*

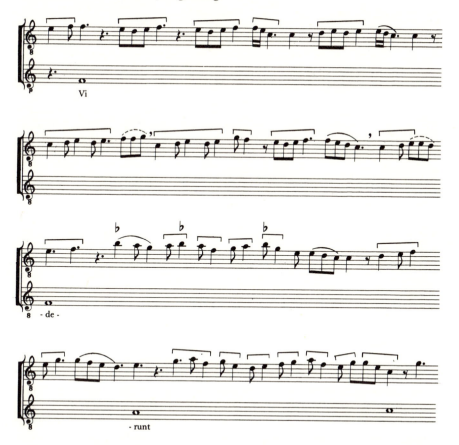

*Transcribed by Edward Roesner

- mnes.

NOTATION ALLOWS FOR A NEW TYPE OF MUSICAL STRUCTURE

As you have heard, the chant melody enjoyed a new life in Leonin's piece, which is just one of many; the composition of *organa* spanned several hundred years. Something quite new was heard in Medieval organum: The main difference was the rhythm. The duration of each tone is drawn out considerably, and only through the notation or familiarity with the style can you even recognize the chant. (Imagine if that melody were *The Star-*

Spangled Banner. Would you recognize it in a similar drawn-out version?) At the crux of this matter are essential differences between *body-based* and *notation-based* music. Body-based music is created and learned without notation. As observed in a previous discussion, Gregorian chant was an oral tradition notated, for the most part, long after its body-based origins. Notation-based music involves the representation of sound *outside the body*. On paper, the chant melody had new possibilities. It could be considered not only as a memorable melody but as a structural element for new musical design. The composer could intellectualize a plan in which the chant interlocked with another melody in counterpoint. This does not mean the composer did not hear the sound of this intellectual manipulation. Animating an intellectual plan with musical sound is one of the basic traditions of Western notated music. Spontaneous musicality—that is, what a person can hear, sing, or play without forethought—is joined with abstract musical concepts. For the accomplished musician in the notated tradition, this interaction becomes so natural that notation-based music, in a real sense, returns to the body.

A Comparison of the Two Pieces

Original Gregorian Chant, *Viderunt omnes*	Leonin, *Viderunt omnes* 9
body-based	notation-based
most likely composed orally, without notation (although later notated)	composed with the aid of notation and in a style whose characteristics depend partially on the ability to consider music as ideas, represented on paper
learned orally, by rote	performed from a notated score
composer unknown	composer known, since notation allows for its creator to be credited
comes from a tradition that was usually nonintellectualized, based more on spontaneous experience*	incorporates originally spontaneous elements in a fixed and intellectualized structure

*There are some important exceptions to this idea which are discussed in the final chapter.

THE NEW TRADITION WAS FIRMLY ROOTED IN THE LIVING LANGUAGE

Successful artistic innovations are rarely, if ever, completely new. In fact, the opposite is true. Most often, new techniques are based on deeply ingrained models or traditions. The new polyphony of Medieval music still contained a most basic element of the living musical language of the time—Gregorian chant. Not only were these chant melodies known to all, they also embodied the spiritual beliefs of a civilization. So a composer using a Gregorian chant as the cantus firmus of a polyphonic texture was starting from an internalized musical reality, a reality that provided a common ground between composer, performer, and populace.

NOTATED POLYPHONY Polyphonic music composed with the aid of notation. This practice evolved in Medieval Europe.

ORGANUM   A Medieval genre in which additional melodies were added to Gregorian chant.

CANTUS FIRMUS   A term applied to a Gregorian chant melody when it was used as a basis for a polyphonic composition.

BODY-BASED MUSIC Music created and performed without the aid of notation.

NOTATION-BASED MUSIC   Music composed and performed with the aid of written symbols.

The Changing Musical Language

We will now trace some aspects of the changing musical language during Span I:

1. The growth of notated instrumental music
2. Melodic styles
3. Rhythmic practices
4. Polyphonic techniques
5. The growth of harmony

In order to identify certain musical characteristics of the three style periods, we will make considerable use of the following music, chronologically organized:

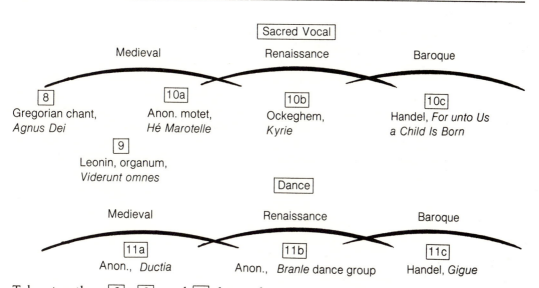

Sacred Vocal

Medieval · Renaissance · Baroque

8 Gregorian chant, *Agnus Dei*

10a Anon. motet, *Hé Marotelle*

10b Ockeghem, *Kyrie*

10c Handel, *For unto Us a Child Is Born*

9 Leonin, organum, *Viderunt omnes*

Dance

Medieval · Renaissance · Baroque

11a Anon., *Ductia*

11b Anon., *Branle* dance group

11c Handel, *Gigue*

Taken together, 8, 9, and 10 form a larger sequence demonstrating the sacred vocal tradition. Sequence 11 traces the instrumental dance tradition. When comparing different selections from the sequences, it is not always necessary to listen to the entire piece.

THE GROWTH OF NOTATED INSTRUMENTAL MUSIC

In 11 we consider the emerging sophistication of notated instrumental music.

Ductia 11a (anonymous, thirteenth century): Medieval instruments have their own particular timbre, which seems especially suited to the music of that era. In fact, when played on modern instruments, Medieval music loses much of its vitality. Although the melodies of this dance were notated, the choice of instruments was not indicated. Performers were free to use whatever was available or whatever suited the moment. Medieval musicians were especially fond of striking contrast between timbres. The purposeful juxtaposition of tone color often influenced their choice of instruments.

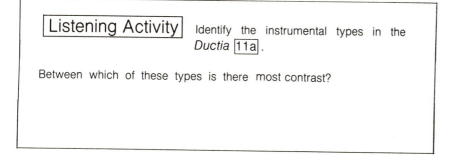

Listening Activity   Identify the instrumental types in the *Ductia* 11a.

Between which of these types is there most contrast?

Branle dance group 11b (anonymous): The *Branle* was a court dance which became popular in the sixteenth century. Like their Medieval predecessors, Renaissance musicians were also fond of contrasts between timbres. But of even greater importance to the Renaissance ear was a blended, homogeneous sound. To accomplish this Renaissance musicians often used *consorts* —sets of instruments from the same family. For example, in this piece you will hear a consort of strings (or viols, as they were called). The smooth, blended sound of these bowed strings is contrasted with the more biting quality of wind instruments.

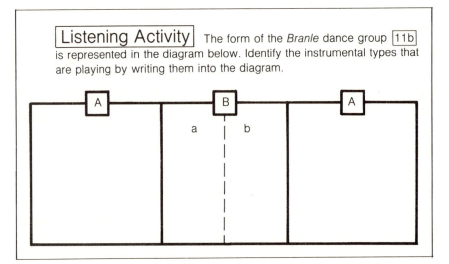

Listening Activity   The form of the *Branle* dance group 11b is represented in the diagram below. Identify the instrumental types that are playing by writing them into the diagram.

Gigue 11c (by George Frideric Handel, eighteenth century): The most obvious characteristic of this dance is the virtuosity of the trumpet part. A solo instrumentalist of that time was expected to improvise upon and ornament the written part. (*Ornamentation* is the spontaneous invention of short, decorative patterns added to the melodic line.*) In this piece, we can also hear the beginnings of the modern orchestra. The various instrumental sections of the Baroque ensemble are still the basis of today's symphony orchestra.

In contrast to his predecessors, the Baroque composer more often specified the instruments for which he was writing. This led to notated music that was idiomatic (suited) to specific instruments. However, in practice, it was not uncommon to substitute one instrument for another. For example, an oboe might play the flute part, since both are melody instruments and have a similar range.

Another typically Baroque sound you will hear in this piece is made by

*Instrumental ornamentation and virtuosity were also features of the Medieval and Renaissance styles. This will be elaborated upon in a forthcoming book by Timothy McGee, *An Approach to Early Music Performance.*

the *harpsichord,* a keyboard instrument played by depressing the keys to activate a mechanism which plucks a tuned string. This action gives the harpsichord its characteristic metallic sound, a timbre primarily associated with the Baroque era.

Instrumental Styles in Span I—Summary

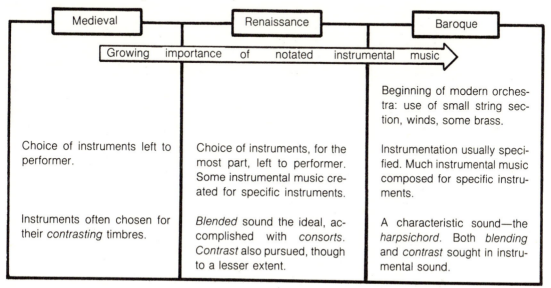

Medieval	Renaissance	Baroque
Growing importance of notated instrumental music →		
		Beginning of modern orchestra: use of small string section, winds, some brass.
Choice of instruments left to performer.	Choice of instruments, for the most part, left to performer. Some instrumental music created for specific instruments.	Instrumentation usually specified. Much instrumental music composed for specific instruments.
Instruments often chosen for their *contrasting* timbres.	*Blended* sound the ideal, accomplished with *consorts. Contrast* also pursued, though to a lesser extent.	A characteristic sound—the *harpsichord.* Both *blending* and *contrast* sought in instrumental sound.

MELODIC STYLES

Compare the melodic style of the Gregorian *Agnus Dei* [8] with the opening vocal line from Handel's *For unto Us a Child Is Born* [10c] . The Gregorian melody is calm and gentle; it employs many stepwise and other easily singable intervals. The rhythm is also relatively simple. In comparison, the Baroque melodody is complex and active, using a variety of intervals and driving, busy rhythms. The Gregorian melody is in an ancient vocal style; the Baroque melody is in a new melodic style, in which both instruments and voices weave complicated melodic patterns. This transition from a gentle vocal style to a complex melodic style is quite apparent when you compare the notation of both these pieces.

Agnus Dei

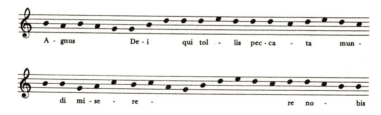

Handel, *For unto Us a Child Is Born* (excerpt, choral parts)

Handel's vocal line illustrates an important aspect of Baroque melodic practice—the way a single motive seems to drive toward a goal. An example of this may be heard on the words "Unto us a son is given."

Compare the Medieval *Ductia* [11a] with the Baroque *Gigue* [11c] . The melodic style of the *Ductia* is quite simple, with stepwise intervals in lively repeated rhythms.* Such a melody was easily learned by rote and most likely represents an oral rather than a notated tradition. It consists of a few simple patterns repeated with some variation. In contrast, the Baroque melody illustrates a much more complex, notation-based organization. Although there is repetition, it is handled in a more intricate manner. This melody, with its neatly stated motives and sequences, reflects the powerful organizational influence of notation upon musical structure. Perhaps the most important characteristic differentiating Baroque melodic style from earlier practice is this type of incessant repetition and development. In this recording, we hear the melody stated as written, then ornamented through improvisation. The instrumentalist had many standard ornaments available, the *trill* (a rapid alternation between two adjacent tones) being one that was retained in later musical styles.

Listen to the characteristic melodic style of the Renaissance in 10b . Renaissance melodic style, like that of the Middle Ages, is primarily vocal in character. In fact, during the Renaissance, Gregorian chant became the ideal for most melodic writing, and smoothness of line was the primary consideration. Even lively Renaissance dance melodies (the *Branle* dance group 11b , for example) were created with stepwise and other easily singable intervals.

Notated Melodic Styles—Span I

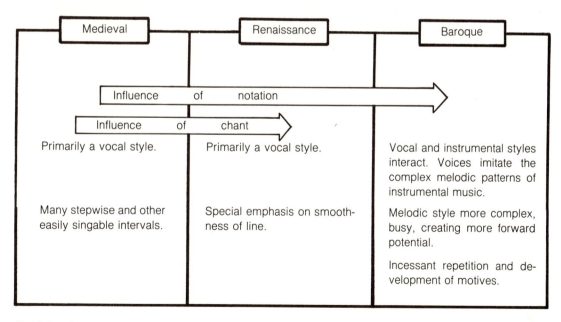

*In Medieval practice, such melodies were most likely ornamented by the instrumentalist and thus may have become quite complex.

RHYTHMIC PRACTICES

Compare the Gregorian chant $\boxed{8}$, the Renaissance *Kyrie* $\boxed{10b}$, and the Baroque *For unto Us a Child Is Born* $\boxed{10c}$. The Medieval chant is in a free, nonmetered rhythm.* It has a gentle pulse supporting the words. The Renaissance *Kyrie* begins as if it will have a definite meter, but as the various parts enter, only the pulse is evident; this is the typical Renaissance "floating rhythm," with its characteristic flexibility. In sharp contrast to both is the Baroque piece, whose strict meter has a relentless regularity.

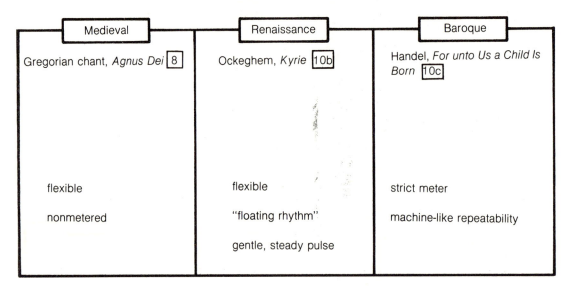

Medieval	Renaissance	Baroque
Gregorian chant, *Agnus Dei* $\boxed{8}$	Ockeghem, *Kyrie* $\boxed{10b}$	Handel, *For unto Us a Child Is Born* $\boxed{10c}$
flexible	flexible	strict meter
nonmetered	"floating rhythm"	machine-like repeatability
	gentle, steady pulse	

This does not mean that regular meter was unknown in the Middle Ages and Renaissance. As we shall see, regular meters were found throughout these eras, especially in dance music. Both the Medieval *Ductia* $\boxed{11a}$ and the Renaissance *Branle* dance group $\boxed{11b}$ employ regular meter.

$\boxed{\text{Listening Activity}}$ Leonin, *Viderunt omnes* $\boxed{9}$

Listen for the absence or presence of meter. Describe the rhythm with this in mind.

---

*There is growing evidence that some early chant did, in fact, employ regular meter.

Another aspect of changing rhythmic practices in Span I may be heard by comparing the Medieval motet *Hé Marotelle* 10a with the Renaissance *Kyrie* 10b . You will notice that in the motet various rhythms sound quite different. Medieval composers delighted in such *rhythmic polyphony*. By comparison, the rhythmic elements in the Renaissance *Kyrie* are similar to one another, and when combined, produce a far more blended rhythmic texture.

| Listening Activity | Handel, *For unto Us a Child Is Born* 10c |
Is the rhythmic texture made up of similar or contrasting patterns?

Rhythm in Span I—Summary

Medieval	Renaissance	Baroque
Continuing influence of dance ➔		
Influence of chant rhythm ➔		
	Growing trend toward regular meter in all music ➔	
Nonmetered and metered.	"Floating" nonmetered rhythm with a pulse. Metered rhythms, especially in dance music.	Strict, regular, meter.*
Use of *rhythmic polyphony*— the purposeful combination of very separate rhythms.	Combinations of very similar rhythms for a blended effect.	Combinations of different rhythms, but in machine-like synchronization.

*Among the exceptions to this statement is a nonmetered Baroque recitative rhythm discussed in the following section.

POLYPHONIC TECHNIQUES

To trace some of the styles of polyphonic composition in Span I, we use 15, as well as 9, 10, and 11. Since it is possible that listening carefully to polyphony will be a new experience for you (as it was for the Medieval listener), it would be useful to review certain aspects of polyphony discussed on page 61.

Medieval polyphony favored *linear* organization. As we move into the Renaissance and Baroque periods, composers become increasingly aware of the harmonic implications of counterpoint. Thus, the texture of polyphony gradually evolved from an emphasis on the linear to the growing equality of harmonic and linear considerations.

Leonin, *Viderunt omnes* 9 (twelfth century): As we have already heard, this two-voice organum is an example of early polyphonic art. Characteristic of this style are long durations of cantus firmus tones sounding with faster, dancelike rhythms in the higher melody. Compared with the polyphony that follows, this piece is relatively simple.

Anonymous motet, *Hé Marotelle* 10a (thirteenth century; see page 152 for text): This Medieval motet reveals a strong emphasis on linear elements. Written for three parts, there are two different sets of lyrics which sound at the same time. In this recording, one voice sings a fragment of a Gregorian chant without the words. The chant is also played on bells. As we have discovered in the previous section, the independence of the separate elements is reinforced by contrasting rhythms. In addition, the harmony is often dissonant. In short, there is little blending in this piece. Instead, there is what one might call purposeful opposition among the various parts. Musically, the repeated chant melody, sung and played in a dancelike manner, seems to hold the individual elements together. For composer and singer, the beauty of this piece seems to lie in the delightful combining of opposites.

Johannes Ockeghem, *Kyrie* 10b from *Missa Au travail suis* (early sixteenth century): One of the fundamental differences between Renaissance polyphony and that of the Medieval era is the blending and equality of voices characteristic of the later period. In this *Kyrie*, there is only one text; each voice sings it on a similar melody. In the opening, you will hear the same motive repeated as each voice enters. *Imitation* is a prominent characteristic of Renaissance style.

As we have discovered in the discussion of the rhythm of this piece, the melodies are woven together like threads of the same color, blending into a unified texture. The Renaissance composer began to be concerned with the kind of homogeneous sound that *emphasizes the chordal, harmonic structure*. In contrast with Medieval motets, where voices seemed isolated from each other, Renaissance polyphony focuses the listener on simultaneous awareness of linear and harmonic aspects. We call the resulting texture *equalized polyphony*.

Purcell, excerpt from *Dido and Aeneas* 15 : This is an excerpt from a Baroque opera; it will be discussed in more detail on page 174. For the moment, we will concern ourselves only with its texture as a reflection of Baroque practice. Baroque texture ranges from homophonic to polyphonic, as the two sections of this excerpt will show. In the first section, we hear a clear presentation of a melody with accompanying harmony. The accompaniment is provided by two instruments: a harpsichord playing chords and a low, bowed string instrument emphasizing the bass melody. Together, they make up the *continuo*, a standard instrumental feature of Baroque music. Above the strong harmonic sound of this *continuo*, a voice sings the melody. This is a clear homophonic texture—a primary melody supported by a chordal accompaniment.

After the words "Death is now a welcome guest," a solo melody initiates a new section. The voice then enters, accompanied by harpsichord and other strings. This texture is called *polarized polyphony*. It is polyphonic in that there are combined, independent melodies (bass and voice). Enhancing this polyphonic design is a harmonic accompaniment played by the harpsichord and strings. Thus, in a real sense, polarized polyphony combines elements of both polyphonic and homophonic texture. The term *polarized* comes from the different roles that the various parts play. Unlike Renaissance *equalized polyphony*, where all voices are similar, the voices in Baroque polyphony are apt to take on individualized roles. For example, in this excerpt, the outer voices are polarized: they are heard as distinctly separate lines using different melodic material. The harmony unifies the entire structure.

Baroque Polarized Polyphony

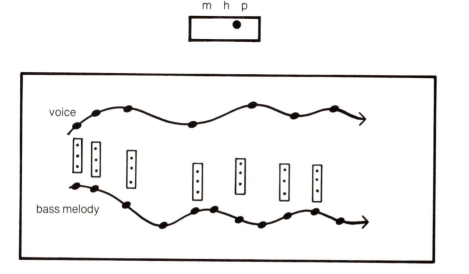

Linear-Harmonic Interplay in Span I—Summary

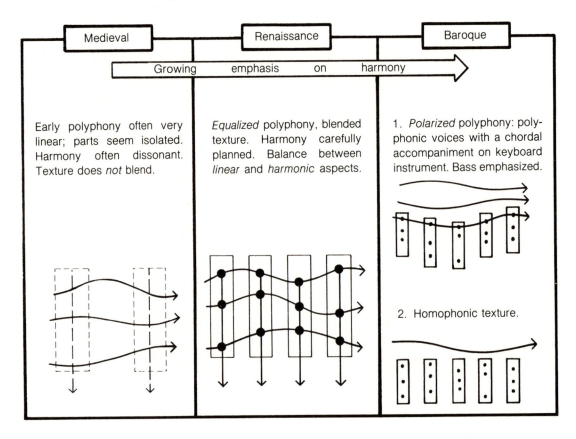

THE GROWTH OF HARMONY

There is no harmony in the Gregorian chant, since it is monophonic. In the thirteenth-century motet *Hé Marotelle* [10a] we hear Medieval harmony, which was often dissonant. In the Renaissance *Kyrie* [10b], the harmony is more consonant and smooth. Chords seem to float along in gentle combinations. Since this is *modal* harmony, the chords do not create the urgent forward potential that listeners have come to expect from more modern progressions. Finally, in *For unto Us a Child Is Born* [10c] we hear the forward-moving harmonic progressions characteristic of the major–minor tonal system which, by the Baroque period, had been firmly established.

Harmony in Span I—Summary

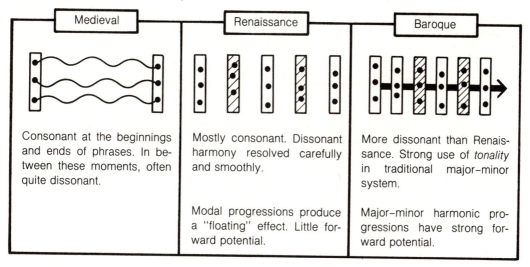

Medieval	Renaissance	Baroque
Consonant at the beginnings and ends of phrases. In between these moments, often quite dissonant.	Mostly consonant. Dissonant harmony resolved carefully and smoothly.	More dissonant than Renaissance. Strong use of *tonality* in traditional major–minor system.
	Modal progressions produce a "floating" effect. Little forward potential.	Major–minor harmonic progressions have strong forward potential.

ORNAMENTATION   The spontaneous invention of short, decorative patterns added to the melodic line.

POLARIZED POLYPHONY   A polyphonic texture in which independent melodic lines are joined with a harmonic accompaniment. Typically, in Baroque polyphony, the bass and treble lines are clearly differentiated.

EQUALIZED POLYPHONY   A polyphonic texture in which all the voices perform a similar role in a blended sonority. Typically, in Renaissance polyphony, there is little differentiation between the melodic characteristics of the voices.

RHYTHMIC POLYPHONY   A complex musical texture made up of very different rhythms.

CONSORT   A group of instruments from the same family; the instruments differ in size and pitch range. For example, a consort of recorders (flute-type instruments) might include a bass, tenor, alto, and soprano recorder.

CONTINUO   The usual instrumental accompaniment to a Baroque piece, consisting of a cello or other low-pitched melodic instrument and a harpsichord or organ. The continuo supplies the bass melody as well as the chord progressions of the music.

BRANLE   A popular dance of the Renaissance.

GIGUE (JIG)   A lively dance popular in the Baroque era.

Important Genres

Turn to the genres chart on page 484. It demonstrates an idea already suggested: An essential element in the continuity of artistic tradition (music, painting, literature, etc.) lies in the existence of basic models. The Western notated musical tradition is no exception. To a great extent its development is the story of these genres: how they came into being; how some continue while others are rejected; how a procedure or form associated with one genre is used in another; etc. Please take particular note of the following features of the chart: A genre may continue throughout various eras. A time period in which the genre is very important to the mainstream of musical practice is indicated by a wide line. A thin line shows that although the genre continues to be used, it is no longer quite so important. For example, consider the *Mass*: It is a basic genre in the Medieval and Renaissance periods; therefore, the line is wide. In subsequent eras, many important Masses were composed, but the genre was no longer a dominant influence on musical styles; therefore, the line is thin.

The Changing Society

The momentous changes in the musical language that occurred between the Middle Ages and the Baroque paralleled equally momentous changes in society. These social and cultural developments, outlined below, provide a background for understanding the evolution of notated music. In this regard, we are concerned with shifts in both *sensory awareness* and *intellectual tradition*, since both influence the aesthetic environment in which music is created and heard. These changes did not occur overnight. At any moment in history, the old and new exist simultaneously. We are not really concerned with the exact moment when things happened. Our interest is more flexible, more involved with the long-range developments. For example, the *Age of Reason* (see below), which occurred approximately in the middle of the eighteenth century, has its roots in earlier traditions. Thus, these basic transformations will be considered within a general chronological framework.

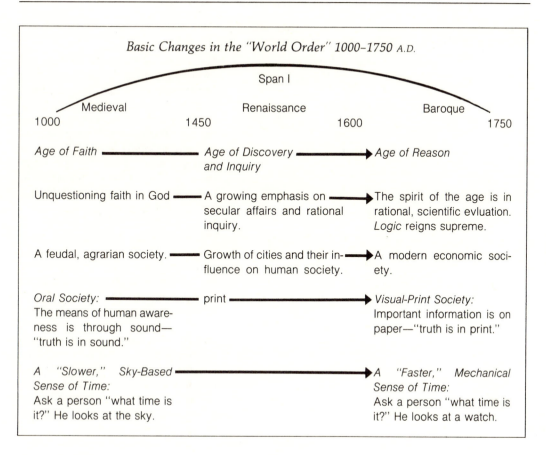

Basic Changes in the "World Order" 1000–1750 A.D.

Span I

Medieval   Renaissance   Baroque

1000   1450   1600   1750

Age of Faith —— *Age of Discovery and Inquiry* ——▶ *Age of Reason*

Unquestioning faith in God —— A growing emphasis on secular affairs and rational inquiry. ——▶ The spirit of the age is in rational, scientific evluation. *Logic* reigns supreme.

A feudal, agrarian society. —— Growth of cities and their influence on human society. ——▶ A modern economic society.

Oral Society: —— print ——▶ *Visual-Print Society:*
The means of human awareness is through sound—"truth is in sound."   Important information is on paper—"truth is in print."

A "Slower," Sky-Based Sense of Time: ——▶ *A "Faster," Mechanical Sense of Time:*
Ask a person "what time is it?" He looks at the sky.   Ask a person "what time is it?" He looks at a watch.

Musical Developments

The development of polyphony. The polyphonic art was only possible with the technology of musical notation.

Polyphony created a new dimension of musical awareness—the listener responds to the linear and harmonic aspects simultaneously.

Cultural Developments

European society was changing from a primarily *oral* culture to one dominated by the *visual sense*, which was given further impetus by the technology of printing. This visual transformation is basic to the experience of the modern "rational" world.

The use of perspective in art created a new dimension of visual space.

Musical Developments	*Cultural Developments*
A growing sense of harmony.	As the focus shifted from God to man, a sense of the beauty of the human body was found in all the arts. The nude figure returned to painting and sculpture. Portrayed in both sacred and secular art, the human form was considered to be the perfect model of proportion and balance, a relationship combining the physical and intellectual worlds. Musical harmony was considered to be related to this sense of beauty and proportion.
From a flexible to a regular and strict sense of rhythm.	The sense of time was becoming faster and more exact. In the Medieval world, time was slower, based on the sun and the rhythms of a society bound to the land. Today one can still feel this slowing down of time in the country, at sea, or on a farm. Clocks first appeared in towers in the twelfth century but only rang out hours. By the eighteenth century, clocks measured minutes and seconds and were widely available. Ancient time, recorded by the skies, was giving way to modern time, measured by new precision machines.
Musical expression became more individualized. There was a transition from an anonymous, universal style of musical expression to a highly personalized style of individual expression.	People like Dante (1265–1321), Leonardo (1452–1519), and Descartes (1596–1650) reflected the increasing influence of the individual on society. The Renaissance ideal was one of personal growth and fulfillment. Print ended the anonymity of oral culture; print allowed the authorship and ownership of music, literature, philosophy, and ideas to be acknowledged and used for personal advancement.
The increase of forward potential.	Society in general was being continually changed at an ever-increasing rate. There was a sense of things happening "faster," with more determination, and with more specific goals.

QUESTIONS

1. Write the correct style period (Medieval, Renaissance, or Baroque) for each of these statements.

   (a) The beginning of polyphony.

   (b) Harmony is often unplanned and dissonant.

   (c) The ideal sound is a blended, homogeneous texture.

   (d) The era of virtuoso vocal and instrumental music.

   (e) The era in which a small modern orchestra may be found.

   (f) The era in which organum is composed.

   (g) The era in which Gregorian chant is no longer a main influence in music.

   (h) Use of instrumental families to create blended timbres.

   (i) The era of polarized polyphony.

   (j) The harpsichord is characteristic of the instrumental sound of this era.

   (k) The first era in which every moment of harmony is carefully planned and controlled.

   (l) The era in which music has the most forward potential.

   (m) The era in which the major–minor tonal system is fully established.

For the following questions, find any false statement(s) and correct them by changing the word(s) in italics. More than one statement may be false; all the statements may be true.

2. Considering the notated musical tradition that developed during Span I:

   (a) It *developed* from a living language of sacred chant.

   (b) Church requirements played an *unimportant* role.

   (c) It had a *minimal* effect on the subsequent developments in musical culture.

   (d) It exploited *body-based* musical practices.

3. Concerning a comparison between body-based and notation-based music:

   (a) Notation-based music *increases* reliance on the body.

   (b) Notation-based music allows for *more intellectualized* musical creation.

   (c) Body-based music was the *earlier* of the two.

4. Considering Leonin's *Viderunt omnes* 9 :

   (a) The Gregorian melody was *widely known*.

   (b) It uses a basic element of the living language as a *cantus firmus*.

   (c) It demonstrates the principle that new procedures of art *rarely* use practices of the past.

   (d) Its genre classification is *motet*.

5. Concerning notation:

   (a) It encourages the *anonymity* of the composer.

   (b) It adds the *visual sense* to musical perception.

   (c) It was developed in the *Renaissance*.

   (d) Some music originally composed orally was *later notated*.

6. Concerning instrumental music in the Medieval era:

   (a) Many of the instruments were *ancient* in design.

   (b) Composers *did not* indicate which instruments played notated music.

   (c) Dance music was a *minor* part of instrumental composition.

   (d) Notated Medieval dance music demonstrates the *interplay* between body-based and notated music.

7. Concerning instrumental music in the Renaissance:

   (a) Instruments were often chosen with the *blending* of timbres in mind.

   (b) It developed the prominent use of *instrumental families*.

   (c) The *juxtaposition* of timbres was also an important practice.

8. An instrumental family

   (a) was also known as a *consort*.

   (b) is created by similar instruments often different in *size*.

   (c) can create a chordal sound which emphasizes the role of *melody*.

   (d) is a basic component of the *modern orchestra*.

9. Concerning instrumental music in the Baroque:

   (a) It was the age of *virtuosic* instrumental playing.

   (b) A standard instrumental practice was use of the *continuo*.

   (c) The *harpsichord* was a characteristic timbre in Baroque sound.

   (d) Solo instrumentalists often *ornamented* their parts.

10. Concerning instrumental music during Span I:

   (a) *Dance music* played a vital role in its development.

   (b) By the *Renaissance*, we find the beginning of the modern orchestra.

   (c) Instrumental music becomes *less* important in musical culture.

   (d) Notated instrumental music *declines*.

11. Concerning the changing melodic styles during Span I:

   (a) The general trend is from *simplicity toward complexity*.

   (b) Melodic style is influenced by the growing importance and sophistication of notated *instrumental* music.

   (c) Melodic styles are influenced by *notation*.

   (d) Melody generally became *less* "busy" and "active."

12. Concerning the melodic style of the Middle Ages and the Renaissance:

   (a) Both were *deeply influenced* by the smooth melodic shape of the Gregorian chant.

   (b) *Both* utilize many stepwise and other easily singable intervals.

   (c) Renaissance composers *increased* the emphasis on smooth, easily singable melodic patterns.

13. Concerning Baroque melody:

    (a) It is a *busy, complex* style.

    (b) It often has an active, *forward-moving* quality.

    (c) Both vocal and instrumental melodies demonstrate a new level of *virtuosity*.

    (d) A motive is often continually repeated by *sequences*.

14. Concerning rhythm during Span I:

    (a) The general direction is toward *regularity and strict meter*.

    (b) Dance music has a *continuing affect* throughout the span.

    (c) The rhythmic affect of chant is *strongest* in the Baroque.

    (d) There *is some* metered music in both the Medieval and Renaissance eras.

15. Concerning rhythm in the Medieval era:

    (a) Some music was greatly affected by the rhythmic structure of *Gregorian chant*.

    (b) Some music was affected by the rhythmic structure of *dance music*.

    (c) Sacred vocal music and secular dance music had *different* rhythmic qualities.

    (d) Chant rhythms were dependent on the *text*.

16. Concerning rhythm in the Renaissance:

    (a) Rhythms of sacred vocal music often had a *floating feeling*.

    (b) There was a *difference* in rhythmic characteristics between sacred vocal music and instrumental dance music.

    (c) Nonmetered and metered rhythm were *both* found in music.

    (d) Meter was *more evident* in sacred music than in dance music.

17. Concerning rhythm in the Baroque:

    (a) Meter *was* indicated by composers.

    (b) The standard practice was *regular meter*.

(c) Pieces often have a few rhythmic motives which continually *repeat*.

(d) Compared with the previous eras, there is *less difference* between the rhythmic structure of sacred vocal and instrumental dance music.

18. Concerning the development of polyphony during Span I:

(a) Some of the earliest polyphony was created with *Gregorian chant* as a musical basis.

(b) Notation was *essential* to the practice of polyphony in each era.

(c) There was a general *decrease* in awareness of the harmonic aspect.

(d) Polyphonic techniques *did not* cross over into secular music.

19. Concerning polyphony in the Medieval era:

(a) It often emphasized the *harmonic* aspect.

(b) The voices sometimes seem *isolated* from each other.

(c) In Medieval motets it was common for different parts to have different texts, thus *decreasing* the independence of the voices.

(d) It demonstrates that musical innovation *rarely* grows out of preexisting practices.

20. Concerning Renaissance polyphony:

(a) The Renaissance ideal was a *balanced, blended texture emphasizing harmony*.

(b) The harmony was primarily *consonant*.

(c) The bass *was* emphasized.

(d) Imitation is *frequently* heard.

21. Concerning Baroque texture:

(a) Baroque polyphonic texture is described as *equalized*, reflecting the separate roles each part played.

(b) The bass *was* emphasized.

(c) Harmonic accompaniment was provided by the *continuo*.

(d) Polyphonic *and* homophonic textures were utilized.

22. Concerning the development of harmony during Span I:

(a) *Medieval* harmony sometimes sounds strange to modern ears.

(b) The traditional major–minor harmonic system was standardized in the *Renaissance*.

(c) Renaissance harmony is mostly *dissonant*.

(d) The harmonic progressions of the Baroque have *more* forward potential than those of the previous eras.

23. Concerning Span I:

(a) There is a general growth in *harmonic awareness*.

(b) There is an *increasing* ability to coordinate linear and harmonic aspects.

(c) Harmony is *more* dissonant in the Baroque than the Renaissance.

(d) The most consonant style is that of the *Renaissance*.

6
Medieval
and Renaissance
Music

Medieval Reality

A popular theme of science fiction is the traveler from the past arriving in a spectacular and confusing present. We delight in imagining a shocked confrontation with the technological advances of our world. Suppose we consider such a journey from a musical point of view. Selecting a church musician from the year 1200, we transport him from this time (it would be a *he* in that era) to the present. Skipping the obvious (planes, trains, tall buildings, computers, etc.), we introduce our guest to the following musical scenes: a rock concert, the performance of a Beethoven symphony, an electronic music and light show, and a record store where he could hear his thirteenth-century music from a "revolving plate." Certainly, to a person from the Middle Ages, these musical experiences would seem quite strange. It would be very difficult for him to understand them without the cultural conditioning of our time. Although this bit of science fiction may seem a touch whimsical, it is not as far off as one might think. In a profound sense, we experience a similar time shift—but in the other direction—by listening to a recording of thirteenth-century music. Through notation and electronic reproduction, a part of that distant reality has traveled through time to this moment. Unless you are a student of Medieval history, you are just as unprepared for this cultural time shift as our thirteenth-century friend. Vital to developing a listening perspective for music of the past is some understanding of what it was like to live in that time.

149

Of the historical eras of Western European civilization considered within the scope of this book, the Medieval is the most distant in time and the most different in culture. Consider the following ideas:

1. Generally, we respond to the past through a modern cultural filter. The basic tenets and notions of reality that make up our views were formed after the Middle Ages in the great shifts of awareness that have occurred with increased intensity since the Renaissance.

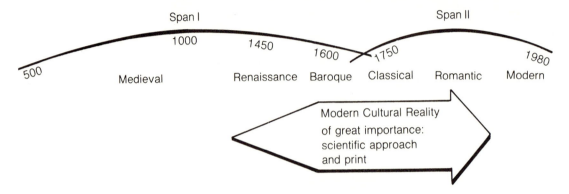

2. In terms of the details of day-to-day life, Medieval culture is closer to its ancient past than its immediate future:

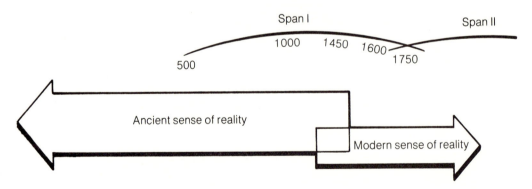

These ideas suggest that in order to temper our modern view about Medieval culture, we are obliged to *approach it from the past*, discarding modern notions and perceptions, while reconstructing (as best we can) something of that distant reality.

MEDIEVAL SENSE OF TIME

No perception is more important to musical response than that of time. This response is a culturally determined phenomenon. People in different societies often experience the passage and meaning (the "essence") of time in different ways. Compared with our own, the Medieval sense of time may be described as circular, slower, and less goal-directed. Time was not, as it is with us, a tangible commodity. One couldn't "gain it" or "lose it." It grew from an ancient reality based in the long rhythms of life, sky, and season. It was understood through the interlocking cycles of day and night, planting and harvesting, life and death. It was measured, internalized, and made sacred through the ritual of the Church. Bells, chants, and prayers measured daily existence. These daily rites interlocked with a longer plan of seasonal celebrations, the whole system representing the rhythms of God's universe.

Medieval music, then, exists in a different time plane. For the modern listener, many Medieval pieces seem to be too long or "to go nowhere." One way for us to bypass this response is simply to slow down. An interesting activity, especially while listening to chant and organum, is to breath more slowly than usual, perhaps coordinating that breathing with long impulses of the piece. This music was never intended merely to be heard. It was meant to be experienced as timeless, symbolic, ritual—a reflection of the cosmos.

LACK OF SENSORY CLUTTER

Look at the picture of a Medieval cathedral (C9) on page 509. You will notice that the clutter of modern civilization (the industrial smokestack, etc.) is competing with the church for our visual attention. Like the other sacred structures in that pictorial sequence, the Medieval cathedral originally rose high above the landscape, its visual impact undisturbed. This uncluttered quality of Medieval space has its parallel in music. While we have become accustomed to living in an environment of sensory overkill—radios, Muzak, television, records, car noise, sirens, etc.—the sound spectrum of the ancient world was less stressful. There was, in fact, far more of that phenomenon essential to the meaning of music—*silence*.

SOUND AS TRUTH

We live in a culture where the *visual sense* is the most important mode in shaping reality. In our world, "truth" is usually honored and identified visually, *in print*. We even speak of reality in visual terms. For example, "view" is often used to mean "idea" ("What's your view?" or "I see" in place of "I understand.") But in the Middle Ages, and since the dawn of humanity, truth was experienced *in sound*. In a culture where sound was truth, music carried a great and magical power. Gregorian chant was more than music: it encoded and communicated the very essence of a civilization. Today, such principles that may hold society together are *read* in the Bible (or other sacred texts) or in documents like the Constitution. In the Middle Ages, long before literacy was widespread, this all-important cultural fabric was *heard* in prayer and chant.

UNITY OF SACRED AND SECULAR EXPERIENCE

In our culture, sacred and secular phenomena are considered separate. In the Medieval world, there was less distinction between religious and secular life. As evidence of this, consider the thirteenth-century motet, which became

> a microcosm of the cultural life of its time. The structure of the motet, with its motley concourse of love songs, dance tunes, popular refrains, and sacred hymns, all held together in a rigid formal mold based on Gregorian plainsong, is analogous to the structure of Dante's *Divine Comedy*, which likewise encompasses and organizes a universe of secular and sacred ideas within a rigid theological framework.*

This merging of sacred and secular—for most of us, a mismatch of cues—is evident in the simultaneous singing of both Gregorian chant and melodies with more worldly texts, as in *Hé Marotelle* (already discussed in another context on page 136):

 Listen *Hé Marotelle*** 10a

Melody 1

Hé, Marotelle! Alon au bois juer,	Hey, Marotelle! Let's off to the woods to play,
Je te ferai chapiau de flour de glai,	I'll make you a hat of rush flowers
Et si orrons le roussignol chanter en l'aunoi:	And we're sure to hear the nightingales sing all together:
"Oci, oci cels qui n'ont le cuer gai,"	"Oh see, oh see those who haven't a light heart,"
Douce Marot, grief sont li mal qui j'ai.	Sweet Marot, great is my woe.
Amours ai, qu'en ferai?	Love is my trouble, what shall I do?
Dieus! Je n'i puis ces mals endurer.	God! I can't stand it any more,
Marot, que je sent pour toi.	Marot, all I feel for you.
Il l'enbracha, sour l'erbe la jeta,	He hugged her, threw her down upon the grass,
Si la baisa, puis li fist sans delai	Kissed her, and then in haste
Le jeu d'amours, puis dist de cuer gai:	Made love to her, then said with a light heart:
"Douce Marot, grief sont li mal que j'ai."	"Sweet Marot, great is my woe."

Melody 2

En la praerie, Robins et s'amie	In the meadow, Robin and his girl friend
Font lour druerei desous un glai;	Are flirting under the rush trees;
Marote s'escrie par grant esmai:	Marot cries out emotionally:
"Aimmi, Dieus! aimmi! qu'en ferai?	"Ah me, God! Ah me! whatever shall I do?
Tu mi bleiches trop a ton "ne sai quoi."	You are hurting me a lot with your *je ne sais quoi*.
Ains mais a tel jeu certes ne juai,	I never before played such a game,
Je sui pucelete, foi que te doi!	I am a maiden, by my word!

*Donald Jay Grout, *History of Western Music*, third ed. (New York, 1980), p. 115.

**Titles of medieval motets are usually made up of the first few words of each melody, therefore a more precise title for this motet would be *Hé, Marotelle—En la praerie—Aptatur*.

Onques mais n'amai,	Never have I loved before,
Pour Dieu! Espargne moi,	For the Lord's sake! Spare me,
Fai tost, lieve toi!"	Have done with it, get up."
Robins sans delai a fait son dornoi,	Robin, without delay, got on with it,
Si l'a enbraciee, et dreciee envers soi	Kissed her, stood up,
Et dist de cuer gai:	And said with a light heart:
"Marot, ja ne te faudrai."	"Marot, I'll never let you down."

Melody 3 Aptatur.   Gregorian chant

THE IMPORTANCE OF RITUAL IN MEDIEVAL SOCIETY

As we've hinted in previous sections, Medieval society was permeated with ritual. We should not underestimate the importance of this observation. Such societies are rooted in a profoundly different reality than our own, and it is this aspect that presents the widest chasm between the Modern and Medieval mind. Since music, like the other arts, was created and experienced within this utterly different mode of being, it cannot be fully understood outside this crucial cultural context. How do we reconnect ourselves to this lost part of our own past? We can begin by examining instances in which ritual has survived.

The importance of ritual of all types in Medieval society is suggested by this four-teenth-century illustration of the *Roman de Fauvel*, a satirical allegory whose hero was half man, half donkey. Such traditions, ritualized in poetry, song, and drama, existed outside the church. From our standpoint, the term *folk ritual* seems an appropriate description.

An obvious and important source for this understanding is the formal religious practices of today. Of special interest is the Catholic Mass (which will be discussed in more detail later), since it was the central rite of Medieval society. To witness the Mass in its original setting (in church, not on a recording) is to experience an ancient and powerful mode of religious celebration—the universal sacred drama—enacted again and again with unquestioned faith. The meaning of the Mass cannot be considered in fragments, but only as an accumulated correspondence of details, interwoven into a unity. Everything in the Mass—music, word, action—combines to create one powerful experience.

There are other contemporary sources for understanding ritual which at first may not seem appropriate because of their secular orientation. (Here it will be useful to remember that the strict dichotomy between sacred and secular life did not exist in the Medieval world.) Do you have friends who believe in astrology, and plan their lives according to movements in the heavens? Have you heard that plane crashes (or deaths) come in threes? Have you ever been kissed under a branch of mistletoe? Have you ever responded to some situation automatically by quoting a proverb (e.g., "A stitch in time saves nine.")? These actions, which basically lie outside modern notions of rational behavior, are "folk rituals," repeated unquestioningly for generations. These examples hint at an ancient, pre-print, pre-scientific consciousness, when such notions were not considered odd, but were the ingrained truths of an entire culture. Now, imagine the rituals described above (both church and "folk") as a continuous, interwoven fabric of daily existence. Imagine a world in which all actions, thoughts, and natural events were experienced and explained as part of this accepted order. In such a world, questions and doubts were answered with the intonation of a prayer, chant, spell, or riddle, perhaps in correspondence with a "sign" in the heavens. *One of the most important understandings about such an ancient reality is that it fosters a nonfragmented experience of the world.* Stated in another way: *the perception of one thing flows into the next.* For example, three stars, three prayers, and three phrases of a song—each might be experienced in a ritualistic correspondence with the other. Nothing existed outside the sacred, rhythmic web of life. Nothing existed alone.

|Listen| Gregorian chant, *Agnus Dei* |8| (text on page 166)
The simple, repetitive phrase design of the chant cannot be evaluated in strictly musical terms. The symbolic experience of "threeness" is basic to the meaning of this music. Here we encounter musical ritual in all its fullness—word, melody, rhythm, form, and sacred symbolism—in a total unity of heightened experience.

South transept of Lausanne Cathedral, Switzerland, c. 1220.

THE MEDIEVAL CATHEDRAL—MUSIC AS SACRED SCIENCE

As another example of how the perception of one phenomenon merged with another, the proportion, form, and aesthetics of Medieval architecture were related to the simple ratios that produce tones from a single string (see "The Magic of the String," pages 70–71). To the learned Medieval mind, sacred architecture was the visual representation of a religious-musical truth:

> the simple ratios of the musical consonances are not only elements of aesthetic beauty, but also scientific laws that assure the stability and order of the Universe. And by these laws the medieval architect had to abide, just as the modern architect has to abide by the laws of science.*

The picture above is of an inner wall and window of the Lausanne Cathedral in Switzerland (thirteenth century). Its design was derived from sacred musical measurements. Basic to the structure are the proportions 1:2:3 (simple divisions of the string). These same proportions produce the chord often heard at the beginning and end of a phrase in medieval sacred music. Thus, to the medieval architect, the wall "sings" and mirrors religious truth. Music, then, was a "sacred science" through which the measurements and patterns of religious architecture were revealed. (See also comments below concerning Dufay's motet *Nuper rosarum flores.*)

Isorhythm—Mathematical Abstraction in Medieval Music

The *Agnus Dei*, like other musical structures involving threefold patterns, was a relatively simple example of the Medieval sacred practice of making

---

*Otto von Simson, "The South Transept of Lausanne Cathedral," in *Man through his Art: Music* (Greenwich, Conn., n.d.), p. 29.

numbers audible through music. A far more complex practice was *isorhythm*, a highly elaborate, abstract procedure used in the composing of some late Medieval polyphonic genres, especially the motet. The isorhythmic plan may be likened to an abstract mathematical puzzle. The two main components of that puzzle were a specific rhythm and a certain order of intervals. The composer juggled these elements in various ways—for example, the rhythmic pattern might be cut in half (the music then sounding twice as fast). The order of intervals might start again before the pattern of rhythm was complete. These elements could be manipulated to express hidden mathematical relationships. All of this would be happening, not in one voice, but in a polyphonic maze of interlocking design. If you think this all sounds quite complex, you're right! Isorhythmic procedures are a perfect example of the extent to which logical, mathematical designs can be applied to musical structure. The trick was, of course, to make such a mathematical puzzle sound good. And there you have again the interplay between body-based musicality and notation-based abstractions. Combining the two impulses into musical experience has been the forge on which the Western notated musical tradition has been fashioned.

Suggested Listening | This chart, like many that will follow, is meant to be used as a resource for your present and future listening.

The following works were composed with isorhythmic techniques. You will not hear the complex mathematical "puzzle" that underlies these pieces. Simply be aware that the musical sound reflects a highly ordered, abstract plan.*

Span I

Renaissance

Medieval   Baroque

Machaut, *Agnus Dei*   Dufay, motet
from the *Notre Dame*   *Nuper rosarum*
Mass (14th c.)   *flores* (1436)

Vitry, motet
Garrit gallus (c.1360)

Of special interest is the motet *Nuper rosarum flores* by Guillaume Dufay (c. 1400–74). Although considered an early Renaissance work, it retains the Medieval practice of isorhythm. Dufay composed the motet to honor a new cathedral in Florence. An important proportion used in the architecture of that structure was 6:4:2:3. This same proportion is encoded in Dufay's motet through a variety of rhythmic procedures. To cite one of many examples, the total number of pulses in each of the motet's four sec-

*All three selections may be found on the *Recordings to Accompany A History of Western Music* by Donald J. Grout (W.W. Norton).

tions is 168:112:56:84 (6:4:2:3). Thus the motet is a sounding model of the cathedral. This highly complex rhythmic structure was not meant to be heard, but intended as a "sacred puzzle." The manipulation of tone, number, and architecture into secret correspondences of religious intention is a cultural strand that reaches back to antiquity. The practice of music as a sacred science ties the early Western notated tradition to some four thousand years of ancient civilization (for example, the civilization that created the pyramids shown in Picture Sequence C on pages 508–10).

Text

Nuper rosarum flores	Recently roses [came]
Ex dono pontificis	as a gift of the Pope,
Hieme licet horrida,	although in cruel winter,
Tibi, virgo coelica,	to you, heavenly Virgin.
Pie et sancte deditum	Dutifully and blessedly is dedicated
Grandis templum machinae	[to you] a temple of magnificent design.
Condecorarunt perpetim.	May they together be perpetual ornaments.
Hodie vicarius	Today the Vicar
Jesu Christi et Petri	of Jesus Christ and Peter's
Successor EUGENIUS	successor, Eugenius,
Hoc idem amplissimum	this same most spacious
Sacris templum manibus	sacred temple with his hands
Sanctisque liquoribus	and with holy waters
Consecrare dignatus est.	he is worthy to consecrate.
Igitur, alma parens,	Therefore, gracious mother
Nati tui et filia,	and daughter of your offspring,
Virgo decus virginum,	Virgin, ornament of virgins,
Tuus te FLORENTIAE	your, Florence's, people
Devotus orat populus,	devoutly pray
Ut qui mente et corpore	so that together with all mankind,
Mundo quicquam exoravit,	with mind and body, their entreaties may move you.
Oratione tua	Through your prayer,
Cruciatus et meritis	your anguish and merits,
Tui secundum carnem	may [the people] deserve to receive of the Lord,
Nati domini sui	born of you according to the flesh,
Grata beneficia	the benefits of grace
Veniamque reatum	and the remission of sins.
Accipere mereatur.	Amen
Amen.	

The Renaissance

The term *Renaissance* is forever linked to the image of a vibrant society immersed in the arts. And with good reason. Beginning sometime in fourteenth-century Italy, this great cultural movement spread through the centers of European intellectual and artistic life, effecting momentous developments and achievements in painting, sculpture, architecture, poetry, drama, and music. These accomplishments were the visible and audible manifestations of a deeper change. European civilization was realigning its basic traditions and societal mechanisms, changes which would eventually cause a rapid, explosive sprint into modern culture.

The Renaissance had many far-reaching effects on music making. There was, in fact, a "spectacular increase of musical culture."* The profound changes in society were paralleled by important transformations in the composition, transmission, and utilization of music in the culture. Among the important developments were the following, each related to the others:

1. *More notated music was being composed than in the previous era.* During the Medieval period the practice of notated polyphony had been limited to a relatively small number of churches and courts. The Renaissance witnessed the rapid expansion of this tradition, not only in churches and aristocratic centers, but in other segments of society as well (see below).

2. *The advent of music printing.* A critical factor contributing to the increase of music culture was the new technology of print. Within decades after movable type had been perfected by Johann Gutenberg for producing books (1454), it was applied with success to music notation. Not only did this technology promote the diffusion of music, it helped raise the composer's status in society. With this development, music became more of a commodity: it could be bought, used, and studied. With music printing came the institution of publishing, which radically changed the composer's relationship to society. (The far-reaching changes wrought by music printing may be compared to a twentieth-century technological development of equal importance to musical culture—the advent of recording technology; see pages 423–25.)

3. *The expansion of secular patronage.* With the Renaissance came new support for music (and other arts) from various segments of secular socity. Basic to this trend was a flourishing commercial economy producing a new middle and upper class eager to support music both as recreation and as a symbol of social status. Church patronage still remained a vital and important source of employment for many musicians.

4. *The growth of notated secular genres.* Paralleling humanist interest in secular affairs, the Renaissance musical culture witnessed a flourishing of notated secular genres of many types, both vocal and in-

*Grout, *History of Western Music*, p. 171.

strumental. (Some of these are discussed on the following pages.)

5. *Increased interplay among regional styles.* The growth of economic and cultural connections within Renaissance Europe naturally lead to increased interplay among regional traditions. For example, the harmonic style of English music influenced the general trend toward consonant harmony on the continent. Musicians had a new mobility, traveling and finding employment in places distant from their region of birth. In short, the collective genius of many subcultures was being united to create a mainstream of musical activity, which, in turn, enriched and changed regional traditions.

6. *The universal European style.* All this interaction fostered the development of a common notated musical language. This universal approach was especially apparent in sacred music. Secular genres, on the other hand, were more apt to reflect regional differences. This was due to their relationship to local languages and folk-popular musical traditions.

This dynamic musical culture fostered a body of works that, in some ways, remains unparalleled in the synthesis of certain aesthetic and stylistic elements:* sensuous harmony was made audible by crafted polyphony; folk-popular song and dance merged imperceptibly into learned compositional procedures; poetry joined with song; the secular spirit was tempered by pas-

*These items are not found in all Renaissance music; different genres will reflect some, not all of these elements. This description seeks a broad view of the stylistic accomplishments of an age and thus must be flexible.

Vanity by Luigi Genovesino Miradori (d. 1651), Italian. The Renaissance ideal of balance and proportion among various elements functions on both a visual and a philosophical level in this painting. Music, an earthly delight (or vanity) is juxtaposed with death. Although the skull occupies only a small portion of the picture, its emotional impact balances that of the girl and lute.

sionate faith. Central to the expression of these elements was an important Renaissance ideal—a sense of balance, proportion, and harmony (in the general sense) among various elements. This ideal was not only to be sensed in music; it was considered the universal principle revealing truth and beauty; it separated order from chaos. It was the mediator between humankind and the universe.

THE HARMONY OF THE SPHERES

While it is true that Renaissance culture is closer to our own than Medieval, it still retained certain qualities that looked back to a more ancient reality. Despite the growth of scientific discovery and thought, it was still a society based to a certain degree on older notions of religious and folk ritual. The great shifts of awareness that were beginning to shape a modern society had not yet occurred on a widespread basis. It is not surprising, then, to find that the basic religious image and belief surrounding music was the *Harmony of the Spheres*—a broad, composite notion that reaches back beyond the Medieval into pre-Christian times. The various ideas encompassed by the Harmony of the Spheres include:

1. The planets revolving around the earth produce a "heavenly harmony." (See picture B7 on page 506: "The Lord as Ruler of the Cosmic Harmony.")
2. This harmony is related to the tones produced by dividing the string into simple ratios. (See pictures on page 71.)
3. This circular motion in the sky represents a "sacred dance," often portrayed by angels singing, dancing, or playing instruments. (See page 505.)
4. Music has the power of good and bad. Good music, created within this sacred framework, insures the harmony of the world, while bad music encourages chaos and evil.

The Harmony of the Spheres was the central musical image of Christianity through the Renaissance. The modern reader should not underestimate its importance in that time because it seems so wildly unscientific; remember that the full impact of scientific thought upon society had not yet occurred. To thinkers of that time, it was science. The Harmony of the Spheres presents a fascinating interplay between religion, "science," art, music, and dance. Within this ritualistic conception of the universe, *sacred polyphony was a reflection of the cosmic order*. An interesting way to listen to Renaissance polyphony is with the various motifs of the Harmony of the Spheres in mind. (Also, see the discussion of Thomas Tallis, pages 473–74.)

The Renaissance Motet

Listen *I Am the Resurrection* 12 , by Orlando Gibbons (1583–1625)
English composers have always had an affinity for consonant harmony. It was the English in the early Renaissance who first transformed the somewhat dissonant, linear polyphonic practices of the late
Middle Ages into a more consonant style. They were also among the
last to give up the Renaissance ideal. Some of the most remarkable and
awesome examples of Renaissance polyphony are to be found at the
end of that era, around 1600. The *anthem* (the English term for *motet*) *I
Am the Resurrection*, by Orlando Gibbons, is an example of one of
these late Renaissance masterpieces. Unlike the Medieval motet, the
Renaissance anthem or motet had a single sacred text.*

Text

I am the resurrection and the life, saith the Lord: he that believeth
in Me, yea, though he were dead, yet shall he live with his
Redeemer. And whosoever liveth and believeth in Me shall not die
forever.

Listening Activity

Consider the opening motive on the text "I am the Resurrection." Does its

melodic shape rise or fall? _____ Consider the clos-
ing motive on the text "shall not die." Does its shape, as you most often hear it,

rise or fall? _____

CONTINUOUS IMITATION

The Gibbons anthem demonstrates an important type of polyphonic texture
found in much Renaissance music—continuous imitation. In pieces employ-
ing this texture, imitation among the voices (for instrumental parts) continues throughout. In a vocal setting, continuous imitation is fairly easy to
hear, since each new line or phrase of the text often has its own motive. This
motive is then taken up by the voices in back-and-forth interplay. The
resulting musical fabric seems complex yet unified.

*The anthem could also be a homophonic setting of a hymn.

Madrigal and Related Vocal Genres

The Renaissance was an age in which the secular spirit was felt throughout the arts. One musical result of this cultural development was the proliferation of secular vocal genres like the *madrigal*. Whereas the Mass and motet tended to be universal in style, the secular genres were more likely to reflect the language and popular musical traditions of their place of origin. Learned polyphonic techniques were blended with the body-based melodies, rhythms, and forms of popular song and dance. A madrigal might be close in style to a sacred motet, or it might have more popular characteristics. Italian in origin, it became wildly popular in England, where it blended with that country's folk song and dance traditions.

Listen *Since Robin Hood* 13a , by Thomas Weelkes (c. 1575–1623) Thomas Weelkes was an English composer of the Elizabethan era (c. 1560–1610), a late Renaissance period that witnessed the flourishing of music, drama, and poetry. (William Shakespeare was also an Elizabethan.) The catchy tune and the dancelike rhythms of this madrigal reflect the influence of popular music on the mainstream of the European notated style. (In a similar process, certain twentieth-century classical composers were influenced by the rhythm and structure of jazz.) Madrigals were composed as entertainment, so it is not surprising that many were humorous or risqué. A popular technique of the period was *word painting*, the evocation of textual meaning through graphic musical patterns. An example of word painting is heard in this madrigal.

Listening Activity

Text

Since Robin Hood, Maid Marion,
　And Little John are gone,
The hobby horse was quite forgot,
　When Kempe did dance alone.
　　He did labour
　　After the tabor.
　　For to dance
　　Then into France
　　He took pains
To skip it in hope of gains,
He did trip it on the toe,
Diddle diddle diddle doe.

Circle the words the composer emphasizes with word painting. Explain how the music represents that idea.

Dance and music were basic activities in social life throughout the Middle Ages and Renaissance. German woodcut from *Die Weltchronik*, 1493.

Listen *Ríu, ríu, chíu* 13b , Anonymous, Spain (Renaissance)

This is a *villancico*, a popular Spanish piece in the dance-song tradition. A relative of the villancico is the English *carol*, still known to the world in surviving Christmas music. The text of *Ríu, ríu, chíu* is a folk expression of religious belief. Strictly speaking, this makes the piece sacred, not secular, in origin. As usual, it is wise to be flexible with such terminology. The style of this piece is related more to the informal style of secular music than to the "learned" style of the Church Mass or motet. The form is *binary*: verses alternate with a closely related *refrain*. The refrain ("Ríu, ríu . . .") begins the piece.

Text

Ríu, ríu, chíu, la guarda ribera:
Dios guardó el lobo de nuestra
    cordera.
El lobo rabioso lo quiso morder,
mas Dios poderoso la supo defender;
quísola hazer que no pudiesse pecar,
ni aun original esta Virgen no
    tuviera.
    Ríu, ríu, chíu. . .

Ríu, ríu, chíu, the river bank
    protects it:
As God kept the wolf from our
    lamb.
The rabid wolf tried to bite her,
But God almighty knew how to
    defend her;
He wished to create her impervious
    to sin,
Nor was this maid to embody
    original sin.
    Ríu, ríu, chíu. . .

Este qu'es necido es el gran monarca,	He who is born is the great King,

Este qu'es necido es el gran
  monarca,
Cristo patriarca de carne vestido;
hanos redimido con se hazer
  chiquito,
aunqu'era infinito, finito se hiziera.
  Ríu, ríu, chíu. . .

He who is born is the great King,
Christ God made flesh;
He has redeemed us by making
  Himself as a child,
Although everlasting He made
  Himself finite.
  Ríu, ríu, chíu. . .

Yo vi mil garçones que andavan
  cantando
por aquí bolando, haziendo mil
  sones,
diziendo a gascones Gloria sea enel
  cielo
y paz en el suelo, pues Jesús
  naxciera.
  Ríu, ríu, chíu. . .

A thousand singing herons I saw
  passing
Flying overhead sounding a
  thousand voices,
Exalting "Glory be in the heavens
  and Peace on Earth
For Jesus has been born."
  Ríu, ríu, chíu. . .

Este viene a dara los muertos vida
y viene a reparar de todos la
  caída;
es la luz d'l día aqueste moçuelo;
este es el cordero que San Juan
  dixera.
  Ríu, ríu, chíu. . .

He comes to give life to the dead
He comes to redeem the fall of Man;
This child is the light of day;
He is the very Lamb Saint John
  prophesied.
  Ríu, ríu, chíu. . .

Listening Activity

What instrument sounds throughout this piece?

In one place a consort of instruments *replaces* the singers. Is that place in the form the verse or refrain?
The instruments in that consort are of what type?

Describe the end of the piece in terms of who plays and/or sings.

 Pase el agoa, ma Julieta [13c], Anonymous, Spain (Renaissance)

This song—another example of the notated popular style from the Spanish Renaissance—is noteworthy for its infectious dancing quality, derived in part from its Mediterranean heritage (cf. Sequence [5]). A strumming guitar would not be out of place as an accompaniment to this piece, and it is quite likely that just such accompaniments were provided. (You may remember that in the Renaissance, composers still did not specify instrumentation.) The text is not presented here in its poetic form, but in a manner that makes correlation with the music easier.

Text

Pase el agoa, ma Julieta dama	Cross the water, my Juliet; lady
pase el agoa. Venite vous a moy.	cross the water. Come to me.
Pase el agoa, ma Julieta dama	Cross the water, my Juliet; lady
pase el agoa. Venite vous a moy.	cross the water. Come to me.
Ju me'n anay en un vergel,	I went into a garden,
Ju me'n anay en un vergel,	I went into a garden,
tres rosetas fui coller. Ma	I went to pick three roses. My
Ma Julioleta, dama,	little Juliet, my lady,
pase el agoa. Venite vous a moy.	cross the water. Come to me.
tres rosetas fui collar. Ma	I went to pick three roses. My
Julioleta, dama.	little Juliet, my lady,
pase el agoa. Venite vous a moy.	cross the water. Come to me.

(Entire text repeats.)

Listening Activity

Name the instrumental types that accompany this song.

Tap a steady pulse to the music (see marks above the beginning of the text.) Circle any words or syllables that seem to have a syncopated rhythm.

The Mass

The most important musical genre through the Renaissance was the *Mass*, a musical setting of the five sung texts that are invariable parts of the daily rite of the Roman Catholic service. Originally sung in Gregorian chant, the Mass took on polyphonic characteristics in the late Medieval era.

THE SECTIONS OF THE MASS

Kyrie

Kyrie eleison,	Lord have mercy,
Christe eleison,	Christ have mercy,
Kyrie eleison.	Lord have mercy.

The opening prayer is in Greek, a reflection of the early centuries of Christianity before Latin became the official language. The prayer derives its basic form from the sacred number three, symbolically represented in the phrases of the chant.

Gloria

Gloria in excelsis Deo	Glory to God in the highest
Et in terra pax hominibus	And on earth peace to men
bonae voluntatis	of good will
[opening only]	

A hymn of praise to God.

Credo

Credo in unum Deum	I believe in one God
[opening line only]	

The Credo is the central statement of essential beliefs among Christians, and also includes some of the most dramatic imagery of the Mass—the crucifixion and resurrection.

Sanctus

Sanctus, Sanctus, Sanctus	Holy, holy, holy
Dominus Deus Sabaoth	Lord God of Hosts
[opening lines only]	

Like the Gloria, a hymn of praise to God. Another pattern of three may be heard in the opening words.

Agnus Dei

Agnus Dei,	Lamb of God,
qui tollis peccata mundi,	who takest away the sins of the world,
miserere nobis.	have mercy upon us.
Agnus Dei,	Lamb of God,
qui tollis peccata mundi,	who takest away the sins of the world,
miserere nobis.	have mercy upon us.
Agnus Dei,	Lamb of God,
qui tollis peccata mundi,	who takest away the sins of the world,
dona nobis pacem.	grant us peace.

The closing section is a prayer for salvation and peace on earth.

You have already heard two excerpts from the Mass—the Gregorian *Agnus Dei* [8] and the Ockeghem *Kyrie* from his complete *Missa Au travail suis* [10b] . A *Sanctus* by Giovanni Gabrieli will be discussed shortly.

THE IMPORTANCE OF THE MASS DURING SPAN I

To Christianity, the Mass was a central rite; to music, it was a central genre, which helped unify and spread the European musical language. The music of the Mass reflects one of the basic ideas of Western culture—*expression within the boundaries of restraint*. Because of its sacred purpose, composers conceived of the Mass within definite, self-imposed, stylistic boundaries. The great works in this genre evoke the wonder of a profound religious experience. The Mass has many dramatic moments. For example, the word *crucifixus* (crucified) might well be set off from the musical flow in a passage of sudden pathos. Such dramatic qualities, which entered the tradition at various times, were kept in check by the essentially reflective purpose of the rite. Thus, a long-range balance was created between the composers' dramatic tendencies and the Church's insistence that the Mass style not get out of hand. In fact, the calm solemnity characteristic of Gregorian chant was retained in the Mass through the Renaissance.

THE MASS IN CULTURAL CONTEXT

Not only is the Mass important in the development of our musical traditions, but also as a model that illustrates the vital connections between life rhythms and the art of music. The following observations relate the Mass to some of the basic ideas already discussed in Chapter 4.

THE ANCIENT UNITY

The Mass is a religious ritual and as such is a heightened experience. It may also be considered a powerful group drama. Each time the Mass is celebrated, the worshipers not only recreate a symbolic dramatic action, but participate in that drama. Historically, music, dance, and drama were integral parts of sacred ritual. In the Mass, however, dance was eliminated as incompatible with Western Christian doctrine, although the Mass retained certain prescribed movements (for example, genuflection and the taking of Communion).

PATTERN AND FORM

The form of the Mass grows directly from the life rhythms of worship. The basic plan of the text is a ritual with a definite order, rigidly maintained within the religious calendar. The text is a basic factor in the musical form. For example, we may note patterns of three, a sacred Christian number, in the Kyrie, Sanctus, and Agnus Dei. The religious significance of the number three may influence the musical form when the composer sets these texts.

THE MASS BEYOND STYLE

Like the basic shapes that unify the picture sequences (see pages 500–11) the form of the Mass transcends boundaries of style and time. There have been thousands of Masses composed from the Middle Ages to the present day, a time span of a thousand years. Comparisons among them can be quite interesting, reflecting the myriad differences of time and place, but retaining the continuity of one basic plan.

Suggested Listening

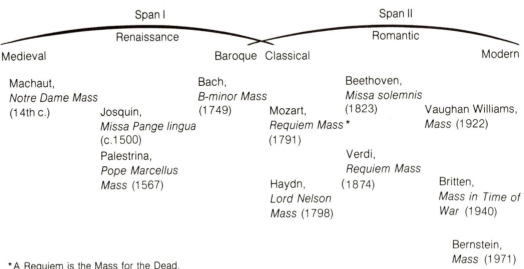

Span I		Span II
Renaissance		Romantic
Medieval	Baroque Classical	Modern

Machaut,
Notre Dame Mass
(14th c.)

Josquin,
Missa Pange lingua
(c.1500)

Palestrina,
*Pope Marcellus
Mass* (1567)

Bach,
B-minor Mass
(1749)

Mozart,
Requiem Mass *
(1791)

Haydn,
*Lord Nelson
Mass* (1798)

Beethoven,
Missa solemnis
(1823)

Verdi,
Requiem Mass
(1874)

Vaughan Williams,
Mass (1922)

Britten,
*Mass in Time of
War* (1940)

Bernstein,
Mass (1971)

*A Requiem is the Mass for the Dead.

Listen *Sanctus* 14 , by Giovanni Gabrieli (1557–1612)
Giovanni Gabrieli, a late Renaissance composer, was an organist at the Cathedral of St. Mark in Venice. The music he wrote for performance in this great eleventh-century building was especially dramatic due to a particular technique—*antiphony*. In an antiphonal texture, different groups—choral and/or instrumental—create musical interest through a dramatic interplay of musical sound sources. Often, they are positioned in different locations—in this case, the opposite sides of a church. This *Sanctus* is written for three separate groups of voices with instruments, a total of twelve separate melodies in the polyphonic texture. In the recording, the left-right split between speakers hints at the magnificent antiphonal effects the work produced in the echoing space of the cathedral.

Listening Activity Describe the various sound sources you hear.

CONTINUOUS IMITATION   A polyphonic design in which imitation proceeds throughout a long section or an entire piece.

ANTIPHONY (ANTIPHONAL)   A texture in which two or more groups (vocal or instrumental) create musical interest through an interplay of sound sources. Often the groups are positioned in different parts of a stage or church.

MADRIGAL   A secular vocal genre of the Renaissance, often influenced by popular musical traditions.

MOTET   In Medieval practice, a polyphonic vocal genre in which several texts are sung at the same time. In Renaissance practice, a polyphonic vocal genre with one sacred text; in England, it became the *anthem*.

VILLANCICO   A popular notated genre of the Renaissance, which was both sung and danced.

ISORHYTHM   A late Medieval procedure in which a basic rhythm and order of pitches were manipulated in an abstract, mathematically based manner.

MASS   The solemn daily rite of the Roman Catholic Church. Although the texts of certain parts of the Mass change from day to day, there are five main sections whose texts are always the same—*Kyrie, Gloria, Credo, Sanctus,* and *Agnus Dei.* These sections are often set to music as a complete work.

AFTERTHOUGHT

In the past, people always looked to the sky for both comfort and warning. Around 1600, a new, extremely bright star appeared in the heavens (we know now that it was a supernova). For seventeen months, its presence helped dramatize an uncomfortable awareness that had been developing in European thought, that the old order was about to change. For the heavens had always been constant and unchanging, the ultimate symbol of unquestioned faith in a universal design. This faith, and the society it had helped to create, dominated by a central church, had long been under siege from many sides: Scientists were discovering a new, rational universe in which human beings, not God, could explain the cosmos with logical principles rather than religious dogma. This change became known as the Copernican Revolution. The Catholic Church was being challenged by a powerful Reformation, which for the most part supported new ideas and a growing sense of man as an independent, religious, social, and economic entity. A city-based middle class was eroding the rigid social structure of agrarian feudalism. The intellectual isolation that characterized the Medieval mind was no more. Ideas from a great Italian city like Venice could reach the far-off world of the English countryside through a new medium—the printed book. All along the interlocking chain we call culture, the ideas of the Renaissance were bringing an ancient order to an end. The old order had meant unquestioning faith and acceptance of the world as it was; the new order meant a more active participation in the creation of one's own values, social position, and destiny. This was possible with the technological tools of print and machines, as well as the new intellectual tools of rational, scientific inquiry. The Baroque age was beginning.

QUESTIONS

For the following questions, find any false statement(s) and correct them by changing the word(s) in italics. More than one statement may be false; all the statements may be true.

1. Concerning the Medieval era:

    (a) The sense of time was *less* goal-directed than our own.

    (b) The aesthetic environment was *less* cluttered than our own.

    (c) Sound was *less* important than the written word.

    (d) Various types of *ritual* permeated the cultural fabric.

2. Concerning the isorhythmic motet:

    (a) It was a musical design shaped in part by a *mathematical plan*.

    (b) The mathematical aspect is *easy* to hear.

    (c) In Dufay's isorhythmic motet "Nuper rosarum flores," the mathematical plan reflects certain dimensions of a *cathedral*.

    (d) Notation plays a *minimal* role in the creation of this genre.

3. During the Renaissance,

    (a) There was an *increase* in the composition of notated music.

    (b) The new technique of *notation* was developed.

    (c) There was a *decrease* in the composition of notated secular genres.

    (d) There was *increased* contact among regional musical styles.

4. Concerning the Harmony of the Spheres:

   (a) It was a central image for Christianity through the *Baroque*.

   (b) It was considered a *science* at that time.

   (c) It was *not involved* with number.

   (d) It included the image of a sacred *dance* in the sky.

5. Concerning the Renaissance motet:

   (a) In England, it was called a *madrigal*.

   (b) It had *one* text.

   (c) It often employed *continuous imitation*.

   (d) It was *more* dissonant than its Medieval predecessor.

6. Concerning the madrigal:

   (a) It tended to be *universal* in style.

   (b) It *rarely* had a dance impulse.

   (c) It might be similar in style to a *sacred motet*.

   (d) It was especially indebted to *folk-popular* traditions.

7. Concerning the Mass:

   (a) It was the most important genre through the *Renaissance*.

   (b) Originally it was sung in *polyphony*.

   (c) By the Renaissance, its style tended to be *universal* (throughout Europe).

   (d) It is *related* to the ancient unity.

8. Concerning the antiphonal effects in the Gabrieli *Sanctus* [14]:

   (a) They are related to the interplay between *soloist and group*.

   (b) They are one feature of the music which reflects a *dramatic impulse*.

   (c) They are created by *different* sound sources.

   (d) They were intended to be heard in different sections of a *concert hall*.

7
The Baroque

Opera: The Musical Drama of Europe

The genre that most captured the spirit and imagination of the Baroque was *opera*. Opera is musical drama—a play that is sung either in whole or in part. Unity of dramatic action with song is its most important characteristic. Dance may provide yet another kind of theatrical action. The result is a continuous interaction of music, movement, and drama. Perhaps in the description of opera, you recognize the essential components of the ancient unity (see page 100). Considered in long-range perspective, this genre, which first appeared in Italy around 1600, was a new vehicle for one of humanity's most basic impulses. In the Baroque, opera was surrounded by a sense of pageantry and celebration, and to this day retains something of that quality. For seventeenth-century audiences, the magnificent sets and staged effects (people rising to heaven and volcanoes erupting, for example) combined with music and drama to create a unique, heightened experience. To use modern terms, Baroque opera was a "state-of-the-art, multimedia production," combining the latest musical style and theatrical technology with a well-established dramatic tradition.

THE CULTURAL ROOTS OF OPERA

As discussed previously, innovative artistic practices usually do not come out of thin air; opera's origins were rooted in the anonymous traditions of Christian ritual and popular celebration. Musical-dramatic events had been part of Christian ceremony for centuries. For example, the *mystery play*—a drama with music—was a staged enactment of Christian allegory in which members of the community took part. (The people of Elche, a town in Spain, still perform their mystery play today in a continuing tradition traceable to the thirteenth century.) Outside the Church, a variety of popular spectacles involving music, dance, and drama flourished. Such festive activities centered around special celebrations: carnivals, fairs, visits of important figures, and traditional holidays.

That opera first flourished in Italy is not surprising. There, as in other European-Mediterranean societies, pageantry held an honored position in the culture. Even more significant to opera's development, however, was the warm lyricism of Italian song. The desire to sing and celebrate, so much a part of Italian culture, became the primary source for the European operatic tradition. And when opera quickly spread throughout Europe, Italian singers and composers were usually imported to do the job. Starting with the Renaissance, the Italian spirit began to breathe a sort of emotional humanism into European music as well as art.

THE FLORENTINE CAMERATA

Opera came into being through a remarkable cultural interaction. A group of Renaissance humanists, dedicated to the study of art, music, literature, and history, played a decisive role in the formation of the new style. Two primary interests of this group, which came to be known as the *Florentine Camerata*, were literature and ancient Greek culture. What interested them was a manner of singing in which the text of a musical drama would be dominant. They argued that polyphony, in its many-voiced complexity, obscured the importance and meaning of the words. In contrast, they cited the Greek drama, in which music and word were part of a single unity. Influenced by these ideas, the musicians of the group advocated a simplification of texture, from polyphonic to homophonic. By setting a single melody with a simple accompaniment, the text could be projected in a dramatic manner. They evolved a special type of melody whose rhythms and shape followed the dramatic inflections of poetry and speech. The style—*recitative*—is named for its relationship to the spoken word (it is derived from the Italian word for "declaim"). Although it was perceived as something new, recitative is really based in a universal impulse—the interplay between melody and speech. Aside from its potential for conveying dramatic action, the heightened emotional style of the recitative allowed the singer greater theatrical possibilities. Recitative alone, however, was not sufficient to maintain musical interest. Therefore, within the first decades of the seventeenth century, the following practices developed as part of operatic form:

RECITATIVE A style of singing deriving its rhythmic and melodic shape from an imitation of speech. It is homophonic in texture and often without meter. Because the text is so easily understood in recitatives, they are used for dramatic sections—to carry the plot forward—rather than for more reflective moments. Not all operas have recitatives.

(*continued on next page*)

> ARIA   A solo vocal piece in a traditional melodic style. Unlike the recitative, with its starts and stops and speechlike melodic structure, an aria is basically a song, usually with orchestral accompaniment. While the recitative advances the dramatic action, the aria is often a reflection on some emotional state (joy, sorrow, love, etc.).
>
> CHORUS   In many operas, the chorus is used to comment on or participate in the dramatic action and is often used to represent the "community." The choral texture contrasts both musically and dramatically with the solo passages.
>
> OVERTURE, PRELUDE   An orchestral piece played before the operatic action begins.
>
> INCIDENTAL MUSIC   Most operas include such orchestral pieces as dances, interludes, and marches woven into the dramatic action. Like the choruses, such pieces provide contrast of a musical and dramatic nature.

The intensity with which opera took hold was remarkable. By the nineteenth century, there were opera houses in every major city in Europe, as well as in far-off places like New Orleans, San Francisco, and Rio de Janeiro. From its origins as a theoretical recreation of the ancient unity, opera became a major influence on the musical traditions of the world.

HENRY PURCELL, *DIDO AND AENEAS*

Henry Purcell (1659–95) was a renowned English composer of the Baroque period. His *Dido and Aeneas* is one of the great operas of the seventeenth century. The story is based on a section of the *Aeneid*, the epic song-poem by the Latin poet Vergil. The plot revolves around Dido, Queen of Carthage, and her love for Aeneas, a visiting prince. Needless to say, things don't go smoothly, and the opera ends in tragedy as Dido kills herself over the loss of her lover. The following excerpt is taken from the end of the opera, as Dido laments Aeneas's departure. It begins with a recitative in which Dido sings of her impending death. The expressive melody and harmonic accompaniment in the continuo create a somber mood. Like many recitative sections, there is no strong pulse or meter. After the last lines of the recitative ("Death is now a welcome guest"), we hear a solo theme of mournful character in the bass. It may not be stretching musical symbolism too far to suggest that this theme represents death, and, symbolic of death's inevitability, is repeated throughout the aria in ostinato fashion. Above this dirgelike melody, Dido sings a passionate farewell to life. The chromatic harmonies and slow triple meter (heard "in three") create the effect of a tragic lullaby. The opera comes to a gentle close as the chorus sings, mixing the bittersweet images of love with death.

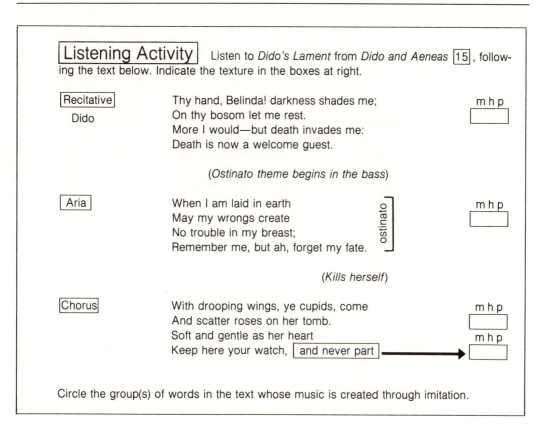

| Listening Activity | Listen to *Dido's Lament* from *Dido and Aeneas* 15 , following the text below. Indicate the texture in the boxes at right. |

Recitative
Dido

Thy hand, Belinda! darkness shades me;
On thy bosom let me rest.
More I would—but death invades me:
Death is now a welcome guest.

m h p

(Ostinato theme begins in the bass)

Aria

When I am laid in earth
May my wrongs create
No trouble in my breast;
Remember me, but ah, forget my fate.

ostinato

m h p

(Kills herself)

Chorus

With drooping wings, ye cupids, come
And scatter roses on her tomb.
Soft and gentle as her heart
Keep here your watch, and never part

m h p

m h p

Circle the group(s) of words in the text whose music is created through imitation.

BAROQUE EVOCATION OF FEELING: DOCTRINE OF THE AFFECTIONS

One characteristic of the Baroque style is its purposeful representation of emotions. A living musical language often involves nonmusical cues (see page 104). Baroque music is no exception. A perfect example of this is Purcell's use of chromatic harmony to represent sorrow in the excerpt you have just heard. (A similar relationship between music and emotion may be found in the contemporary use of "blues" harmony and melody to express the particular pathos of our time.) The nonmusical cues of Baroque style were so important and widespread that they were codified by theorists and called the *Doctrine of the Affections*. This codification of Baroque musical language identified specific melodic motives as representing specific emotions or feelings. Purcell uses one of these specific motives to represent sorrow on the words "soft, soft" in the final chorus of *Dido and Aeneas*. These image-laden motives were not confined to vocal music, but often occurred in instrumental settings as well.

Purcell, *Dido and Aeneas*

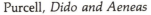

soft,   soft

Bach, *Fugue in C-sharp minor*

Although the rhythm is different, the same pitch design—the Baroque "sorrow" motive—may be found in both pieces.

Sorrow was not the only emotion that might be expressed through musical symbolism. Rage, heroism, mystery, and many other human sentiments had their own musical representation. These emotional cues instilled Baroque style with a heightened sense of drama and feeling quite appropriate for the age.

Opera Beyond Style

Of all musical genres, opera is the most dependent on nonmusical cues. The perception of opera is related to a host of stylistic details that range from language and regional taste to aesthetic values and social self-image. It is no wonder, then, that response to opera is as varied as operatic style itself. This has been true wherever the operatic tradition has flourished. Yet *the basic principles of the music drama clearly transcend limitations of style.* Historically, this universal impulse has found expression in many guises. When Italian seventeenth-century opera spread throughout Europe, it met with both enthusiasm and hostility. The French, Germans, and English blended Italian tradition with styles more suited to their regional languages and tastes. *Dido and Aeneas*, for example, is an English opera. Parts of it are Italianate in style, while others seem more English. Various regional styles have continued to evolve well into the twentieth century.

DIDO AND AENEAS AND WEST SIDE STORY

Opera presents fascinating possibilities for listening beyond style. On the one hand, in no other listening experience are we so style conscious; on the other hand, no other genre sheds its outer details so easily, once the inner structure of dramatic action is revealed. Comparisons among music dramas of many styles may enrich your understanding of any single work. To prove this point, we shall cut across traditional stylistic perceptions and compare certain aspects of *Dido and Aeneas* with Leonard Bernstein and Stephen Sondheim's *West Side Story*. That many do not consider *West Side Story* a true opera need not concern us.* The American *musical* was one of

---

*In Europe, the bastion of operatic tradition, this work is performed in many opera houses as part of the standard repertory.

those styles that developed from the universal music-drama principle to meet regional tastes. The real differences between *Dido and Aeneas* and *West Side Story* are matters of style, not substance. Both are staged music dramas in which the *music is essential to the dramatic action*. Both are based on dramatic models of the past: Purcell's work is drawn from Vergil's *Aeneid*, while Bernstein and Sondheim's music drama is based on Shakespeare's *Romeo and Juliet*. Both stories are about a love destined to end in tragedy. Thus, both fall into the love-and-death genre of world drama, a popular theme throughout the ages. At this point, we need to become more acquainted with *West Side Story*.

| Listen | Excerpts from *West Side Story* | 29 |

One Hand, One Heart: This is a duet between the lovers Tony and Maria, in which they exchange marriage vows. The play is set in New York City and draws on the friction between white and Puerto Rican street gangs. Tony is a former member of the Jets; Maria's brother is the leader of the rival Puerto Rican gang, the Sharks. The young lovers each sing alone and then together in *unison*. (Both sing the same melody, symbolizing the oneness of the song's theme.) Toward the end, they sing briefly in harmony, only to find each other, again symbolically, by ending on the same pitch.

> Make of our hands one hand,
> Make of our hearts one heart,
> Make of our vows one last vow:
> Only death will part us now.
>
> Make of our lives one life,
> Day after day, one life.
> Now it begins, now we start
> One hand, one heart;
> Even death won't part us now.

Listening Activity

Tap out the meter ("in three") with the music. Coordinate it with the
  1   2   3   1   2 3
words "Make of our hands . . ." etc. Continue tapping through at least half the song.

Is the pulse exactly periodic? _____

Read the definition of *rubato* on page 485. Does this term apply to the

rhythm of *One Hand, One Heart*? _____

The Rumble: In this dance, the inevitable happens—a violent fight between the two gangs. As the action unfolds, Bernardo, Maria's brother, stabs Tony's friend, Riff. Tony then stabs Bernardo. The gangs flee at the approach of a police car.

Listening Activity

Is the rhythm syncopated or nonsyncopated? _____

Does the harmony tend toward dissonance or consonance?

_____

Finale: The various conflicts of the drama come to a head. Tony is told that Maria has been killed (which is not true). As he wanders the streets in despair, Maria finds him. For a brief moment, they are reunited; then Tony is shot by another member of the Sharks. In the *Finale*, the stunned members of both gangs sing the line "There's a place for us." Tony and Maria sing together before he dies. The gangs join to carry his body off stage.

> There's a place for us,
> A time and place for us.
> Hold my hand and we're halfway there.
> Hold my hand and I'll take you there
> Somehow, some day!

Listening Activity

Does the musical motive for "There's a Place for Us" ever sound for

instruments alone? _____

Aside from their general resemblance in story type, each work employs a number of similar musical-dramatic devices:

Dido and Aeneas	*West Side Story*
Closing Scene	*Finale*
Dido, unable to face life without Aeneas, who has left her, kills herself.	Tony and Maria spend their last moments together before his death.

In both works, the drama comes to a tragic end, made more poignant by the gentle yet tragic musical atmosphere. Images of love and death mix freely. In both finales, the chorus serves as a universal voice, commenting on the meaning of the drama.

(The following comparisons require the complete recordings of each work; both will be found in most libraries.)

The Dance of the Furies   *The Rumble*

> Both are musical representations of wild, frenzied action.

The Dance of Witches and Sailors   *Jet Song*

> Many operas include scenes in which a group's particular characteristics are portrayed in song and dance.

Duet of the Witches   *Officer Krupke*

> Many dramas employ comic relief as an emotional contrast to tragedy. In both cases, the music supports this comic impulse.

George Frideric Handel

Handel (1685–1759) was a German who made his fortune in England composing Italian operas. He was one of the best known, most widely traveled and commercially successful composers of the late Baroque. While still a young man, Handel left Germany for Italy, to experience and absorb Italian song in its natural Mediterranean setting. He recognized that opera was the most commercial music of the time. It had become fashionable throughout Europe, especially with the aristocracy. After a brief return to Germany, Handel voyaged to London, where he created a sensation with his Italian opera *Rinaldo*.

Handel's operas and the Italian singers he imported to sing them were, for a decade, a great success. But Italian opera went out of favor with the English public for a variety of reasons. As noted before, no other genre is more rooted in the perception of style than opera, and many English found Italian operatic style objectionable. What was for Italians a native language was foreign and strange to the English. The mythological plots, which in Italian opera were often no more than vehicles to unleash a display of virtuoso singing, seemed backward to an audience familiar with the powerful dramatic tradition of a William Shakespeare. In short, they simply didn't like the style. But the universal principle of the music drama, existing as it does *beyond style*, was to find another avenue of expression through Handel's genius.

Handel was a practical man. His biographer Paul Henry Lang tells us that, "Handel recognized no artistic absolutes; he wrote a great deal out of necessity, for money, or because he wanted to beat the opposition."* So when the public taste changed, Handel was quick to produce dramatic music more suited to his London audience—the English *oratorio*. Like an opera, an oratorio has recitatives, arias, and choruses; what it does not have is staging. Many oratorios have a sacred theme, with the dramatic action carried solely by the music and text. Oratorio, then, is a type of "sub-dued" opera. Handel's musical genius lay in his ability to capture the essence of drama in melody.

Although Handel's main output was in the vocal genres of opera and oratorio, he also wrote some very fine instrumental music (his *Gigue* [11c], for example). But the energy of the theater was the driving force in Handel's art, and from this dramatic impulse he fashioned his greatest works. *Messiah* (from which you have heard the chorus *For unto Us a Child Is Born* [10c]) has become an all-time favorite, and with good reason. This oratorio, based on various biblical texts, is among the finest creations of sacred vocal music. Its many moods range from the peaceful beauty of the aria *Oh, Thou, that Tellest Good Tidings to Zion*, to the fury of *Thou Shalt Break Them with a Rod of Iron*, to the awesome grandeur of the *Hallelujah Chorus*. It was music like this, with its straightforward biblical imagery and appealing melodies, that made Handel a major influence on English music for a hundred and fifty years.

Handel: Additional Listening

Messiah. In addition to [10c], *Overture, Comfort Ye, Ev'ry Valley, O Thou, that Tellest Good Tidings to Zion, Thou Shalt Break Them with a Rod of Iron, Let Us Break Their Bonds Asunder, Hallelujah Chorus.*

ORATORIO   An unstaged choral work which is dramatic in nature, usually on a religious subject. Like opera, it has arias, choruses, and recitatives.

The Baroque Concerto: Solo Concerto

One of the most important instrumental genres of the Baroque was the *concerto*. We will now discuss the *solo concerto*, a work for one instrument and a small orchestra. Central to its musical organization is the *contrast between soloist and group*. You are familiar with this basic principle of musical orga-

*Paul Henry Lang, *George Frideric Handel* (New York, 1966), p. 7.

nization from previous listening examples. We have already noted how soloist and group create *unity and variety*. Traditionally, the soloist exhibits more musical diversity, while the group "holds things together" by the repetition of familiar material. The Baroque concerto is no exception to this universal pattern.

ANTONIO VIVALDI

Antonio Vivaldi (1648–1740) was an Italian composer of the late Baroque. Although he wrote in many genres, he is best known today for his remarkable output of concertos (he composed over 450). The Italians had a great tradition of instrumental virtuosity, which is not surprising, considering their connection to the musical culture of the Mediterranean (cf. Sequence 5 , page 113). Moreover, Italians continued to lead European music in the Baroque toward greater freedom of emotional expression. Thus, the performance of Vivaldi's music requires a high level of technical competence and the ability to play with many shades of expressive nuance.

Listen Vivaldi, *Concerto for Oboe and Orchestra in C minor*, third movement 16
The Baroque concerto is comprised of *movements*—extended sections that seem complete in themselves and help sustain interest in compositions of some length. Movements are usually juxtaposed in contrasting tempos and moods. This concerto has three, in the fast-slow-fast configuration standard during this period.

I	II	III
Allegro (fast)	Largo (slow)	Allegro (fast)

We will consider the last movement. It opens with a *ritornello* theme, so named because it will return periodically, played by the full orchestral ensemble (*tutti*—all). This theme serves as the primary unifying element of the movement. Listening to the opening tutti, we hear that the ritornello material consists of two ideas (we will call them *a* and *b*), which are presented in *aba* design. Following the first ritornello, the soloist enters with new music, accompanied by a pared-down version of the orchestra, which provides immediate contrast in texture, timbre, and dynamics.

This interplay between tutti and soloist continues throughout the movement, and is the main compositional procedure on which the piece is based. The tutti returns with various bits of the ritornello theme, while the soloist continues to play contrasting material. The movement is summed up by a final tutti statement of the ritornello theme.

Listening Activity

The diagram below illustrates the relationships between the soloist and the group. First, listen to the music while following the visual representation; then repeat, as needed, to complete the instructions that follow:

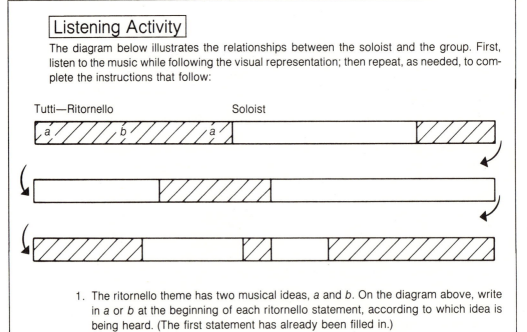

1. The ritornello theme has two musical ideas, *a* and *b*. On the diagram above, write in *a* or *b* at the beginning of each ritornello statement, according to which idea is being heard. (The first statement has already been filled in.)
2. Describe the various elements that create contrast in this musical design.

Listening Comparison   Donald Byrd, *Speculation* 36

The basic principle of the Baroque concerto was not utilized only in that period. Compare the Vivaldi with this contemporary selection.

Describe some similarities of musical design:

Describe some differences:

The Baroque Concerto: Concerto Grosso

| Listen | Bach, *Brandenburg Concerto No. 2*

Another type of concerto popular in the Baroque period was the *concerto grosso* (grand concerto). There is one important difference between the two versions of the concerto: soloist and tutti provide the contrast in the solo concerto; in the concerto grosso, several solo instruments replace the single player. In this Bach work, for example, the solo group is comprised of trumpet, violin, flute, and oboe. With a group of solo instruments—called *concertino* (little concert)—there is greater potential for interesting contrasts of timbre and texture.

The *Brandenburg Concerto No. 2* by Johann Sebastian Bach is in three movements. Like Vivaldi, Bach uses a ritornello in his first movement, but it is developed into a more complex design. (Bach rarely used traditional models without developing them.) The movement begins with a clear alternation between a tutti ritornello and concertino passages. But as the movement unfolds, this relationship becomes more flexible.

Two important qualities that help shape this form are tonal design and contrapuntal richness. In the last movement of the Vivaldi concerto, the piece modulated away from the tonic and moved through one key center before returning home. Bach also uses a tonal design which moves away from the tonic and returns. But typical of his genius for harmony, this piece moves through a maze of keys with deceptive simplicity. The other trait that characterizes all of Bach's works is contrapuntal richness. He explores the relationships between instrumental lines (or voices) systematically and often pursues their possibilities in an almost mathematical way. Such organization is evident in the concertino passages of this movement. As noted before, there are four solo instruments. Each time the concertino plays, we hear a different combination of soloists in the polyphonic texture. In one section, we hear violin and oboe, in another trumpet and violin, and so on. This technique is one of many by which Bach creates the fascinating acoustic patterns that continually hold our interest.

Second Movement: while there is a lyrical singing quality to this movement, Bach's melodies still unfold in highly elaborate polyphony. The tutti is silent; the movement is played by three solo instruments and continuo (cello and harpsichord). The main motive is stated by the violin, then imitated by the other instruments. This pattern is followed throughout the movement, which may be thought of as a lyrical, polyphonic dialogue among three voices. The continuo provides both a harmonic and a rhythmic base. Each has invented an elaborate contrapuntal structure that, despite its density, still sounds ravishingly lyrical. The ability to compose in a learned polyphonic style without losing the magic of spontaneity is a measure of his genius.

Third Movement: marked *allegro assai* (very fast), this movement ends the concerto with a display of instrumental virtuosity. The difficult trumpet part was not written for the instrument we know today, but for a smaller Baroque trumpet. There is a great deal of forward potential in this music, generated by the insistent rhythms, chord progressions, and the buildup of a tense polyphonic texture; all of this drives toward the final cadence which brings the movement to a close.

CONCERTO   A piece for solo instrument(s) and ensemble. A basic feature of concertos is the musical juxtaposition of soloist(s) and group. If there is only one soloist, the piece is a *solo concerto*.

CONCERTO GROSSO   A Baroque concerto for a group of soloists (called the *concertino*) and small orchestra (called the *tutti*).

RITORNELLO   In a Baroque concerto, the musical material which returns throughout the piece. It is usually played by the ensemble and sets off the solo passages.

Fugue

As an introduction to this genre, consider the following:

1. A fugue has a highly polyphonic texture.
2. It is built around a special motive—the *fugue subject*. First heard at the opening of the piece, this subject is repeated many times.
3. The most important compositional procedure in a fugue is *imitation*.

Note: In order to develop the listening skills necessary for structural understanding of fugue, it is essential that you listen to the following piece several times.

Listen   *Example 22a*, Bach, *Fugue in F major*
This is a *three-voice fugue*—three melodic lines make up the contrapuntal texture. Even in an instrumental piece, it is customary to iden-

tify each line as if it were sung by a human voice; accordingly, the three lines are called soprano, alto, and bass. These designations will be helpful when we discuss fugue structure.

While you are listening to the music, follow the diagram, which indicates the various statements of the fugue subject. This performance is on electronic synthesizer in order to emphasize the fugue subject. (A more traditional performance follows at *Example 22b.*) The emphasized fugue subjects on the recording correspond to the rectangular symbols in the diagram. The three lines represent the three voices of the polyphonic texture.

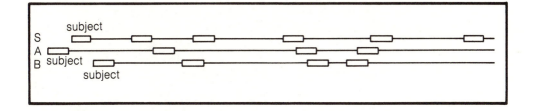

Consider the placement of the fugue subjects "boxed". We may use the diagram and the music to help identify certain aspects of fugue structure:

1. *Fugue is a continuous form.* Since most fugues proceed without any strong interruption of the rhythmic flow or any division into clearly set-off sections, we speak of fugue form as *continuous.*

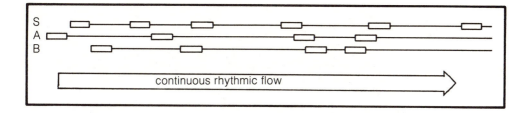

Continuous form helps to create a high level of forward potential, which drives the music toward the final cadence.

2. *Passages of presentation.* As the fugue subject sounds in various voices, distinct patterns result. These are passages of presentation, also called fugal expositions.

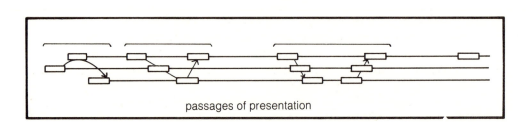

passages of presentation

In the passages of presentation, we hear a dialogue in which each voice takes its turn at sounding the fugue subject. Such passages are the structural pillars of fugue form. They invariably open the piece and reappear several times in the course of the work. (There are, of course, exceptions.) In this fugue there is a lone statement of the subject near the end. In other fugues there may be many such statements not immediately "answered" by another voice.

3. *Episodes*. As you will notice in the diagram (and hear in the music), the fugue is not made up exclusively of passages of presentation. Between these passages, there are sections in which there is no complete statement of the subject. These sections are called *episodes*. They seem to flow out of the passages of presentation. The reasons are simple: First of all, the rhythmic movement is uninterrupted. Secondly, the material of the episodes grows directly from the fugal subject. Episodes are freer structurally than passages of presentation, and may induce a more relaxed response from the listener. (This is not true of all fugues, however; sometimes, episodes are used for the opposite reason—to create tension.)

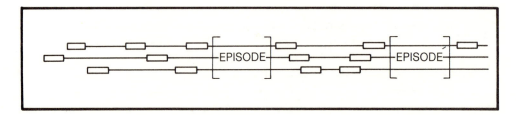

4. *Stretto*. In several places, certain entries of the subject overlap —one enters before the other is finished. This kind of subject entry is a *stretto*. It is most often found toward the end of a fugue for the following reason: when subjects are piled up on one another, an exciting tension results. Thus, a stretto toward the end raises the level of forward potential and gives the fugue

an extra push toward its ultimate conclusion—the final cadence. The *F-major Fugue* also has a brief stretto in the second passage of presentation.

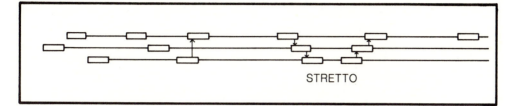

STRETTO

5. *Use of different tonal centers.* In *Examples 14b* and *14c* (poly-phonic settings of the Demonstration Melody), you heard how tonality can help organize polyphony. Basically, the same prin-ciple applies to a fugue. We experience a tonal center at the opening of the piece. The music then travels through various keys, the modulations creating a sense of forward potential toward the tonic. Most fugues finally reach the tonic some-where near the end.

Listen   Bach, *Fugue in G minor for Organ* 17

Listen to this fugue without concern for details. You will most likely recognize its basic features because of the previous discussion.

The *G-minor Fugue* offers some interesting contrasts with the *F-major Fugue*: the subject is much longer; it is in four voices; the pace is somewhat more relaxed; there are no strettos; while the *F-major Fugue* is a tight, compressed musical structure, the *G-minor Fugue* unfolds in long, relaxed spans, yet still creates a powerful sense of for-ward potential.

This piece demonstrates another feature found in many fugues—a *countersubject.* A countersubject is designed to complement the fugue subject. In the diagram below, the countersubject is represented by a wavy line:

Bach, *G-minor Fugue*: Opening Passage of Presentation

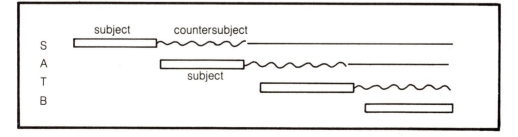

Use of a countersubject provides another opportunity for inventive design in passages of presentation. In this fugue, the countersubject follows after the fugue subject from the highest to the lowest voice. Some fugues have more than one countersubject, which increases the possibilities for interesting contrapuntal patterns. Listen again to the *G-minor Fugue*, following this diagram:

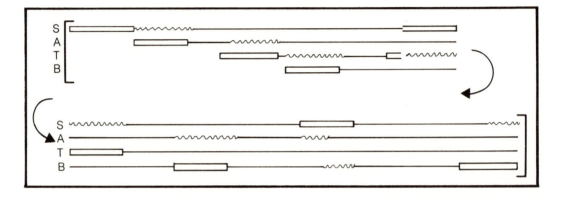

Listen   *Kyrie* 18 from the *Mass in B minor*, by Bach

This vocal fugue is the second of two fugal *Kyries* in Bach's *Mass in B minor*. It is a four-voice fugue with a powerful stretto toward the end. Sit back and listen to the piece without consciously isolating any aspects of fugue technique.

FUGUE   A type of composition in which a main idea—the fugue subject—is systematically imitated in a polyphonic texture.

FUGUE SUBJECT   The main melody of a fugue, supplying the basic melodic and rhythmic material of the piece.

COUNTERSUBJECT   A secondary melody which consistently sounds against the fugue subject.

PASSAGES OF PRESENTATION   Fugue passages in which the subject is presented in various voices.

EPISODE   A fugal passage that contains no complete statements of the subject. The musical material of an episode is drawn from the passages of presentation.

STRETTO   A section in which fugue subjects overlap one another. Strettos are most often found toward the end of a fugue, since they build tension and forward potential toward the final cadence.

FUGUE AS CONTINUOUS FORM   Since it proceeds as an unbroken flow of rhythmic activity without clearly set-off sections, fugue form is described as continuous.

THE DEVELOPMENT OF FUGUE

The opening of a Baroque fugue is quite similar to that of a Renaissance Mass or motet. In each of these, a subject (as it is called in a fugue) is initially stated and then imitated by every voice. Compare the opening sections of the Ockeghem *Kyrie* 10b , Gibbons's *I Am the Resurrection* 12 , and Bach's *G-minor Fugue* 17 .

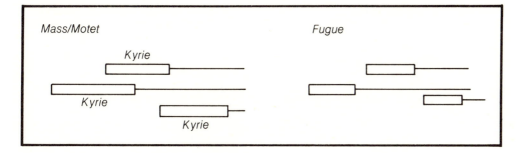

The similarity is not accidental. The continuous imitation characteristic of Renaissance vocal style is an ancestor of the Baroque fugue. Although originally identified with vocal music, it found its way very easily into instrumental music. Singing was often supported by instrumental accompaniment, and when an organist, for example, played the vocal parts of a motet (or any other polyphonic piece), a musical structure similar to a fugue was in his fingers. The important difference between fugue and the continuous imitation of Renaissance Masses and motets is the unity of melodic material associated with the Baroque genre. In Renaissance practice, each new phrase of text was set with a new melody; by contrast, a fugue is built around one subject.

The development of fugue illustrates the type of long-range connections essential for understanding the growth of Western music. Bach could not have composed his fugues, considered among the great achievements of Western culture, if polyphonic techniques had not been developing continually for several hundreds of years.

From Renaissance to Baroque: Musical and Cultural Change

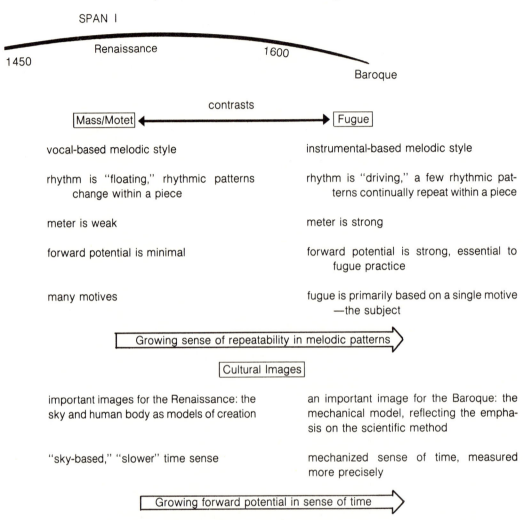

SPAN I

Renaissance 1600

1450

Baroque

contrasts

Mass/Motet ←————————————→ Fugue

vocal-based melodic style	instrumental-based melodic style
rhythm is "floating," rhythmic patterns change within a piece	rhythm is "driving," a few rhythmic patterns continually repeat within a piece
meter is weak	meter is strong
forward potential is minimal	forward potential is strong, essential to fugue practice
many motives	fugue is primarily based on a single motive —the subject

Growing sense of repeatability in melodic patterns ⟩

Cultural Images

important images for the Renaissance: the sky and human body as models of creation	an important image for the Baroque: the mechanical model, reflecting the emphasis on the scientific method
"sky-based," "slower" time sense	mechanized sense of time, measured more precisely

Growing forward potential in sense of time ⟩

This chart does not mean that cultural phenomena for the Baroque were not found in the Renaissance, and vice versa, but only suggests a gradual change in philosophical and cultural emphasis. One contributing factor in the shift toward precise measurement and exact repeatability was the emergence of both printed music and books.

FUGUE AFTER BACH

Fugue has continued as an important genre well into the twentieth century. It represents for many composers a special realm for the exercise of musical logic, expressed through the time-honored craft of counterpoint. Fugue is recognized as one climax of the polyphonic tradition, a unique achievement of possibilities created by polyphonic organization of musical sound. It is quite an accomplishment to compose a good fugue. Those composed "by the rules" without inspiration can be tedious and dry. It takes considerable gifts and skill to follow in the shadow of the unchallenged master of this genre, J. S. Bach. In this sense, no matter how modern they sound, later fugues look back to Bach and the great polyphonic tradition he inherited. A composer who writes a fugue today consciously reaffirms the connection to a centuries-old tradition.

Span I

Span II

Bach

Mozart, *Kyrie*
from *Requiem* (1791)

Beethoven,
Credo from
Missa solemnis (1823)

Berlioz, Fugue from
The Damnation of Faust (1846);
Fugue from
The Childhood of Christ (1854)

Stravinsky,
Symphony of Psalms (1930),
second movement

Bartók, *Music for
Strings, Percussion,
and Celesta* (1936),
first movement

Hindemith,
Ludus tonalis (1943)

Loesser, *Fugue for
Tinhorns* from
Guys and Dolls
(1950)

The Dance Suite

Like Gregorian chant, the European dance tradition is rooted in an ancient past. It is hard for us to imagine how important dance was to a society that had no television, records, movies, and few books. Dance was more than entertainment; it was a rhythmic activity vital for the well-being of the community. Through the Renaissance, and to some extent the Baroque, dance still functioned at the center of daily life. Perhaps the most vivid examples of dancing as heightened social experience were the Medieval outbreaks of dance frenzies intended to avoid the plague. Entire cities were swept with this madness for entire days at a time. Imagine for a moment the entire population of a city today dancing endlessly in order to avoid the latest strain of the flu! A more realistic analogy would be the present-day carnival celebrations in New Orleans or Rio di Janeiro.

To the nobility, dance was an essential social grace. It served to identify and reinforce social image. It was in this setting that the learned traditions of notated music interacted with the older, body-based folk traditions to produce dances like the *Ductia* 11a and the *Branle* dance group 11b. Since dance music was meant to accompany actual dancing, it isn't surprising that the pieces were often arranged in groups. The result was called a *suite*. Notated suites begin to appear during the late Renaissance and early Baroque. This type of presentation is certainly as old as dance itself. Modern musicians who play for dances today call such groupings a *set*. Suite or set, the principle is the same: Keep the people dancing with a variety of tempos, moods, and meters. The suite soon acquired an additional identity—it became purely musical entertainment. Baroque composers began to write suites or *partitas*, as they were also called, intended to be played and heard only, and not to be danced. Bach's *Gigue* 19 from his *Partita in D minor for Violin* is an excellent example of this tradition.

| Suggested Listening | Bach, *Partita in D minor for Violin* (complete)
Bach, *Suite in C minor for Cello*
Bach, *French Suite in G for Harpsichord* |

> SUITE   A work consisting of several dances. Another term sometimes used for the suite is *partita*.

Johann Sebastian Bach

On any given day, musicians in every corner of the world perform, study, and listen to the music of Johann Sebastian Bach (1685–1750). Some are beginners, barely able to struggle through Bach's easy pieces; others are acknowledged masters of our time—composers, performers, conductors—returning again and again to the musical world of this great man. Although he has been dead for over two hundred years, his music has never been more alive. The works of Bach represent one of the fundamental models for understanding the craft of musical composition. This was no ordinary being.

In 1685, Bach was baptized in a Lutheran Church in the German town of Eisenach. From that symbolic moment, he who would shape so many musical lives received his sacred charge: a life of unquestioning devotion to the art of music in the service of God. The organist who played for the ceremony was one of Bach's relatives. This was no mere coincidence; the child was born into a family of musicians whose ancestry could be traced back some five generations. Like his father and grandfather, brother and cousin,

Oil painting of J. S. Bach by
Haussmann.

no other life than that of a musician was ever possible for Johann Sebastian. The Bach family were proud, obedient servants of their society. They valued religion, tradition, and musical craft. Bach, then, was born into a secure world, where the motto for a youngster might certainly have been "obedience without question." His childhood was filled with music from the beginning. He played harpsichord and violin, and also sang. He learned the art of improvisation and the careful skill of composition. If we can reconstruct something of his childhood character from his later personality, he must have been quite a determined little fellow. Yet we can only imagine the impact upon a nine-year-old child when, in a year's time, first mother, then father died. The seventeenth century was an era when orphaned children might be abandoned to the street. But this would have been unthinkable to the close-knit Bach family. The youngster continued his musical apprenticeship in the home of an older brother, an organist in a nearby town. Young Bach contributed his earnings as a professional singer to the household. Thus, by the age of ten we find Johann Sebastian already functioning as a responsible professional musician.

At fourteen, Bach ventured out completely on his own. Hearing that a school in Lüneburg, two hundred miles away, welcomed talented apprentice musicians, he applied and was accepted. Within a few years, he was earning a livelihood in the service of church and nobility, as he would do for the rest of his life.

BACH'S SOCIAL STANDING

In Bach's time, a musician was not much more than a respected servant. Although he was famous as an organist, and highly renowned among knowledgeable musicians and patrons, his daily life was controlled by petty bureaucrats. When he petitioned his superiors, he did so from a servant's stance. The following excerpt is typical of the relationship between Bach and the officials who often ruled his life. (The letter concerns a petty problem at the church where Bach was organist. Our interest lies in Bach's subservient position, not the actual dispute.)

> To their Magnificences, the Most Noble, Most Distinguished, Steadfast and Most Learned, also Most Wise Gentlemen, the Burgomasters and Members of the Most Worshipful Town Government of the Town of Leipzig, My Most Highly Honored Masters and Patrons.
>
> Your Magnificences, Most Noble, Steadfast and Most Learned, also Most Wise, as well as Most Highly Honored Gentlemen and Patrons!
>
> There will still be present to Your most gracious memory, Your Magnificences and You, Most Noble Sirs, what I felt compelled to report to Your Honors concerning the disorders that were caused eight days ago during the public divine service by the actions of the Rector of the Thomas-Schule here . . . [The rest of the letter, omitted here, details the problem.]
>
> I remain, Your Magnificences and Most Noble Sirs, Your obedient Johann Sebastian Bach.*

We must consider this letter in the light of its time. This overblown style was customary when addressing superiors. And yet we may be astounded at the irony of the great Bach groveling before "Your Magnificences"; for the judgment of the world would humbly bestow all these praises on Bach—magnificent, steadfast, most learned, and noble—but unfortunately not until after his death. A musician in 1736, no matter how talented, rarely attained secure social standing.

But times were beginning to change, as one defiant action by Bach demonstrates. The early eighteenth century was still within what some historians have called the *Age of Absolutism* (see page 217). Characteristic behavior for a person of Bach's social position was total obedience to his superiors, be they local nobility, clergy, or king. But a new spirit—an *Age*

The Bach Reader, ed. by Hans T. David and Arthur Mendel, rev. ed. (New York, 1966), p. 146.

of Reason (see page 217)—was having a liberating effect on the middle class. The new sentiment valued an individual's self-esteem, measured in terms of deeds and accomplishments. In 1717, Bach was offered a better position as a court musician. In order to accept the offer, he needed the approval of his current patron. Several of Bach's forefathers had, in fact, been prevented from improving their lot by their employers' refusal to let them go. Bach's patron did just that! For Bach's father and those before him, that would have been the end of it. But Johann Sebastian was determined to take the new position. He protested at such length that he was imprisoned. And there he sat, refusing to give in, for an entire month. Fifty years later, Mozart would take such liberties to an even greater degree, and soon after that, Beethoven would symbolically overthrow the establishment with his open defiance of all social restrictions. But Bach lived most of his life under the strict rules of the old order. For one who had always accepted the social code without question, his action was extraordinary. He must have been convinced that he was right and that his cause would inevitably triumph.

BACH'S MUSICAL STYLE

"Rightness" is a quality that describes not only Bach's convictions, but also his music. From the first notes of a Bach piece, one senses the inevitability of the outcome. The music unfolds so logically that its course always seems clear, even perfect; and yet, it is a course that only Bach could have taken. Playing, studying, or listening to a Bach piece, you may experience a wondrous sense of discovery: "*This* is how music works!" In point of fact, Bach, like all composers, was faced with an infinite number of choices; he simply made all the right ones.

Bach's art can be considered a summation of centuries of musical traditions. The following chart shows some of these traditions and their impact on Bach's style.

Traditions Evolving since the Middle Ages	*Effects on Bach's Music*
1. *The establishment of the major–minor tonal system*	
The major–minor tonal system had become well established by the Baroque. By this time, harmony, counterpoint, and musical form had all come under its strong tonal sway.	Bach's music rests firmly in the major–minor tonal system. He had an extraordinary sense of harmony within the major–minor tonal framework. The melodic and harmonic elements in Bach's polyphony are inseparably intertwined.

Traditions Evolving since the Middle Ages	Effects on Bach's Music

2. *The development of polyphony*
The evolution of notated polyphony lay at the heart of the Western musical tradition.

Bach's music is recognized as a unique fulfillment of the possibilities of polyphonic organization. His fugues (and other works) are a high point, not only in music, but also in the Western intellectual tradition.

3. *Importance of genres for composers*
Musical culture was animated by a rich variety of genres which had evolved from a living culture. Sacred genres, like chant, organum, Mass, motet, oratorio, and cantata* grew out of religious life. Secular genres, many of them dance-derived, flourished as entertainment. All these genres, begun in the anonymous traditions of Medieval society, had evolved into highly stylized models that formed a basis for the living language of European notated music.

Bach's art was built squarely upon the existing genres of the Baroque. He studied, copied, and absorbed a rich variety of models which he then transformed into his own unique creations. His works are simultaneously conventional and unique (because his version of each standard genre was shaped by his genius). The only important Baroque genre in which Bach did not compose was opera. Evidently, opera, the most important secular genre of the era, was far too worldly for this deeply religious man. Nonetheless, Bach's sacred vocal music was profoundly related to operatic practice. His more than two hundred cantatas, the two Passions,** and the *Mass in B minor* all used recitatives, arias, and choruses. But the connection between Bach's music and opera goes well beyond these obvious matters of form. Every aspect of the Baroque musical language had been affected by opera. Although the conservative

*Cantata: A semidramatic musical work without staging, similar to the oratorio, but usually far less theatrical or dramatic.
**Passion: An oratorio-like composition whose subject is always the life and death of Jesus according to any of the four Evangelists—Matthew, Luke, John, or Mark; for example, Bach's *Passion according to St. Matthew* and *Passion according to St. John*.

Traditions Evolving since the Middle Ages

Effects on Bach's Music

and deeply religious Bach would have been out of place in an Italian opera house, his art, nourished by operatic practice, demonstrates the cultural interactions that create a living language.

4. *The cross-fertilization of music by regional styles*
The development of Western music was made possible by a rich interplay of various European traditions.

Bach never left Germany. But he avidly studied the music of other traditions, which enriched his immediate musical world.

5. *Cues that related musical style to ideas and feelings*
As we have seen, a living musical language often involves cues from a variety of other human experiences. As examples, we may cite musical structures related to the number three, the Harmony of the Spheres, word painting, and the Baroque Doctrine of the Affections.

To consider Bach only as an intellectual composer is to miss the essence of his art. His music evolved from a powerful world of religious ideas and feelings.

6. *Church patronage*
The innovative techniques of Western notated music were born, nourished, and developed within the cultural context of the Church.

Bach's religious beliefs and his practical duties as a church musician are the dominant cultural influences upon his style.

7. *The patronage of the nobility*
An alternative source of livelihood for a musician up to the eighteenth century was service to the aristocracy. Music was central to the social life of the European nobility. Opera is one of many genres that owes its existence to aristocratic patronage.

During Bach's service to the nobility, he produced many instrumental masterpieces for the enjoyment of his patrons. (The suites for unaccompanied violin and cello and the *Brandenburg Concertos* are examples.) Bach was a master of the living language which had evolved under the dual influence of church and aristocratic patronage.

BACH BEYOND STYLE

The music of Bach may be perceived at many simultaneous levels of awareness. At one level, it is clearly music of the Baroque. At another, it sums up many earlier traditions. In addition, Bach's music served as an important model for many composers who came after him. Finally, and most vital to this discussion, Bach's basic impulses seem to survive all manner of stylistic presentation. The same fugue can be performed on organ, piano, or wind band without losing its aesthetic integrity. In other words, no matter how the tones are produced, one may still experience Bach's musical intentions without distraction. Perhaps the best way to make this clear is through a comparison: imagine a piece by the Rolling Stones played by a symphony orchestra. Even if the pitches and rhythms were identical to the original, the musical intention would be obscured. It would be a hopeless mismatch of stylistic cues. A Bach fugue, on the other hand, can survive such transformations without losing its meaning. Played on Baroque harpsichord, a symphony orchestra, a twentieth-century synthesizer, or some as-yet-unknown instrument of the future, something of its essence remains intact. There is a universal quality in Bach's music that enables it to survive such a mixup of stylistic cues.

What makes Bach's music so special? There is no simple answer, but one possibility is worth considering: the music of Bach has always invited descriptive adjectives like "mathematical," "intellectual," and "abstract." Viewed from this perspective, a Bach work may be considered as patterns of pure thought expressed in musical terms. Perhaps it is the universality of these patterns that allows the same piece to be played effectively on so many different instruments. Like a mathematical principle, the inner structure remains constant beyond the limits of style and time.

It is a profound mistake to consider that its intellectual qualities make Bach's music dry or devoid of emotion and feeling. His musical language was shot through with an intense religious mysticism. The composition of mathematically inspired musical structures may be understood within a well-established and quite ancient tradition: the interplay between sound and number was a mystical representation of "God's Order." According to this philosophy, musical composition had to follow a preordained plan, much in the same way that "God had planned the heavens." Through the experience of this music, one could be in touch with universal truth. We have already encountered this idea in "The Magic of the String" and "The Harmony of the Spheres." Bach considered many of his creations to be "cosmic puzzles" which ultimately represented his relationship to God. His symbolism often involved hidden correspondences between sound, number, and idea. This concept will become much clearer with some specific examples: in a section of Bach's *St. John Passion* the chorus (when asked to judge Jesus) sings: "It is not lawful for us to put any man to death." The motive

Bach uses for the German word *töten* (to kill) is a strange chromatic succession consisting of *five* notes. You can easily play this "death motive" by following the keyboard diagram below:

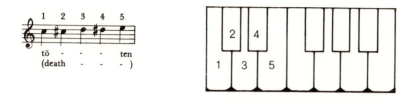

The sliding, uneasy sound of this motive is another example of how Baroque chromaticism was used to convey a feeling. But Bach's symbolism goes deeper. The five notes evidently refer to the fifth commandment ("Thou shalt not kill"). The motive occurs exactly *ten* times, representing the ten commandments.

Another type of symbolism commonly used in that time involved a substitution of numbers for letters of the alphabet according to the following plan:

A — 1	G — 7	N — 13
B — 2	H — 8	O — 14
C — 3	I, J — 9	P — 15
D — 4	K — 10	Q — 16
E — 5	L — 11	R — 17
F — 6	M — 12	S — 18

Using this table, Bach's name had a particular cryptic quality when translated into number:

$$\text{B \quad A \quad C \quad H}$$

$$2 + 1 + 3 + 8 = 14$$

$$\text{J. \quad S. \quad B \quad A \quad C \quad H}$$

$$9 + 18 + 2 + 1 + 3 + 8 = 41$$

These two numbers—14 and 41—show up in Bach's music from time to time as a kind of hidden signature. For example, the theme of the *Three-part Invention in F minor*, one of Bach's most "mathematical" creations, consists of fourteen notes. In *The Musical Offering*, Bach "signs" the work with fourteen entrances of the theme. Perhaps the most moving instance of Bach's personal numerology occurred shortly before his death. The composer, now blind, was dictating one of his last pieces—the organ chorale

Before Thy Throne, My God, I Stand. Bach manipulated the tune in such a way that the first line consists of fourteen notes, while the entire melody has forty-one, "as if the composer wanted to express that BACH, J. S. BACH was now preparing to enter the heavenly abode."* For some composers in Bach's time, such mystical correspondences between tone and number were still part of music's philosophical basis. The eighteenth-century German philosopher Leibnitz expressed this ancient notion with these words: "Music is a secret exercise in the arithmetic of the soul, unaware of its act of counting."**

Connections in the Bach Discussion

Social position of the composer.
Absorption of a living musical language.
The importance of genres in musical culture.
The interplay of regional styles.
Use of an abstract mathematical plan in musical design.

QUESTIONS

For the following questions, find any false statement(s) and correct them by changing the word(s) in italics. More than one statement may be false; all the statements may be true.

1. Concerning the beginnings of European opera:

    (a) It was a new style born of a *universal impulse*.

    (b) It *had* its roots in the anonymous traditions of religious ritual and folk celebration.

    (c) It first flourished in *France*.

    (d) The tradition of pageantry and celebration common in Mediterranean societies *helped* create the cultural environment in which it was born.

2. Concerning the Florentine Camerata:

    (a) They were a group of men who met to consider art, music, history, literature, and other matters in *France*.

*Quoted from Karl Geiringer, *Symbolism in the Music of Bach* (Washington, D.C., 1956), p. 14.
**Ibid.*, p. 11.

(b) They considered the *polyphonic* tradition ideal for the expression of a text.

(c) They believed that the music should be *more* important than the text.

(d) Their cultural background is part of the Renaissance *humanist* tradition.

3. Recitative

(a) is essentially *polyphonic*.

(b) was the Camerata's theoretical re-creation of the style of the *ancient Greek theater*.

(c) usually has a *strong* meter.

(d) was an *essential* element for the origins of European opera.

4. Which of the following were direct or indirect ancestors of European opera? (Cross out the wrong one[s].)

(a) *the ancient unity*

(b) *the mystery play*

(c) *Greek drama*

(d) *motet*

5. Concerning recitative, aria, and chorus:

(a) They are basic components of *Baroque* opera.

(b) They developed in the early *eighteenth* century.

(c) They provide continual *contrast* in the flow of operatic form.

(d) Except for *recitative*, they are sung by soloists.

6. The Baroque Doctrine of the Affections

(a) identified musical sound with *specific* emotions.

(b) is an example of how *nonmusical cues* may be important in a living musical language.

(c) may be understood as part of the *growing* use of music to portray specific human emotions.

(d) is an example of how response to a musical style may be deepened by an understanding of its *cultural perspective*.

7. The comparison between *West Side Story* and *Dido and Aeneas* illustrates the following ideas:

   (a) The American musical is one of many styles *evolving* from the European operatic tradition.

   (b) Although these works are different in musical style, they have *basic similarities* of musical-dramatic structure.

   (c) The *contrasting* styles of the two works illustrate how the music-drama impulse may be adapted to a certain region or time.

   (d) The pieces reflect an important historical fact: the opera tradition begins in Span I and *does not continue* in Span II.

8. These two music-dramas demonstrate the following principles:

   (a) Creativity (in all arts) is *often* based on preexisting models.

   (b) Musical traditions are *rarely* enriched by the interplay of regional styles.

   (c) Any moment of musical style is *related* to the past.

   (d) A musical style may be a *blending* of traditions.

9. Concerning Bach's childhood:

   (a) He was born into a family of *musicians*.

   (b) He learned his craft at an *early age*.

   (c) He was instilled with a sense of *religious duty*.

   (d) He was raised in an atmosphere of *discipline and obedience*.

10. Concerning Bach's professional career:

    (a) He assumed his first professional duties *as an adult*.

    (b) Throughout his life, he was never more than a *well-respected servant*.

    (c) He wrote over two hundred cantatas as part of his duties as a *church* composer.

    (d) The "Gigue" from his "Partita for Violin" ⟨19⟩ was composed for one of his *church* employers.

11. Concerning Bach's reaction to his patron's refusal to grant his leave:

    (a) It was *uncommon* for a musician of the eighteenth century to assert himself in this manner.

(b) His insistence on his rights conforms to the social order of the *Age of Absolutism*.

(c) He eventually *won* his fight for professional nobility.

(d) His defiance of authority *was typical* of Bach's character.

12. Concerning Bach's musical style:

(a) He *created* in many genres.

(b) He *was influenced* by Baroque operatic practice.

(c) His harmony belongs to the *modal* tonal system.

(d) There is an *unequal* relationship between the melodic and harmonic elements of his style.

13. Concerning Bach's position in the musical culture:

(a) His music represents a high point in *homophonic* organization.

(b) His art not only reflects the accomplishments of an individual, but also of a *culture*.

(c) Like other professional musicians, Bach relied on the *patronage of church and nobility* for his livelihood.

(d) His religious beliefs *were* central to his musical practices.

14. Concerning Bach's fugues:

(a) They are widely acknowledged masterpieces which have continued to influence musical practices *up to the present*.

(b) They were composed *only for instruments*.

(c) Bach *created* the genre.

(d) *Imitation* is an essential procedure in fugue composition.

15. Write Baroque *fugue*, Renaissance *Mass/motet*, or *both* after each statement:

(a) A heightened sense of forward potential: _____

(b) Preceded the other in time: _____

(c) Polyphonic texture: _____

(d) Use of imitation: _____

(e) Use of continually changing motives: _____

(f) Continual use of a single motive: _____

(g) The same rhythmic motive continually repeated: _____

(h) "Floating," gentle rhythm: _____

(i) Vocal-based melodic style: _____

(j) Instrumental-based melodic style (for the most part): _____

(k) Essential genre in the Western tradition: _____

(l) Strong meter: _____

(m) Weak or no meter: _____

8

The Classical-Romantic Continuum

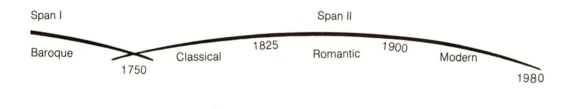

Span I   Span II

Baroque   Classical   1825   Romantic   1900   Modern

1750   1980

The Second Span, 1750-1980

With this chapter, the second long span in our historical survey begins. It is framed approximately by the years 1750–1980. During this time, the related cultures of nineteenth-century Europe and America rapidly evolved into the modern world we know today. Music also reflects this transformation as certain traditional practices evolve into what we call "modern music." Tracing this development, we encounter constant interaction between two forces: the weight of continuing tradition and the growing need for change. From the music historian's view, the cultural patterns that emerged as a result of this dynamic interplay fall into three broad style periods: *Classical* (1750–1825), *Romantic* (1825–1900), and *Modern* (1900–present). These dates are only approximate, since the characteristics of style periods inevitably overlap.

One strand of continuity within Span II is composers' continued use of certain traditional genres (see Main Genres Chart, page 484). Several of these genres constitute what we may call the *sonata-symphony group*. The genres in this group are closely related, often following a traditional model; it is this model we now study. As an introduction, consider these terms:

SONATA   A composition for a solo instrument with or without accompaniment. Traditionally it is comprised of several related movements of contrasting tempos and content. Sonatas range in length from relatively short works (8 min.) to longer ones (40 min.–1 hr.).

SYMPHONY   A composition for orchestra, usually conceived on a large scale. Like the sonata, it is usually comprised of several related movements.

TRIO, QUARTET, QUINTET   Each of these describes a work in several movements for a small group of instruments: *trio*—three instruments; *quartet*—four instruments; *quintet*—five instruments. A similar work for six instruments is called a *sextet*; for seven instruments, a *septet*; and for eight, an *octet*. Various combinations of instruments may comprise each group.

CONCERTO   A large-scale, multimovement work for a solo instrument(s) with orchestra.

Traditional Format of the Sonata-Symphony Group

The genres above (sonata, symphony, trio, quartet, etc.) are often considered as a group, because they all resemble one traditional model involving a basic design and certain musical procedures. First, we consider the basic design:

Traditional Designs of the Sonata-Symphony Group

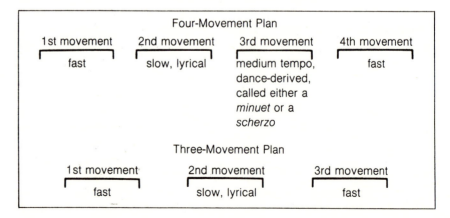

THE SONATA PRINCIPLE: A STUDY IN FORWARD POTENTIAL

The first movement of the sonata-symphony group developed from a compositional procedure called the *sonata principle*. At the heart of this principle is the juxtaposition of different tonal centers causing a sense of imbalance (see page 78). This imbalance creates a sense of forward potential. The following diagrams and explanation review this musical phenomenon by visual representation.

The Juxtaposition of Two Tonal Centers

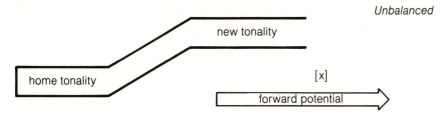

This diagram represents a musical structure in which a "home" tonality is juxtaposed with a new tonality. At letter *x* we experience increased forward potential, because we expect a return to the home tonality. Since the diagram above does not show a return to the home key, it can be described as *unbalanced*.

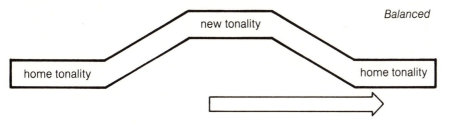

A return to the home tonality completes a cycle of stability–instability–stability. The second diagram can be described as *balanced*. This tonal design is a fundamental aspect of the *sonata principle*.

As we have just seen, the sonata principle is set in motion by the contrast of two tonal centers. Usually this contrast also involves two *different themes*—Theme I and Theme II:

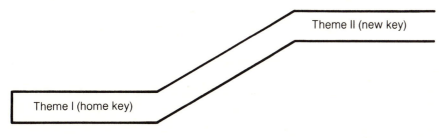

Now we really have a situation that generates forward potential: 1) the juxtaposition of two key centers, creating a need for the return to the home key; and 2) the juxtaposition of two melodic ideas, creating dramatic musical questions: What is going to happen to these themes? How will they interact?

THE TRANSITION

There is a considerable amount of musical activity between Theme I and Theme II that doesn't seem to belong to either. This is called the *transition*; its purpose, in this case, is to take us to the new tonality (to modulate). Thus we can revise the diagram above by showing this *transition section:*

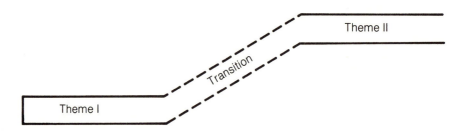

The transition section has no tonality of its own.

THE EXPOSITION

The presentation of these conflicting elements—two tonalities and two themes—has a certain dramatic effect, comparable to the beginning of a play. Often in the first act, we meet certain characters in a particular situation, from which the subsequent action will develop. But before the real conflict begins, the first act must come to a close. So we experience a partial ending, not at all complete as we await the inevitable action that will follow. We have the same kind of partial ending at this point in the movement, and we call it a *closing section*. The *closing section* follows Theme II and seems to bring the conflict between the two keys and themes to a temporary halt. It sums up the action so far. At this moment, we have reached the end of the *exposition*. Since the *closing section* is in the *new key*, we are still in a state of expectation. The diagram now looks like this:

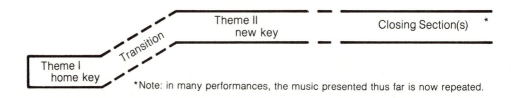

*Note: in many performances, the music presented thus far is now repeated.

We can now summarize the structure and musical intention of the exposition: two themes and tonal centers have been "exposed." The contrast between them has created a certain tension and forward potential. A closing section brings the music to a temporary moment of rest. We are left hanging, awaiting the resolution of tonal imbalance.

Listen   Mozart, *Symphony No. 40*, Exposition (through measure 100)

Note: These instructions assume that you are in a classroom situation. Listening to a section of a movement requires some guidance. The independent reader is referred to *The Norton Scores*, 3rd ed., Vol. I, p. 500ff.

THE DEVELOPMENT

The sonata principle continues its forward momentum in the *development section*. Left with a slightly unbalanced feeling by the juxtaposition of two tonal centers and two contrasting themes deprived of resolution, we are ready for more action. Far from resolving the tonal-dramatic conflict, *the development will take us further into unstable regions*. Tonally, the development seems to wander around, passing through many distant keys, resulting in a very unstable but exciting quality. While shifting through these distant tonalities, the composer may explore and develop various elements of the thematic material. The texture, also, may change, becoming more polyphonic, which, in comparison to the homophonic exposition, makes the development seem all the more unstable. The diagram will now look like this:

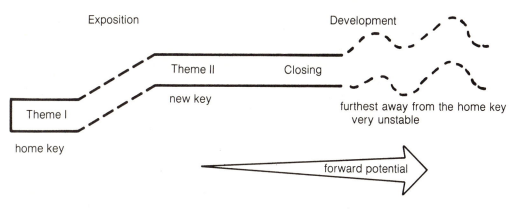

THE RECAPITULATION

By the end of the development, we have been led through various states of instability. The original sense of imbalance in the exposition between the home tonality and the new tonality has been intensified. To put it simply, we are quite ready for a return to the home key. This is accomplished in the final section, or *recapitulation*, when the various tensions and conflicts of the movement are resolved. Themes I and II *both* sound in the tonic key; the transition between them does not modulate. The movement ends with the closing section in the home key. The drama is complete.

Listen Mozart, *Symphony No. 40*, complete first movement. Follow the diagram.

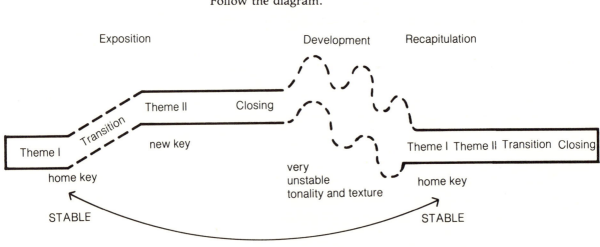

SOME SHORT-RANGE DETAIL
Now that the long-range form of this movement has been delineated, we consider some of the details that give it shape. You may want to review the discussion of the opening theme on page 51. This theme, and indeed the entire movement, seems to grow out of the short, three-note impulse (da-da-dum). Throughout the movement, this motive is heard in many guises: at the beginning of phrases; in forceful cadences; as the subject of the imitative dialogue in the development; and finally, at the recapitulation, when it reintroduces Theme I with a gentle insistence that is one of the most wonderful moments in all music.

SONATA-ALLEGRO FORM
What has emerged from our analysis of this movement is *sonata-allegro form*, perhaps the single most utilized design since the eighteenth century. Many composers used this model in a somewhat predictable fashion, while others created masterpieces. Like the various forms in the picture sequences on pages 500–511, the sonata-allegro design transcends style and time. Like all models, it provides a flexible plan for the composer, not a rigid formula.

There are many possible variations in the sonata-allegro plan. The details of this design may vary in response to a specific handling of the basic principles. For example, the composer may use three themes instead of two. Variations in detail increase as we move toward the twentieth century.

Although the *sonata principle* is associated with the first movement of the sonata-symphony group, it is used in many other musical situations. We may find it in subsequent movements of a sonata or symphony (for example, in Mozart's *Symphony No. 40* it is used in the first, second, and fourth movements). It may turn up in a piece which does not fit into the sonata-symphony group at all, for example, the Overture to Mozart's opera *The Magic Flute* (to be discussed shortly).

Discussions about musical form sometimes communicate an unintentional but profound misunderstanding of how composers actually work. While it is correct to think of sonata-allegro form as a plan that fits neatly into boxes on a diagram, this static image has little meaning for the composer. To the composer, form is less a noun (like "table," "book," or "thing") than a verb ("to make," "to create," "to form"). Composers do not pour their inspiration into forms; it is form that is created by their inspiration.

SONATA PRINCIPLE   A compositional process rooted in tonal juxtaposition to create various tensions, eventually resolved.

SONATA-ALLEGRO FORM   The form created by the sonata principle. It consists of three sections: exposition, development, and recapitulation.

EXPOSITION   The opening section of a sonata-allegro form, in which two tonal centers and sometimes two themes are introduced.

DEVELOPMENT   The section of sonata-allegro form in which the various musical ideas are explored. The tonal feeling of the development section is generally unstable.

RECAPITULATION   The section that resolves the conflict set in motion by the exposition and further heightened by the development. In the recapitulation, the home key is reaffirmed.

CLOSING SECTION   A section of sonata-allegro form which concludes the exposition. It also describes the end of the recapitulation.

TRANSITION   A musical span which leads from one part of the form to another. In sonata-allegro form, transitions are usually found between Theme I and Theme II.

MOZART, *SYMPHONY NO. 40*, SECOND MOVEMENT

The second movement in the sonata-symphony group is traditionally slow and lyrical. In the *Symphony No. 40*, the slow movement bears witness to Mozart's deep relationship with the great Viennese lyrical tradition. (The symphony was written in the Austrian capital, where Mozart spent his last ten years.) Vienna, because of its geographical location, was an ideal meeting ground for Italian and German musical influences. Here, close to the source, German composers were especially receptive to the warm lyricism of Italian melody. (We shall return to discuss this strand of the European notated tradition—Viennese lyricism—in later chapters.)

Mozart's melodic genius is legendary. As already mentioned, no one can be taught to write a great melody; it seems to be a gift that only a few human beings possess. Mozart had this gift. Beautiful melodies abound in his works, each one a spontaneous, graceful miracle. In this particular movement, Mozart presents his melody in quite an interesting way: we hear it first in a gentle polyphonic dialogue, which soon gives way to a clear homophonic texture. Usually, polyphony does not lend itself to such lyricism, yet Mozart's counterpoint is so smooth that one can still respond to the flowing melodic shape.

The form of this movement is generated by the sonata principle, but you will not hear the dramatic juxtaposition of themes, as in the first movement. In fact, there is really only one theme for which the broad tonal outlines of sonata-allegro form serve as a background. This is a perfect example of the flexibility of the sonata principle: it is not a rigid design, but rather an internalized tradition, active, flexible, and natural within the composer's living language.

Listening Activity

The way Mozart uses meter in this movement is particularly elegant. The music seems to flow in an especially graceful manner within the metrical structure ("in six"). While the music moves within the metrical grid, it is also *set free* by the meter.

A physical activity may help demonstrate this freedom:

With the right hand tap out the rhythm of the opening notes. Continue this pattern:
(in music notation)

RH ♩♪♪♪♪♪♪♪♪♪

When you have this rhythm going, *add* the slower beat in the left hand. The rhythmic structure is a layered combination of faster threes and slower twos:

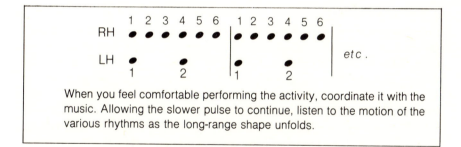

When you feel comfortable performing the activity, coordinate it with the music. Allowing the slower pulse to continue, listen to the motion of the various rhythms as the long-range shape unfolds.

THIRD MOVEMENT: MINUET AND TRIO

You have encountered the term *dance-derived* in connection with the third movement in the sonata-symphony group. The actual history of the derivation is very interesting. You will remember the Renaissance *Branle* dance group, 11b , in which one dance was followed by a second, after which the first dance returned:

Dance I	Dance II	Dance I

By the Baroque era, this plan had evolved into the formal design of the *minuet and trio*. It was written as a functional dance for the aristocracy, but was also adopted as the third movement of the symphony. The *trio* is simply a contrasting dance, often played by a smaller ensemble than the opening minuet.

Minuet	Trio	Minuet

repeat

No one gets up to dance to the minuet of a Mozart symphony, although of all its movements, this one, coming directly from the dance, is most likely to evoke the dance impulse. If you were to imagine an actual dance to this music, it certainly would not contain the delicate gestures associated with the aristocratic minuet. The trio, by contrast, has something of that subdued aristocratic elegance.

MINUET   A dance genre popular in the seventeenth and eighteenth centuries. The minuet was adopted as a movement in the symphony.

MINUET AND TRIO   The traditional format of the dance movement in the sonata-symphony group, whose form is

A	B	A
Minuet	Trio	Minuet

FOURTH MOVEMENT

Composers use various forms for last movements in the sonata-symphony group. In this symphony, Mozart has chosen to repeat the sonata-allegro form. The movement opens with a *rocket theme* (so-called because of its soaring melodic shape and energetic rhythm). Although the form of this movement is practically identical with that of the first, it is not a simple repetition of a formal concept. Here Mozart uses the sonata principle to fashion a high-energy finale for the work. Within the concise sonata-allegro form, the music is restless and forward moving, and seemingly has but one purpose—to get to the end. Again, the flexibility of the sonata principle is evident.

Wolfgang Amadeus Mozart

"There is a touch of the miraculous, something both childlike and god-like, about all of this . . ."—Donald Grout

By the year 1766, the name of Wolfgang Amadeus Mozart was on the lips of Europe's musical connoisseurs. He had just completed a three-year odyssey through the courts and cities of northern Europe. Audiences were amazed with his talents both as a performer on the violin and keyboard and as a composer. Not only did Mozart play his written compositions, but he often improvised pieces for his audiences. He could perform the most difficult concerto at sight. As a challenge, a local court musician might present an unfinished fugue for Mozart to complete, which he would do by improvising effortlessly. And according to all contemporary accounts, whatever Mozart played was always in elegant "taste" (the word used for "style" in the eighteenth century). In 1766, Mozart was acknowledged among the greatest musicians of the world. In 1766, Wolfgang Amadeus Mozart was ten years old.

MOZART'S NATURAL GENIUS

Mozart (1756–1791) was among the most gifted musical geniuses the world has ever known. But there are really three geniuses in the Mozart legend. Wolfgang's sister, "Nannerl," achieved a remarkable level of musicianship at an early age, but like so many gifted women of the past, her career was submerged by the traditional social restrictions of the eighteenth century. The third genius, and the controlling force over the other two, was their father, Leopold Mozart.

It seems that a fair number of natural geniuses are born into the world; but the realization of their potential remains a mysterious mix of variables. In the case of Wolfgang Amadeus Mozart, we know a great deal about one of those variables—the influence of his father. Leopold Mozart was an

Leopold Mozart and his children in performance, from a contemporary engraving.

accomplished musician in his own right. Talented and knowledgeable, he provided a sophisticated musical environment for his children in which professionalism of the highest order was the norm. Not only was Leopold a skilled violinist and composer, but he had a special talent as a teacher. He was, in fact, the author of a widely read book on violin pedagogy. It was not surprising, then, that the notebooks of pieces and exercises he compiled for his son's instruction (many of which have survived) show a high level of professionalism tempered by a sensitive awareness of the young student's personal needs. Wolfgang's extraordinary talent was well matched with Leopold's extraordinary gift as an educator.

That Wolfgang was a natural genius was evidenced in many ways. For example, he had a special sensitivity to timbre. As a child, he was afraid of the trumpet's sound and actually fainted on one occasion when the instrument was played in his presence (or so the story goes). In contrast, he found the timbre of a particular violin so attractive he called it "butter-fiddle." Mozart's response to musical sound, then, seems always to have been of a very special order, much in the way a visual artist may have a heightened sense of color. His sensitivity to timbre would later be reflected in the delicate orchestral sonorities of his mature works, for example, the second movement of the *Fortieth Symphony*.

The boy's skills grew rapidly under his father's guidance. Studies in keyboard, violin, singing, composition, and counterpoint were his daily fare. Each time a new piece was mastered, Leopold would record the achievement on the music itself. "The preceding eighth minuet Little Wolfgang learned in the fourth year of his age," wrote the proud father. Another inscription read: "Little Wolfgang learned this minuet and trio on January 26, one day before his fifth year, at half past nine in the evening, in half an hour."

MOZART'S EARLY PIECES: IMITATIONS OF EXISTING MODELS

Many of those first pieces that Mozart learned were minuets (some with trios). It was no surprise, then, that when the five-year-old Mozart began composing, his first efforts were of this same genre. Once again, we have encountered an instance where a traditional model is important to the perpetuation of a living musical language. We may imagine that the five-year-old Mozart created his own minuets in a spontaneous and natural manner. Teachers who have taught talented five-year-olds will confirm that, at this age, composing does not proceed from rules or technical planning, but rather through spontaneous, creative imitation. Although Mozart undoubtedly picked up the basic minuet style easily, there were probably many small technical errors in his harmony or counterpoint. Father Leopold, who notated the boy's early pieces, would correct these mistakes. By this dynamic learning process, Mozart's natural gift was fine-tuned through the acquisition of technical skills.

One does not acquire such skills without many hours of practice. But it would be wrong to think of the young prodigy reluctantly slaving away; by all accounts Wolfgang made no distinction between fun and work. Undoubtedly this was in part due to his remarkable talent, but also important were the habits and values fostered by Leopold. The Mozart household reflected the customs of a middle-class family of eighteenth-century German society. Respect for tradition and order were joined to a strong sense of self-worth. There were always reasonable answers to any question. "Papa" was a tyrant, but a benevolent one. Each night, after a day filled with both music's pleasures and its duties, young Wolfgang would kiss the end of "papa's" nose and promise "always to keep him in a little glass box." This was a house where authority was tempered with love and purpose.

THE MOZARTS AS EIGHTEENTH-CENTURY MUSICIANS

Leopold Mozart was a very ambitious man; as we shall see, this trait was to play a vital role in Wolfgang's early life. To understand this interaction, we need to discuss the social position of the eighteenth-century musician, which was an important reality for the Mozart family.

As the conflict between J. S. Bach and one of his patrons demonstrated (page 194), a musician in the eighteenth century was not usually his own man. Professional musicians (for the most part) belonged to the middle class. Today, the term *middle class* has primarily economic connotations; but in the eighteenth century its social implications were far more important. For centuries, European society had been strictly divided into various classes, with the aristocracy at the top of the social ladder. Society functioned under the firm belief that power and prestige were the natural birthrights of the nobility.

Social stratification influenced many aspects of everyday life, from political rights to dress and demeanor. Basically, musicians in the service of the aristocracy were no more than trumped-up servants. They wore uniforms and wigs, ate at the servants' table, and behaved accordingly in the presence of their "betters." A musician's destiny was controlled by the whims of his patron.

Within this rigid social order, the musician's life was a curious anomaly: on one hand, he was considered socially inferior to the aristocracy; on the other, it was his talent and sensibilities that provided an essential commodity of aristocratic life. Through close contact with the nobility, and in creation of aristocratic musical taste, musicians participated vicariously in the aristocratic life style. Service to the aristocracy represented social and monetary security. The more prestigious the aristocrat, the greater the honor to be in his employ. Up until the eighteenth century, this social doctrine was rarely questioned. Servitude and duty rooted in social distinctions were believed to be the natural law, preordained by God. But in the mid-eighteenth century, the situation was beginning to change, its disintegration hastened by an intellectual movement called the *Age of Reason*.

THE AGE OF REASON

The Age of Reason (also termed the *Enlightenment*) was an era marked by a basic change in social and political awareness. It displaced a more rigid social order, the *Age of Absolutism*. You may remember that in the Baroque period, absolute power was exercised by the aristocracy. The time frame in which these social phenomena occurred is somewhat flexible, but may be generally considered thus:

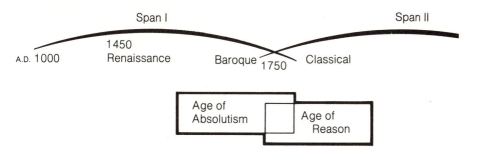

We have considered the life of a musician under the yoke of Absolutism in our earlier discussion of Bach (see page 194–95). This era of unquestioning obedience to authority ended as European society began a transition toward a more modern social order. Above all else, the Enlightenment is characterized by a powerful faith in *reason* and *scientific thought* as the basis for human values. Long-held traditions of religion and society were questioned in the light of rational thinking. At the heart of the Enlightenment was the middle class, whose industrious self-image had outgrown their inferior status. They sought not only long-overdue political rights, but also legitimacy and respect as a social class. The Enlightenment was an optimistic age; its adherents were filled with a spirit of self-confidence. More and more, the person not born to social privilege, but possessed of talent, energy, and discipline, was ready to make a success of his life. Such a man was Leopold Mozart.

THE "LITTLE WIZARD"

Leopold understood that Wolfgang's talent could be used to improve the Mozart family's situation. So, from the age of six until early adulthood Wolfgang was to spend much of his life touring the great aristocratic centers of Europe. Leopold was an ambitious entrepreneur with a practical skill for "show business," as this press notice he wrote for a London paper demonstrates.

COURTESY MOZART MUSEUM, SALZBURG

Press notice in the London *Public Advertiser*, July 11, 1765.

To All Lovers of Sciences

The greatest Prodigy that Europe, of that even Human Nature has to boast of, is, without Contradiction, the little German boy WOLFGANG MOZART; a Boy, Eight Years old, who has, and indeed very justly, raised the admiration not only of the greatest Men, but also of the greatest Musicians in Europe. It is hard to say, whether his Execution on the Harpsichord and his playing and singing at Sight, or his own Caprice, Fancy, and Compositions for all Instruments, are most astonishing. The Father of this Miracle, being obliged by Desire of several Ladies and Gentlemen to postpone, for a very short Time, his

Departure from England, will give an Opportunity to hear this little Composer and his Sister, whose musical Knowledge wants not Apology. Performs every Day of the Week, from Twelve to Three o'clock in the Great Room at the Swan and Hoop, Cornhill. Admittance 2 (£) 6d. each Person. The two Children will play also together with four Hands upon the same Harpsichord, and put upon it a Handkerchief, without seeing the Keys.

The child Mozart became a celebrity in the courts of Europe. His talent, charm, and tender age allowed him an intimacy with royalty that was unthinkable for the ordinary person of his station. "Little Wolfgang jumped on the Empress' lap, threw his arms around her neck, and kissed her good and thoroughly," wrote proud father Leopold to his wife. Emperor Francis I was so won over by the boy that he called him the "Little Wizard."

In his home town of Salzburg, Austria, Mozart was no more than the child of a local musical servant. But in Paris, Vienna, London, and Rome, the "Little Wizard" was the wonder of his age. The effects of such a life upon this child already gifted beyond most cannot be underestimated. The prodigy moved with confidence and ease through the centers of musical culture. He learned to speak several languages. He associated with the musical elite of his time. In London, he came into contact with Johann Christian Bach (one of J. S. Bach's sons), whose musical style became a major influence on the younger composer. Like the young media personalities of today, skyrocketing through the movie-television scene, Wolfgang Amadeus Mozart lived a near-fantasy existence, caused by and, in turn, nourishing his remarkable genius. It was, however, a fantasy that would end.

As Mozart reached adulthood, several related conflicts began to affect his life. At the center of these troubles lay his relationship with Leopold. Throughout those early years, Mozart had submitted totally, willingly, and joyfully to his father's plans and aspirations. Control was total. Dissent never occurred. But as he grew to adulthood, Wolfgang began to disagree with Leopold on important matters. Central to their differences was Mozart's refusal to enter the service of a noble patron in order to provide financial security for himself and the family. Already acknowledged by many as the greatest living composer, he was simply unwilling to become a servant, and was easily offended by situations in which his inferior social status was a factor. In a letter to his father, he said that he wished he had told a patron who insulted him: "I could sooner acquire all your orders than *you* could become what *I* am." To Leopold, despite his enlightened ways, such attitudes were unthinkable. The ties between father and son were finally undone when Mozart married at the age of twenty-six. Although they maintained a cordial relationship which included a steady correspondence on musical matters, the close emotional bond had been broken.

After his marriage, Mozart would live only nine years, and those were

Mozart at the age of twenty-six (unfinished painting by Josef Lange).

marked by many personal troubles. Although he earned a great deal for a musician of his time, Mozart was incredibly careless with money. In the final years, he was constantly borrowing in order to survive on a day-to-day basis. In many ways, he never became a responsible adult. The fantasy world of his childhood had never prepared him for practical realities. In truth, he "lived his real life in the inner world of his music, to which his everyday existence often seems only a troubled and shadowy parallel."*

THE MOZART STYLE
In a brief lifetime of thirty-five years, Mozart composed over six-hundred works.** Those written in his last ten years, while he was living in Vienna, represent a mature style synthesized from many influences into a unique Mozartean language. In these wondrous creations, formal German tradition lives side by side with inspired Italian lyricism. Dancing Viennese rhythms are joined to contrapuntal intricacy. (In his later years, Mozart became very interested in the music of Bach.) One after another, symphonies, concertos, chamber works, and operas poured from his pen with incredible speed, each crafted with extraordinary care.

THE MAGIC FLUTE
One of the last works Mozart completed was an opera on a German text, *The Magic Flute*. Most of Mozart's operas are in Italian, for, like Handel before him, he was at home with the Italian language and operatic tradition.

*Grout, *History of Western Music*, 3rd ed. (New York, 1980), p. 503.
**A complete catalogue of Mozart's music was prepared by L. von Köchel, whose name (or the initial K.) appears before a number identifying each work.

Lyrical melody had become an integral part of his style, as it had for many other composers from northern parts of Europe. But you will recall that opera had found many regional manners of expression. In Germany, it was the *singspiel*, a type of popular musical comedy with spoken dialogue not unlike our Broadway musical in its direct appeal to audiences. But in the hands of Mozart, *The Magic Flute* was to be more than an ordinary singspiel. Much as Leonard Bernstein transformed *West Side Story* into something beyond the traditional Broadway musical, Mozart expanded a regional tradition into a universal statement.

There is no simple way to describe what *The Magic Flute* is about; it is about everything. Like most great works of art, it functions at many levels and means different things to different listeners. The main protagonist is Tamino, a young man of noble birth. He is searching for Pamina, his love. Tamino's comic companion, Papageno the Bird Catcher, also seeks his mate, Papagena. Pamina's mother, the Queen of the Night, is a curious figure who embodies both good and evil. Finally, Sarastro, a mysterious priest, seems to represent some higher force. The name of the opera refers to a flute (actually a panpipe, an ancient instrument; see page 451) with magical powers, which was given to Tamino to protect him.

Suggestions for Listening *The Magic Flute* should ideally be enjoyed in the theater, but a good recording with a translation is a reasonable substitute. It is suggested that you listen to the recordings over a period of time, rather than at one sitting.

1. *Overture*. The overture to *The Magic Flute* is a fine example of a universal principle discussed in Chapter 4: namely, *the interplay of basic forms and models to create new musical designs*. The basic genre of this section is the *overture*, a piece used to introduce the action of most operas. Overtures are written in various forms; this one is in *sonata-allegro* design. But woven into the sonata-allegro procedure are passages of *fugal* writing. For example, the one important theme, although not an actual fugue, is presented in fugal texture. The basic sonata-allegro outline is generated by the juxtaposition of key centers, making for a very tight design. It is charged with an energy that propels the listener into the drama. A wonderful dramatic tension is created by the short development section, in which unstable harmonies and dense layers of polyphonic melodies create an "unbearable" feeling of forward potential that leads the listener to the return of the home key.

2. *Characterization through music*. Mozart was a superb musical dramatist. He was able to capture something essential about a character, situation, or feeling, and communicate it to his audience. The opening scene of the opera (directly after the overture) readily demonstrates this point.

In a short space of time, we are led through a series of rapid dramatic changes. For example, the scene begins on an ominous note, supported in the music by frenzied rhythms and sliding chromatic harmony, which create an unstable effect charged with forward potential. Suddenly, a heroic statement sounds, characterized by a shift into a major key and a fanfare-type melody.

A delightful characterization is provided for Papageno, the Bird Catcher. Whereas Tamino and Pamina sing in a soaring, lyrical style that represents their noble birth, Papageno, an ordinary fellow, is given a down-to-earth German folk-song style. Sarastro and his priests intone in a solemn oracular fashion. The choral parts of some of these sections present a hushed, mysterious sound that seems to encode something of fate and eternity. In one of the most fantasy-laden scenes of the opera, the Queen of the Night performs a hysterical aria which is cast, for effect, in a virtuosic Italian style. Throughout the work, different persons and groups are portrayed in different musical languages. In *The Magic Flute*, the purposeful juxtaposition of musical styles is a vital means of dramatic communication.

3. *Symbolism*. It has already been suggested that the opera functions at many levels. One of the most intriguing is its symbolism drawn from Freemasonry. The Masons were a secret cult of intellectuals dedicated to the humanitarian and democratic ideals that had been given impetus by the Age of Reason; Mozart was among them. Something of the rituals of the Masonic order is evidently portrayed in the drama, the most obvious being the many mystic representations of the number three. Rather than point these out, perhaps it is more in the spirit of *The Magic Flute* to seek examples of the threefold symbolism on your own—not because they are hard to find (most are quite obvious), but because the search may reveal other unexpected levels of the drama. Seeking one thing and finding another is, in part, what the opera is about.

THE MAGIC FLUTE AS A SUMMATION OF MOZART'S ART

Mozart died within months of the first performance of *The Magic Flute*. Haunted by his impending demise, sick and somewhat out of his mind, he labored unsuccessfully to complete a Requiem Mass. (The *Requiem* was completed by a student and is in the current concert repertory.) Perhaps, for the following reasons, *The Magic Flute* may be considered something of a Requiem in a broad, humanistic sense. For all its apparent confusion and fantasy, certain themes are unmistakable: one is love and brotherhood; another, that music is a life-giving force in the face of death. Furthermore, *The Magic Flute* brings together in a single work the many sides of Mozart as a person and composer.

History has miscast Wolfgang Amadeus Mozart in a mold of aristocratic saintliness. But anyone who has studied this remarkable man understands him to be not only the noble Tamino but also the down-to-earth Papageno. He could compose music of great solemnity (Sarastro's aria) only to follow with comic playfulness (the duet between Papageno and Papagena). Mozart's letters reveal a childlike, loving man given to spontaneous expression of feelings and playful vulgarities. To some observers, the latter are aberrations; to others they speak only of Mozart's humanity. For the listeners of Mozart's time, *The Magic Flute* was popular entertainment, based directly in a popular genre, and to some extent, a popular musical style (for example, Papageno's folklike melodies). In the history of the Classical-Romantic-Modern span, this opera was among the first musical works to call out for democracy and humanism. (The next great examples of this would be Beethoven's opera *Fidelio* and his *Ninth Symphony*.) That it embodies a variety of styles—German and Italian, popular and serious, comic and solemn—seems perfectly fitting. That all of these apparent diversities are molded into a single unified creation not only summarizes Mozart's genius, but suggests the ultimate theme of this book: that one must go beyond stylistic definitions to fully grasp the meaning of great art.

Connections in the Mozart Discussion

The importance of traditional models in a living language.
The emerging role of the independent composer in society.
The relationship between an artist and culture.
The importance of stylistic interaction between various European traditions in the development of Western notated music.

Mozart: Additional Listening

SYMPHONIES

Symphony No. 25 ("Little G minor"), K. 183
Symphony No. 35 ("Haffner"), K. 385
Symphony No. 38 ("Prague"), K. 504
Symphony No. 41 ("Jupiter"), K. 551

OPERAS

The Marriage of Figaro (in Italian)
Don Giovanni (in Italian)

CONCERTOS

Piano Concerto in D minor, K. 466
Piano Concerto in A major, K. 488
Violin Concerto in G major, K. 216

CHAMBER WORKS
Clarinet Quintet, K. 581
String Quartet in G, K. 387
Piano Quartet in G minor, K. 478
String Quintet in G minor, K. 516

Rondo

| Listen | Franz Joseph Haydn: *Finale* from the *Piano Sonata in E minor* 24a

As we discussed at the beginning of this chapter, the sonata-symphony group includes several genres, among them the solo sonata. Franz Joseph Haydn (1732–1809), another composer of the Classical era, wrote many sonatas for the keyboard. The *Sonata in E minor* is in three movements. The last movement, or *finale*, is a *rondo*—a form closely related to the ritornello design heard in the last movement of Vivaldi's *Concert for Oboe and Orchestra* (see page 181). Like the ritornello, the rondo opens with a catchy tune that returns throughout the movement.

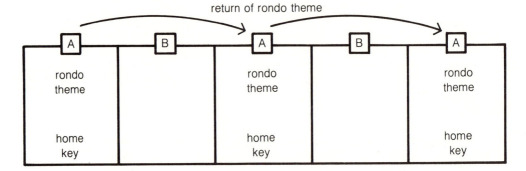

The tonal contrast in this piece is created by an interesting juxtaposition. The home key is *E minor* (that is, the melody and harmony use tones from the E-minor scale). The *B* sections are in *E major*. Thus, there is tonal contrast created by the alternation between minor and major keys of the same tonic pitch.

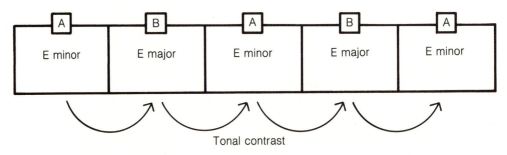

In between statements of the rondo theme, one also expects contrasting material. This rondo provides contrast in a somewhat unusual way (compared with most examples of this form). Instead of presenting completely new material, the *B* section is a variation of the rondo theme; but owing to its *major* quality and the considerable changes in its melodic design, it is perceived as a contrast in the fullest sense.

A	B	A	B	A
rondo theme	variation on theme	rondo theme	another variation on theme	rondo theme
E minor	E major	E minor	E major	E minor

> RONDO   A musical design based in contrast and return, in which a main theme alternates with other material. The rondo theme usually returns in the original key.

The Classical Aesthetic

The term *classical* has evolved a variety of widely used but somewhat disparate meanings. For this reason, we must approach it with caution, flexibility, and patience, suspending our need for exact definitions. Words that have become obscured by overlapping meanings often reflect a dynamic process, a traditional heritage too rich to abandon. The way we will now use this term describes *an approach to artistic creation*. In order to differentiate this meaning from others, the term *classical aesthetic* will be employed in this book. To explore the meaning of the term, we have only to reflect on the general style of Mozart's *Fortieth Symphony* and Haydn's *Rondo*.

> *Traits that Evoke the Classical Aesthetic*
>
> *Clarity of Form*. The form of both works is always clearly presented. Each section has a definite purpose. There is a sense of neatness in the way the composers have used the sonata-allegro and rondo designs.

(continued on next page)

> *Expression within the Boundaries of Restraint.* In both works, one may feel a quality of restraint that keeps dramatic expression within traditional boundaries. Understatement and economy of means also describe this quality.
>
> *A Sense of Tradition.* Both pieces fit into the traditional forms and practices of their day. A classical aesthetic indicates a respect for tradition. Opposite qualities are innovative and revolutionary.

It may be helpful to remember that these are flexible perceptions and should not be considered as absolutes. And we need not stay within the eighteenth century to find the classical aesthetic; this creative approach may be found in other traditions and styles, as the following music suggests.

Listen Hindemith, *Trauermusik* (Funeral Music), last section 3c
Paul Hindemith (1895–1963) was a twentieth-century composer whose approach to music fulfilled the classical aesthetic. This music is the last section of a work composed in memory of King George V of England at his death in 1936. Although there is a sweeping lyricism in this musical conception, it has a pervasive mood of *controlled* intensity. This is one essential aspect of the classical aesthetic: expression within the boundaries of restraint. Also present are the other two characteristics discussed above: *the form is clear,* as is the unmistakable *continuity with tradition.* The excerpt is based on a traditional religious hymn (which many know as *Praise God from Whom All Blessings Flow*). (See additional discussion on page 89.)

Listen John McLaughlin, *Thousand Island Park* 37b
This piece, recorded in 1973, exemplifies the classical aesthetic in several ways. The form is absolutely clear. Moreover, there are only three instruments playing—all acoustic—bass, piano, and guitar, suggesting an economy of means. Finally, compared with most popular music of today, there is an absence of rhythmic drive, another feature that suggests restraint.

Listen The Heath Brothers, *Atherdoc Blues* 35d
As in *Thousand Island Park,* the rhythm of *Atherdoc Blues* (recorded in 1978) is restrained (or in popular terms, "laid back"). Even more basic to the classical aesthetic is the form. The piece is a traditional twelve-bar blues (see page 388). The classical aesthetic is rarely associated with innovation, especially that of form; more often, the composer chooses traditional models. Part of the charm of this piece lies in

the special way the musicians have used a well-known model for a personal statement—a perfect example of *expression within the boundaries of restraint*.

Attributes of the Classical Aesthetic found in Mozart's Symphony, *Haydn's* Rondo, *Hindemith's* Trauermusik, *McLaughlin's* Thousand Island Park, *and Heath Brothers'* Atherdoc Blues

economy of means
sense of restraint
clear, concise form
sense of balance in form and texture
use of traditional model (except the McLaughlin)

The Romantic Aesthetic

The classical aesthetic has a fluid counterpart in what we may call the *romantic aesthetic*. This approach to artistic activity embraces rather contrasting qualities, as the next selection demonstrates.

Listen   John McLaughlin, *Sapphire Bullets of Pure Love* 37a
This very short piece by the same musicians who created *Thousand Island Park* is certainly not characterized by a sense of restraint; on the contrary, it seems far more uninhibited and wild. Interestingly, on the original album, it comes right before *Thousand Island Park*; thus, heard in order, the pieces provide a stark contrast in artistic approach —the unrestrained burst of *Sapphire Bullets of Pure Love* followed by the delicate and restrained *Thousand Island Park*. Listen to both pieces again, this time in order.

Thousand Island Park	*Sapphire Bullets*
controlled	unleashed
delicate	wild
restrained	unrestrained

We can now discern a flexible continuum of artistic approach in which these two related aesthetics—classical and romantic—are juxtaposed. It must be stressed that this comparison is not absolute, yet the concepts have been relevant to artistic activity in many styles and eras.

A common misconception about romanticism stems from its automatic association with romantic love. In the sense that we use the term *romantic* in this book, love is only one of the feelings that may be evoked by the romantic aesthetic. Consider, for example, the blood-and-thunder heroes of old Hollywood movies: the swashbuckling pirate was a romantic figure not only because of his amorous affairs, but even more because of his wildly adventurous escapades, in which danger, courage, and unbounded heroism were the order of the day. *The fact that an emotion has been unleashed is far more important to the romantic aesthetic than the particular character of that emotion.* Let us consider a classic-romantic continuum:

Classical Aesthetic ⟵⟶	*Romantic Aesthetic*
a sense of restraint, order, tradition	a sense of unstrained and often innovative artistic activity
economy of means	extended use of all available resources and often a search for something *new*
form tends to be clear and traditional	form tends to be less clear and more innovative
the composer functions within chosen boundaries of restraint	the composer throws off all restraint and seeks any means of self-expression
traditional form and musical language more important than personal expression	personal expression more important than form and musical language

These are very general, even stereotyped descriptions, yet they do represent the extremes of a discernible artistic environment.

To explore the interplay between the classical and romantic aesthetics, place each of the following statements to the right, left, or somewhere in the middle on the continuum. (Do not approach this exercise expecting exact answers. We are dealing with aesthetic responses which can never be absolutely quantified. Don't actually write the statement, just the number of the statement.) For example, the first statement, "Music is an art of logic, order, and tradition" evokes qualities associated with the classical aesthetic. Therefore, write the number 1 on the left side of the continuum.

1. "Music is an art of logic, order, and tradition."
2. "I . . . call upon your feeling and taste for order and discipline . . ."
3. "I will seize fate by the throat."
4. "Wearing a straw hat, an old grey shirt . . . and gun or guitar in hand, I would set off, not caring where I spent the night . . . I would stop . . . to jot down in my notebook some symphonic idea that had

just occurred to me; always, whatever I did *drinking to the full, the unutterable delight of complete and absolute freedom.*"

5. "Gratuitous excess spoils every substance, every form that it touches."

6. "Less is more."

Classical Aesthetic	*Romantic Aesthetic*

A FLEXIBLE APPROACH

The purpose of using a continuum is not only to show contrasts, but more important, to suggest an *interplay*. This middle ground is especially relevant to the classical–romantic continuum, since these are terms denoting *emphasis* rather than *separation*. For example, you have just heard both approaches in two works by the same composer, John McLaughlin. He even presents them back-to-back, as if to say, "My sense of beauty embraces both these traits." In the final analysis, the characteristics of either the classic or the romantic aesthetic are measurable only in terms of the other (*more* restrained, *less* restrained) and, as these examples suggest, both impulses may flow from the same source.

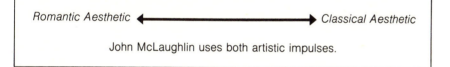

John McLaughlin uses both artistic impulses.

Another possible representation of this interplay appears in the following diagram. Here, the continuum suggests an emphasis on the romantic aesthetic, but with some elements from the classical. (The piece is *The Childhood of Christ* by Hector Berlioz, a composer discussed on pages 260–87).

A Representation of Berlioz's *The Childhood of Christ*

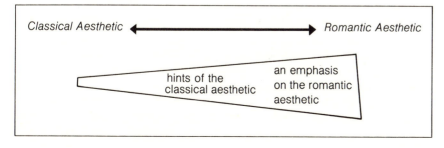

These responses may vary, depending on the cultural filters of the listener. To many musicians of the early nineteenth century, Mozart's *Symphony No. 40* fulfilled the romantic aesthetic.

The Early-Nineteenth-Century Response to Mozart's *Symphony No. 40*

Classical Aesthetic ◄──────────────────────────► Romantic Aesthetic

Mozart
Symphony No. 40

To many musicians of the twentieth century, however, the *same* symphony is perceived clearly within the classical aesthetic.

Classical Aesthetic ◄──────────────────────────► Romantic Aesthetic

Mozart
Symphony No. 40

The Classical Era

In the preceding section, the classical and romantic aesthetics were discussed as artistic tendencies in various eras. Both approaches may be found in any musical culture. However, at certain times, one or the other has been so predominant that historians have used the aesthetic term to characterize the style and spirit of the entire period. Whenever an entire group of artists works with the same basic models, and when tradition, not innovation, is the spirit of the day, a classical phase of creative activity exists. Thus, we may speak of a classical era in Greek drama (fifth century B.C.) or a classical revival in French and English architecture (eighteenth century). Closer to home, the decade of the '50s became known as the era of classic rock and roll, a time when a lean, unself-conscious style expressed in traditional forms lay the foundation for later developments.

Another such period is the Classical era of European notated music. During this time (roughly 1750–1825), a group of composers (including Mozart, Haydn, and, to some degree, Beethoven) wrote music in a style that shared certain traits exemplifying the classical spirit. Among these characteristics are the following:

1. The use of the sonata-symphony group as main genres.
2. The use of the sonata-allegro form as a central element in the musical language. (You will remember from the discussion of the Mozart symphony that balance, proportion, and clarity of form were essential qualities of this design.)
3. A quality of expression within the boundaries of restraint. (This characteristic is especially true of Mozart and Haydn. Beethoven will present a special case in this respect.) Even when the composer is at his most lyrical, there is always a pervasive sense of control. Musical style still reflected the calm, rational qualities of the Age of Reason.

As has been amply demonstrated above, the classical aesthetic transcends chronological time. Thus, it is not surprising to encounter an artistic movement called *neoclassicism* (new classicism) in the twentieth century. Hindemith's *Trauermusik* 3c is a twentieth-century *neoclassical* work.

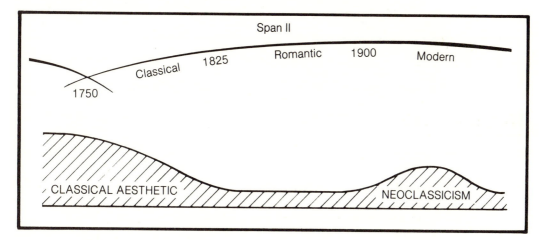

The shaded portion of the diagram above represents, in a general way, the life of the classical aesthetic since 1750. Notice that it does not disappear during the Romantic era, but continues as a distinct, though deemphasized, artistic trait.

The Romantic Era

The romantic aesthetic began to dominate the music culture of Europe early in the nineteenth century. This did not happen overnight. There was no announcement on January 1, 1825, that all composers would hereafter shift to a romantic style. The seeds of romanticism had always been present in the Classical era and were already flowering in the late works of Mozart. This gradual shift might be represented in the following manner:

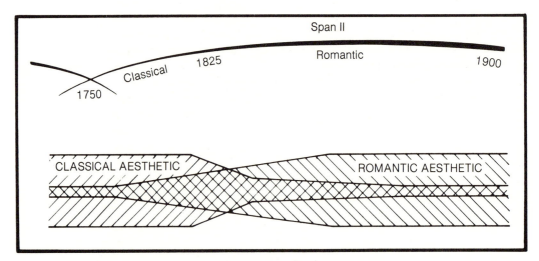

THE CLASSICAL AESTHETIC   A broad and flexible approach to art which includes some or all of the following: expression within the boundaries of restraint, clarity of form, economy of means, and the use of traditional genres and forms. This aesthetic is not limited to any one era of artistic activity.

THE ROMANTIC AESTHETIC   A broad and flexible approach to art which includes some or all of the following: unrestrained expression, the sense that the artist's *persona* dominates all aspects of creation. This aesthetic is not limited to any one era of artistic activity.

THE CLASSICAL–ROMANTIC CONTINUUM   The fluid relationship between these two aesthetics which allows one to consider them as related. The music of a particular composer, for example, may simultaneously reflect both classical and romantic qualities.

THE CLASSICAL ERA   A style period in the European notated tradition which occurred approximately from 1750 to 1825. During this time, several prominent composers created music with similar traits which fulfill the classical aesthetic.

THE ROMANTIC ERA   A style period in the European notated tradition from approximately 1825 to 1900. During this era, many composers created music that reflected the romantic aesthetic.

AFTERTHOUGHT

With this chapter, we have entered the second great span of the European notated tradition. Two vital cultural energies—classicism and romanticism—have been described, not as opposites, but as related aesthetics which may affect, in a general way, the creation of music (as well as the other arts). Classicism and romanticism are qualities that are always present in a culture. However, there are periods when one or the other is more emphasized. Such was the case in the Classical era of European music (1750–1825), the period upon which this chapter has concentrated. The composer we have studied from this period is Mozart. As proof of the relationship between classicism and romanticism, we have taken note that Mozart's late works (the *Fortieth Symphony* and *The Magic Flute*, for example) have qualities that clearly point toward romanticism, the era of European music that is on the horizon (beginning around 1825). All this flexibility and overlapping between the classical and romantic aesthetics strongly suggests that the various musical styles bearing these names often have more similarities than differences.

Another concern of this chapter has been the sonata-symphony group, related genres whose continued use represents one of the most important strands uniting the musical practices of the Classical, Romantic, and, to some extent, the Modern era. An important procedure utilized in many works of the sonata-symphony group is the sonata principle, with its resulting design, sonata-allegro form. With the onset of this tradition in the middle of the eighteenth century, two important differences from music of earliest times (Span I) begin to manifest themselves: 1) Music created with the sonata principle is rooted in tonal and often thematic *conflict*, expressed in purely musical terms. This conflict creates tension and forward potential, which is finally resolved. This kind of musical design, which leads the listener through a long-range journey of stable and unstable musical experiences, was, for the most part, unknown in Span I. 2) The symphonies, concertos, sonatas, etc. by composers like Mozart and Haydn ushered in a new age of instrumental music.

QUESTIONS

For the following questions, find any false statement(s) and correct them by changing the word(s) in italics. More than one statement may be false; all the statements may be true.

1. The sonata principle

   (a) is rooted in tonal *conflict*.

   (b) often presents two themes in *the same key*.

   (c) is rooted in *tonality*.

   (d) works because of the creation of an *imbalance*.

2. The transition section

    (a) *modulates* to a new tonal center.

    (b) has *a definite* tonal center of its own.

    (c) creates an *inactive and stable* feeling.

    (d) *lessens* forward potential.

3. The first closing section

    (a) *sums up* the action so far.

    (b) brings the music to a *final* rest.

    (c) is *in the home* key.

    (d) follows the *transition*.

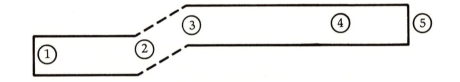

4. Concerning the diagram of an exposition above:

    (a) ① and ③ indicate the position of *Themes I and II*.

    (b) ② indicates the *transition*.

    (c) ④ indicates the *closing section*.

    (d) ⑤ indicates a place in the music where the listener most likely feels a need for *more* musical action.

5. Concerning sonata-allegro form:

    (a) Like all musical forms, it is perceived at simultaneous *short- and long-range* levels of awareness.

    (b) The process that sets this form in motion is the *sonata principle*.

    (c) It is rooted in the *modal system*.

    (d) It derives much of its compositional energy from the perception of *balance*.

6. Concerning the development section:

    (a) It creates a very *stable* feeling.

(b) It *decreases* forward potential.

(c) It may explore musical ideas drawn from the *exposition*.

(d) It *is* in the home key.

7. Concerning the recapitulation section:

   (a) It *resolves* the conflict set in motion by the sonata principle.

   (b) Theme I sounds in *a new key*.

   (c) Theme II sounds in *the home key*.

   (d) Like the *exposition*, it may have a *closing section*.

8. Concerning sonata-allegro form as an example of musical form in general:

   (a) It demonstrates the *importance* of models in musical culture.

   (b) It suggests the *rigidity* of such models.

   (c) It demonstrates that form grows out of a *creative process*.

   (d) It demonstrates that *tonality* may play an important role in the perception of form.

9. Concerning the classical and romantic aesthetics:

   (a) They are *definitely* artistic absolutes.

   (b) They *are not* related.

   (c) They are attitudes which are found in *many* style periods.

   (d) They relate *not only* to music but to other arts as well.

10. Concerning the classical and romantic aesthetics:

    (a) They may be perceived *differently* by various individuals.

    (b) The relative perception of these attitudes may *change* in different eras.

    (c) They form a continuum which may be used to demonstrate their *isolation*.

    (d) Aspects of both aesthetics are *never* found in the same work.

11. The classical aesthetic

    (a) suggests expression *within* the boundaries of restraint.

    (b) suggests a sense of *tradition*.

(c) suggests the use of *clear* form.

(d) *is limited* to "serious" music.

12. The romantic aesthetic

   (a) suggests that expression should have *no restraints*.

   (b) suggests that tradition is *more important* than immediate artistic impulse.

   (c) is *exclusively* related to love.

   (d) emphasizes the role of the *individual* in art.

13. Concerning the Classical era:

   (a) It occurred *exactly* from 1750 to 1825.

   (b) It was the *first* style period in Span II.

   (c) It is followed by the *Romantic* era.

   (d) It was preceded by the *Renaissance* era.

9

Beethoven

Beethoven, Symphony No. 5

Beethoven's *Fifth Symphony* is probably the most famous symphony ever composed. Its direct appeal to so many listeners, on so many different levels, is a primary reason why this great work has remained popular for so long. Before listening, consider these general characteristics:

1. *Motivic unity*. In this symphony, the same rhythmic motive is used in various guises in each movement. Heard in the opening moments of the work, the motive may be characterized as:
   short-short-short-long
   The continual reappearance of this motive creates a powerful unity of melody and rhythm.
2. *Clarity of form*. Beethoven's long-range designs are supercharged with clarity, logic, and a heightened dramatic sense, expressed through the sonata-allegro principle.

Listen Beethoven, *Symphony No. 5*

FIRST MOVEMENT
This movement is in clear-cut sonata-allegro form. It opens with Theme I based solely on the characteristic motive (*s-s-s-l*). This is soon followed by Theme II, which, for a short time, provides a relaxed contrast. The movement develops with urgency and precision, its melodic material limited to these two themes but continually dominated by the opening motive. Unlike many opening movements in sonata-allegro form, this one seems compressed; the sections do not unfold in a leisurely manner, but rather suddenly, with a sense of drama, as if the composer were winding up a spring. At the end of the movement, the listener is left with an unresolved feeling of tension.

237

SECOND MOVEMENT

The listener comes to the second movement with a tremendous sense of forward potential, so that the opening of the movement, with its slower, more lyrical theme, creates a state of suspended dramatic action. Although this is a more relaxed musical environment, some of the powerful energy of the first movement is present, waiting to explode; before long, it does. The theme is soon transformed into a louder, heroic statement, the *s-s-s-l* rhythm supporting its triumphant rising melody. These two sections, the original gentle theme and the loud heroic transformation of the theme, create a pattern we may designate as *AB*:

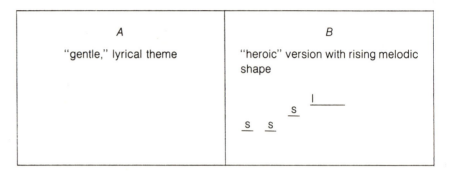

The movement then unfolds as a set of *variations*, based, for the most part, on part *A*. Each time *A* returns, Beethoven ingeniously creates a new variant. Each *A* section, except for one, is followed by the *B* section. The form is a type of *theme and variations*. The *B* section does not undergo the same intense variation process, but rather serves as a climax to each new version of *A*.

A	B	A¹	B	A²	A³	B	A⁴
		Variation 1		Variation 2	Variation 3		Variation 4

THIRD MOVEMENT

Following the traditional symphonic plan, the third movement is dance-derived. Beethoven and his successors usually composed a *scherzo* in place of the *minuet*, the traditional third movement of Haydn and Mozart. Like the minuet, the scherzo is dancelike and often "in three"; however, it tends to be faster and much more lively. The beginning of this movement reveals a similarity to the second—a subdued first section followed by a heroic second theme.

The first theme (*a* in the diagram below) is played by the low strings (cellos and basses). It is a type of melody we have encountered in Mozart, a "rocket theme" (see page 214). But unlike Mozart's rather explosive melody, Beethoven's theme is soft and mysterious. After two phrases of *a*, we hear a sudden, double-forte (*ff*) heroic theme *b*, another restatement of the *s-s-s-l* motive.

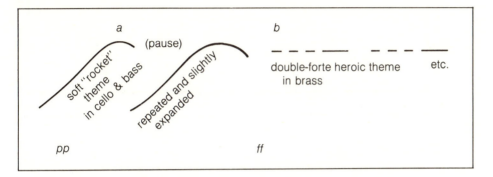

As he did in the second movement, Beethoven again juxtaposes a soft, lyrical theme with a loud, heroic one. With these two themes, Beethoven creates the first long section of the Scherzo, as shown in the diagram below.

Following the traditional form of the scherzo/minuet, we can now expect the trio (see page 213). Beethoven begins this trio with a dancing melody in the low strings in a significantly faster rhythm than the opening. The trio theme is treated polyphonically, each successive entry adding more weight and complexity until the mega-phrase self-destructs in a climactic cadence.

The opening section eventually comes back, but there is an extraordinary turn of events. Beethoven has conditioned us to expect the dramatic juxtaposition of the soft rocket theme *a* and the loud heroic theme *b*. We do hear theme *a* according to plan, but now the unexpected: the heroic theme is played *softly* and by the strings *pizzicato* (plucking instead of bowing). The intention of this sudden dramatic gesture soon becomes clear: it sets the stage for the triumphant finale, whose impact would have otherwise been diffused.

One further surprise, and a startling one for the times: there is no break between the third and fourth movements. They are joined by a *bridge* (a connective passage) which transforms the mood of the Scherzo, leading us into the opening of the Finale.

240

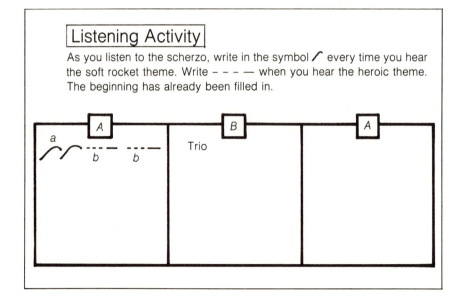

Listening Activity

As you listen to the scherzo, write in the symbol ⌒ every time you hear the soft rocket theme. Write – – – — when you hear the heroic theme. The beginning has already been filled in.

FOURTH MOVEMENT

A striking feature of the Finale is the way the opening theme resolves some of the tension created in the opening notes of the symphony.

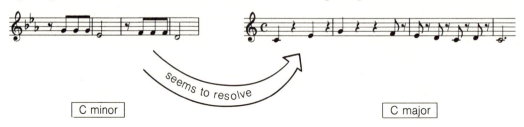

Opening Theme of First Movement   Opening Theme of Last Movement

C minor   *seems to resolve*   C major

This is not accidental. Beethoven was a master of long-range design. He has taken the listener on a thematic journey, transforming a basic melodic idea in each movement, until we are brought inevitably and logically to this moment. The movement races forward with a powerful sense of urgency. About halfway through, we are once again jolted by the unexpected: the heroic theme of the third movement sounds again in its pizzicato version. As it did before, it provides a dramatic shift of focus, which proves to be only temporary. The faster-paced finale theme returns, and the symphony ends with a stubborn, forceful repetition of the tonic chord. It is only now that the accumulated tension is resolved.

SCHERZO   A dance-derived movement developed by Beethoven to replace the Minuet in the sonata-symphony group. Like its predecessor, the minuet and trio, the form of this movement is often:

A   B   A
Scherzo   Trio   Scherzo

Later composers also wrote scherzos as independent compositions.

THEME AND VARIATIONS   A genre in which a melody undergoes various changes of musical detail while retaining its basic shape.

BRIDGE (TRANSITION)   In musical form, a passage which leads from one section to another. (In contemporary popular music, the term *bridge* often refers to a contrasting *B* section.)

A COMPARISON: MOZART'S *FORTIETH SYMPHONY* AND BEETHOVEN'S *FIFTH SYMPHONY*

Comparing these two symphonies can be instructive on several levels. First of all, each work is brought into sharper focus. Secondly, the comparison may animate the changing character of nineteenth-century music in Europe, an evolution in which Beethoven played an important role.

Similarities	*Differences*
Both works use the sonata-symphony format.	Beethoven adds several innovations (joining the third and fourth movements or using a section from one movement in the middle of another, for example).

Mozart's *Fortieth*   Beethoven's *Fifth*

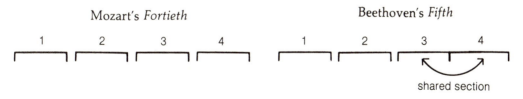

shared section

Both works exhibit clarity of form.	Beethoven's form is more experimental.
Both use the sonata principle, rooted in tonal contrast and a sense of balance and proportion.	In Mozart's piece, these characteristics are handled with classical restraint. By comparison, Beethoven emphasizes the dramatic elements to a much greater degree.

BEETHOVEN'S *FIFTH SYMPHONY* ON
THE CLASSICAL-ROMANTIC CONTINUUM

Consider some of these general descriptions of Beethoven's work in the following context:

Classical Aesthetic	Romantic Aesthetic
clarity of form	a definite feeling that personality dominates form
the use of traditional designs: sonata-allegro and traditional musical language	no sense of restraint; qualities of yearning and searching
emphasis on order and logic	emphasis on freedom and innovation

Beethoven's symphony sits comfortably on both sides of the continuum. There are several valid reasons for this, all important to this study:

1. Beethoven was a unique figure in the history of music. His style may be perceived at various levels, and, as is often the case with genius, descriptions and categorizations only hint at the complete musical reality.
2. As stated before, one must be flexible in assigning aesthetic labels to music.
3. The classical and romantic aesthetics may coexist in the same work.
4. Beethoven's music is a bridge between the late-eighteenth-century Classical and the nineteenth-century Romantic traditions.

Ludwig van Beethoven

If somehow all the known facts about Beethoven were lost, and only his music remained for future generations, one might truthfully say "This is enough." For Beethoven's music communicates a complete world of ideas and feelings in the deepest sense. Without a shred of biographical data or a single page of commentary (like this one), without one of the countless Beethoven anecdotes, the listener can know the man. What was central to Beethoven was expressed in his music in ways that changed the face of art itself.

EARLY LIFE AND PERSONALITY

Beethoven (1770–1827), like Mozart, was born into a family of professional musicians. Both his father and grandfather pursued musical careers, evi-

An engraving of the young Beethoven.

dently without much distinction. Beethoven's childhood was as crucial to his musical development as Mozart's, but in a very different and tragic manner. Mozart's father was a strong, disciplined, loving man, a model of propriety and success. The environment that he carefully created for the young Mozart was very secure (though in the long run it had certain adverse affects). Beethoven's childhood emerges dimly as a dark, troubled period. His father was, among other things, a drunkard, a cheat, and on occasions the local informer. According to later accounts, Beethoven was a withdrawn child and rarely spoke. He was uninterested in school and had few friends. He was often poorly dressed and slovenly. The young Ludwig seems to have been happiest when left alone, and when he could withdraw into his own private world of music.

By the age of twelve, Beethoven had found employment as a professional court musician. At his mother's death four years later, the young Beethoven became head of the family, a responsibility long abandoned by his unreliable father. Beethoven seems to have been the victim of a love-hate relationship with his parent, a trauma destined to affect his later involvements with people. These involvements were characterized by a period of intense warmth leading to an inevitable rupture, brought about by Beethoven. In modern psychological terms, Beethoven continued to reenact the various tensions and longings of his childhood. His personal life was troubled, turbulent, and some might even say unstable. While no one can quantify the mystery of artistic creation, it seems that this early turbulence

Beethoven four years before his death, in a painting by Ferdinand Georg Waldmüller.

was an essential element in Beethoven's personal and musical makeup. Many of his works encode some type of struggle represented in purely musical terms. A sense of searching, whether it be the structural high point of a sonata-allegro form or a mysterious, spiritual transcendence, seems to be present in much of his music.

Beethoven became known as one of the great pianists and improvisers of the day. Many members of the Viennese aristocracy vied for the privilege of being his patron. They took him into their homes and showered him with money and adoration. In an age of rigid social stratification, he enjoyed an extraordinary degree of acceptance from the upper classes. Throughout much of his life, Beethoven, perhaps fulfilling some strange personal fantasy, encouraged the widely circulated stories that he was the illegitimate son of the king of Prussia. His curious relationship with the Viennese nobility—an uncomfortable mixture of contempt and dependency—remains a prophetic sign of the shifting social mores of his time.

A NEW BREED OF MUSICIAN

Beethoven's musical talent was overwhelming. It was common to hear sobs from the audience during one of his rhapsodic improvisations at the piano. On the strength of his early works, he was generally acknowledged to be the successor to Mozart. But he brought a new dimension to music that many conservative listeners found disturbing. In both his playing and his compositions there was a powerful unleashing of physical energy, a quality unlike anything heard before.

He was the first of a new breed. Traditionally a musician, no matter how talented or famous, was nothing more than a valuable servant. Haydn, for example, whose fame had spread throughout Europe, reported daily to his employer, Count Esterházy, for instructions. He always appeared promptly at the designated hour, dressed neatly in a servant's uniform. When dinner was served, Haydn was to be found in the kitchen with the other servants, not in the dining room.

In a real sense, Haydn's music reflects the order and restraint that characterized his social position. The entire situation was very neat. Now if there was ever a word that doesn't apply to Beethoven, it is *neat*. His personality, his appearance, his behavior, his very being personified the opposite of the musician-as-respectful-servant image. Beethoven was arrogant, demanding, and proud. He often acted and looked like a wild man—ill-mannered, sloppy, and boisterous. Goethe, the famous poet, said of our strange hero, "His talent amazed me; unfortunately he is an utterly untamed personality."* When the Viennese aristocrats sat down to dinner after listening to him play, Beethoven would storm out if he found himself seated anywhere but at the main table.

BEETHOVEN'S MUSICAL STYLE

The word *neat* doesn't fit Beethoven's music either. Like Mozart and Haydn, his art was firmly rooted in the Classical tradition, in which the various procedures of the sonata principle are basic (see page 207). But Beethoven used this language with a strongly personal style that shocked many listeners. The neat logic of Mozart and Haydn became a fierce logic for Beethoven, who continually probed the limits to which the standard procedures could be taken. His treatment of the symphony is one example of this exploration of the potentials of traditional form. The chart below compares the general outlines and proportions of his nine symphonies.

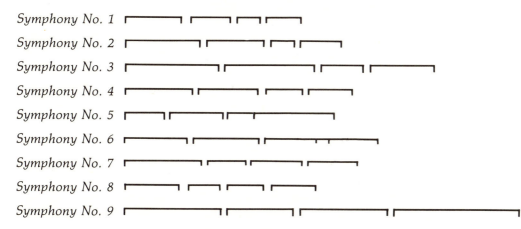

*Goethe, letter to Zelter, quoted in George Marek, *Beethoven, Biography of a Genius* (New York, 1969), p. 444.

The outer shape of these symphonies hints at the experimentation that goes on inside of them: in the *Fifth Symphony* he compressed the first movement; in the third and ninth he stretched out the entire work. He was rarely content simply to recreate traditional models; he was always testing, exploring. Unlike Mozart, who for the most part would write the final version of a piece in the first draft, Beethoven filled many pages with different versions of the same theme. He sometimes worked on ideas for years until they reached their final form. Beethoven's compositional procedures, like his personality, reflected a continuous struggle and restlessness. (Beethoven frequently changed his lodging, by the way. No sooner would he settle in a new apartment than off he would go to find another.) The restless quality in his music is brought into sharper focus when we compare his work with Mozart's. The drama of a Mozart sonata-allegro movement unfolds like a neatly told story: the listener always knows what the characters are going to do. Beethoven's sonata-allegro dramas are more like monumental epics: although we know the end of the story, the characters' actions are less predictable. This is not to suggest that Beethoven had a story line in mind when composing symphonic music; but certain qualities in his music have always lent themselves to extramusical interpretation. Great art never exists in one plane only and can never be fully described in absolute terms.

BEETHOVEN'S DEAFNESS

One of the most tragic ironies ever visited upon a musician was destined to shape most of Beethoven's adult life. By the age of thirty, he was becoming deaf. As if he were the victim of some terrible cosmic joke, this already-troubled genius was thrown into even darker regions. Beethoven recorded some of his agony in a letter to his brothers, a letter which was never delivered and only surfaced at his death:

> . . . what a humiliation for me when someone standing next to me heard a flute in the distance and I *heard nothing*, or someone heard a *shepherd singing* and again I heard nothing. Such incidents drove me almost to despair, a little more of that and I would have ended my life —it was only *my art* that held me back. Ah, it seemed to me impossible to leave the world until I had brought forth all that I felt was within me . . .*

It seems quite certain that this handicap became a major influence on Beethoven's musical life. As he grew older, his hearing became worse. Once one of the greatest pianists of Europe, he could no longer perform. Increasingly all his energies turned to expressing his inner musical universe. Beethoven, like many other musicians, was able to hear the many sounds

*Thayer, *Life of Beethoven*, rev. and ed. by E. Forbes (Princeton, 1967), I, pp. 304–06.

and timbres of his music in his head, much in the same way an artist can visualize a picture before it is painted. He became more and more isolated from society; many of his most disagreeable qualities—arrogance, alienation, egomania—intensified. But though it was often difficult, his friends stood loyally at his side.

THE THREE STYLE PERIODS

Beethoven's works fall into *three style periods*; the *first style period* includes his early music, up to 1803. In these works, Beethoven's close relationship to the Classical style of Mozart and Haydn is especially clear. Although there are definite hints of the more radical style to come, the Viennese public were able to accept these works, which conformed to the taste of the day.

The *second style period* dates from 1803 to about 1816. With the performance of his *Third Symphony*, the "Eroica," Beethoven put the world on notice that it was in for something quite new. This symphony, which today is considered one of the most logically wrought of all musical creations, was ahead of its time for many listeners. One reviewer wrote that it "loses itself in lawlessness" and described certain passages as "glaring and bizarre." But Beethoven's new language communicated something far too powerful to be influenced in the slightest by critical disapproval. Much of the music of Beethoven's second style period has a heroic quality. Epic, sweeping themes, often accompanied by bold sonorous harmonies, abound (as, for example, in the *Fifth Symphony*). His use of the orchestra explored a new world of texture and sound. Where Mozart had used finesse and subtlety, Beethoven treated orchestral sonority as an artist might use primary colors to support and define structure. A heroic chorale may sound in the brass, only to be echoed by the strings. Timpani (orchestral drums) play solo motives with a dramatic power previously unknown in "serious" music. Many of Beethoven's most popular works were written during this second period.

As Beethoven neared the end of his life, his musical style took yet another turn. Alienated from the world by his deafness and his bizarre personality, he created during the *third style period* (c. 1816–1827) a series of remarkable, radical, and visionary works. His musical language became quite mysterious and often seemed to involve a private musical symbolism. His forms became even more personalized and exploratory. Among these late works are two of his greatest and most universal masterpieces, the *Missa solemnis* and the *Ninth Symphony*.

THE BEETHOVEN CULT

As no one before in the European musical culture, Beethoven seems to have unleashed a powerful, even mythical force with his music. Consider the reaction of the French composer Jean François Lesueur to the *Fifth Symphony*, as recorded in the memoirs of his student Berlioz:

I found him [Lesueur] in a corridor, striding along with flushed face. "Well, master?" "Ouf! Let me get out. I must have some air. It's amazing! Wonderful!"*

The next day, Berlioz came to see his teacher to discuss the symphony. Although Lesueur acknowledged Beethoven's greatness, he was disturbed by the music. "All the same, music like that ought not to be written," he said. Although the accuracy of this account may be in question owing to Berlioz's tendency to overstate, it does suggest the powerful effect that Beethoven's music had on musicians and public alike. Beethoven's music brought to Europe and the world a new artistic vision. On the strength and implications of this vision, the Beethoven cult would grow. In the years following his death, everyone who had had some contact with Beethoven added his or her "eyewitness" accounts to the legend. Many were outright fabrications in the romantic manner of the day. On the one hand, this presents a problem to the historian trying to separate fact from fiction; but, on the other, the very existence of these fabrications provides us with a profound insight into human nature. When considering the broader perspective, we are encountering a society seeking to flesh out and canonize the memory of Beethoven's life and music. When a culture mythologizes a human being, it is usually because he or she has evoked an extraordinary and deeply centered response. Consider this romanticized account of Beethoven's death, written long after the event:

. . . There came a flash of lightning accompanied by a violet clap of thunder, which garishly illuminated the death-chamber. . . . After this unexpected phenomenon of nature, which startled me greatly, Beethoven opened his eyes, lifted his right hand and looked up for several seconds with his fist clenched and a very serious, threatening expression as if he wanted to say . . . I defy you . . . When he let the raised hand sink to the bed, his eyes closed half-way. My right hand was under his head, my left rested on his breast. Not another breath, not a heartbeat more! The genius of the great master of tones fled from this world of delusion into the realm of truth!—I pressed down the half-open eyelids of the dead man, kissed them, then his forehead, mouth and hands.—At my request Frau van Beethoven [his sister-in-law] cut a lock of hair from his head and handed it to me as a sacred souvenir of Beethoven's last hour.**

To Beethoven's followers, then, his body and image became sacred, like that of a god or a king! This was part of a romantic trend of the nineteenth

*The Memoirs of Hector Berlioz, ed. and trans. by David Cairns (New York, 1975), p. 105.
**Letter of Anselm Hüttenbrenner, dated August 20, 1860, quoted in Thayer, pp. 1050–51.

century we may call "art as religion" or the "cult of the artist." Beethoven was not the sole cause of this artistic hero-worship, but he became its proto- type—a model still powerful in our own time.

Beethoven: Additional Listening

FIRST STYLE PERIOD

> *Symphony No. 1*
> *"Pathetique" Sonata*, Op. 13*
> *Quartet in G major*, Op. 18

SECOND STYLE PERIOD

> *Symphonies No. 3 ("Eroica"), No. 6 ("Pastoral"), and No. 7*
> *Violin Concerto*
> *Piano Concerto Nos. 4 and 5 ("The Emperor")*
> *"Moonlight" Sonata*, Op. 27
> *"Waldstein" Sonata*, Op. 53
> *"Appassionata" Sonata*, Op. 57

THIRD STYLE PERIOD

> *Missa solemnis*
> *Symphony No. 9 ("Choral")*

The Beethoven Legacy

The Beethoven aftershock nourished Western culture with such potency that it helped to change the social fabric in which the creative artist is related to the world. In a symbolic way, his journey was to be imitated, time and time again, throughout the nineteenth century and in some cases well into the twentieth. The following interrelated discussions document this continuing Beethoven presence.

BEETHOVEN'S MUSICAL INFLUENCE

Beethoven's music had a profound and continuing influence on the com- posers who followed him. It is interesting that composers of quite different stylistic persuasions maintained that their art had stemmed from Beethoven. Nowhere was this influence more manifest than in later symphonies. Any new symphony was measured against Beethoven's nine. Johannes Brahms, a composer of the second half of the nineteenth century, who didn't write his first symphony until late in his career, said, "You have no idea how it

---

*Op. is the abbreviation for *opus* (plural *Opp.* or *opera*), meaning "work." The term is often used to catalogue a composer's work. It is especially useful in cases where this output is substantial.

feels to hear behind you the footsteps of a giant like Beethoven." It is quite easy to sense Beethoven's presence in symphonies that span a period of more than a century after his death. This statement may be confirmed by comparing the openings of any of the following symphonies with that of Beethoven's *Ninth*:

The Beethoven Presence in Later Symphonies

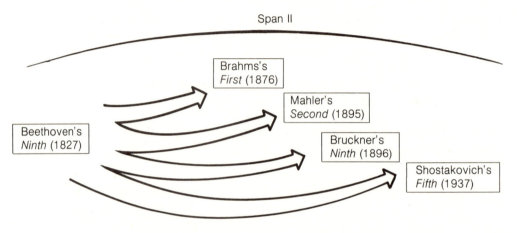

Beethoven's influence may be sensed at various levels. Perhaps the most vital influence lies in subsequent attempts to recreate the sense of power and symbolic meaning that Beethoven had brought to his symphonic works. The image of the symphony could not be divorced from Beethovenian epic drama and struggle. Symphonies had become serious business.

BEETHOVEN'S ACCELERATED STYLISTIC DEVELOPMENT

"He had started as a composer in the Classic tradition and ended up a composer beyond time and space, using a language he himself had forged: a language compressed, cryptic, and explosive, expressed in forms of his own devising."*

If we listen to the opening measures of Beethoven's *First* and *Ninth Symphonies*, we experience a stylistic evolution that is at once profound and prophetic. Other composers had changed stylistically during their lives, but none to this extent! By the end of his career, Beethoven's journey had brought him to a place that defies neat stylistic description and chronological categorization. This evolution, rooted in a personal search for the ultimate, became a potent cultural image for the nineteenth and twentieth

*Harold Schonberg, *Lives of the Great Composers*, rev. ed. (New York, 1981), p. 119.

centuries. Here again, Beethoven was not solely responsible for this trend; it paralleled the general flow of art and society. His musical evolution was a preview of the stylistic changes that began to dominate both individual creation and art in general. There are many parallels in Beethoven's personal journey to be found in our time (among them the career of the singer-composer Joni Mitchell; see pages 428–36).

BEETHOVEN AS HUMANIST

Beethoven was the first of the great composers to address himself to all humanity. In the *Ninth Symphony*, composed during a politically repressive period, Beethoven set Schiller's *Ode to Joy*, containing such revolutionary lines as:

Alle Menschen werden Brüder . . .	All men are brothers . . .
Seid umschlungen, Millionen!	O ye millions, embrace ye
Diesen Kuss der ganzen Welt!	With a kiss for all the world!

Today, we take the concept of brotherhood for granted, but this was not the case in nineteenth-century Europe. In the broad cultural sense, Beethoven—both the man and his music—is symbolic of the struggle for democracy and brotherhood, the main current in world history since the American and French revolutions. How tragic the promise of the *Ninth* may seem in view of the terrible destruction that has haunted the twentieth century. This idea is dramatically presented in *A Clockwork Orange*,* in which musical distortion of the *Ninth Symphony* symbolizes some of the frightful forces that have been let loose in the modern world.

Beethoven's eloquent appeal to humankind is even more moving when we consider its source: Beethoven was not exactly a "nice" person. He was obstinate, spoiled, arrogant, and inconsiderate. But when one enters his life through his letters, the accounts of his friends, and above all, his music, a touchingly human portrait emerges. At heart, Beethoven was childlike and honest. The romantic image of his life and art is, to a certain extent, a valid ideal. No matter how scientific one tries to be, it would be difficult not to respond to the account of Beethoven at the performance of his *Ninth Symphony*: standing on the stage unable to conduct, unable to hear the applause, as the world first heard one of its most beautiful and universal "songs"—music born from this deaf, sad man.

BEETHOVEN BEYOND STYLE

Was Beethoven a composer of the Classical or the Romantic era? This is a question that has elicited different responses from different quarters and reflects the problem of putting definite labels on music. The basic method of

*The book by Anthony Burgess was the basis for Stanley Kubrick's film.

determining the style periods of music history is through the details of musical language. At this level, Beethoven's use of harmony, texture, and sometimes form fall easily within the Classical tradition. After all, Beethoven absorbed this tradition as his living language. And while he extended and developed this musical language, he never really changed the basic materials. If we were to make an analogy with architecture, Mozart, Haydn, and Beethoven used the same "building blocks" joining them—each to the other—in the same manner. To continue the analogy, composers traditionally labeled "Romantic" used different types of building blocks (new types of chords, for example) and joined them together in somewhat new ways. Considered at this short range, Beethoven fits into the Classical style period. But now, let's shift into a longer perspective, that of form. Beethoven used the traditional forms of the Classical period, but created within them a totally new dimension. To return to the analogy with architecture, using the same building blocks, the same technique of joining them together, and the same initial plan, Beethoven erected startling new structures (his long musical forms). The final result was often quite foreign to both the Classical era and the classical aesthetic. In this context, Beethoven's music shifts toward the romantic side of the continuum. One final perspective may be added—that of Beethoven's personality and its relationship to his music. In this regard, Beethoven is the ultimate Romantic—the lone individual from whose emotional life and inner struggle are born grand-scale works in search of life's meaning. To put it simply, at the short-range, detailed level, he may be perceived in the Classical tradition; in the long-range perspective, he is sensed as a Romantic. Seen on the continuum (for example, see page 228) it is clear that Beethoven's world is clearly *beyond* both the classical and romantic labels.

Connections in the Beethoven Discussion

Importance of a basic model in musical tradition.
The flexible development of basic models.
The absorption of a living musical language.
The social position of the composer.
The classical-romantic continuum.
Accelerated stylistic evolution in Span II.

QUESTIONS

For the following questions, find any false statement(s) and correct them by changing the word(s) in italics. More than one statement may be false; all the statements may be true.

1. Concerning Beethoven and Mozart:

   (a) *Both* composers came from families of professional musicians.

   (b) They had *similar* relationships with their fathers.

   (c) *Both men* composed quickly and without much revision.

   (d) Beethoven was much *more assertive* of his rights than Mozart.

2. Concerning Beethoven's childhood:

   (a) It *was* insecure, troubled, and traumatic.

   (b) He *was* a withdrawn child who rarely spoke or played.

   (c) It *most likely* played an important role in the formation of his later musical style.

   (d) He entered professional life *at an early age*.

3. Concerning Beethoven's relationship to the nobility:

   (a) He was often *docile* with them.

   (b) It reflects a *change* in the status of the musician in nineteenth-century European culture.

   (c) He *discouraged* the rumor that he was one of them.

   (d) He sometimes viewed them with *contempt*.

4. Concerning Beethoven's three style periods:

   (a) He was *the first* important composer of Span II to go through a change of such severity.

   (b) This evolution *may have been related* to his growing deafness.

   (c) This stylistic development *is a preview* of normal nineteenth- and twentieth-century artistic life.

   (d) Mozart *went* through a very similar change.

5. Concerning Beethoven's *Fifth Symphony*:

   (a) Its form demonstrates heightened qualities of *clarity and logic*.

   (b) A basic motive is found in *each movement*.

   (c) This motive returns *always in an exact repeat of its original identity*.

   (d) The use of this recurring idea brings a sense of *motivic unity* to the work.

6. Concerning Beethoven's *Fifth Symphony*:

   (a) The first-movement form may be characterized as *leisurely paced*.

   (b) The second-movement form is shaped by the *sonata principle*.

   (c) The third-movement form is called a *theme and variations*.

7. Concerning the comparison between Mozart's *Fortieth Symphony* and Beethoven's *Fifth Symphony*:

   (a) Both use the *sonata-symphony format*.

   (b) Both use the *sonata principle*.

   (c) *Mozart's* form is more experimental.

   (d) *Beethoven's* form includes the joining of two movements.

8. Concerning Beethoven's position on the classical-romantic continuum:

   (a) His music has qualities that fit *both sides*.

   (b) It reflects his role as a transition composer between the *Baroque and Classical* eras.

   (c) It demonstrates the *flexibility* of the classical-romantic concept.

   (d) It demonstrates that the classical-romantic impulse can be found in the *same* artist.

9. Concerning Beethoven's impact on the musical culture:

   (a) Its magnitude was *unprecedented*.

   (b) It became especially apparent in the composition of *fugues*.

   (c) It helped foster the *romantic* view of the artist.

   (d) It furthered the image of *seriousness* in Western notated music.

Romanticism-I

10

Mendelssohn, *Overture to A Midsummer Night's Dream*

Certain pieces of music seem to be magical—they may invoke a special response of wonder and discovery. To the sensibilities of many listeners, the *Overture to A Midsummer Night's Dream* by Felix Mendelssohn is such a work. There are three bits of magic here: first, there is the music, the magic of which you will soon hear. The second concerns an aspect of its creation —it was composed by a seventeen-year-old boy and was immediately recognized as a true masterpiece. The third bit of magic happened two hundred years before Mendelssohn's birth, and a tidy piece of magic it is: *A Midsummer Night's Dream*, the play by William Shakespeare.

Shakespeare lived in Elizabethan England (sixteenth century), a time and place in which late Renaissance culture provided a background for a luxuriant flourishing of the arts. Then, the holiday they called Midsummer's Night had a very special quality. It was, in fact, one of those remnants of the archaic past that survived as folk ritual. On this night people in Elizabethan England celebrated with music, dance, and drama. The special mood surrounding this night, one which Shakespeare was able to capture in his play of make-believe, is described as follows:

> More than any other night in the year, midsummer night suggested enchantment and witchcraft, something Shakespeare has superbly embodied in his fairy world. To an Elizabethan audience, moreover, the play's title would have immediately called to mind the so-called "midsummer madness," which was a state of mind marked by a heightened readiness to believe in the delusions of the imagination that were thought to befall the minds of men after days of great summer heat.*

Then, as now, this drama reveals a world in which sound and motion rule the senses. The play is performed with background music, as well as

*Wolfgang Clemen in an introduction to the Signet edition of the play (New York, 1963), p. xxiv.

songs set to Shakespeare's lyrics. But there is also another music—Shakespeare's poetry. And, bringing the ancient unity to full measure, the characters dance in the course of the story. But there is also another dance—the story itself. Characters appear, disappear, only to reappear, their movements choreographed by Shakespeare's plot. The main play interacts with a smaller "play within a play." In modern terms, we could call Shakespeare's creation a "multimedia" production. In this experience, music, dance, and drama—sound, motion, and idea—are so intertwined that one easily forgets distinctions that may hide their unity.

Now, in one of those connections of genius that seem to transcend time and place, we move from Elizabethan England to nineteenth-century Germany. The year was 1828. Germany, like the rest of Europe, was in the sway of a great artistic and cultural movement—*Romanticism*. At its core, Romanticism was a humanistic movement, seeking out and extolling the natural qualities of human life, which had been obscured by the Age of Reason (or so the Romantics believed). Theirs was not a universe built on systematic explanation, but one rooted in nature, feelings, and adventure. Poets and writers led the way, for part of the new Romantic sensibility was a deep involvement with literature. The past had a special magic to the Romantics. They literally devoured Shakespeare, who previously had been considered "little more than a rough-hewn, ill-mannered poet."* Voltaire, one of the architects of the Age of Reason, had called Shakespeare a "drunken savage." This certainly doesn't fit our present-day image of the great English playwright and serves as an interesting commentary on how different cultures respond to the same stimulus. It also suggests the timelessness of romanticism. Clearly, there are romantic qualities in Shakespeare's plays. As Europe entered the nineteenth century, these qualities came into great favor. So, two hundred years after his death, Shakespeare was alive and well (and in translation) in Germany. It was through this deep cultural channel that *A Midsummer Night's Dream* reached Felix Mendelssohn.

There is a sense of enclosure in the play which also may be reflected in the world of Felix Mendelssohn. In the drama, the interplay of the characters, the sounds, the movement, even nature itself seem to be encompassed within theatrical space. The play within a play also adds to this sense of neat containment; contained yet free, the juxtaposition is a delight. This same sense of enclosed space might be used to describe the garden outside the Mendelssohn estate in Berlin. The garden itself, located within a beautiful private park (seven acres of it!), was the center of Felix Mendelssohn's world of music and literature, poetry and art. His was no ordinary childhood, and he was no ordinary child.

Mendelssohn (1809–47) was born into a world that was carefully controlled by his parents, secure, structured, and disciplined, but where creative expression was normal, encouraged, and expected. From a very

*George Marek, *Beethoven, Biography of a Genius* (New York, 1969), p. 147.

Felix Mendelssohn at age twelve, in a drawing by Wilhelm Hensel, who later became Mendelssohn's brother-in-law).

This portrait of the adult Mendelssohn suggests a formal quality that can also be sensed in his music.

early age he rose each day at 5 A.M. to begin music, language, painting, literature, and other studies. The Mendelssohn home was a center for the intellectual-artistic elite of Berlin. Felix was soon giving concerts at these social gatherings, even conducting his own orchestra (hired by his father). The study of Shakespeare, Goethe, and Beethoven (to name a few) was daily fare for him and his friends. They adopted Shakespeare's world as today's young people may take on life-styles drawn from television and film. In this environment he was inextricably bound to the music, the literature, the ideas, and the feelings of his time. And along with this involvement went the disciplined acquisition of musical skills at the highest professional level. In terms of artistic development, it would be hard to imagine a more perfect environment. This charmed life, like the garden, was a carefully enclosed space, protected and secure. But within these boundaries, both music and nature were wonderfully free. In the summer of 1828, the seventeen-year-old Mendelssohn spent most of his time composing in that garden. He wrote to his sister (who was away at the time), "I've finished two piano pieces there—in A major and E minor—and today or tomorrow I'm going to start dreaming *Midsummer Night's Dream*."

The motion in Shakespeare's play immediately comes alive in Mendelssohn's *Overture*. The opening four chords, which seem to evoke the changing light, introduce a magic world. We hear music which portrays the dancing elfs and spirits, the young lovers, even the "hee-haw" of a donkey (a spell cast on Bottom, one of the characters, transforms his head into that of a donkey). Although the plot is not literally represented by the music, certain features coincide. Mendelssohn described the close of the *Overture* as follows: "After everything has been satisfactorily settled and the principal players have joyfully left the stage, the elves follow them, bless the house and disappear with the dawn. So ends the play, and my overture too."

Listening Activity

Two listening activities are suggested, to be performed either separately or simultaneously:

1. Using the terms *winds*, *brass*, *strings*, and *tutti* (all), indicate the instrumentation of the work as you hear it (you may write more than one term at a time). Bracket them to indicate if they sound together, for example: $\begin{bmatrix} \text{strings} \\ \text{winds} \end{bmatrix}$. Write the instrumentation terms in a horizontal line from left to right, beginning a new line if necessary.

2. Write in any nonmusical images that the music brings to mind. (This is very much in the spirit of this piece.)

Connections in the Mendelssohn Discussion

Artistic activity is often connected to a cultural chain.
The absorption of a living musical language from a culture.
The importance of the ancient unity.

Mendelssohn: Additional Listening

Violin Concerto
Symphony No. 4 ("Italian")
Hebrides Overture
String Octet

Program Music

An important trait of nineteenth-century Romanticism, which you may have experienced in the *Overture to A Midsummer Night's Dream*, is a heightened *interplay of the senses*. Although Mendelssohn represents the world of Shakespeare's play only in sound, his inspiration and conception of the music were directly influenced by an extramusical world. With the title alone, he deliberately encourages the listener to blur distinctions between sight, motion, feelings, and sound. And, as Mendelssohn allowed this interplay in his musical process, we may reexperience our own version of it; the purely musical sound has the capacity to awaken a multitude of life images within us. Because the *Overture to A Midsummer Night's Dream* deals with an extramusical situation, we call it *program music*. In contrast, *absolute music* does not involve life-images and is conceived in purely musical terms.

These terms are by no means mutually exclusive. As usual, we find a pair of concepts that are related in a flexible manner:

Absolute Music ←——————→ *Program Music*	
music as an end in itself	music in an interplay with extra-musical phenomena
form based on abstract designs	form may follow an order of dramatic events, moods, feelings, often adapted from literature
freedom to fully explore musical communication beyond words	titles act as pointers for the imagination, relating music to specific life-rhythms and images

This continuum represents two extremes. As you might suspect, many pieces of music fall somewhere in the middle. For example, although Mendelssohn's *Overture* hints at the events of the play in a general manner, its primary design is sonata-allegro form. Thus Mendelssohn's piece derives energy from both absolute and programmatic traditions.

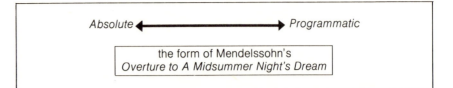

Once again we are in a shifting and flexible environment. One of the most profound shifts is that of the listener's aesthetic sense. Some would prefer to respond to the piece as absolute music, perhaps reflecting a more rational, classical taste. The listener of a more whimsical, romantic persuasion might lean toward the programmatic side, with all its suggestive life-imagery. One's listening preference might vary from day to day according to mood and circumstance. For example, it might be difficult for even the most willing romantic to respond to elves, donkeys, and magic potions in our age of hard-boiled skepticism. Listeners, as well as composers, usually deal with the notion of absolute and program music in a flexible manner.

Berlioz, *Fantastic Symphony*

In 1830, a young, unknown French composer presented to the Paris public an orchestral work which won him immediate recognition. The work was the *Fantastic Symphony (Symphonie fantastique)*. Even before the first notes sounded, the audience must have been intrigued, because Hector Berlioz had published the *program* (or story) describing the dramatic action of the symphony in a newspaper a week before the performance. Like Mendelssohn's *Overture to A Midsummer Night's Dream*, this piece is program music—in fact, we call it a *program symphony*. But Berlioz went much further than Mendelssohn in providing word-imagery for the music. Mendelssohn, after all, had only given his audience a title; everything else was left to their imagination and familiarity with the play. Berlioz wrote a detailed and somewhat sensational scenario, which is generally believed to be autobiographical. There were several versions of this program. The following one was published with the orchestral score. The words are Berlioz's own, except for those in boxes, which are explanatory notes. The symphony is in five movements (they are called *parts* in Berlioz's program); each has a title and description. First, read through the entire story, omitting the boxed comments. The listening instructions will follow.

BERLIOZ'S PROGRAM

The composer's intention has been to develop, insofar as they contain musical possibilities, various situations in the life of an artist. The outline of the instrumental drama, which lacks the help of words, needs to be explained in advance. The following program should thus be considered as the spoken text of an opera, serving to introduce the musical movements, whose character and expression it motivates.

> It is interesting that at the very outset, Berlioz states that the interplay between the drama and the music is essential to the listener's experience. He calls the work an *instrumental drama* and makes a comparison to the genre most dependent on dramatic action—opera.

PART ONE
REVERIES—PASSIONS

The author imagines that a young musician, afflicted with that moral disease that a well-known writer calls the *vague des passions*,* sees for the first time a woman who embodies all the charms of the ideal being he has imagined in his dreams, and he falls desperately in love with her. Through an odd whim, whenever the beloved image appears before the mind's eye of the artist it is linked with a musical thought whose character, passionate but at the same time noble and shy, he finds similar to the one he attributes to his beloved.

This melodic image and the model it reflects pursue him incessantly like a double *idée fixe*.** That is the reason for the constant appearance, in every movement of the symphony, of the melody that begins the first Allegro. The passage from this state of melancholy reverie, interrupted by a few fits of groundless joy, to one of frenzied passion, with its movements of fury, of jealousy, its return of tenderness, its tears, its religious consolations—this is the subject of the first movement.

> Aside from its narrative intent, Berlioz's program introduced a new technique of thematic structure. In this symphony, his beloved is represented by a melody he calls the *idée fixe*. What happens to this theme in the various movements is central to the drama.

PART TWO
A BALL

The artist finds himself in the most varied situations—in the midst of *the tumult of a party*, in the peaceful contemplation of the beauties of nature; but everywhere, in town, in the country, the beloved image appears before him and disturbs his peace of mind.

*Wave of passion.
**Fixed idea or obsession.

> The appearance of the beloved image is signaled by a new version of the *idée fixe* theme in the middle of the movement.

PART THREE
SCENE IN THE COUNTRY

Finding himself one evening in the country, he hears in the distance two shepherds piping a *ranz des vaches** in dialogue. This pastoral duet, the scenery, the quiet rustling of the trees gently brushed by the wind, the hopes he has recently found some reason to entertain—all concur in affording his heart an unaccustomed calm, and in giving a more cheerful color to his ideas. He reflects upon his isolation; he hopes that his loneliness will soon be over.—But what if she were deceiving him!—This mingling of hope and fear, these ideas of happiness disturbed by black presentiments, form the subject of the Adagio. At the end one of the shepherds again takes up the *ranz des vaches*; the other no longer replies.—Distant sound of thunder—loneliness—silence.

> The shepherd's dialogue is achieved by an English horn calling to an oboe, which answers from backstage, as if from a distant hillside. This pastoral mood continues until the *idée fixe* theme reappears, bringing a more turbulent character to the music. Near the end of the movement, we hear the sound of thunder created by the timpani. The movement closes with the English horn once again calling out, but receiving only the thunder of the timpani in reply.

PART FOUR
MARCH TO THE SCAFFOLD

Convinced that his love is unappreciated, the artist poisons himself with opium. The dose of the narcotic, too weak to kill him, plunges him into a sleep accompanied by the most horrible visions. He dreams that he has killed his beloved, that he is condemned and led to the scaffold, and that he is witnessing *his own execution*. The procession moves forward to the sounds of a march that is now sombre and fierce, now brilliant and solemn, in which the muffled noise of heavy steps gives way without transition to the noisiest clamor. At the end of the march the first four measures of the *idée fixe* reappear, like a last thought of love interrupted by the fatal blow.

*Folksong of the Swiss cowherds.

The execution at the end of part four is the most "realistic" representation of dramatic action through music in the work. You will hear the *idée fixe* as the artist's last thought before his death. The fall of the ax is depicted by a sudden chord in the orchestra, followed by a solemn drumroll. This particularly theatrical effect, considered on the absolute–programmatic continuum, is about as far to the right as you can get.

PART FIVE

DREAM OF A WITCHES' SABBATH

He sees himself at the sabbath, in the midst of a frightful troop of ghosts, sorcerers, monsters of every kind, come together for his funeral. Strange noises, groans, bursts of laughter, distant cries which other cries seem to answer. The beloved melody appears again, but it has lost its character of nobility and shyness; it is no more than a dance tune, mean, trivial, and grotesque: it is she, coming to join the sabbath.—A roar of joy at her arrival.—She takes part in the devilish orgy.— Funeral knell, burlesque parody of the *Dies irae, sabbath round-dance.* The sabbath round and the *Dies irae* combined.

A mocking burlesque of the *idée fixe* theme is heard. The *Dies irae* is a Gregorian chant from the Requiem Mass.

| Listen | Berlioz, *Fantastic Symphony*

Now, listen to the music with the story in mind. Read the boxed comments before each movement. The real strength of program music lies in its ability to stimulate the imagination.

PROGRAM SYMPHONY   A symphony influenced by some type of extra-musical idea—for example, a literary plan.

IDÉE FIXE   Berlioz's term for the recurring musical theme representing his beloved in the *Fantastic Symphony*.

AFTERTHOUGHT

The importance of the *Fantastic Symphony* lies not in its story but in its innovative techniques. Among them, we may note the following:

1. *The interplay of sonata-symphony form with a dramatic program.* Despite the narrative elements in its form, the *Fantastic Symphony* is closely related to traditional symphony design. The five-movement plan (instead of the usual four) had already been used by Beethoven in his *Sixth Symphony*. The first movement of the *Fantastic Symphony* actually follows a loosely knit sonata-allegro procedure. The second (*A Ball*) is dance-derived, comparable to the minuet or scherzo. The third movement (*Scene in the Country*) may be compared to the slow, songlike movement of a symphony. The *March to the Scaffold* may be thought of as an additional dance movement, while the *Dream of a Witches' Sabbath* serves as an exciting finale. What Berlioz did, in fact, was to present his drama within an expanded sonata-symphony form.

   This may remind us of two ideas raised in previous discussions: first, *the importance of traditional models to a living language*; and second, *the flexibility of these models in actual use.*

2. *The use of a recurring theme in different movements.* Aside from its dramatic purpose, the use of the *idée fixe* theme in each movement brings a sense of thematic unity to the work. A hint at this procedure was heard in Beethoven's *Fifth Symphony*.

3. *Orchestration.* Berlioz was a superb and imaginative orchestrator. While we may be accustomed today to brilliant orchestral colors and textures like those in the *Fantastic Symphony*, this kind of orchestral display was revolutionary in the 1830s. The entire symphony is filled with dazzling touches of musical-dramatic imagery brought to life, to a great extent, by new orchestral sounds. Berlioz used a much bigger orchestra than had been the custom; he combined instruments to create unusual sonorities and orchestral timbre. We might suggest an analogy between what he did with the orchestra and the advent of color in film. The *Fantastic Symphony* is still considered a model for the student orchestrator, although its secrets cannot be taught or even fathomed in technical terms. As an orchestrator, Berlioz was a genius. The *Fantastic Symphony* became a landmark for composers, demonstrating the possibilities for modern orchestral sound.

BERLIOZ AND ROMANTICISM

Learning the characteristics of a certain stylistic era from a list created "out of the blue" can be very misleading if what one seeks is a basic understanding of how musical styles evolve. After all, composers don't get together and decide that on a certain date they will all change to a new type of harmony or melody to conform with a new style. Such changes usually happen gradually and at a hidden level. No generalizations can capture the rich interaction of an individual artist with the circumstance and ambience of the times which produce a style. However, in the following section, we will seek some insight into this remarkable interaction. Historical style periods come to life through the people that helped create them. Hector Berlioz (1803–69), in many ways, is a perfect personality through whom the essential features of nineteenth-century Romanticism can be revealed.

EARLY YEARS AND TRAINING

In comparison to Mozart, Beethoven, or Mendelssohn, Berlioz's early musical training was rather meager. First of all, he did not learn to play the piano, a fundamental skill for most composers of that era. He played the guitar and flute, only beginning his musical studies at the age of twelve. The inadequacy of his training became apparent when, at age nineteen, he sought admission to the composition class of a noted professor in Paris. He was told he would have to learn the basic rules of counterpoint and harmony, rules which would have been second nature for any competent musician with a thorough background. Berlioz recounts this episode in his *Memoirs*:

> Lesueur [the professor] had the kindness to read carefully through the first of these crude efforts, and he said as he handed it back to me, "There is plenty of feeling here, plenty of dramatic life, but you do not yet know how to write, and your harmony is riddled with mistakes."*

Although noting the lack of competency, Lesueur had the foresight eventually to accept Berlioz as a student.

Berlioz's earliest childhood recollections of music evoke a mysterious and sensuous union between sound and life. Here is his deeply romantic description of his first communion, which he calls his "first musical experience":

> I took my first communion on the same day as my elder sister. . . . It was spring: the sun shone brightly, a light wind stirred the rustling poplars; the air was full of some delicious fragrance. Deeply moved, I crossed the threshold of the chapel. I found myself in the midst of young girls in white, my sister's friends; and with them I knelt in prayer and waited for the solemn ceremony to begin . . . I gave myself to God . . . I was rudely awakened by the priest summoning me . . . I went up, blushing at the unmerited honour, and received the sacrament. As I did so, a chorus of fresh, young voices broke into the eucharistic hymn. The sound filled me with a kind of mystical, passionate unrest which I was powerless to hide from the rest of the congregation. I saw Heaven open—a Heaven of love and pure delight, purer and a thousand times

The Memoirs of Hector Berlioz, tr. and ed. by David Cairns (New York, 1975), p. 50.

lovelier than the one that had been so often described to me. Such is the power of true expression, the incomparable beauty of melody that comes from the heart.*

Berlioz was a dreamer. What he might have lacked in technique was outweighed by pure inspiration. In another era he might have amounted to nothing. But the nineteenth century was a time that was ripe for a dreamer. The Romantics were eager to embrace the mysterious and unattainable. Inspiration was their sacred impulse—and of this Berlioz had plenty to spare.

Berlioz's lack of facility on the piano may have been the factor that led him to develop another type of virtuosity, orchestration. Early in his musical career, he had become fascinated with the technique and timbre of orchestral instruments. While a student in Paris, he was employed as a chorus member in a small opera company, where he could observe the practical problems of orchestral writing. He listened. He asked questions. If he was not sure that something he had written was idiomatic for a certain instrument, he would ask a friend in the opera orchestra to try it out. Each new opera the company performed added to his practical knowledge of the orchestra and its potential—a potential he was destined to help realize.

THE "ROMANTIC REVOLUTIONARY"

Berlioz was born into a world caught in the aftermath of the French Revolution. No matter where one stood within society, the Revolution and its sub-

*Ibid., pp. 31–32.

Hector Berlioz (sketch by Coignet).

sequent aftershocks had a continuing influence. It was, in fact, an Age of Revolution, creating the inevitable climate of change that accompanies all such social upheavals. It had an overall effect of loosening the tightly drawn restraints on society and allowing sudden change to take place at every level of human activity. These changes involved everything from the ownership of land and codes of dress and etiquette to the place where music was performed and the musical styles that audiences accepted. It was only natural that the passionate young Berlioz would be a revolutionary. But his revolution would take place in the concert hall, not in the street.

Berlioz and his young Romantic companions—fledgling painters and writers as well as musicians—dedicated their lives to artistic revolution. They fashioned their revolution not with guns, but with ideas. They were not interested in literally killing the political old guard, but in symbolically overthrowing the artistic establishment. They did not attend secret political gatherings; rather, they were to be found in the concert hall in support of one of their revolutionary heroes, Beethoven, especially when his late works were programmed. Oftentimes, Berlioz and his cohorts might attend a play by one of their group to "make a good showing." Because art was sacred to them, they were especially enraged when a work was presented in mutilated form, an all-too-common occurrence. (For example, Beethoven's *Fifth Symphony* might be performed with a substitute movement from another one of his symphonies; or a conductor might "correct" Beethoven's harmony!) The Romantics' concept of the rights of the artist paralleled the revolutionary doctrines of the Rights of Man. And like true revolutionaries, the young Romantics expressed their opinions rather forcefully. Here is an eyewitness account of the young Berlioz at the opera, berating the orchestra that did not perform the score accurately:

> [Berlioz] rises from his seat and bending towards the orchestra shouts in a voice of thunder: "You don't want two flutes there, you brutes! You want two piccolos! Two piccolos, do you hear? Oh, the brutes!" Having said this, he simply sits down again, scowling indignantly. Amidst the general tumult produced by this outburst, I turn around and see a young man trembling with passion, his hands clenched, his eyes flashing, and a head of hair—such a head of hair. It looked like an enormous umbrella of hair, projecting something like a moveable awning over the beak of a bird of prey.*

As we have already discussed, one of the essential features of a revolutionary age, by definition, is a passion for change. As the restraints of a social order are loosened, long-repressed cultural currents are set in motion. The old ways seem tired, played out, to be replaced by the cult of the new.

*Ernest Legouvé quoted in Harold C. Schonberg, *Lives of the Great Composers*, rev. ed. (New York, 1981), p. 157.

This was a perfect setting for that part of Berlioz's character which adored novelty for its own sake. He loved to be the instigator of cultural shocks, to take the establishment by storm. He confided to a friend, concerning his *Damnation of Faust*, "I want it to astound the entire musical world." The creator of the shocking effects of the *Fantastic Symphony* knew exactly what he was doing. While other traits of Romanticism have fallen into disfavor in the twentieth century, *the continuous search for something new to say and a new way to say it has persisted—even increased—in our present-day world*.

THE DAMNATION OF FAUST

Berlioz's piece is based on the famous poetic drama *Faust*, by the German writer, Goethe. The hero of this drama symbolized the very soul of the nineteenth-century Romantic spirit. Faust is a man who seeks to understand the infinite, to experience the deepest passions that lie beyond conventional life. He is willing to risk all, including eternal damnation, to attain this goal.

Berlioz, like all the Romantics, was deeply influenced by Goethe's work. As early as 1828, before he wrote the *Fantastic Symphony*, Berlioz had composed *Eight Scenes from Faust*, musical settings of portions of the poem. But these were only a prelude to a more ambitious effort (of which the eight scenes became part) completed in 1846—*The Damnation of Faust*. Berlioz continued the innovations of genre and form begun with the *Fantastic Symphony* in *The Damnation of Faust*, which he called a concert opera. It is a dramatic work with orchestra, soloists, and choruses. In the libretto there are descriptions of dramatic action, but these are not played out on a stage. Much of the action happens only in the imagination of the listener. There has been much discussion concerning the genre to which the work belongs, but the answer, if there is one, has no bearing on the impact of the music. *The Damnation of Faust* is a music-drama, with a close kinship to its relatives, opera and oratorio. At the same time it seems to have a sweeping symphonic impulse that connects it to Beethoven, especially his *Ninth Symphony*.

The three main characters in the story are Faust, Mephistopheles, and Marguerite. Faust is a scholar who has spent most of his life absorbed in study. As the work opens, he expresses total boredom with all aspects of conventional life. In contemporary terms, Faust is in the midst of an identity crisis. Mephistopheles is the devil. But in this drama he is a witty and often likable fellow, whose main objective is to get Faust to sign away his eternal soul. He often spouts a rather humorous philosophy that ridicules human values and vulnerability. Marguerite is the girl with whom Faust falls in love. (Mephistopheles arranges for this to happen.) Her character is never developed in the drama; typical of the attitude toward women at the time, she is depicted as a romantic stereotype of the "ideal woman."

The drama unfolds in a series of musical scenes. We meet Faust and learn of his frustrations. Although he loves nature, it alone does not fulfill his yearning for infinite knowledge. He considers the glory of war and dismisses it as an "empty dream." He contemplates suicide but is restrained by images of religious faith. At this juncture, Mephistopheles offers to show Faust "all that is dreamed of in your wildest desire." Faust consents and Mephistopheles states what could have been the Romantic's answer to the Age of Reason—"Let us start then to understand life. And jettison your dull philosophy." They begin a journey through various aspects of human existence. Mephistopheles eventually brings Faust to Marguerite, and the two fall passionately in love. Marguerite is scorned by her neighbors for her lack of virtue (also part of Mephistopheles's plan). While Mephistopheles urges Faust to flee, the lovers swear to meet again the next day. (At this point in the story, the recorded excerpt begins.)

| Listen | Berlioz, *The Damnation of Faust*, scenes 16–19 | 28 |

| Listening Activity |

Berlioz has used the orchestra very skillfully to portray various aspects of the dramatic action, as well as some literal representations of what is happening in the text. As you listen, identify some of these orchestral effects by naming the group of instruments that is used to portray them. (Write this information at the box at right of page.) Also, circle in the text the emotion, action, or object that the orchestra is portraying. For example, you might circle the words "I hear hunters chasing through the woods" and write in the box "horns." Also indicate any section that seems to be in recitative style by writing the word "recitative" in the box.

"O nature—vast, impenetrable, and proud"

© DON HAZELTINE. 1981

Scene 16
INVOCATION TO NATURE
Forests and Caverns

Faust alone

FAUST

Nature immense, impénétrable
  et fière,
Toi seule donnes trêve à mon
  ennui sans fin.
Sur ton sein tout-puissant je
  sens moins ma misère,
Je retrouve ma force, et je
  crois vivre enfin.

Oui, soufflez, ouragans!
Criez, forêts profondes!
Croulez, rochers!
Torrents, précipitez vos ondes!
A vos bruits souverains ma
  voix aime à s'unir.

Forêts, rochers, torrents, je
  vous adore! Mondes
Qui scintillez, vers vous
  s'élance le désir
D'un coeur trop vaste et d'un
  âme altérée
D'un bonheur qui la fuit.

FAUST

O nature—vast, impenetrable,
  and proud,
You alone give rest to my
  unending weariness.
On your all-powerful breast I
  feel my misery less,
I recover my strength and come
  alive at last.

Yes, blow, hurricanes!
Cry out, deep forests!
Crumble, rocks!
Torrents, hurl down your waves!
My voice seeks union with your
  sovereign roarings.

Forests, craigs, torrents, I
  worship you!
Sparkling worlds, toward you
  soars the desire
Of a heart too vast and a
  troubled soul
Deserted by happiness.

Scene 17

MÉPHISTOPHÉLÈS

MEPHISTOPHELES
(climbing up the rocks, approaching Faust)

A la voûte azurée
Aperçois-tu, dis-moi, l'astre
  d'amour constant?
Son influence, ami, serait
  fort nécessaire:
Car tu rêves ici, quand cette
  pauvre enfant,
Marguerite———

In the azure vault of heaven
Tell me, do you see the star
  of constant love?
Its influence, my friend, will be
  very necessary:
For you are dreaming here while
  that poor child,
Marguerite———

FAUST
Tais-toi!

FAUST
Quiet!

MÉPHISTOPHÉLÈS
Sans doute il faut me taire,
Tu n'aimes plus!
Pourtant en un cachot traînée,
Et pour un parricide à la
  mort condamnée———

MEPHISTOPHELES
No doubt I should be silent,
You no longer love!
Nevertheless, dragged off to jail,
And condemned to death for
  parricide———

FAUST
Quoi!

FAUST
What!

MÉPHISTOPHÉLÈS
J'entends des chasseurs qui
  parcourent les bois.

FAUST
Achève! Qu'as-tu dit?
Marguerite en prison!

MÉPHISTOPHÉLÈS
Certaine liqueur brune, un
  innocent poison,
Qu'elle tenait de toi pour
  endormir sa mère
Pendant vos nocturnes amours
A causé tout le mal!
Caressant sa chimère,
T'attendant chaque soir, elle
  en usait toujours.
Elle en a tant usé
Que la vieille en est morte.
Tu comprends maintenant!

FAUST
Feux et tonnerre!

MÉPHISTOPHÉLÈS
En sorte
Que son amour pour toi la
  conduit———

FAUST
Sauve-la,
Sauve-la, misérable!

MÉPHISTOPHÉLÈS
Ah! je suis le coupable!
On vous reconnaît la,
Ridicules humains!
N'importe!
Je suis le maître encor de
  t'ouvrir cette porte!
Mais qu'as-tu fait pour moi
Depuis que je te sers?

FAUST
Qu'exiges-tu?

MÉPHISTOPHÉLÈS
De toi?
Rien qu'une signature
Sur ce vieux parchemin.
Je sauve Marguerite à
  l'instant,

MEPHISTOPHELES
I hear hunters chasing through
  the woods.

FAUST
Go on! What did you say?
Marguerite in prison!

MEPHISTOPHELES
A certain brown liquid, a
  harmless drug
That she got from you to make
  her mother sleep
During your nights of love
Has caused all the harm!
Clinging to her idle fancy,
Waiting for you each night,
  she always used it.
She used it so often
That the old woman died from it.
Now you understand!

FAUST
Fires and thunder!

MEPHISTOPHELES
So that
Her love for you has led her———

FAUST
Save her,
Save her, you wretch!

MEPHISTOPHELES
Oh, so I'm to blame!
You are so easy to recognize,
Ridiculous humans!
No matter!
I am still master at opening
  this door for you!
But what have you done for me
Since I've been serving you?

FAUST
What do you need?

MEPHISTOPHELES
From you?
Nothing but a signature
On this old parchment.
I'll save Marguerite this
  instant,

272

Si tu jures
Et signes ton serment
De me servir demain!

FAUST

Eh, que me fait *demain* quand
  je souffre à cette heure!
Donne!

Voilà mon nom!
Vers sa sombre demeure
Volons donc maintenant!
O douleur insensée!
Marguerite, j'accours!

MÉPHISTOPHÉLÈS

A moi, Vortex! Giaour!
Sur ces deux noirs chevaux,
  prompts comme la pensée,
Montons, et au galop!
La justice est presée.

If you swear
And sign your oath
To serve me tomorrow!

FAUST

Oh! What does *tomorrow* matter
  when I suffer now!
Give it to me!

(Faust signs)

There is my name!
Then let us fly now
To her dismal dwelling!
Oh senseless grief!
Marguerite, I hurry to you!

MEPHISTOPHELES

Here, Vortex! Giaour!
Let's mount these two black
  horses, swift as thought,
And gallop!
Justice hastens us.

Scene 18
THE RIDE TO THE ABYSS
Plains, Mountains, and Valleys

(A stormy wind rages fiercely.
Faust and Mephistopheles galloping on two black horses)

FAUST

Dans mon coeur retentit sa
  voix désespérée . . .
Au pauvre abandonnée!

CHOEUR DE PAYSANS

Her desperate voice still
  echoes in my heart . . .
O poor abandoned girl!

CHORUS OF PEASANTS

(Kneeling before a rustic cross)

Sancta Maria, ora pro nobis!
Sancta Magdalena, ora pro nobis!

FAUST

Prends garde à ces enfants,
  à ces femmes priant
Au pied de cette croix!

Holy Mary, pray for us!
Holy Magdalene, pray for us!

FAUST

Be careful of those children,
  and those women praying
At the foot of that cross!

MÉPHISTOPHÉLÈS

Eh! qu'importe! an avant!

MEPHISTOPHELES

Oh, what of it! Onward!

CHOEUR DE PAYSANS

Sancta Margarita!
Ah!———

CHORUS OF PEASANTS

Holy Margaret!
Ah!———

(Lightning strikes the cross, which falls over.
Cries of terror. The chorus scatters.
The horsemen go by. The rain pours down in torrents.)

The Ride to the Abyss: Faust and Mephistopheles are pursued by a hideous monster and a swarm of great night birds.

FAUST
Dieux! un monstre hideux en
   hurlant nous poursuit . . .

MÉPHISTOPHÉLÈS
Tu rêves!

FAUST
Quel essaim de grands oiseaux
   de nuit!
Quels cris affreux!
Ils me frappent de l'aile!

MÉPHISTOPHÉLÈS

Le glas de trépassés sonne
   déjà pour elle.
As-tu peur? retournons!

     (They stop.)

FAUST
Non! je l'entends! courons!

  (The horses double their speed.)

MÉPHISTOPHÉLÈS
Hop! Hop! Hop!

FAUST
Regarde autour de nous cette
   ligne infinie

FAUST
Oh gods! A hideous monster
   pursues us, howling . . .

MEPHISTOPHELES
You're dreaming!

FAUST
What a swarm of great night-
   birds!
What dreadful cries!
They're beating me with their
   wings!

MEPHISTOPHELES
  (reining in his horse)
The death-bell of sinners
   already tolls for her.
Are you afraid? Let's turn back!

FAUST
No! I hear it! Let's hurry!

MEPHISTOPHELES
Hup! Hup! Hup!

FAUST
See all around us that endless
   line

274

MÉPHISTOPHÉLÈS
Hop!

FAUST
De squelettes dansant!
Avec quel rire horrible ils
   nous saluent en passant!

MÉPHISTOPHÉLÈS
Hop! pense à sauver sa vie
Et ris-toi des morts!
Hop! Hop!

FAUST
(more and more terrified and breathless)
Nos chevaux frémissent,
Leurs crins se hérissent,
Ils brisent leurs mors.
Je vois onduler
Devant nous la terre:
J'entends la tonnerre
Sous nos pied rouler.

MÉPHISTOPHÉLÈS
Hop! Hop! Hop! Hop!
Hop! Hop!

FAUST
Il pleut du sang! . . .

MÉPHISTOPHÉLÈS
(in a voice of thunder)
Cohorts infernales,
Sonnez vos trompes triomphales!
Il est à nous!

FAUST
Horreur! Ah!———

MÉPHISTOPHÉLÈS
Je suis vainqueur!

MEPHISTOPHELES
Hup!

FAUST
Of dancing skeletons!
With what horrid laughter they
   greet us as we pass!

MEPHISTOPHELES
Hup! Think about saving her life
And laugh at the dead!
Hup! Hup!

FAUST
Our horses tremble,
Their manes bristle,
They crush their bits.
I see the ground moving in waves
Before us:
I hear the thunder rolling
Beneath our feet.

MEPHISTOPHELES
Hup! Hup! Hup! Hup!
Hup! Hup!

FAUST
It's raining blood! . . .

MEPHISTOPHELES
Infernal cohorts
Sound your triumphal fanfares!
He is ours!

FAUST
Horror! Ah!———

MEPHISTOPHELES
I have conquered!
(They fall into an abyss.)

Scene 19
PANDEMONIUM

(Hell. Faust is sent to the flames.)

CHOEUR DE DÉMONS ET DAMNÉS
Has!
Irimiru Karabrao!
Has! Has! Has!

LES PRINCES DES TÉNÈBRES
De cette âme si fière
A jamais es-tu maître et
   vainqueur, Méphisto?

CHORUS OF DEMONS AND THE DAMNED
Has!
Irimiru Karabrao!
Has! Has! Has!

THE PRINCES OF DARKNESS
Of this soul so proud
Are you master and conqueror for
   eternity, Mephisto?

Mephistopheles:
"I have conquered!"

MÉPHISTOPHÉLÈS
J'en suis maître à jamais.

MEPHISTOPHELES
I am his master for eternity.

LES PRINCES DES TÉNÈBRES
Faust a donc librement
Signé l'acte fatal qui le
    livre à nos flammes?

THE PRINCES OF DARKNESS
Then Faust has freely
Signed the fatal contract that
    delivers him to our flames?

MÉPHISTOPHÉLÈS
Il signa librement.

MEPHISTOPHELES
He signed freely.

CHŒUR DE DÉMONS
Has! Has!

CHORUS OF DEMONS
Has! Has!

(Infernal orgy. Mephistopheles's triumph)

Tradioun marexil fir tru dinxé
    burrudixé.
Fory my dinkorlitz,
O mérikariu! O mévixé! Mérikariba!
O mérikariu! o mi dara caraibo
    lakinda, merondor dinkorlitz,
Merondor dinkorlitz, merondor.
Tradioun marexil,
Tradioun burrudixé,
Trudinxe caraibo.
Fir ome vixe merondor
Mit aysko, merondor, mit aysko!
    oh! oh!
Diff! diff! merondor, merondor aysko!
Has! Has! Satan! has! has! Belphégor!
Has! has! Méphisto!
Has! has! Kroïx!
Diff! diff! Astaroth!

Tradioun marexil fir tru dinxe
    burrudixe.
Fory my dinkorlitz,
O merikariu! O mevixe! Merikariba!
O merikariu! o mi dara caraibo
    lakinda, merondor dinkorlitz,
Merondor dinkorlitz, merondor.
Tradioun marexil,
Tradioun burrudixe,
Trudinxe caraibo.
Fir ome vixe merondor
Mit aysko merondor, mit aysko!
    oh! oh!
Diff! diff! merondor, merondor aysko
Has! Has! Satan! has! has! Belphegor!
Has! has! Mephisto!
Has! has! Kroïx!
Diff! diff! Astaroth!

Diff! diff! Belzébuth!	Diff! diff! Belzebuth!
Belphégor! Astaroth! Méphisto!	Belphegor! Astaroth! Mephisto!
Sat, sat rayk ir kimour.	Sat, sat rayk ir kimour.
Has! has! Méphisto!	Has! has! Mephisto!
Has! has! Méphisto!	Has! has! Mephisto!
Has! has! has! *etc.*	Has! has! has! *etc.*
Irimiru karabrao.	Irimiru karabrao.

The last scene of the drama takes place in Heaven. Marguerite has been saved from eternal damnation. A chorus sings, "She has loved deeply . . . Come, Marguerite, come."

Connections in the Berlioz Discussion

The classic–romantic continuum.
Flexibility of basic musical models.
Use of a basic model or genre.
The ancient unity.
Artistic creation may be connected to a cultural chain.

Berlioz: Additional Listening

L'enfance du Christ (The Childhood of Christ)
Nuits d'été (Summer Nights)
Requiem

The Basic Traits of Nineteenth-Century Romanticism

Berlioz was one of the few well-known composers who was also a writer of some accomplishment. His wildly Romantic *Memoirs* are perhaps too emotional and overblown for the modern sensibility, but they mirror Romantic thought and feeling at its most extreme. Consider this excerpt, in which he describes his wanderings in the Italian countryside:

Wearing a straw hat and an old grey shirt, with half a dozen piastres [Italian coins] in my pocket and gun or guitar in hand, I would set off, not caring where I spent the night, knowing that I could always find shelter if need be in one of the countless wayside caves or shrines. Sometimes I went at a great pace, sometimes I would stop to examine an old tomb, or from the top of those melancholy hillocks that dot the dusty Roman plain, listen to the boom of the bells of St. Peter's, whose golden cross gleamed on the horizon, or break off the pursuit of a flock of lapwing [a type of bird] to jot down in my notebook some symphonic idea that had just occurred to me; always, whatever I did, drinking to the full the unutterable delight of complete and absolute freedom.

Sometimes, when I had my guitar with me instead of my gun, I would station myself in the midst of a landscape in harmony with my mood, and some passage from the *Aeneid*, dormant in my memory since childhood, would come back to me, set off by the character of the country into which I had wandered. Then, improvising a strange recitative to a still stranger harmony, I would sing the death of Pallas, the despair of the good Evander, ...

Under the combined influence of poetry, music and association I would work myself up into an incredible state of excitement. The triple intoxication always ended in floods of tears and uncontrollable sobbing. The most curious part of it was that I was able to analyze my feelings . . . I longed for those poetic days when the heroes, sons of the gods, walked the earth in glittering armour, casting delicate javelins, their points set in a ring of gleaming gold. Quitting the past for the present, I wept for my own private disappointments, my uncertain future, my interrupted career; until, collapsing in the midst of this maelstrom of poetry, and murmuring fragments of Shakespeare, Virgil and Dante . . . . I fell asleep.*

We can use this quote, which includes many of the characteristics of nineteenth-century Romanticism, as an introduction to these traits, which are:

1. Reverence for Nature
2. Pursuit of the Bizarre, the Irrational, and the Mythical
3. Nationalism and the Folk Element
4. Interplay of the Senses
5. The Quest for the Unattainable
6. Freedom of Artistic Expression
7. Individualism

Romanticism not only affected music; it was one of the most important cultural energies since the nineteenth century. Although the Romantic era ostensibly ended in 1900, many of the artistic and cultural forces it set loose are still active today.

REVERENCE FOR NATURE
Berlioz's wanderings in the countryside in search of inspiration was a typical pastime of the nineteenth-century creative artist. Nature, for the

Memoirs, pp. 171–72.

Romantics, was the sacred model for art; its spirit and imagery flow through Romantic music, poetry, painting, and literature as a basic and unifying theme. A new purpose for music was the imitation of nature and her sounds. E. T. A. Hoffmann, one of the period's most influential figures, wrote:

> There is about the imperceptible beginning, the swelling and the dying of the tones of nature, something which has a most powerful and indescribable effect on us; and any instrument which could be capable of reproducing this would undoubtedly affect us in a similar way.*

The translation of nature into musical sound was accomplished through new combinations of harmony, melody, texture, and timbre. Berlioz was influential in creating this language. While it is almost impossible to quantify this rather mysterious relationship between nature and music, a few specific examples from Berlioz's style may be useful. The long, asymmetrical phrases (phrases of uneven length) of many of Berlioz's melodies can be compared to the horizon line of the French Alps, his boyhood home. His juxtaposition of textures can be likened to contrasting light effects on the landscape, where one patch may be darkened by the shadow of a passing cloud. One of the great Romantic celebrations of the earth is the "Invocation to Nature" from Berlioz's *Damnation of Faust*, in which harmony, texture, and orchestral timbre are used to evoke nature's awesome and powerful presence. The reflection of nature in music became a standard theme for the nineteenth century and continued, though to a lesser extent, into the twentieth, as the following chart indicates:

Music and Nature in Span II

Vivaldi, *The Four Seasons* (1725)

Haydn, *The Creation* (1798); *The Seasons* (1801)

Vaughan Williams, *Pastoral Symphony* (1922)

Beethoven, *Pastoral Symphony* (1808)

Smetana, *The Moldau* (compl. 1879)

Mendelssohn, *Overture to A Midsummer Night's Dream* (1826); *Italian Symphony* (1833)

Debussy, *Afternoon of a Faun* (1894); *La Mer* (1905)

Copland, *Appalachian Spring* (1944)

Stravinsky, *Rite of Spring* (1913)

*R. Murray Schafer, *E. T. A. Hoffmann and His Music* (Toronto and Buffalo, 1975), p. 7.

PURSUIT OF THE BIZARRE, THE IRRATIONAL, AND THE MYTHICAL

The "strange recitative to a still stranger harmony" that Berlioz improvised in the Italian countryside reflects Romantic fascination with strange phenomena. In contrast to the rationalism of the Enlightenment, the Romantics purposely sought out what was irrational, bizarre, and mythical. They found mystery in the past (for example, Berlioz's wanderings in caves and shrines). Images of death, drugs, myth, and fantasy—in short, anything they felt invested life with danger and passion—are found throughout Romantic art. While much of twentieth-century "serious" music turned away from such exotic pursuits, this tradition flowed directly into our popular culture in the form of movies (and their musical scores based directly on nineteenth-century program music), novels, and superhero comics. The science fiction, Gothic, and horror traditions have their roots in nineteenth-century Romanticism. (That is why so many horror movies are set in the nineteenth century!)

Pursuit of the Bizarre, the Irrational, and the Mythical

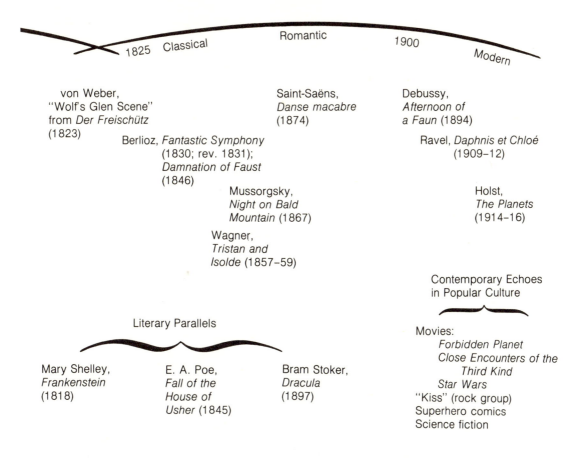

NATIONALISM AND THE FOLK ELEMENT

As you have read in his account, Berlioz did not set out into the countryside dressed in aristocratic finery, but wearing a "straw hat and an old grey shirt." Like many nineteenth-century Romantics, Berlioz sought a kinship with the common people. Folk culture, with its popular tunes, myths, and natural modes of experience, had become a Romantic ideal. (It should be pointed out that this was basically an artistic rather than a social phenomenon. Artists continued to woo the aristocracy with as much fervor as ever.) Of all the "serious" musical styles of Span II, Romantic music most closely reflects the popular taste of its day. Romantic melodies are often folklike or folk-based. Moreover, the music appeals directly to the listeners' emotions.

The interest in folk culture was closely related to the growing sense of nationalism which was shaping the modern boundaries of Europe. Many composers began to write music that reflected their cultural heritage. To accomplish this, it was necessary to blend musical material from the native culture with learned styles. For example, Chopin, the great Polish composer, wrote many *mazurkas* and *polonaises*, piano pieces based on Polish folk dances. Modest Mussorgsky composed music based on Russian folk themes and harmonies. Berlioz's music has a subtle but distinct French flavor.

Nationalist and Folk-Inspired Music in Span II

Classical   1825   Romantic   1900   Modern

1750   1950

Chopin,
Mazurkas (1824–49);
Polonaises (1817–46)

Wagner,
The Ring (1854–74);
Tristan and Isolde (1859)

Mussorgsky,
Boris Godunov
(1869; rev. 1871–72)

Brahms,
Songs (1853–96);
Liebeslieder Waltzes
(1868–69)

Dvořák,
Slavonic Dances
(1878; 1886)

Debussy,
Pelleas et Melisande
(1892–1902)

Sibelius,
Finlandia (1899)

Bartók,
*Rumanian Christmas
Songs* (1915);
String Quartets
(1908–39)

Stravinsky,
Firebird (1909–10);
Rite of Spring (1913)

Vaughan Williams,
*Fantasy on a Theme by
Thomas Tallis* (1910)

Orff,
Carmina Burana
(1935–36)

Joaquin Rodrigo,
Concierto de Aranjuez
(1939)

Copland,
Appalachian Spring (1944);
A Lincoln Portrait (1942);
Billy the Kid (1938);
Rodeo (1942)

Bernstein,
West Side Story
(1957)

In the first half of the nineteenth century, the great German instrumental tradition dominated the musical scene. The preeminence of this tradition is easily understood when you consider even a few of its masters: Bach, Haydn, Mozart, Beethoven, Mendelssohn. It is no wonder, then, that many European composers imitated German models and style. As nationalism grew, so did efforts to break away from this German tradition and create music that reflected regional cultures. The nationalist influence did not end with the nineteenth century, but has lived on in the works of many modern composers, including some prominent Americans.

INTERPLAY OF THE SENSES

> . . . Under the combined influence of poetry, music, and association I would work myself up into an incredible state of excitement. . .

We have already discussed the interplay of the senses in Mendelssohn's *Midsummer Night's Dream* and program music in general. The Romantics did not invent the idea of the interplay of the senses; on the contrary, it has always been a vital part of many kinds of heightened experience (music, myth, drama, poetry). What the Romantics did was to bring this interplay into greater prominence. Again, a familiar concept reappears: *stylistic trends are often shaped by an emphasis on elements always present in the culture.*

The heightened interplay between sound, sight, emotion, ideas, etc. became a Romantic quest for a *fusion of the arts*:

> We should strive to bring the arts closer together and search for bridges from one to the other. Statues will come alive to become perhaps paintings; paintings will become poems; poems will become music; and who knows, perhaps solemn religious music will rise up again as a temple in the sky.*

Berlioz's *Damnation of Faust* may be considered a model of sensory fusion. The sounds that Berlioz uses to represent the dramatic elements evoke distinct and inescapable visual images. Significantly, Berlioz specifically uses verbal descriptions to conjure up a musical-visual interplay.

The interplay of the senses continues to be a potent influence in the Modern era. One can only guess at how delighted Berlioz would have been with the recent twentieth-century fusion of sound and sight, by film, videotape, and holography. Would he be repelled by the "unnaturalness" of the new technology, or drawn to the possibilities of "unutterable and absolute freedom"?

*August Wilhelm Schlegel, in *E. T. A. Hoffmann*, p. 8.

THE QUEST FOR THE UNATTAINABLE

> I longed for those poetic days when the heroes, sons of the gods, walked the earth . . .

Romantics like Berlioz were at their best when they wanted something they couldn't have. The allure of the past, with its heroes and gods, was but one tantalizing mystery beyond their reach. The quest for the unattainable was a central theme in *The Damnation of Faust*. For the true Romantic, the search itself became the meaning of life.

Translated into musical terms, the quest was expressed through vast orchestral forces in grandiose symphonic forms. Through works that grew louder and larger, the extremes of orchestral color were explored. The prototype was Beethoven's *Ninth Symphony*, and the quest has had reverberations well into the twentieth century (for example, Shostakovich's *Fifth Symphony*). In certain parts of today's culture, there is a distinct reaction against such a self-indulgent aesthetic. But in other quarters, the Romantic quest continues; this is especially evident in movies, novels, and popular songs. *The hero in search of meaning is one of the oldest images in human culture*. The Romantics did not create this motif; but they gave it new and powerful meaning.

FREEDOM OF ARTISTIC EXPRESSION

> . . . Whatever I did, drinking to the full the unutterable delight of complete and absolute freedom.

With these words, Berlioz has proclaimed the Romantic credo. Romantic music is filled with this sense of freedom. While Haydn and Mozart composed within the discipline of existing genres and forms, Romantics such as Berlioz were impelled to create new ones (which often grew out of the old ones in quite logical ways). For example, *The Damnation of Faust* is part symphony and part opera-oratorio. The nineteenth-century orchestra provided another source of freedom with its greater size and technical capabilities. Another kind of freedom was released by the astounding new level of virtuosity exhibited by such legendary performers as Liszt (piano) and Paganini (violin). These men were able to execute incredibly difficult technical passages with an ease that allowed for the creation of totally new instrumental effects. Throughout the arts, there were daring explorations of theme and topic; *sensationalism became the norm*.

The concept of artistic freedom is so basic to twentieth-century thought that we may lose sight of its roots in nineteenth-century Romanticism. It was the Romantics and their impassioned, almost innocent quest for total artistic freedom that set loose this cultural energy. Their insistence on the validity of a personal art laid the groundwork for stylistic diversity. Later composers, when feeling the constraints of a current musical language, would simply throw it out and create a new one. *Radical changes in style increasingly dominated the music of the Romantic and Modern eras.* Unlike some other traits of Romanticism which eventually diminished in a twentieth-century backlash, the concept of artistic freedom has continued to increase with intensity into our own time.

INDIVIDUALISM

> . . . I wept for my own private disappointments, my uncertain future, my interrupted career; until, collapsing in the midst of this maelstrom of poetry, and murmuring fragments of Shakespeare, Virgil and Dante . . . I fell asleep.

Closely related to the freedom of artistic expression was the heightened role of the individual. Above all else, what he or she feels is the ultimate justification for artistic creation. The Romantic "liberation of the individual" had a vital effect on subsequent musical culture. Individualism is another word for freedom, and with freedom comes diversity. The cultural history of the last two centuries has been dominated by increasing stylistic diversity. Composers more and more find themselves in a curious quandary—on the one hand, they have a need to absorb a "living language" from the culture, but on the other, they are expected to transform that language into something personal and new. In the nineteenth century, and with increasing intensity in the twentieth, *musical styles tend to be defined by individual composers' methods.* To illustrate, consider this change. The term *Baroque harmony* has a clean and decisive meaning. It identifies a standard tradition with specific technical practices shared by a large group of composers for 150 years. By comparison, the phrase *Romantic harmony* is very vague. While it denotes certain broad characteristics, any attempt to define it precisely results in contradictions. It becomes easier to describe a harmonic practice of the Romantic and Modern eras with the name of its practitioner; for example, we may speak of *Brahmsian harmony* (that of Johannes Brahms) or *Debussyan harmony* (that of Claude Debussy).

To summarize, since the Romantic period, there has been a distinct tendency for each composer to seek a *personal* musical language. Thus, Romantic individualism was yet another reason for the growing diversity of musical styles in the twentieth century.

Mendelssohn and Berlioz: A Contrast in Style

Mendelssohn and Berlioz were contemporaries. They knew each other personally and they knew each other's music. We may call both of them Romantic composers and, in doing so, evoke certain qualities common to both their musical styles. But Mendelssohn and Berlioz were very different people, and their music was as different as night and day. These differences can provide a perspective for understanding not only Romanticism, but, more important, how the general trends of an era relate *flexibly* to the real world of the composer.

It is not always the case that a composer's personality seems to fit his music. But there are many instances when such correlations are not only tempting, but probably valid. One may certainly sense a relationship between the "cosmic order" of Bach's music and his deeply religious nature. Beethoven's defiant character is manifest in his powerful musical style. And as we have seen, both Mendelssohn and Berlioz wrote music that in many ways reflected some aspect of their personalities. In this chapter Berlioz has represented Romanticism in the extreme. His flamboyant personality and innovative musical style qualify him as a "radical Romantic." But what of Felix Mendelssohn? He represents a different current in nineteenth-century music. As a man, he was the opposite of Berlioz—conservative, cautious, and traditional. He led a tidy and proper life which had a counterpart in his tidy and proper music. His musical style has a distinctly classical strain. It is this quality that allows us to consider him a "conservative Romantic." Using the classic–romantic continuum as a diagram, it is possible to compare the styles of Mendelssohn and Berlioz in musical terms. The examples cited are from the pieces discussed (and heard) in this chapter.

Classical Aesthetic	*Romantic Aesthetic*
Genre and Form	
A large part of Mendelssohn's output was *absolute* music. His program music usually follows a traditional form—for example, the *Overture to A Midsummer Night's Dream* is in a clear sonata-allegro form. In his program music, the dramatic impulse never gets out of hand.	Berlioz's output is entirely *programmatic* or operatic in nature. He experimented with the creation of new genres and forms—for example, the *Fantastic Symphony* is a program symphony; *The Damnation of Faust* is an operatic symphony. In Berlioz's works, the dramatic impulse far overshadows traditional musical design.
Melody	
Mendelssohn's melodies are far more traditional than Berlioz's. They are more tuneful, falling neatly into symmetrical phrases. Their beauty lies in a sort of	Berlioz's melodies fall into many categories, among them a new style of emotion-charged, start-stop, long-spinning melody associated with extreme romantic

Mozartian lightness mixed with a bit of romantic sentiment. Mendelssohn's melodic style is closer to Mozart's than to Berlioz's.

expression of emotion—for example, the *idée fixe* from the *Fantastic Symphony*.

Harmony

Mendelssohn's harmony was mostly *diatonic*; he shied away from the daring chromaticism associated with extremes of romantic expression. Mendelssohn's harmonic style is closer to Mozart's than to Berlioz's.

Berlioz was an innovator exploring bold, new harmonic relationships that included *chromatic* and *modal* harmony—for example, "To Nature" from *The Damnation of Faust*. He was one of the first composers to conceive of harmony totally integrated with texture and timbre. Unlike Mendelssohn, some of his harmonic ideas cannot be separated from their orchestral settings—for example, one cannot play them on the piano and still experience their effect.

Texture—Timbre

Mendelssohn used inventive orchestral textures and timbres in a wonderful but conservative manner. His orchestral textures tend to be delicate and subtle.

Berlioz explored the possibilities of texture and timbre as no one had before. He often used daring and dramatic instrumentation to produce musical effects.

Considering the comparison above, one might be tempted to ask, "Was Mendelssohn really a Romantic composer at all?" And here we must deal with the wonderful contradictions that always arise with the categorization or labeling of artistic experience. The answer to the question reveals no exact information in the scientific sense, but hints at a living art in which reality is as much one thing as another. Yes, Mendelssohn was a Romantic composer, and we can cite certain features of his music that relate his style to that of the nineteenth century. His program music may evoke an elegant interplay of the senses (*A Midsummer Night's Dream*, for example); the role of timbre and texture in his orchestration (when compared to an orchestral work by Mozart) are clearly within nineteenth-century practice. But there is a better way to get hold of Mendelssohn's Romanticism, and it speaks to music's ultimate power: no matter what we say about music in technical terms, there is always that other dimension that cannot be described. If you listen to the *Overture to A Midsummer Night's Dream* with your senses wide open, you may experience emotions in that sort of dreamy, magical way that was the lifeblood of nineteenth-century Romanticism. But Mendelssohn was not a romantic personality. Both Beethoven and Mozart were far more romantic characters than Mendelssohn. He was a composer with a classical aesthetic living in a time when the culture took a big swing toward romanticism. He was to some degree caught up in that swing. But his conservative nature and classical aesthetic held him in check; and the resulting musical style—a careful and delicate romanticism—is precisely what is wonderful about his music.

Berlioz was one of the composers ready to go as far as the romantic swing would take him, and even further. His friend Mendelssohn found his music to be a "frightful muddle." Berlioz, on the other hand, clearly recognized Mendelssohn's genius. Upon hearing the complete music for *A Midsummer Night's Dream*, he wrote to the composer, "I have never heard anything more deeply Shakespearean than your music . . . I would have given three years of my life to embrace you . . ." (How typical of Berlioz! Mendelssohn would probably have had difficulty accepting the embrace, much less the three years.) Mendelssohn did not live long enough to understand the importance of Berlioz's music. He died in 1847 at the age of thirty-eight; Berlioz lived until 1869. Berlioz's career was a mixed one. His grand-scale successes were matched by equally grand-scale failures. The oft-heard cliché "He was ahead of his time" certainly applied to Berlioz. As the first leader of a succession of radical Romantic composers, Berlioz played an important role in the evolving musical language of the nineteenth century. Aside from expanding the resources of that language through new concepts of orchestration, harmony, melody, form, texture, and timbre, his revolutionary music, like Beethoven's, helped to create a climate for change. What seemed "a muddle" to Mendelssohn would become an artistic beacon for many composers of the second half of the nineteenth century. Even later conservative composers who could not respond to Berlioz's aesthetic and style would benefit from the many innovations he had brought into the musical language.

Perhaps an example from our time will help make clear the type of musical-cultural interplay just described. In the late 1960s, a performer named Jimi Hendrix unleashed a daring, loud distorted electric guitar style into rock music. At the heart of this style was an uninhibited expression of energy and emotion in a manner which thoroughly fits the radical side of the Romantic aesthetic. In fact, you have heard something similar in the brief *Sapphire Bullets of Pure Love* by John McLaughlin 34a . The response to Hendrix's radical style was similar in some ways to the nineteenth-century response to the radical Romantics. Some listeners were immediately drawn to it, others felt it had gone too far. The latter were, by and large, adherents of a more classical style of rock and roll. This "hard rock," as it was called, was simply too extreme and wild. In time, the general tolerance to this type of sound was increased. The extremism of Jimi Hendrix and others altered what was considered the norm. Within a matter of years, the distorted guitar sound (or fuzz-tone) became a standard component in many popular styles, including the more subdued, traditional ones. It is common today to hear a rock song in a ballad style (a very traditional, classical type of rock) with a guitar solo that uses this distorted timbre. Thus, the more radical romantic style of a Jimi Hendrix expanded the language of more traditionally oriented musicians.

SUMMARY

At any given time, there are contrasting personalities in a musical culture. They add to and take from that culture in various ways. Mendelssohn and Berlioz were contrasting personalities who lived in the Romantic era. From that culture each man absorbed a living musical language that reflected his personality and aesthetic. To that culture, each became a standard-bearer—Mendelssohn the "conservative Romantic" and Berlioz the "radical Romantic." Together they framed two sides of the early-nineteenth-century classical–romantic continuum within which many styles of Romantic music would flourish.

QUESTIONS

For the following questions, find any false statement(s) and correct them by changing the word(s) in italics. More than one statement may be false; all the statements may be true.

1. Concerning the *Fantastic Symphony*:

   (a) It is *absolute* music.

   (b) At its first performance it was Berlioz's intention that the audience *should not* have read the story beforehand.

   (c) The form is related to the traditional *sonata-symphony* design.

   (d) Placing this work on the classical–romantic continuum, most listeners would position it toward the *left*.

2. Concerning Mendelssohn's *Overture to A Midsummer Night's Dream* and Berlioz's *Fantastic Symphony* and *The Damnation of Faust*:

   (a) Each work was shaped under the influence of the *Romantic movement*.

   (b) None of these works falls under the category of *absolute* music.

(c) Each work was influenced to some degree by *poetry* or *drama*.

(d) Each work incorporates a cultural thread from the *past*.

3. Concerning the three pieces mentioned above:

(a) They reflect the Romantic tendency toward *isolation* of the senses.

(b) The one that has the least resemblance to opera is *A Midsummer Night's Dream*.

(c) Although each piece reflects something of music's place in the ancient unity, the *Fantastic Symphony* is the work that reflects this connection in the most direct manner.

4. Concerning nineteenth-century Romanticism:

(a) One of its characteristics was a reverence for *nature*.

(b) One of its characteristics was a *decrease* in the importance of the individual in art.

(c) One of its characteristics was an *increase* in the awareness and importance of national identity.

(d) It made "serious" music *less* compatible to the popular taste.

5. Concerning nineteenth-century Romanticism:

(a) It was one of the *most important* cultural energies of Span II.

(b) It fostered a new interest in *rationality*.

(c) It had *no* continuing effect in the twentieth century.

(d) It *decreased* the importance of orchestral timbre in music.

6. Concerning the importance of the individual to the Romantics:

(a) *Beethoven* was among the first composers to be viewed in this way.

(b) Romantic individualism promoted *conformity* of musical style.

(c) It was an idea that *ends* in the twentieth century.

(d) The character of *Mephistopheles* from Goethe's poem symbolized the image of the "personality crisis" for the Romantics.

7. Concerning Mendelssohn and Berlioz:

(a) They *were not* contemporaries.

(b) They are both considered *Romantic* composers.

(c) On the classical–romantic continuum, Mendelssohn would most likely be placed to the *right* of Berlioz.

(d) Differences in their personalities *correspond* to differences in their musical styles.

11
Romanticism - II

The Romantic Miniature

The grandiose symphonic works of the nineteenth century had their counterpart in short, more intimate genres, the *romantic miniatures*. Usually intended for one or two musicians and most often performed at private gatherings, these pieces captured the essence of the romantic spirit in its purest state. In such miniatures, a feeling could be explored with brief, reflective intensity. Among the most popular examples of this type are the short piano piece and the song.

The Song

A song (*Lied* in German; *melodie* or *chanson* in French) with piano accompaniment became a favorite genre of the Romantic era, fulfilling one of its avowed goals, the union of music and poetry. Romantic songs were often set to poems by great writers like Goethe, and the poetry was considered as important as the music. In this genre, the singer and pianist are partners in a total musical experience.

SCHUBERT AND THE GERMAN LIED
Franz Schubert (1797–1828), a Viennese composer whose short career spans both the late Classical and early Romantic periods, was a master of the German lied. Like Beethoven, Schubert does not fall neatly into either period, suggesting, once again, that these designations must be applied with flexibility. In any event, Schubert's romanticism was especially evident in his *lieder* (songs). A genius with melody, he composed over 600 songs, many of which have become favorites with singers and audiences throughout the world.

Listen *Lied der Mignon* (Mignon's Song), by Franz Schubert **27a**

Mignon, a character in one of Goethe's novels, is the lost child of aristocratic parents brought up by gypsies. This poem, set to music by Schubert in 1826, was also set by many other composers, including Beethoven. The simplicity of the music is in sharp contrast to the symphonic works of Berlioz heard in the previous chapter. This is another side to Romanticism, in which simplicity is the key to the expression of deeply felt emotion. To heighten the emotional impact, Schubert uses chromatic harmony, especially on the line beginning "Es schwindelt" (I faint).

Lied der Mignon

Nur wer die Sehnsucht kennt,	Only one who knows longing
Weiss, was ich leide!	can understand what I suffer!
Allein und abgetrennt	alone and bereft
Von aller Freude	of all joy,
Seh' ich ans Firmament	I look at the sky
Nach jener Seite.	yonder.
Ach! der mich liebt und kennt,	Ah, he who loves and understands me
Ist in der Weite.	is far away.
Es schwindelt mir, es brennt	I faint. Fire burns
Mein Eingeweide.	within me.
Nur wer die Sehnsucht kennt,	Only one who knows longing
Weiss, was ich leide!	can understand what I suffer!

Listening Activity

Describe an element of *contrast* in the song.

Describe an element of *balance* in the song.

Circle the lines in the text that seem the most *unstable* in the music.

AFTERTHOUGHT: SCHUBERT AND STEVIE WONDER

It would be avoiding the central idea of this book if we did not discuss, for a moment, the problems for some listeners in responding to the German lied. We have reached another crossroad where your response to music as good or bad can have little meaning. This is not only good music, it is great music. Whether or not you are able to respond to it reflects neither your ability nor the validity of your taste. For many listeners, the German lied represents a distant cultural tradition. How would Schubert have reacted to a song by Stevie Wonder or Joni Mitchell? Could he distinguish between good or bad music in a style that flows from a culture so far from his own? Stylistically, Schubert and Stevie Wonder may seem worlds apart (as indeed their respective cultures are), but beyond style, they share a common ground. Exploration of that common ground may serve to enrich the experience of both styles.

German lied is a living language. Among its primary sources are German folk song and poetry. It was the interplay of these traditions with the learned style of composers like Schubert that gave life to this art. Your reaction to it may depend on your familiarity with German culture and the Romantic tradition. By the same token, current masterpieces of popular song by such artists as Stevie Wonder and Joni Mitchell also reflect a living musical language that has grown from a culture. Response to these songs may also depend upon familiarity with the cues that bind popular song to contemporary experience. *Song, because of its direct connection to the language and melodic traditions of a society, may trigger many cultural cues in the listener.* There is no rule or yardstick by which we can evaluate a person's willingness to respond to a particular style. But regardless of how we feel at the surface level about the songs of either Schubert or Stevie Wonder, we can understand the cultural threads that unite them *beyond style*:

Common Cultural Ground for Songs of Schubert and Stevie Wonder

Each is in a living musical language that reflects the song traditions of its culture;

Each draws on contemporary traditions of poetry and speech (contemporary popular lyrics have their own value as poetry, just as ballads of past eras are still studied as verse);

Each involves cues that connect the musical experience to its surrounding world.

THE SONG CYCLE AND ITS COUNTERPART, THE RECORD ALBUM

Sometimes composers organized songs into *cycles*, in which a common idea, feeling, or other element ties the songs together in a dramatic unity. Some of the famous song cycles of the nineteenth and twentieth centuries are listed below. You may listen to them according to their availability.

The song cycle has a counterpart in some contemporary popular record albums, in which the various songs are loosely connected by some organizing plan. The Beatles' *Abbey Road* and *Sgt. Pepper's Lonely Hearts Club*

Band were trailblazers in this recorded genre. Putting aside the irrelevant labels of "popular" and "serious" we find no real difference in the basic procedures used in the works listed below.

Suggested Listening

Song Cycle

Span II

Classical — 1750 — 1825 — Romantic — 1900 — Modern — 1980

Schubert, *The Miller's Beautiful Daughter (Die schöne Müllerin*; 1823)
Winter's Journey (Winterreise; 1827)

Schumann, *The Poet's Love (Dichterliebe*; 1840)

Berlioz, *Summer Nights (Nuits d'été*; 1856)

Mussorgsky, *Songs and Dances of Death* (1877)

Debussy, *Songs of Bilitis (Chansons de Bilitis*; 1897)

Schoenberg, *Book of the Hanging Gardens (Das Buch der hängenden Gärten*; 1908)

Beatles, *Abbey Road* (1969)

Joni Mitchell, *Hejira* (1976); *Blue* (1970)

Stevie Wonder, *Songs in the Key of Life* (1976)

Billy Joel, *The Stranger* (1976)

Frédéric Chopin

The early nineteenth century witnessed a great leap forward in the sophistication and perfection of musical instruments. At the same time, composers were becoming more aware of timbre and texture as vital elements in their music. We have already discussed the part that Hector Berlioz played in the expansion of the orchestra into a "machine" of virtuosity, capable of producing wondrous new colors, textures, and technical brilliance. *What Berlioz did for the orchestra, Chopin would do for the piano.*

Frédéric Chopin (1810–49) was an early Romantic of Polish origin who revolutionized the art of composing for the piano. A phenomenal pianist with a unique and virtuosic manner of playing, he wrote compositions for a variety of effects, colors, and textures. Can various textures be created on a piano? The answer is yes. The piano allows for *simultaneous combinations* of rhythms, melodies, harmonies, dynamics, etc., which result in characteristic textures. Chopin's style was thoroughly romantic, and at the heart of each piece are emotional qualities that a good performer will bring to life.

To get some idea of how new and different Chopin's pianistic style must have seemed in the early nineteenth century, compare the end of the *Rondo* by Haydn 24a with the opening of the *Revolutionary Etude* by Chopin 24b .

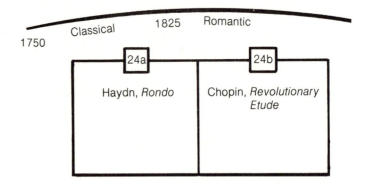

Aside from obvious differences of mood, the Chopin piece demands far more from a technical standpoint. You may notice that the combination of colors and textures create quite a different effect than the more reserved style of Haydn. As an example, the repeated pattern that we hear at the very beginning of the piece (in the lower register, very fast) builds a wall of sound above which the main melody is heard. The *etude*, a genre that entered Western music culture during the nineteenth century, reflects two Romantic traits: 1) *the growth of virtuosity*: an etude explores some technical problem on an instrument, often at the virtuoso level; thus, Chopin's *Revolutionary Etude* challenges the pianist's ability to play fast, complex passages with the left hand; 2) *the exploration of a feeling or mood*: this etude has been called "Revolutionary" because its fiery, impassioned mood supposedly represented Chopin's anger when the Russians captured the Polish city of Warsaw in 1831. However we interpret it (and it probably reflects a mood without a programmatic connection), it certainly expresses a powerful feeling in the Romantic manner.

Listen   Chopin, *Revolutionary Etude* 24b

Chopin: Additional Listening

Any of Chopin's works in the following genres is recommended:

ballade—a piano piece whose title suggests a connection to some unstated dramatic plan.
impromptu—a miniature which has the quality of an improvisation.
waltz—the famous dance in triple meter associated with Vienna.
mazurka—a lively Polish dance, also in triple meter.
nocturne—night piece.

LIED The German word for song. Traditionally, the term *lied* describes a notated song for singer and accompaniment.

SONG CYCLE A group of songs by one composer usually connected in some manner through music, feeling, or text.

ETUDE A piece in which a composer explores a specific instrumental technique.

Brahms, *Concerto for Piano and Orchestra in B-flat major*

Johannes Brahms was a late Romantic composer whom we will be discussing shortly. No work better demonstrates his style than his second piano concerto, a luxurious, intensely lyrical exploration of the *sonata-symphony* plan. In comparison to a Mozart symphony, Brahms's symphonic conceptions are not only longer, but are far more given to that romantic quality of "unleashed emotionalism."

First Movement, Allegro non troppo (not too fast). The movement opens with a typical Brahms theme—a noble, heroic statement (played by a solo horn, in dialogue with the piano and followed by strings) quickly followed by an agitated, faster idea played by the piano. The opening theme, then, has two parts, which immediately provide dramatic conflict. After a full orchestral statement of the original horn material, the second theme, in a new key, is presented. Its character is typically Brahmsian—a haunting,

Viennese melody played by the strings to a "dancing" pizzicato accompaniment. The basic thematic material presented, the composer proceeds to unfold a sonata-allegro design in long, lyrical spans.

There is a distinct difference between this movement and the one you first heard as an example of sonata-allegro form (pages 210–11). The Mozart has a "tight," "compact" form, typical of the Classical era. By contrast, the form of this movement is shaped by a romantic expansiveness. The tonal conflict, so vital to a Mozart symphony, is stretched so much longer in a Brahms symphonic form, that it may not be much of a factor in influencing long-range response. Instead, our attention is focused toward the dramatic interplay between piano and orchestra, fantasy-like sections and formal themes, haunting and heroic moods—in short, the listener's response shifts toward the romantic aesthetic.

Second Movement, Allegro appassionato (fast and passionate). In contrast with the luxurious length of the first movement, this movement—a scherzo—is quite compact in design. We know that in the traditional dance-derived movement we expect a three-part plan with a trio in the middle. Brahms does not disappoint us, but we are in for a bit of a surprise as to the nature of the trio. The form of the movement is presented below. This diagram may seem more similar to the sonata-allegro design than to the minuet and trio. It has qualities of *both*. Once again, we encounter the flexibility of models—an interaction between two forms—another example of a composer dealing with form as an active, changing process, rather than a static set of rules.

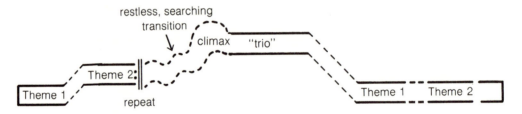

Third Movement, Andante (fairly slow). Brahms often composed intensely lyrical melodies with lullaby-like qualities. The theme of this movement, first played by a solo cello, is certainly one of these. Bittersweet and sad, this music is especially prominent in the overall plan of the concerto, for Brahms has switched the order of the second and third movements so that the slow one comes at an even more dramatic moment, after the agitated scherzo and right before the finale. In typical Brahms fashion, the lyrical "lullaby" is juxtaposed with a more agitated and restless *B* section, which finally leads back home to the original material. The overall form, then, is *ABA*.

Fourth Movement, Allegretto grazioso (somewhat fast and graceful). In this movement, the dance impulse is especially prominent. The opening theme, first heard in the piano, returns several times throughout the movement, giving it a *rondo* shape. A secondary lyrical theme provides further contrast. This rondo format is a good deal more intricate than the Haydn example you have heard; however, the basic *rondo* principle is still evident.

Brahms and Viennese Lyricism

During his lifetime, Johannes Brahms (1833–97) was accused of being stuffy and academic because of his preoccupation with traditional genres and techniques. All of his music reveals a remarkable control of details, especially motivic construction, but the popularity of Brahms's music has had little to do with his careful execution of musical designs. It is, rather, those bittersweet melodies that appeal to so many listeners. *At the heart of Brahms's style is an interplay between highly formal musical structure and a sentimental, romantic lyricism.* That special brand of lyricism came from a special city, Vienna.

What does a musical style have to do with a particular place? Sometimes, everything. If you are a fan of contemporary popular music, you may have heard of the "Nashville sound" or the "Motown sound." Each describes a style that was born in a certain place. Through some indescribable interaction between people, place, and circumstance, some cities (or regions) may provide the spark and nourishment for the development of a musical style. One could not imagine the development of jazz without the city of New Orleans. It would be equally strange to imagine the history of classical music since the eighteenth century without the city of Vienna.

Brahms at the age of twenty (drawing by J. B. Laurcus).

Whatever it was about Vienna that nurtured musical genius, it spawned several generations of great composers. From the late eighteenth century on, the men who would shape the European musical mainstream were there: Haydn, Mozart, Beethoven, and Schubert all lived and worked, for at least part of their lives, in Vienna. They were to be followed by other important composers, among them Brahms. Among the traits that tie these composers together is Viennese lyricism. Like the elusive term "soul" in today's popular music, Viennese lyricism is difficult to define. It may be described as a singing quality, which is "bittersweet" and "sentimental." Another of its trademarks is chromaticism. You can hear Viennese lyricism in the slow movement of Mozart's *Symphony No. 40*, Schubert's *Lied der Mignon*, and the lyrical sections of Brahms's *Piano Concerto in B-flat*.

INFLUENCES ON VIENNESE LYRICISM

Where does this singing quality come from? One very strong influence is German folk song, part of the living musical language for many composers of German descent. But there was another musical influence in Vienna that has already been mentioned; its proximity to Italy made it a place where both German and Italian musical traditions interacted and flourished. The Italian musical tradition, so influenced by "warm" Mediterranean song, added a special ingredient to the Viennese style.

Viennese lyricism sometimes involves a dance impulse. Vienna was the legendary home of the waltz, a dance that captured the fancy of nineteenth-century Europe, and found its way into the dance movement of the sonata-symphony group. For example, *The Ball* from Berlioz's *Fantastic Symphony* is, in fact, a waltz. In 1937, the Russian Dmitri Shostakovich composed his *Fifth Symphony*, a work very much in the sonata-symphony tradition. The trio of the scherzo movement sounds like a cross between a Viennese waltz and a Russian peasant dance (the emphasis depends a good deal on the performance). However, its connection to the dance tradition of Vienna is unmistakable.

The Viennese spirit comes to life in the music of Brahms in a special way. His melodies have the unmistakable qualities associated with Viennese lyricism. He also loved dance music and was a great fan of the Viennese waltzes by Johann Strauss. There are some places in his music where this is quite obvious; for example, it is possible to hear a remarkable similarity between a Strauss waltz and the lyrical theme of the last movement of Brahms's *B-flat Piano Concerto*.

Brahms lived in the second half of the nineteenth century, a time when Romanticism reached its most radical and revolutionary stage. *With his interest in traditional genres, forms, and techniques, Brahms's Romanticism had a distinctly conservative tinge.* In an age when many were obsessed with a musical radicalism, Brahms's art looked back to an idealized past. He "became a singer of the past, believing, perhaps, that singing of the past, he might serve the future."*

Connections in the Brahms Discussion

A composer's living language may be related to a city (or region).
Viennese lyricism.
Stylistic interplay of different musical traditions.
Continuing importance of the sonata-symphony group.
Flexibility of basic models.

Brahms: Additional Listening

Symphonies No. 1–4
Short piano pieces, Op. 117
Piano Quintet in F minor

Viennese Lyricism

influences	*qualities*
German and Italian folk song Viennese dance tradition	a "bittersweet," singing quality, sometimes including chromaticism

---

Richard Wagner

Only one other composer of the nineteenth century had an impact on European culture comparable to that of Beethoven: Richard Wagner, whose followers considered him to be the only true Beethoven heir. Wagner's musical style and related philosophy swept through Europe under the revolutionary slogan "the music of the future."

Any discussion of the life and music of this controversial composer is filled with potential traps. Without question, he was one of the most remarkable, original artists of the Classical–Romantic–Modern span. At the root of the Wagner "problem" is his personal philosophy, which ranged from racial purity to "the true path of art." There are those who would say, "Never mind Wagner's theories, just listen to his music." But Wagner would not have been among them. He wrote volumes on the philosophical-social

---

*Paul Henry Lang, *Music in Western Civilization* (New York, 1941), p. 896.

basis of music. As it happens, his most basic premise is one that concerns us deeply—the *ancient unity*. Although he might have been unable to respond to "Soul Train" (see page 99), a vital force in his life and art was the Greek drama. In the following passage, Wagner describes his vision of the ancient Greek dramatist Aeschylus (525–456 B.C.) in the throes of creative ecstasy:

> When the voices, ringing full, sounded forth the choral song, singing the deeds of the gods . . . while they gave to the dancers the mastering measure that meted out the rhythm of the dance. Which dance itself, in graceful movements told the story of those deeds . . . when to all the rich elements of spontaneous art . . . he joined the bond of speech, and concentrating them all into one focus, [Aeschylus] brought forth the highest conceivable form of art—the drama.*

A musician who calls *drama* the ultimate art! This is not surprising when you consider the Romantic quest for unity among the arts. Wagner's dream was to create the *Gesamtkunstwerk* (literally, "combined-art-work"). We already know its basic elements—music, dance, and drama. Wagner found his version of the ancient unity in a highly personal approach to music-drama. (The one element that was not included was dance.) He wrote his own texts, considering himself as much a dramatist as a musician.

Reflecting Wagner's desire to bond musical sound to drama was his use of *leitmotives*, a procedure that resembles Berlioz's use of the *idée fixe* (see page 263), but taken to far greater extremes. In a Wagner opera, each important element—person, object, idea—has its own orchestral motive. As the plot unfolds, the orchestra becomes an integral part of the drama through these life-laden musical statements. (An example is provided in the discussion that follows.) This procedure combines a logical, intellectualized scheme with a powerful and emotional lyricism in an attempt to capture that elusive Romantic dream: to blur the distinctions between music, drama, and life.

TRISTAN AND ISOLDE

Wagner's most famous opera is *Tristan and Isolde*. The cultural chain that provided him with its dramatic model, as well as its strange theme, is quite remarkable and bears comment. You will remember that the Romantics delved into myth as part of their general fascination with the past, the irrational, and the fantastic. The story Wagner used for his opera was a Medieval legend. The links to the past, however, go back much further. According to some scholars, *Tristan and Isolde* is but one version of a

*Wagner on Music and Drama, trans. by H. Ashton Ellis (New York, 1964), p. 77.

worldwide mythical tradition dating back to prehistoric times that has been called the love-death ritual.* It deals with the powerful energies generated by the relationships between life, death, and the role of fertility as a life-force. In the same sort of process described on pages 114–16 (the discussion of the ballad), this tradition spawned countless variants, some closely related, others only vaguely. One group of variants reached Medieval Europe as the Celtic legend of Tristan and Isolde. How were the legends communicated? One way was through song (or chant). In the closing centuries of the Middle Ages, these sung legends became models for written song-poems, which then entered European culture as literature (in most cases, only the text was written down). The version of the Tristan and Isolde legend that reached Wagner was one of these song-poems composed about 1210 by Gottfried von Strassburg. As you might expect with the reworking of a basic model, be it a myth, a sonata-allegro design, or the mother-child configuration of the picture sequence on page 500–503, the original details are inevitably shifted around a bit to suit the new creative situation. The plot of *Tristan* unfolds as follows:

Act I (The act takes place on the deck of a ship). Tristan is bringing the Princess Isolde back to Cornwall to marry his uncle, King Mark. Tristan has killed the man Isolde was to wed and now seems indifferent to the love she reluctantly bears him. She accuses him of having forgotten his knightly vows to make amends for the wrongs he has done and to seek forgiveness of his enemies. Tristan offers her his sword so that she may kill him, but Isolde suggests, instead, that they both drink from a "cup of peace" which she has had prepared. Isolde believes the drink to be poison by which they will both die, but it is really a love potion, which causes them to fall deeply and passionately in love. The act ends as the ship's crew hail the impending appearance of the groom-to-be, King Mark.

Act II (King Mark's castle). Isolde is now married to King Mark. Tristan is unable to leave the castle because of his obsessive love for his uncle's wife. Days are unbearable to the lovers, for then they must hide their feelings; the night takes on symbolic mystery as their real world of truth and passion. They sing a hymn to the night, but at its climax, they are discovered by Mark. Tristan, rather than defend himself, hurls himself upon his adversary's sword in order to commit suicide.

Act III (Tristan's castle in Brittany). Tristan, gravely wounded, has been carried back to his own castle across the sea. Isolde is eventually brought to him, but it is too late; united once again with his beloved, he dies. King Mark, who has learned of the love potion they inadvertently drank, comes to forgive the star-crossed lovers. He arrives in time to hear Isolde's heartrending song of farewell as she dies beside Tristan's body.

* Joseph Campbell, *The Masks of God*, 4 vols. (New York, 1959–68).

Suggestions for Listening

Ideally, Wagner's opera should be experienced in the setting for which it was conceived—a darkened theater. Since it is in German, it is important, under any circumstances, to be familiar with the text. (Most recordings include a line-by-line translation of the libretto.*) Some innovative features of Wagner's operatic style should be mentioned:

1. *The role of the orchestra.* Compared with earlier operatic practice, the orchestra plays a heightened role in Wagner's operas, while the independent role of the singer has been somewhat subordinated. In a way, Wagner's operas are like symphonies with vocal lines woven in. In many sections, the removal of the vocal part would leave a thoroughly accurate musical statement intact.
2. *Continuous musical form.* As an extension of the previous idea, Wagner's operatic form abandons, to some extent, the juxtaposition of recognizable sections such as recitative, aria, and chorus. Instead, we hear a more continuous musical line. In the more traditional operas, the listener may have a comfortable feeling of recognition— "Ah, here comes a recitative. And now the aria!" etc.—but such expectations have no place here. To follow Wagner's long-range continuous musical form, the listener is obliged to become actively involved with the meaning of the drama. Stated another way, you cannot separate Wagner's musical design from its dramatic intent. And that is exactly what he was after.
3. *Innovative chromatic harmony.* Wagner's late works, beginning with *Tristan and Isolde,* are marked by a very personalized and innovative use of chromatic harmony. This is discussed in the following section.

The *Prelude to Tristan* is often played apart from the opera as a concert piece. It provides a microcosm of the opera's legendary chromaticism. Therefore, we shall listen to it primarily for its implications considering tonality.

Listen | *Prelude to Tristan and Isolde*

Tristan and Isolde is about love, adultery, and death. The mood of the prelude is dark, tragic, and sensual. Throughout the opera, Wagner identifies the passion of the two lovers with a specific leitmotive. The *Prelude* opens with this "passion motive," heard three times, moving up in sequence. It is a chromatic melody, growing out of some very unstable chromatic harmony. You will notice that the motive is always

*A *libretto* is the text of a music-drama.

"left hanging." It does not resolve, but creates a restless forward potential. In fact, Wagner does not resolve the motive until the end of the opera, at Isolde's death. The message is clear: The sexual passion between Tristan and Isolde can only be resolved in death. This is an example of how Wagner's long-range musical form can only be understood in relation to the plot. It also demonstrates how he used leitmotives to create dramatic meaning.

Listening Activities

Consider three aspects of the *Prelude*: tempo, meter, and "arrivals at home base."

Describe the tempo:

Is there a meter?

How many times does the music reach a firm feeling of stability at a "home base"?

THE IMPORTANCE OF *TRISTAN AND ISOLDE*

The influence of *Tristan and Isolde* on the musical language of Span II cannot be overstated. It changed the course of European musical culture. What was there about this music that was so revolutionary? It was the chromaticism. In earlier music you have heard in which chromatic harmony and melody are present (Purcell's *Dido and Aeneas* and Schubert's *Lied der Mignon*, for example), chromaticism functions within the context of a "home base." Its instability resolves to a strong *tonality*. But what of the *Tristan Prelude*? You probably found few, if any, stable moments in the music. Even in the moments of silence, the harmonic tension remains.

Wagner's use of chromaticism tends to obscure tonality. In the *Prelude to Tristan*, it is difficult to discern the tonic key. The music seems to wander in a restless search for home. Without a clear key center, the listener is left in a continual state of expectation. This might become clearer if we compare *Tristan* to a more traditional harmonic structure: an *ABA* design with a modulation from the *A* section to the *B* section (discussed on page 78).

Traditional *ABA* Tonal Design

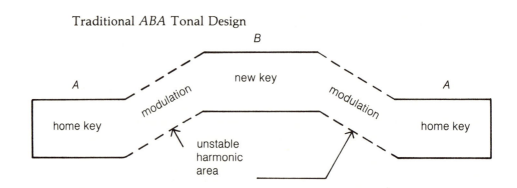

We know that a modulation passage feels unstable and creates a sense of forward potential. In the *Prelude*, the tonal goal is so far off and obscure that the listener may never hear it. The tonal journey of the *Prelude* might be represented as follows:

Prelude to Tristan

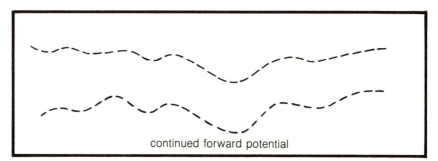

In *Tristan and Isolde*, Wagner challenged one of the most basic elements of the European tradition—tonality. He wasn't the first to do so. For decades, the Romantic composers' search for new chromatic harmonies had been exploring the limits of the major–minor tonal system. But with *Tristan*, it seemed that a bridge had been crossed, leading to new regions of harmonic organization. We will pick up this important strand in the evolution of musical language in the next chapter, where we discuss the composers Claude Debussy and Arnold Schoenberg.

TRISTAN BEYOND STYLE

The force of *Tristan*'s impact, not only on Western notated music, but on European culture as a whole, is evidence of a power of communication that warrants closer study. Style is, after all, only the outer layer of an experience, and though it is an all-important means of artistic communication, there are deep-seated strands of human musicality underneath these details.

TRISTAN AND THE ANCIENT UNITY

There is no doubt that Wagner was an innovator. The obscure tonality of the *Prelude* clearly points to a new type of musical organization. But it should not be overlooked that this innovation functions within one of the oldest inventions of humankind: the music-drama. We have already observed that innovation is often based on some preexisting model or practice that acts as a lifeline, something that both composer and audience can hang on to. Furthermore, it may be suggested that Wagner discovered and refined his personal musical language under the direct influence of the universal dramatic impulse. Clearly, one path to the creation of the "new" is to immerse oneself in the deep channels of human musicality that exist beyond style and to use the energy and impulses of that channel as a guiding force. Time and time again, composers have used the ancient unity as a vehicle for generating stylistic details.

TRISTAN AS RITUAL

Wagner considered his music to be more than art; it was the expression of a personal philosophy that was comparable to a religion (though far removed from the Judeo-Christian concept of what a religion is). He was, in fact, the ultimate exponent of that Romantic notion of "art as religion." He conceived of his operas as full-fledged rituals, in which the audience was expected to take part both emotionally and philosophically. While we will not enter into any discussion of Wagner's philosophy, it is interesting to consider the musical means with which he accomplished this ritualistic purpose.

It may be suggested that *the success of any ritual depends upon the willingness of the participants to enter a heightened state of awareness, for a certain length of time, during which the message is experienced.* Consider for a moment, some of the things you have discovered about the *Tristan Prelude* that may lead the listener into this ritualistic realm:

1. The lack of a clear tonal center (home base) keeps the listener in a continual state of expectation.
2. The slow tempo increases the solemnity of this effect. The forward potential created by the restless chromatic harmony and the unresolved leitmotive happen in a sort of slow-motion world that may seem to suspend normal reality.

Considering the complete work, we find another level at which the listener is drawn into a long-range ritual. To follow Wagner's form, one must follow the ideas of the drama. At the end of the opera, when the "passion" leitmotive is resolved at Isolde's death, the *willing* listener has been led through a solemn, timeless ritual of music, emotions, and ideas.

CUES RELATING *TRISTAN* TO LIFE-IMAGERY

But not all listeners are willing. In Chapter 4 we discovered that an important aspect of some musical languages are cues that relate music to ideas, life-rhythms, etc. *Tristan* is legendary for its evocation of sexuality. For many listeners, the "passion" motive moving through its many chromatic harmonic settings produces a type of tense, sexual urgency. It is no secret that the long-range musical form may be considered symbolic of the sex act itself. But these cues are by no means universal. To other listeners, the same musical sounds may seem trite, or even boring. There can be no absolutes in this matter. Clearly, the same musical cues can mean different things to different listeners, depending upon background and temperament. Although the cues themselves are not universal, the *use of cues relating music to life* is a universal feature that contributes much to *Tristan*'s success.

WAGNER'S ROLE IN THE TRANSITION TO MODERN MUSIC

We shall soon be discussing the music of the twentieth century, or *modern music*, as it is called. Wagner played an important role in the passage from Romanticism to Modernism in two key areas:

1. Wagner's chromaticism and long-range form represented a new type of musical organization that contributed to the breakup of the major–minor tonal system's preeminence in musical practice.
2. In a cultural sense, Wagner was perceived as the ultimate Romantic. His music, interwoven with his personality and philosophy, had brought European Romanticism to a climax. (And many observers place that long-range climax at *Tristan*.) Although Romanticism continued in many guises, its full energies had been spent, dissipated by Wagner's one-of-a-kind romantic ecstasy.

Wagner and his work have always elicited extreme reactions—both positive and negative—from the public and musicians alike. But no one doubts either his genius or his role in changing the course of musical culture. More important are the many levels of understanding at which his music functions—another set of keys to the connective web of the world's music. It may be something of a shock to realize that the singers in *Tristan and Isolde* have unnamed counterparts in Dutch New Guinea, where a more ancient version of the love-death ritual is performed in a tribal ceremony of chanting, drumming, and dancing. And though the style of their music would be far different from *Tristan*, nonetheless the final effect in cultural terms is very much the same. Both music-dramas—Wagner's *Tristan* and its distant cousin, the love-death ritual of New Guinea—use various elements of the ancient unity to lift their participants out of temporality and "into the no-place, no-time, no-when, no-where of the mythological age, which is here and now."* Shifting gears into a shorter perspective, we find in *Tristan* a musical language that ultimately would affect many twentieth-century harmonic styles, including jazz. That so many different doors of musical understanding may be opened to reach *Tristan*, and are in turn opened by *Tristan*, speaks ultimately of the universality of musical experience, beyond the boundaries of style.

Connections in the Wagner Discussion

The ancient unity.
Music as heightened experience (ritual).
Artistic activity may be part of a cultural chain.

Brahms and Wagner: A Contrast in Style

The artistic lives of Brahms and Wagner were at their apogee during the second half of the nineteenth century. As you may have already deduced, they related to each other in much the same way that Mendelssohn and Berlioz did. Considered on the classical–romantic continuum, Brahms appears as a conservative Romantic and Wagner a radical one. (You may wish to write in some of the features of their personalities and music which support this perception.)

classical aesthetic ⟵————————————⟶ romantic aesthetic
                          Brahms   Wagner

Although Brahms had no deep stylistic connection to his conservative predecessor Mendelssohn, Wagner's musical style and musical philosophy did owe something to Berlioz. Both Wagner and Berlioz tried to unite music with drama in a grand-scale fusion: each tried to create a revolutionary art that would capture the soul, senses, and spirit of the public; each saw revolutionary change in musical style as the "true path of art" for the future; each had experimented with genre, form, and other musical techniques to

*Campbell, *The Masks of God*, Vol. 1: *Primitive Mythology*, p. 170.

accomplish his vision. Although there was some personal tension between Wagner and Berlioz, there was also an acknowledgement of the common ground they shared.

While Wagner had continued on the radical path staked out by Berlioz, Brahms became the standard-bearer of musical conservatism in the late nineteenth century. His symphonies and chamber works, crafted along traditional sonata-symphony lines, and noticeably devoid of the sensationalism of Wagner's music, continued as a Romantic echo of the Classical ideal. Here we can acknowledge, once again, the Beethovenian presence in the musical culture of the nineteenth century. Both Brahms and Wagner sought the "true path" that led from the man they both recognized as their master. Wagner publicly proclaimed himself Beethoven's "true successor," that he had picked up the cosmic threads of Beethoven's *Ninth Symphony*. Brahms's claim to the lineage was far less flamboyant. He simply turned out one masterpiece after another, dominated by the Beethovenian sonata-symphony ideal. Who was right? Which of them had indeed inherited the Beethoven mantle? This question will be answered shortly.

The Quest for Legitimacy

The musical split between Wagner and Brahms became the subject of quite a heated controversy in the second half of the nineteenth century. The music of each man was the rallying point for two distinctly opposed camps. This war of aesthetics was part of a cultural phenomenon we will call the "quest for legitimacy" and was often heated, petty, and curiously vicious. Consider, for example, this review of a Brahms symphony by the Wagnerite Hugo Wolf, a composer himself:

> Brahms . . . exercises about as much influence on the history of art as the late Robert Volkmann [a popular composer of the nineteenth century] . . . which is to say *no* influence at all. . . . The man who has written three symphonies and apparently intends to follow with another six* . . . is only a relic from primeval ages and no vital part of the great stream of time.**

Stylistic controversy and related judgmental views concerning the relative value of a particular musical style (and by implication of an audience's musical taste) are certainly familiar in our time. Rather passionate and sometimes amusing battles still rage between supporters of various musical styles, for example, jazz versus rock in popular music; the "abstract-intellectual" versus the "subjective-emotional" in "serious" music.

*Wolf apparently thought Brahms was merely rewriting Beethoven's nine symphonies.
**Quoted in Schonberg, *Lives of the Great Composers*, rev. ed. (New York, 1981), p. 296.

In fact, evaluating musical styles has become a powerful tradition in our culture. Critical appraisal of music has always been fashionable, but it reached a new intensity in the nineteenth century. Hugo Wolf's comments contain the essential ideas in this quest for legitimacy. Since this trend is basic to understanding the cultural environment of the modern world, a closer look at part of the quote and its implications will be useful:

Brahms . . . exercises about as much influence on the history of art as the late Robert Volkmann . . . which is to say *no* influence at all. . . .

1. The quote supports the tendency to dismiss a composer's work (in this case, both Brahms's and Volkmann's) in a superior and scornful manner. This is certainly a style of response with which we may be familiar, whether it be in books, articles, or conversation.
2. The quote implies that the legitimacy of a composer is measured by his influence on the evolution of the art. The idea that society and art are continually evolving to higher states dominates much of nineteenth-century thought and continues to do so today. This mode of thinking places tremendous value on change as a natural phenomenon. Thus, musical styles which do not fit the evolutionary plan are relegated to oblivion. (See also page 123, "The Idea of Evolution in Musical Styles.")
3. By implication, the writer suggests that there is only one legitimate path for musical style. The idea of a mainstream of music evolving since the Middle Ages is a powerful one. According to this tradition, certain composers are "legitimate," while others lie outside some predetermined path of stylistic development. Composers who "go down the wrong path" receive less than courteous treatment in critical evaluations.

That these beliefs are defended with great vigor simply reflects how important music can become: It has the capacity to encode the very image of a person, group, or culture. In the words of a present-day musician reacting to an audience indifferent to his solo improvisation, "Hey, out there, these ain't just notes . . . this is my life!"

The same idea—that music can become life itself—certainly applies to Brahms and Wagner. Each was totally immersed in composing. Each found a personal musical language within his culture. Each found inspiration in the music of Beethoven. They were different people with different temperaments. And most important, they lived in an age that was both stimulated and fragmented by stylistic diversity. Later, less passionate observers would understand that *both styles were legitimate*. How could it be otherwise when millions of people have found the music of both composers to be important in their lives? The rivalry between the supporters of Brahms and Wagner seems petty, even pointless a century later. In retrospect, we recog-

310

nize this battle as part of a continuing phenomenon destined to increase in intensity during the twentieth century, creating choices and problems for composers and listeners alike.

Giuseppe Verdi

The giant of nineteenth-century Italian music was Giuseppe Verdi (1813–1901). At the center of his art was the gift of Italian lyrical melody; the genre in which he found expression, quite naturally, was opera. (He wrote few pieces not intended for the stage.) Verdi's name has become a legend in operatic circles, and his works form a substantial part of the world's operatic repertory.

Verdi's art is rooted in the passion and spontaneity of drama and song. Though his music is crafted with precision, brilliance, and skill, it is never encumbered with stodgy intellectualism. From its inception, Italian opera had always been a "popular" art, concerned with a direct appeal to the emotions. In Italy, opera is, in the best sense, a national art—a living musical language of an entire culture. Verdi is in a direct line of composers reaching back to the Florentine Camerata and beyond to the dramatic song traditions of the Mediterranean cultures (see pages 172–73).

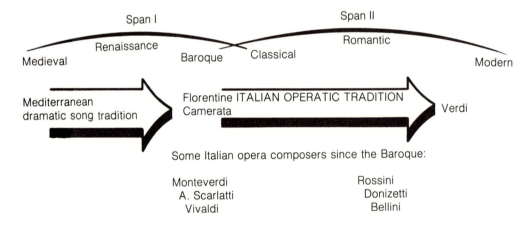

Some Italian opera composers since the Baroque:

Monteverdi
A. Scarlatti
Vivaldi

Rossini
Donizetti
Bellini

AÏDA

By the middle of the nineteenth century, the premiere of a new Verdi opera was quite a prestigious event. Undoubtedly this was what prompted the ambitious director of a new opera house in Cairo, Egypt, to commission a new work for its opening from Verdi. The result was *Aïda*—an opera about Egypt on a French libretto translated into Italian and performed by Italians in Cairo in 1871! While the idea of ancient Egyptians singing in Italian may seem a bit odd, it amply demonstrates the power and prestige of the Italian operatic tradition, which persists to this day. Finally, we must remember that *Aïda* was really intended for Europeans. Thus, it is but one of many representations of an exotic, non-Western culture, part of a practice that flourished in the nineteenth century and continues in our time, especially in fiction and film.

Verdi liked to set stories with lots of action, passion, and emotional contrast. Underlying all his operas are basic human situations; *Aïda* is no exception. The plot revolves around the love of an Egyptian general, Radames, for Aïda, the daughter of an Ethiopian king at war with Egypt. To complicate the situation, Amneris, the daughter of the Egyptian king, is in love with Radames. Thus we have a well-established formula: the eternal triangle. As the drama unfolds, it becomes clear that the lovers are doomed. As in *West Side Story*, eternal love is in conflict with earthly responsibilities. Aïda's father persuades her that, in order to save her native land, she must trick Radames into betraying information about a planned attack of Egyptian troops. When this has been accomplished, Aïda and her father flee, leaving the dishonored Radames to face charges of treason. Act IV begins as Amneris begs Radames to renounce Aïda in return for his life.

| Listen | *Aïda*, by Giuseppe Verdi, Act IV

AFTERTHOUGHT
The following ideas will help put *Aïda* into a broader perspective, as well as provide insights for your listening experience:

1. Verdi's art focuses on the human voice, unlike Wagner's operas, in which the orchestra plays an equal—if not superior—role with the singers. With Verdi, the soul of the work cannot be separated from its emotion-laden melody. In this sense, a Verdi opera is more direct than Wagner's, in which the orchestra provides more intellectualized commentary on both the action and its meaning.
2. Notwithstanding the prime importance of the voice, Verdi's orchestra plays a crucial supporting role. The orchestral material captures the mood of each scene with astonishing musical-dramatic accuracy. Consider, for example, the role of the drum in Act IV, as well as the "heavenly" accompaniment to Aïda's "angel of death" passage. Verdi's use of harmony, texture, and orchestration is an important part of his genius. And he had an infallible sense of timing: he knew just when to use a particular effect or sound. Once you are familiar with the story of *Aïda* (or any other opera), it can be fascinating to focus your listening on the orchestral part to gain another perspective on the work.

Modest Mussorgsky

Any discussion of the works of Modest Mussorgsky (1839–81) must include two important concepts: *nationalism* and *realism*. We have already described nationalism as a basic trait of nineteenth-century Romanticism (see pages 280–81). You will recall that many composers became more conscious of the relationship between their music and their homeland, especially in areas outside France and the regions that are now Italy, Germany, and Austria. (Austrian music is generally considered part of the German music tradition.) The music of these last-named regions had dominated the Western notated tradition since 1600. In the Classical–Romantic span, German music had become the most influential, primarily in recognition of the great masterpieces in the sonata-symphony group by such composers as Mozart, Haydn, Beethoven, Schubert, Mendelssohn, and Brahms. The term *nationalist composer* is generally applied to composers who tried to break away from this central tradition by writing music that drew on regional folk styles. There is no better example of a nineteenth-century nationalist than the Russian Modest Mussorgsky.

Born the son of a wealthy landowner, his early life reflects one of the cultural mechanisms that perpetuated the diffusion of the Western notated tradition: *the association of "serious" music with aristocratic taste*. As was the custom of the Russian nobility (or those who wished to assume the various aspects of its life-style), Mussorgsky was raised in an environment that held foreign culture in high esteem. Through this cultural channel, the young Mussorgsky absorbed a basic musical language from the European tradition. A fascinating image of Mussorgsky as a young military officer suggests something of his aristocratic self-image, and more important to us, the place of music in it:

Mussorgsky shortly before his death (portrait by Ilya Repin).

Mussorgsky was at that time a very callow, most elegant, perfectly contrived little officer: brand-new, close-fitting uniform, toes well turned out, hair well oiled and carefully smoothed-out, hands shapely and well cared for. His manners were polished and aristocratic. He spoke through his teeth, and his carefully chosen words were interspersed with French phrases and rather labored. He showed, in fact, signs of a slight pretentiousness; but also, quite unmistakably, of perfect breeding and education. He sat down at the piano and, coquettishly raising his hands, started playing delicately and gracefully, bits of *Trovatore* and *Traviata* [at that time, the latest Verdi operas], the circle around him rapturously murmuring "Charmant! Delicieux!"*

This image of Mussorgsky as man and musician could not be further from that which the world was destined to know. The currents of history would lead him on another path.

An unresolved tension existed in nineteenth-century Russian society between those who wished to pattern art on Western European ideas and those who sought an independent Russian culture, free from outside influence. This conflict affected not only music, but literature and painting as well. Soon after the time referred to in the quote above, Mussorgsky became involved with a group of Russian composers who urged him to follow the nationalist path. The young man did a complete about-face: he wrote to one of his friends, "You know I have been a cosmopolitan, but now I have undergone a rebirth: I have been brought near to everything Russian."

*M. D. Calvocoressi, *Modest Mussorgsky* (Fair Lawn, N.J., 1956), pp. 18–19.

Two years later, in 1861, the Russian serfs were emancipated. As a direct result of this social upheaval, Mussorgsky was deprived of his inheritance. In keeping with the Romantic cult-image of the artist, he dropped out of normal society (although he worked, on and off, as a civil servant for most of his remaining days) and joined a commune of radical young intellectuals, whose activities included discussions of the latest ideas about art and philosophy. It was during this time that Mussorgsky embraced the second concept that would shape his music: *realism*. The idea of realism is quite simple: *art should depict life as it is, not as we would like it to be*. The young Russian had many opportunities to test out the theory, since the rest of his life included a series of traumatic episodes involving alcoholism, depression, poverty, abandonment by friends, and the creation of a few masterpieces that would ensure his place among the major composers of Western music.

BORIS GODUNOV

Mussorgsky is known to the world by a handful of compositions, among them the opera *Boris Godunov*. It is a drama about a sixteenth-century czar who has gained the throne by murdering a child who was the rightful heir. It should be mentioned that this was not some imaginary legend to nineteenth-century Russian audiences, but history. At a time when there was still an absolute monarch in power, *Boris Godunov* was a very realistic subject. (Compare this, for example, with *The Damnation of Faust*, which is clearly a fantasy.) The main focus of the drama is the character of Boris, who goes mad and dies as the enormity of his crime is revealed. The following discussion concerns the general musical style of the work, and two specific scenes, the Death of Boris and the "Fool Scene".

| Listen | *Boris Godunov*, Act IV, Scene 2, The Death of Boris and Act IV, Scene 3, Lament of the Fool. |

THE MUSICAL STYLE OF *BORIS GODUNOV*

How did Mussorgsky translate the twin concepts of nationalism and realism into musical sound? The nationalistic aspect is easier to describe: Mussorgsky's musical language was based directly in the folk traditions of Russia. His melodic style is drawn from the living language of Russian folk music, characterized by modal themes, repeated motives in near-ostinato patterns, and complex meters. The modal harmonies reflect Russian tradition, influenced by both folk and church practices. To the nineteenth-century European listener, this was very exotic music, which lay far outside the traditional major–minor tonal system.

The realism is somewhat more difficult to pin down. That the music was based in everyday Russian traditions is, in itself, realistic. But Mussorgsky went further than that: he believed that music should reflect the spoken language. To this end, he observed the rhythms, inflections, and melodic shape of the Russian language and experimented with representing specific speech-types through music. (In his songs, for example, we find melodic imitations of the slurred speech of a drunk, as well as the sound of a woman scolding her husband.) Consider, as an example of this imitative style, the "wailing" motive of the Fool ("ah! ah! ah!") who confronts Boris with his crime. Here is a musical motive taken directly from life. (As an experiment, say "ah" to yourself in a natural manner. Notice the melodic shape of that emotion-based sound.) This realistic approach to melody might well be thought of as a kind of musical photography. The connection between the sung melody and the spoken word takes on even greater meaning when we realize that the motive is also played in the orchestra throughout the drama. But there is more: the melody the Fool sings has a "fool-like" rhythm: starting, stopping, mindlessly repetitive. Was Mussorgsky's melodic style a new discovery? Not really. Like the origin of recitative (see page 173), Mussorgsky's melodic realism is another regional expression of a deeper impulse—*the universal potential for interplay between speech and melody.* Another realistic sound is the "tolling bell" motive heard in the death scene and echoed throughout the opera. It is juxtaposed with a religious chorale, first heard in the background. The two musical ideas, both taken from life, create a powerful, even awesome effect as Boris dies. *Realism, in the universal perspective, is simply an emphasis of the potential bond between music and life.*

FROM ROMANTICISM TO REALISM

Realism was one inevitable result of the Romantic search for "truth." Romanticism proclaimed a passion for the infinite and a desire to attain the fullest measure of existence. But what happens when you go looking for the truth without a safety net? You might not like what you find. This is, in part, what realism is about.

The early Romantics tended to be idealists. After all, nineteenth-century Romanticism suggests that there is some noble truth in life that we can attain through a personal quest for a state of transcendence. The subjects of Romantic music and art often included mythical beings and heroic deeds of the past. Despite all the realistic touches in Berlioz's *Damnation of Faust* (the vocal cries, the orchestral portrayal of the monster), something tells us, "This is not the way life really is." A step toward realism, yes; but realism? No.

To Mussorgsky, music had no value as an end in itself. Its only purpose was to reflect and communicate reality. There is no better illustration of this realistic approach than Mussorgsky's harmony, which was frequently dissonant and bleak. In fact, the most often-performed version of *Boris* is a romanticized arrangement by another Russian composer, Rimsky-

Korsakov. After Mussorgsky's death, he "corrected" what he considered to be harmonic errors and replaced Mussorgsky's bare-sounding orchestrations with a more ornate and mellifluous version. It may be said that Mussorgsky's realism was, and continues to be, too harsh for many listeners. But that is what Mussorgsky's art was about: a nonidealistic representation of life as he saw it. *The rejection of the idea that music should be beautiful and pleasing for its own sake is a decisive step toward modernism.* And in this respect, *Boris Godunov* reflects a cultural energy that would dominate many musical styles in the twentieth century.

Connections in the Mussorgsky Discussion

A living musical language may be tied to a culture or region.
The ancient unity.
The potential bond between music and life.
The association of Western notated music with aristocratic taste.
Potential interplay between speech and melody.

Mussorgsky: Additional Listening

Night on Bald Mountain (1867)
Pictures at an Exhibition (1874)
Songs and Dances of Death (1875)

REALISM   The idea that art should reflect life.

QUESTIONS

For the following questions, find any false statement(s) and correct them by changing the word(s) in italics. More than one statement may be false; all the statements may be true.

1. Concerning Franz Schubert:

    (a) He is well known as a composer of the *chanson*.

    (b) His music was influenced by *both* the classical and the romantic spirit.

    (c) His song style reflects a relationship to *German folk song*.

    (d) His "Lied der Mignon," set to a poem by Goethe, reflects the Romantic interest in the *union between music and poetry*.

2. Concerning the Romantic miniature:

    (a) It describes song and *sonata*, among other genres.

    (b) It is the *fulfillment* of the Romantics' tendency toward grandiosity.

    (c) It was often concerned with the *portrayal of an intense feeling*.

    (d) It was conceived as *concert music*.

3. Concerning Viennese lyricism:

    (a) It is one example of the *relationship of a musical style to a city or region*.

    (b) You can hear its influence in the music of *Mozart, Schubert, and Brahms*.

    (c) One of its important components was the music of *France*.

    (d) Another important component was the *dance*.

4. Concerning Brahms and Wagner:

    (a) Brahms was the *conservative* Romantic.

    (b) *Wagner* composed pieces mainly in the sonata-symphony group.

    (c) Each man was deeply influenced by *Berlioz*.

    (d) The music of *Brahms* better demonstrates direct relationships to the ancient unity.

5. Concerning the "quest for legitimacy":

    (a) It suggests that the music best follows an *evolutionary* course.

    (b) It suggests that those who lie outside this course are *inferior* composers.

    (c) It *decreased* in intensity as music moved into the twentieth century.

    (d) It places great value on *change* in musical style.

6. Concerning Wagner:

    (a) An important element in his music was the use of *modal* harmony.

    (b) In terms of the European musical culture, he was a *radical* innovator.

(c) In a long-range perspective of musical culture, his art is directly based in some of the *oldest human impulses and traditions*.

(d) In terms of musical aesthetics, he was closer to *Mendelssohn than Berlioz*.

7. Concerning Berlioz's *idée fixe* (previous chapter), Wagner's system of leitmotives, and Mussorgsky's realism:

(a) Each technique is somewhat *related to the other*.

(b) Each grows out of the universal tradition of *the ancient unity*.

(c) Each leans toward the concept of *absolute* music.

(d) Other than opera, they are most closely related to the Baroque tradition of *fugue*.

8. Concerning Verdi:

(a) In universal terms, the most basic musical impulses in his works are drama and *dance*.

(b) He stands in a long line of Italian opera composers reaching back to *1750*.

(c) In contrast to Wagner's operas, Verdi's are centered around the *orchestra*.

(d) Compared to Wagner, Verdi's approach to opera was more *radical*.

9. Concerning Mussorgsky:

(a) He found his living musical language by turning to the traditions of *Russia*.

(b) Two important features of his work are *nationalism and realism*.

(c) His musical language explored regions *outside* the major-minor tonal system.

(d) Basic sources for his melodic style were *Russian folk song and instrumental practice*.

12

The Modern Era

As the nineteenth century came to a close, Romanticism was losing its hold on the musical culture. Three composers—Debussy, Schoenberg, and Stravinsky—were to take new paths that would greatly expand the musical language. Innovation continued to exist side by side with tradition. The sonata-symphony group, its history reaching back over a hundred years to the Classical era, continued in various guises. Above all, *diversity dominated the musical scene*. No single musical style gained supremacy. But the quest for legitimacy continued with the same intensity. At the same time, the culture of the world became more complex and interconnected. There was more to know and more to experience. And the cultural cues that identify a living musical language were becoming more numerous.

Claude Debussy

As a student at the Paris Conservatory, Claude Debussy (1862–1918) had a reputation as an upstart. He often gathered together a group of students and improvised wild and "dangerous" music on the piano for them. In these improvisations he purposely broke all the traditional rules, especially those of harmony. This activity was more than just a student rebellion; Debussy was experimenting with the raw material of a highly personal style destined to influence the course of modern music.

Debussy's music represents a turning away from German Romanticism which had become, for him, a collection of trite formulas. He was not very fond of Beethoven's music, although he recognized the importance of the *Ninth Symphony*. For Debussy, its lesson was "not to retain old forms . . . but to open our windows onto a free sky." As we have discovered, German music had dominated the European scene throughout the nineteenth century. It was Debussy's intention to reaffirm the French aesthetic, and his music may be understood as part of the general trend toward nationalism. Early in his career, Debussy had been under the sway of Wagner's ideas and music. And, though he would eventually disavow this influence, he incor-

Claude Debussy (oil painting by Forcade).

porated certain Wagnerian practices of harmony and orchestration in his early works. *Once again we discover that a living musical language reflects the blending of many sources and styles.* Rejecting Wagnerism, Debussy found inspiration in the decidedly non-German style of Mussorgsky. Here was music more suited to the French taste. Debussy felt quite at home with Mussorgsky's modal melodies and harmonies and its emphasis on simplicity and directness. His appraisal of Mussorgsky is an implied criticism of the German tradition:

> No one has spoken to that which is best in us with such tenderness and profundity; he is unique, and will be remembered for an art without rigid procedures or arid formulas. Never before has such a refined sensibility expressed itself with such simple means.*

That good music does not have to be difficult or overloaded with "significance" was central to Debussy's aesthetic. Although we shall discover that his technique is quite complex, the result always sounds effortless, an elusive interplay of moods and feelings.

*Claude Debussy, *Monsieur Croche* (Paris, 1971), p. 29.

Listen | Debussy, *Prelude to "The Afternoon of a Faun"* (1894)

Prelude to "The Afternoon of a Faun" was Debussy's first major orchestral achievement and has remained his best-known symphonic work. The musical conception was inspired by a poem of Stéphane Mallarmé. Sensual and exotic, the poem tells of a mythical being, half man and half goat, and his dreamlike encounter with three nymphs. The setting is a wooded landscape. At its first performance, this work was so enthusiastically received that the conductor was compelled to repeat it. The poet, upon hearing it, said, "This music prolongs the emotion of my poem and fixes the scene much more vividly than color [painting] could have done."*

Listen | Debussy, *La Mer* (The Sea) (1905)

    I. *De l'Aube à midi sur la mer* (From Dawn till Noon on the Sea)
    II. *Jeux de vagues* (Play of the Waves)
    III. *Dialogue du vent et de la mer* (Dialogue of Wind and Sea)

Debussy chose a painting by the Japanese artist Hokusai for the title page of *La Mer*. The composer was not suggesting that his piece was a musical version of the painting, but that both the painting and his piece shared a similar region of aesthetic experience. *La Mer* is filled with images of *light evoked in sound*. In reference to its composition, Debussy said, "What I am doing might be like painting a landscape in a studio." It is in the spirit of Debussy's intentions for us to let music suggest visual images. Sound, sight, light, and imagination are all invited into the musical experience.

DEBUSSY'S IMPRESSIONISM

The term *impressionism* has become synonymous with the music of Debussy. Although the composer was unhappy with it, the word does evoke certain qualities of his style. Impressionism, both in music and art, is concerned with the creation of a mood, a feeling (an *impression!*) through simple but elusive means. *Light* and its changing effects in the visual world play an important role in impressionistic music. How can music be concerned with light? Since music allows action in time, it is especially suited to the portrayal of changing patterns of light. *La Mer* can be considered a study of light interacting with the motion of the sea.

Unlike Romantic composers, poets, and painters, whose subjects were often monumental, epic themes, the impressionists sought out the commonplace world and found it filled with miracles; a familiar landscape or a figure in the park could be an appropriate subject for their art. Totally

* Leon Vallas, *Claude Debussy*, trans. by M. and G. O'Brien (New York, 1933), p. 102.

absent from impressionist music and art is the Romantic's struggle for meaning. In Debussy's music, as in the works of the impressionist painters, "meaning" is sensory experience.

DEBUSSY'S HARMONY

Debussy's harmony, which was influenced by both Wagner's chromaticism and Mussorgsky's modal harmony, had an immediate impact on musical tradition. For the most part, he gave up the standard progressions of the major–minor tonal system and its heightened sense of harmonic forward potential.

To review: In the traditional major–minor tonal system which had dominated European music since 1600, each chord is sensed as part of a chain moving toward a harmonic goal:

In a typical Debussy progression, the chords "float" without creating a strong sense of forward potential:

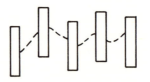

Debussy joined chords together in new ways. His progressions often seemed "circular," their ultimate destination often obscure. Debussy's harmony is frequently but incorrectly called "vague"; it is actually incredibly precise. The slightest change in any chord would upset a most fragile harmonic balance. One of Debussy's unique accomplishments was the creation of nameless "harmonic moods" within a long-range harmonic plan. Such harmony might be presented in this manner:

mood 1 mood 2

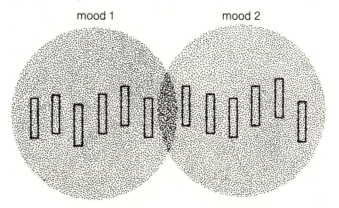

THE WHOLE-TONE SCALE

Debussy often created harmony and melody from scales considered non-traditional at the time. His *modal harmony* was related to ancient church modes. He also used the *whole-tone scale*, comprised totally of whole steps (see pages 41–42). A whole-tone scale may be easily played on any keyboard. You will notice that it has only six tones:

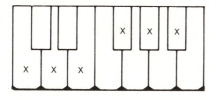

Especially characteristic of the whole-tone scale is the *absence of a tonal center*. You can start the scale on any of its pitches, and it will always sound pretty much the same. When harmony is created from this scale, it, too, has no tonal center. Thus, whole-tone melody and harmony, when compared with traditional major–minor music, seems to "go nowhere." Debussy's use of the whole-tone scale is another instance of the breakup of the major-minor tonal system.

DEBUSSY'S TEXTURE

Debussy's orchestral texture cannot be accurately described by such terms as *homophonic* or *polyphonic*, although at moments one may hear either of these textures with varying degrees of clarity. Melody, rhythm, harmony, timbre, create a continuous interplay in which *no single element is consistently more important than another*. His musical textures may be compared to a collage (a unified visual creation of many diverse elements). The collage effect becomes more apparent when you compare a Debussy work with, for example, the opening of Mozart's *Fortieth Symphony*: the latter is clearly homophonic. There is no question about the presence of a clearly differentiated melody and harmony. In a like manner, consider a Bach fugue: we recognize the various voices and the resulting polyphonic texture without any difficulty. In a Debussy work, especially an orchestral piece, such textural categorization is much more problematic. A melody appears, only to disappear within the mass of sound. The foreground–background relationship is often blurred, sometimes nonexistent.

| Listen | Debussy, Etude, *Pour les Degrés chromatique* (For the Chromatic Scale), 24c (1915) |

This interesting piece is quite short and should be listened to several times. At first hearing, consider the two motivic ideas that interact in the work:

1. A *faster* chromatic scale passage: we first hear this motive moving rapidly downward. It is the basic technical concern of the etude and continues throughout the piece.
2. A *slower* (but not by much) tuneful melody: this idea sounds from time to time in various guises as the etude unfolds and is always in a lower register than the chromatic motive.

Essential to this musical structure are the various rhythmic textures that result from the interplay of these two ideas. This is characteristic of Debussy's general style, in which *texture has become a central concern in the compositional process.* We have only to contrast this piece with Chopin's *Revolutionary Etude* to understand the significance of this textural emphasis. In the Chopin, a single melody is presented as a *theme*—that is, in a related group of phrases—and is the basic thread in the musical design. In the Debussy etude, the theme is heard in brief fragments. While these fragments are important, the concept of a main theme has lost its position of supremacy. This is significant in light of evolving styles. *In twentieth-century music, melody is often fragmented, manipulated, and in some cases, even disappears.*

You may also notice that this etude's harmony is at times quite dissonant, and the sense of a tonal center is not very strong. The piece does have a home base, with a distinctly modern twist: Debussy has mixed both major and minor harmony so that at the end of the piece we hear both simultaneously. This unconventional mixture reflects *the trend of twentieth-century composers to expand the possibilities of tonality beyond the limits of the major–minor system.*

DEBUSSY AND ROMANTICISM

Debussy's style bridges nineteenth-century Romanticism and twentieth-century Modernism. Although he reacted against the grandiose impulse of many nineteenth-century composers, that mysterious life-force of Romanticism—emotional freedom—flows quite freely in Debussy's music. His was a toned-down Romanticism, distinctly French in essence, effect, and eloquence. Another Romantic aspect of Debussy's art was its commitment to the interaction of music and the visual scene. It was Debussy, more than any other composer, who fulfilled the Romantic quest for a union of sound and sight.

DISTANT INFLUENCES ON DEBUSSY'S STYLE

Debussy's musical world extended well beyond the then-current boundaries of the European tradition. One of his interests was Medieval music, and certain Medieval harmonic techniques, such as organum (see pages 125–28), found their way into Debussy's modern language. He was also intrigued by non-European folk music. Today, many composers have similar interests, but Debussy was among the first of his time to seek out practices from distant cultures, absorbing them into his living language.

At first glance, it may not seem very remarkable that a composer would be influenced by a style from the past. Have we not been tracing such connections throughout this book? But Debussy's interests were unique in that they were focused *far back in time*. Until the late nineteenth century, composers absorbed the practices of their contemporaries and recent predecessors.

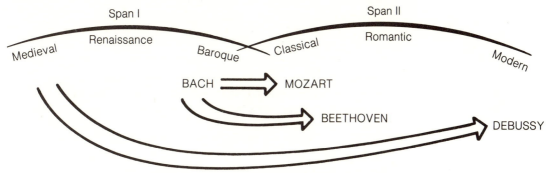

As the new century approached, there was increased interest in the music of the past. This paralleled the increase in scholarship of all types and the greater dissemination of information. Music that had long ceased to be directly influential in the creation of a composer's living language was once again available. The past began to pour into the present. This trend was given considerable impetus by the Romantic fascination with antiquity. At the same time, there arose an excitement about music of the non-European world. Debussy was drawn to these exotic traditions because they provided him with a fresh musical outlook. The significance of his involvement with these musics has been summed up as follows:

> Debussy opened up the music of Western Europe to the music of the rest of the world. He absorbed a profound influence from the Indonesian gamelan and occasionally he made use of Afro-American ragtime. What he learned from these exotic musics helped him to loosen European conventions, and to promote a further free give-and-take, not only of influence but of values, among people sensitive to music all over the world.*

Debussy's absorption of disparate influences represents a new trend that has continued to dominate the twentieth century. As the world was getting smaller, the stylistic choices for the composer were becoming more numerous.

*William Austin, *Music in the 20th Century* (New York, 1966), p. 2.

Connections in the Debussy Discussion

Musical style may be a blend of many influences.
Influence of distant musical traditions.
Continuing influence of the Romantic impulse.
Exploration of new musical language outside the major–minor tonal system.
Music can be related to life-rhythms.
Music can be related to a culture or region.

IMPRESSIONISM   A style in music and art concerned with the creation of a mood, often with subtle and elusive means. Impressionistic music and art originated in France in the late nineteenth century.

WHOLE-TONE SCALE   A scale comprised of whole steps, characterized by a weak or nonexistent tonal center.

Arnold Schoenberg

The essence of the German "serious" music tradition might be described as an interplay between musical *logic* and *lyricism*. This *does not* mean that other musical languages are not logical. It only suggests that historically, German composers have held in esteem those musical procedures in which logic and formal design play a heightened role—for example, *fugue* and *sonata-allegro form*. You have encountered this logical lyricism in composers from Bach to Brahms; the music "sings," yet has been carefully crafted into *highly formal structures*. The Viennese composer Arnold Schoenberg (1874–1951) was to mold musical logic and lyricism into a radical style destined to have a revolutionary influence upon twentieth-century musical culture.

Schoenberg considered his music to be traditional in the deepest sense. One aspect of his connection to earlier musical styles is Viennese lyricism, a vital impulse despite the dissonant sound of his music.

| Listen | Arnold Schoenberg, Song Two from *The Book of the Hanging Gardens*, Op. 15 27b (1908)

This lied is from a song cycle (see page 292). Although you may find the musical language modern, you will also hear a lyrical quality traceable to the Viennese tradition. It will be helpful to read the translation of the text before you listen to the song.

Song Two from *The Book of the Hanging Gardens*

Hain in diesen paradiesen	Groves in blissful paradises
Wechselt ab mit blutenwiesen	interweave with flowering meadows
Hallen buntgemalten fliesen	halls and brightly painted flagstones
Schlanker storche schnabel krauseln	Beaks of pikestiff storks stipple
Teiche die von vichen schillern	ponds where iris fishes shimmer
Vogel-reihen matten scheines	beadlike strings of duncoat birds
Auf den schiefen firsten trillern	trill along the crooked ridgepoles
Und die goldnen binsen sauseln—	and the golden rushes whisper—
Doch mein traum verfolgt nur eines.	yet my dreaming eye sees you alone.
—Stefan George	trans. by Robert Erich Wolf

To place this song within the German lied tradition, as well as Viennese lyricism, listen to it together with Schubert's *Lied der Mignon* 27a .

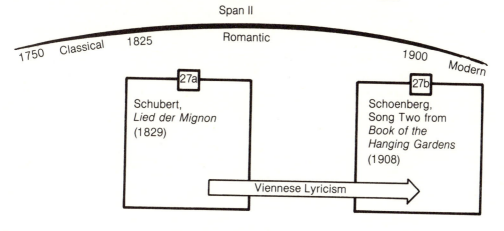

Span II

Romantic

1750 Classical 1825 1900 Modern

27a

Schubert,
Lied der Mignon
(1829)

27b

Schoenberg,
Song Two from
*Book of the
Hanging Gardens*
(1908)

Viennese Lyricism

Listening Comparison

Describe one contrast between these two songs.

Describe one similarity.

Listen | Schoenberg, *Pieces for Orchestra*, Op. 16, Nos. 1 and 2 (1909)

Notice the titles of the pieces before you listen to the music:

No. 1, *Vorgefuhle* (Premonitions)
No. 2, *Vergangenes* (The Past)

Since the composer has provided us with titles that describe extra-musical subjects, this is *program music*. Here we encounter another one of Schoenberg's connections with tradition. Despite its modern sound, this work may be considered a direct descendant of Romantic program music.

In both *The Book of the Hanging Gardens* and the *Pieces for Orchestra*, Schoenberg accomplished what Wagner had prophesied in *Tristan*: music conceived outside the confines of the traditional Western tonal system. In recognition of this quality, some describe Schoenberg's music as *atonal* to indicate the *absence* of a home key center. *The deliberate and successful denial of tonality represents a momentous break with tradition.* How Schoenberg came to this point of departure is of special interest to our study.

THE EVOLUTION OF SCHOENBERG'S LIVING LANGUAGE

Born in Vienna in 1874, Schoenberg grew up in a time and place where a composer's greatness was still measured not only by critical acclaim but by whether or not people were humming his tunes in the streets. So it is not surprising that he fervently wished that audiences would also respond to his personal brand of lyricism:

> There is nothing I wish for more earnestly (if I wish for anything else at all) than to be regarded as a superior sort of Tchaikovsky—for goodness' sake, a little superior, but that is all. Or at the very most, that my melodies should be known and whistled.*

It is fairly safe to say that there is little chance for "Schoenberg sing-alongs" in the near future. In fact, there are quite a few professional singers who find Schoenberg melodies difficult. Those melodies, like other aspects of his style, represented a new level of musical complexity for both listeners and performers alike. What led Schoenberg down this new stylistic path?

Schoenberg believed wholeheartedly in the ideas that comprise "the quest for legitimacy" (see page 308). He accepted that there was a right and wrong direction for Western music; he believed in the importance of finding that course. The Darwinian concept of evolution from a lower state of being

*Austin, *Music in the 20th Century*, p. 95.

Arnold Schoenberg conducting an ensemble in New York, 1940 (sketch by Dolbin).

to a higher one is an important image in such a philosophy. An example of its influence may be found in Schoenberg's criticism of composers, like Bartók (whose music we will soon encounter), who included popular-folk elements in their musical language. Popular-folk music, for Schoenberg, was "by nature primitive"; only formal music was "appropriate to a more evolved type of thought." Schoenberg stopped composing for a time in order to create a system that would simultaneously fulfill his need for a personal musical language and for a position in the evolutionary chain. From this interaction between culture and composer came Schoenberg's *twelve-tone technique* (also called *serialism*), one of the landmarks in the Western musical tradition.

Listen   *Gigue* [20] from Schoenberg's *Suite for Piano*, Op. 25 (1921–23)

The *Suite for Piano*, of which this *Gigue* is the last movement, was one of Schoenberg's early works composed in the new twelve-tone technique. You have already heard this piece as a modern example of a European dance-derived genre. We may note at this point that while the piece has a dancelike quality, it is far removed from traditional dance rhythms. There is no tune to whistle. Schoenberg's style represents a deliberate break with such accessible qualities as easily singable tunes and foot-tapping rhythms.

SCHOENBERG'S TWELVE-TONE TECHNIQUE

That special moment of genius, when an inevitable shift of awareness is crystallized into comprehensible form, is often a moment of simplicity. Schoenberg's solution in his search for a legitimate living language is such a moment. It is at once simple and profound. Schoenberg's twelve-tone technique involves an *order of pitches in which each pitch must be sounded once before it can be used again.* This order of tones is called a *twelve-tone row* (or series). Each row has its own unique qualities. It is easy to experience the inner life of a row: the following are by two different composers. (If a keyboard is available, play each one, a finger at a time.)

Twelve-Tone Row from *Trio*, Op. 20, by Webern

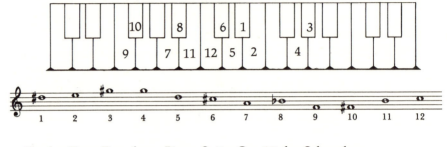

Twelve-Tone Row from *Piano Suite*, Op. 25, by Schoenberg

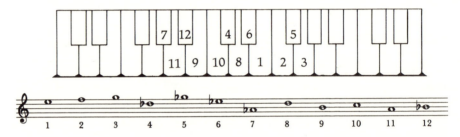

From this order of pitches the composer draws all melodic and harmonic material. The intervals of a row are usually chosen so that no tonal center is established. *It was Schoenberg's intention to free the composer from traditional concepts of tonality.*

The melodic aspect of the twelve-tone row represented a break with long-established practices. The intervals are difficult to sing when compared to more traditional melodies. Yet there is something distinctly musical that holds a row together. In fact, a *twelve-tone row reflects a new type of musical awareness that rests in a twentieth-century sense of how tones may relate to one another.* Although a description of these relationships is far beyond the scope of this book, it is important to understand that the basis of the twelve-tone technique grows from human musicality taken to a very advanced stage. There are many principles and techniques in the compositional process that Schoenberg and his followers employed to turn a twelve-tone series into an actual piece. These involved the interplay of musical sounds with abstract and sometimes mathematically inspired plans. The result was a new and dissonant modern style, which was bewildering to many listeners. Traditional melody and harmony were no more.

In short, what others had only partially accomplished, Schoenberg took the whole way: in the rejection of traditional melody, harmony, rhythm, and tonality, Schoenberg abandoned the basic language long shared by composer and audience. In order to understand this new style, one needed a new set of cues.

SCHOENBERG'S STYLE AND TWENTIETH-CENTURY TRENDS

The following observations relate Schoenberg's music to certain general trends in "serious" music during the twentieth century.

1. *In many instances the traditional cues shared by composer and audience have been abandoned.* As a result, certain twentieth-century musical styles are appreciated by a relatively small group of persons.
2. *The music of Schoenberg, like that of many twentieth-century composers, comes alive through intense study.* Thus, in order to respond to this music, audiences must be willing to put more effort into the listening experience.
3. *Compared with music of the previous era, Schoenberg's style reflects a new emphasis on intellectual-analytical qualities.* One may state with a fair amount of accuracy that to "feel" certain twentieth-century musical styles, the listener must first be willing to enter a distinctly intellectual-analytical environment. In the search for new links in the evolutionary chain of musical style, many twentieth-century composers have unmistakably raised the abstract and sometimes mathematically inspired qualities of music to an unprecedented level of importance.

THE SCHOENBERG LEGACY

Schoenberg's innovative technique did not make an immediate impact on most of his contemporaries. In the early part of the century, his influence was limited to a group of staunch disciples, among them Anton Webern (1883–1945) and Alban Berg (1885–1935). Most composers remained unmoved and even hostile toward the twelve-tone method. This situation changed rapidly after World War II, when the works of Schoenberg, Webern, and Berg found a sudden and vibrant response in the musical community. Schoenberg's original principle found its way into the living language of many composers, and was transformed into various styles. Even the art of jazz musicians Ornette Coleman, Charles Mingus, and Cecil Taylor may be understood as deriving energy and techniques from atonality. In short, the principle functions beyond style.

Schoenberg's living language is a difficult one. To a great extent, it has remained largely within the domain of the professional musician and the highly trained listener. This does not make the music "good" or "bad." It simply implies that it takes time and motivation to learn the cues. Schoenberg's wish that his melodies would achieve the popularity of composers like Tchaikovsky remains an unrealized dream. The evolutionary theory of musical style has led many twentieth-century composers down a fascinating though quite private path. The "quest for legitimacy" in our time has meant for some a profound separation from the majority of listeners. Schoenberg's stylistic evolution, which was honest and powerful, reflects the growing diversity of styles that can exist in our culture. His greatness, like that of many twentieth-century musicians, lies scattered among those who understand and appreciate the cues that make up his musical language.

Connections in the Schoenberg Discussion

Continued importance of traditional genres.
The use of an abstract mathematical plan.
The "quest for legitimacy."
The emergence of music outside the major–minor tonal system.
Stylistic evolution of a composer.
Growing stylistic diversity in modern culture.

Additional Listening Each of the following works demonstrates the twelve-tone technique:

Schoenberg *Moses and Aaron* (opera-oratorio) (1932)
String Trio (1946)

Webern *Symphony* (1928)

Berg *Wozzeck* (opera) (1921)
Violin Concerto (1935)

ATONALITY The absence of a tonal center or "home base."

TWELVE-TONE MUSIC (SERIALISM) A style of composition originated by Arnold Schoenberg in which the composer's basic musical ideas come from a specific order—or row—of twelve pitches, each used only once.

Stravinsky, *The Rite of Spring*

Throughout history, there have been intermittent attempts to tame what many have called "primitive" and "uninhibited" rhythm. Nowhere has this been more evident than in the Western world. As Christianity turned away from the rites of ancient religions, European culture fostered the negative image of rhythmic intoxication through music and dance. An interesting long-term phenomenon is the way this suppressed rhythmic impulse seems to erupt periodically into the social fabric. One example is the *dance of death* craze in the Middle Ages. The sight of a wild, delirious mob dancing in the streets for days in an attempt to ward off the plague is not an image that sits well with traditional notions of civilization.

Although it adapted many dance rhythms, "serious" European music virtually abandoned the uninhibited body rhythms of the archaic past. European composers sought more restrained, "refined" rhythmic styles. One might consider the minuet the ultimate example of this more "refined" rhythm and movement. (Here we encounter the word "refined" in a socio-cultural context where subdued, stylized, and controlled body movements are primary components.) It is not until the Romantic era that some of this primitive rhythmic impulse returns to "serious" music, perhaps taking its cue from the cultural pounding that Beethoven's rhythms had released into the world. The twentieth century is the era in which this impulse has reasserted itself, full-bodied and in many guises. In 1913, it reappeared in all its shocking glory in Igor Stravinsky's ballet music *The Rite of Spring.*

The Rite of Spring is no minuet! Composed for a Russian ballet company active in Paris early in the century, it was an exotic expression of Russian nationalism through music, dance, and primitive theme. Stravinsky described his vision later in these words:

I saw in imagination a solemn pagan rite: sage elders, seated in a circle, watched a young girl dance herself to death. They were sacrificing her to propitiate the god of spring.*

Listen | Igor Stravinsky, *The Rite of Spring* (Part I)

Adoration of the Earth
Dance of the Adolescents
Game of Abduction
Spring Dance
Games of the Rival Cities—Entrance of the Sage—Dance of the Earth

In *The Rite of Spring*, Stravinsky expanded the traditional sense of harmony, rhythm, melody, and tonality into a distinctive musical language that sounds simultaneously modern and archaic. The manner in which this is done defies simple description, but we may cite a few of the elements that reflect Stravinsky's genius:

*Igor Stravinsky, *An Autobiography* (New York, 1936; 1962), p. 31.

Texture: As in Debussy's music, texture plays a vital role in the Stravinsky sound. His textures, like Debussy's, are continuously changing. Melodies appear and disappear. Deceptively simple chord patterns begin suddenly, as do melodic fragments and phrases, only to end unexpectedly. A basically homophonic texture may be transformed quickly into a dense contrapuntal display. All of these procedures are given life by a dazzling use of orchestral sound. Instruments often play in their most extreme registers to obtain new and exotic effects. Although we are describing elements of the texture as isolated entities, any of these considered separately from the complete sound mass rarely retains any essential quality of the work. To illustrate this point, we have only to compare *The Rite* with a typical Classical symphony. If you sing or hum the main theme of Mozart's *Fortieth Symphony*, something quite essential of the spirit and meaning of the work will survive. This is not true of *The Rite*. Any isolated theme from the piece (with the notable exception of the opening solo) conveys little by itself. This speaks to one of the essential trends of the late nineteenth and twentieth centuries: *the growing position of texture and timbre as a primary focus of the compositional process.*

Rhythm: At the basis of a Stravinsky texture are unique combinations of rhythms. Perhaps the most startling rhythmic textures of *Rite* are the jagged synchronizations of irregular patterns which repeat incessantly, starting and ending with abrupt precision. These rhythms, both primitive in their forcefulness and modern in their sophisticated logical interplay, encode a special moment of musical-cultural history that has never been duplicated.

Harmony: *The Rite of Spring* is legendary for its "emancipation of dissonance," especially those famous chords that begin the *Dance of the Adolescents*. However, the real impact of this dissonance is derived from the rhythmic setting, which suggests once again that no musical element may be isolated from its rhythmic identity. It is the forceful repetition of Stravinsky's dissonance that creates this powerful impact. Dissonance not only remains unresolved, it often merges into a sort of mega-consonance through continued imprinting into the senses.

In *The Rite*, Stravinsky did not abandon tonality; he redefined and enlarged its potential. In fact, he returned to one of the most ancient tonal practices: tonality by assertion. Throughout the work, tonal centers are often created through obstinate repetition of ostinatos and melodies. Another harmonic characteristic of *The Rite* is *polytonality*—simply, the sounding of melodies in two or more tonalities at the same time.

Melody: The melodic material of *The Rite* is either drawn from actual folk songs or deliberately created in folk style. In addition to these melodies, which comprise the main threads of the work, there are many thematic fragments typically twentieth-century in style, with their complex rhythms and jagged intervals. The two types of melodies complement each other in a remarkable synthesis.

While texture, rhythm, harmony, and melody have been discussed as if they were separate entities, it must be pointed out, as always, that these elements are not isolated from one another; they grow organically from one potent impulse that bonds them together in a powerful union. *The Rite* has a quality that we have already observed in Bach (see page 195)—a total synthesis of inspiration and craft. As one enters deeper into its dual world of spirit and logic, that same voice may say once again, "*This* is how music works."

THE RITE AS THE ROCK MUSIC OF ITS TIME

Although there are obviously profound differences between this work and rock, there are also some interesting parallels. Both *The Rite* and the rock style of the sixties unleashed a powerful, almost mythical response to rhythm. The powerful rhythmic patterns in the low register of Stravinsky's orchestra are not unlike the bass, drums, and rhythm guitar of the rock group. Both share continual, incessant repetition as part of their aesthetic. It is possible, then, that beyond the differences of style, time, and place, both tap into a similar vein. *The Rite* and rock have each become symbolic of the rhythmic, dissonant unrest of our century.

IGOR STRAVINSKY

In his autobiography, Igor Stravinsky (1882–1971) recalls this moment from his childhood in pre-Revolutionary Russia (sometime in the 1880s):

> Another memory which often comes back is the singing of the women of the neighboring village. There were a great many of them, and regularly every evening they sang in unison on their way home after the day's work. To this day, I clearly remember the tune, and the way they sang it, and how, when I used to sing it at home, imitating their manner, I was complimented on the trueness of my ear. This praise made me very happy . . . And it is an odd thing that this occurrence, trifling though it seems, has a special significance for me, because it marks the dawn of my consciousness of myself in the role of musician.[*]

Stravinsky was not one to indulge casually in romantic whimsy. An essential characteristic of the man and composer was a reserved personal style, the opposite of the romantic aesthetic. So, when he reflects on such a "trifle,", we know that it must be important. We can use the story as a starting point in our discussion.

[*]Ibid., p. 4.

Caricature by Jean Cocteau of Stravinsky playing *The Rite of Spring*.

First, an observation applicable to creative artists in general (composers, poets, painters, writers, etc.): it has often been acknowledged that some deeply felt experience can later become meaningful in a creative life. This may reveal itself in countless ways, on both a grand and a minute scale. The experience may find its way into a particular work, or reappear in different guises throughout the creator's life. It may be used as a spark for creation; it may become significant in the artist's aesthetic value system or working principles; or it may simply be a memory, as in Stravinsky's case, which seems to frame the artistic present with the past. The important idea is that a life experience directly or indirectly affects the creative process. In ways often beyond quantifiable analysis, the experience is transformed into sounds, shapes, or words.

A second idea concerns Stravinsky's use of Russian folk melody in his early works. In *The Rite*, as well as his other works of the same period, Stravinsky used both actual folk melodies and his own folklike creations. His original melodies sound as authentic as those taken directly from the folk tradition. Stravinsky himself has provided a reasonable explanation in the reminiscence quoted earlier. The music one hears and sings as a child is internalized as a living musical language. But Stravinsky's use of these folk memories was to be very distant from that Russian peasant world.

In Stravinsky's aesthetic, the intellectual-analytical traditions of the West were held in high esteem. His personality emerges in his writings: brilliant and witty, but always reserved and formal. One may sense something essential about Stravinsky and his music in these words from his lectures at Harvard University in 1939: "Throughout my course and on every hand I shall call upon your feeling and taste for order and discipline." So it is not surprising that when Russian folk melody is heard through a "Stravinsky filter," the very nature of folk song has been transformed. A traditional folk song is an end in itself: simple, direct, complete. In Stravinsky's music, it has no life of its own; it is but one component in a crafted structure in which formal design reigns supreme. Despite the use of folk melody, the *nationalist* character of *The Rite of Spring* is far different from that of Mussorgsky's *Boris Godunov*. It is more reserved and less emotional. We are drawn not so much into the world of ancient Russia as into Stravinsky's own transformation of that world.

STRAVINSKY'S STYLISTIC EVOLUTION

The war of 1914 and the Russian Revolution sent many Russian artists into exile; Stravinsky was one. First settling in Switzerland, he returned in 1920 to Paris, where *The Rite* had first been performed. During the years 1914–20, his musical style underwent the first of several radical transformations. He abandoned his Russian heritage and turned to new sources: the classical models of the past. The music he created in this style is called *neoclassical*—literally, new-classical (see page 231). *Symphony of Psalms* is one of the most successful works from this period. In the second movement, Stravinsky has created a modern fugue cast in the tradition of J. S. Bach. The manner in which he recreates the Baroque master's tonal logic in a twentieth-century idiom can only be described by that overworked word *genius*.

| Listen | Stravinsky, *Symphony of Psalms*, second movement

Text

Expectans expectavi Dominum,
  et intendit mihi et exaudivit
  preces meas;
et exduxit me de lacu miseriae,
  et de luto faecis. Et
  statuit super petram pedes
  meos: et direxit gressus meos.
Et immisit in os meum canticum
  novum, carmen Deo nostro.
  Videbunt multi, videbunt et
  timebunt: et sperabunt in
  Domino.

I had waited patiently for the Lord,
  when he inclined himself unto me,
  and heard my cry.
And he brought me up out of the
  noiseful deep, out of the miry
  clay, and he set up my feet upon a
  rock, making firm my steps.
And he placed in my mouth a new song,
  a praise unto our God: many will
  see it, and fear: and they will
  trust in the Lord.
—Psalm XXXIX:2–4

Stravinsky's life in the twentieth century, when many other notable composers have had to struggle both artistically and financially, was one of comparative security. In 1939, he settled in the United States, where he continued to compose with typical craftsmanship and ingenuity. He personally conducted recordings of all his major works, thereby becoming the first composer to do so. With his close associate Robert Craft, he produced a series of books which reveal his personality, aesthetic values, and musical processes in detail. During his lifetime, he was lionized, revered, well-paid —in short, he was the most successful composer the twentieth century had produced. Secure in this position, he undertook a last stylistic adventure: composition in the twelve-tone techniques of Schoenberg and Webern. It was only natural for one of music's most gifted intellects to experiment with one of its most logical processes. The result, although twelve-tone, had a distinctly Stravinskian sound. Like other traditions that had passed through the Stravinsky filter, this one, too, emerged with the unique stamp of a great master.

Connections in the Stravinsky Discussion

The absorption of a living musical language at a young age.
Stylistic evolution.
Classical aesthetic.
The connection between a musical style and a region.
The influence of musical traditions from the past.

Stravinsky: Additional Listening

The Firebird (1909)
Petrushka (1911)
The Wedding (1917–23)
Symphony of Psalms (1930) (all three movements)
Symphony in Three Movements (1945)
Threni (1958)

POLYTONALITY   More than one tonal center heard at the same time.

NEOCLASSICAL   Literally, "new classical." Refers to the resurgence of the classical aesthetic in the twentieth century.

The Sonata-Symphony in the Modern Era

Despite the great diversity of musical styles that have come into being since the time of Mozart, there have also been many unifying strands. One of them is the continuing sonata-symphony tradition. While some composers of the Modern era have turned away from these genres, others have continued to find them useful. The composer of the twentieth century who used this model had to find a new style in which to express it. Because we are dealing with a model which often retains its basic architecture even when stylistic details are changed, comparisons within the sonata-symphony group offer an ideal opportunity for listening beyond style.

| Suggested Listening | Sonata-Symphony Group in the Modern Era |

1900

1950

Stravinsky, *Symphony in C* (1938–40)

Prokofiev, *Classical Symphony* (1917)

Debussy, *String Quartet* (1893)

Shostakovich, *Symphony No. 5* (1937)

Ravel, *String Quartet* (1902–3)

Samuel Barber, *Symphony No. 1* (1943) *Piano Sonata* (1949)

Bartók, *String Quartet No. 2* (1917) *Piano Concerto No. 2* (1931)

Leonard Bernstein, *Symphony No. 3* ("Kaddish") (1961–63)

Hindemith, *Piano Sonata No. 2* (1936)

Vaughan Williams, *Symphony No. 6* (1944–47)

BARTÓK, *QUARTET NO. 4*, SECOND MOVEMENT

Composers of the early twentieth century found various ways to expand their musical language. One of the most inventive and successful was Béla Bartók (1881–1945). Bartók was a Hungarian whose love for his native folk music (and other related traditions) led him to incorporate melodic, harmonic, and rhythmic elements of these traditions into his musical style. The result was a vibrant, modern musical language, which Bartók often used to rework traditional genres. Among his most successful works are six string quartets, which despite their modern style, may be considered descendants of Beethoven's works in this genre. You will listen to the second movement of *Quartet No. 4*. It has several features that illustrate twentieth-century trends:

1. The rhythm is very complex; its various meters, accents, and syncopations give the music an exciting rhythmic vibrancy.
2. The harmony is very dissonant.
3. The melodies are based on scales outside the major–minor tonal system.
4. Changing timbres and textures are vital elements of the form. It is extraordinary that the dazzling effects in this movement are produced by only four string instruments. To accomplish this, Bartók calls upon the instrumentalists to produce a variety of timbres with unconventional use of their fingers and bows.

Listen   Bartók, *String Quartet No. 4*, Second Movement (1928)

Listening Activity

Rhythmic polyphony is a continuing feature of this movement; but are there moments when all the instruments play the exact same rhythm at the same time?

Does the form lean toward *sectional* or *continuous* shape?

Are there any *sliding* pitches?

Would you describe the overall effect of the harmony as *stable* or *unstable*?

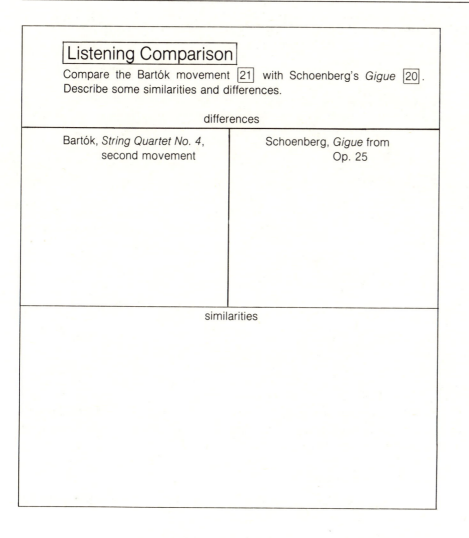

The Interplay between Innovation and Tradition

At an immediate level, it was the innovative features in the styles of
Debussy, Stravinsky, Schoenberg, and Bartók that seemed the most important to their audiences. And certainly, innovation has been the principal
short-range concept that has fueled the efforts of many twentieth-century
composers. But the outer layer of these musical styles can obscure more
important connections to tradition. As a review of this chapter, make at
least one connection between each of these composers and the traditions of
the previous century:

Connections between the Music of Four Important Modern Composers and the Traditions of the Nineteenth Century

```
┌─────────────────────────────────────────────────┐
│                                                   │
│   Debussy                                         │
│                                                   │
│                                                   │
│                                                   │
│   Stravinsky                                      │
│                                                   │
│                                                   │
│                                                   │
│   Schoenberg                                      │
│                                                   │
│                                                   │
│                                                   │
│   Bartók                                          │
│                                                   │
│                                                   │
│                                                   │
└─────────────────────────────────────────────────┘
```

QUESTIONS

For the following questions, find any false statement(s) and correct them by changing the word(s) in italics. More than one statement may be false; all the statements may be true.

1. Concerning Debussy:

    (a) As a student, he often improvised in a style that broke the traditional rules of *harmony*.

    (b) His harmony was influenced by both *Mussorgsky* and *Wagner*.

    (c) In a general sense, he turned away from *Wagnerism* as a musical philosophy.

    (d) His music may be understood as a *rejection* of German musical traditions.

2. Concerning Debussy and Romanticism:

    (a) He *turned away* from the excesses of Romanticism.

    (b) His music may be considered a bridge between *Romanticism and Modernism*.

(c) He *rejected* the Romantic quest for the union of sound and sight.

(d) He *rejected* the tradition of program music, an established practice of the Romantic era.

3. Concerning Debussy's impressionism:

   (a) It describes a style of *both music and art*.

   (b) It was, for the most part, an artistic movement that reflected *German* ideas about music and art.

   (c) Among its qualities in both music and art are a concern for the *changing effects of light on the world*.

   (d) Impressionism leans toward concepts associated with *absolute* music.

4. Concerning Arnold Schoenberg:

   (a) He believed in the *evolution* of music toward a higher state.

   (b) To this end, he created his *twelve-tone system*.

   (c) The twelve-tone principle was based in *tonality*.

   (d) Schoenberg's language accomplished a harmonic result that had been hinted at in Wagner's *Tristan*.

5. Schoenberg's music

   (a) demonstrates the German musical tradition of *logic and lyricism*.

   (b) *drew heavily* on folk music.

   (c) *excludes* the Romantic tradition of program music.

   (d) continues the tradition of Viennese lyricism found in such composers as *Mozart, Schubert, and Debussy*.

6. Concerning Igor Stravinsky:

   (a) His early music shares some common ground with that of *Mussorgsky*.

   (b) Some time after *The Rite of Spring*, he turned away from all traits of nationalism and adopted the *classical aesthetic* as a guiding force.

   (c) His final style period incorporated the *twelve-tone system*.

   (d) A Baroque composer who influenced Stravinsky was *Mozart*.

7. Concerning *The Rite of Spring*:

   (a) It falls into the *sonata-symphony* genre.

   (b) It has qualities that may be perceived as radically new or very ancient, *but not both*.

   (c) In universal terms, it reveals the human impulse toward *refined and controlled* rhythmic response.

   (d) One of its most basic impulses is the *dance*.

8. Concerning the melodies of *The Rite*:

   (a) Some were drawn from *actual* Russian folk music.

   (b) Some were created by Stravinsky but in a *primitive* folk style.

   (c) Combined with the folk melodies is another type of very modern melody characterized by *easily singable* intervals.

   (d) Sometimes two melodies sound simultaneously in *two different tonal centers*.

9. Concerning the harmony of *The Rite*:

   (a) It is primarily *consonant*.

   (b) Its effects are deeply related to the *rhythmic* character of the work.

   (c) An example of how Stravinsky expanded traditional notions of tonality was his use of *polytonality*.

10. Concerning Bartók's *String Quartet No. 4*:

   (a) It was influenced by the string quartets of *Bach*.

   (b) It is characterized by *simple* rhythmic procedures.

   (c) The melodies are based on scales *outside* the major–minor tonal system.

   (d) The harmony is *very dissonant*.

13

The Full Impact of Modernism: Overview of Span II

Modern architecture, modern music, modern philosophy, modern science—all these define themselves not *out* of the past, indeed scarcely *against* the past, but in independence of the past. The modern mind has been growing indifferent to history because history, conceived as a continuous nourishing tradition, has become useless to it.

—Carl E. Shorske*

Messiaen, Ligeti, and Stockhausen: The Full Impact of Modernism

Debussy, Schoenberg, and Stravinsky opened up certain pathways to modern music. Although we have discovered that each had important connections to the European notated tradition, their musical languages represented a distinct break with long-established practices. Their music exemplified the single most important trait of modernism: *Anything is possible.* No tradition is sacred; it is the composer (or artist, or writer) who makes his or her own rules. As trailblazers, they may be considered first-generation moderns (although both Stravinsky and Schoenberg continued to compose

Fin-de-siècle Vienna (New York, 1980), p. xvii.

and influence the musical culture for some time). But what happens with the second and third generations, for whom the music of Debussy, Stravinsky, and Schoenberg represents the traditional? It is in these composers' works that the full impact of modernism is felt. We will consider three later moderns—Messiaen, Ligeti, and Stockhausen—chosen from a field of many possibilities.

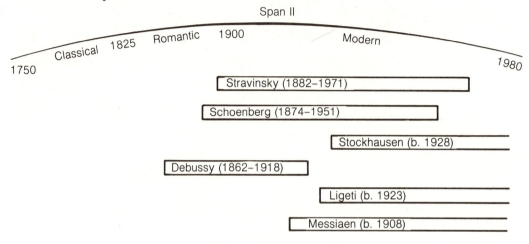

OLIVIER MESSIAEN

Messiaen is one of the most fascinating figures of modern music. As you will discover, his musical language reflects a staggering fusion of many diverse elements.

As a child, Messiaen absorbed many traditional influences. His parents were poets. His father translated Shakespeare into French, and, by the age of eight, the boy had read all of Shakespeare's plays aloud. The composer has said that his mother's poetry "surely influenced my character and fate." Among his earliest musical experiences was the singing and playing of operas by Mozart, Berlioz, and, most significant, the one such work by Debussy. Messiaen felt an affinity for Berlioz, identifying himself as "a Frenchman of the mountains, like Berlioz." Although separated by a century, there is more than a passing resemblance between the two men's personal aesthetic. For example, compare any of Berlioz's writings (Chapter 10) with the following description by Messiaen of a movement from his masterpiece, *The Quartet for the End of Time* (1940). The movement is entitled *Cluster of rainbows, for the angel who announced the end of Time.* Notice the fusion of feelings and ideas with music:

> The night angel appears, and in particular the rainbow that envelops him (the rainbow, symbol of peace, of wisdom, of every quiver of luminosity and sound). In my dreaming I hear and see ordered melo-

Olivier Messiaen surrounded by a group of students.

dies and chords, familiar hues and forms: then, following this transitory stage, I pass into the unreal and submit ecstatically to a vortex, a dizzying interpenetration of super-human sounds and colors. These fiery swords, these rivers of blue-orange lava, these sudden stars: Behold the cluster, behold the rainbows!

There is no question that, although his musical language sounds modern, Messiaen is a romantic spirit. Few composers of the twentieth century would describe their music with such uninhibited emotion and blending of the senses. (Compare, for example, with Stravinsky's words: "I shall call upon your feeling and taste for order and discipline"—words that clearly fall within the classical aesthetic.) But unlike Berlioz, Messiaen's living language was formed in the twentieth century, and in many ways it is far removed from that of his French predecessor.

Messiaen entered the Paris Conservatory, the same school attended by Berlioz and Debussy, at the age of eleven. For the next ten years, he distinguished himself in studies of counterpoint, fugue, harmony, improvisation, piano, organ, history, and composition. During this period he came into contact with the music of Stravinsky and Schoenberg, among other moderns. Ultimately, each of the "big three"—Debussy, Stravinsky, and Schoenberg—influenced the young man. If we were to stop right now, we would already have accumulated quite a list of different musical languages that affected Messiaen's style, but there is more, for he incorporates many diverse traditions, impulses, and influences into his art:

1. *Ancient Greek rhythm and scales.* (You will remember that ancient Greek rhythm was directly related to dance and verse—see "The Ancient Unity," page 97.)

2. *Hindu rhythms.* Messiaen studied these complex rhythmic patterns from a thirteenth-century manuscript.

3. *Christian mysticism.* An overriding concern of Messiaen's music is its direct relationship to various aspects of Christianity. For Messiaen, the study of the Scriptures is just as vital to his music as any formal technique.

4. *The songs of birds.* Throughout his life, Messiaen has studied bird calls. Preserved both in notation and on tape, they have provided a major source of his melodic material.

5. *Color.* For Messiaen, musical sound cannot be separated from actual colors. His musical language is influenced by a personal perception of synthesis between sound and sight. He often speaks of his sound as a "rainbow."

All this may seem quite fanciful. At this moment in the discussion, you would have little choice but to place Messiaen on the Berlioz side of the classical–romantic continuum. But wait: Messiaen had something for everyone. He has used some of the most rational and scientific approaches to music. One of these highly rational procedures is called *total serialism*.

Total serialism is an extension of Schoenberg's twelve-tone technique. You will remember that in this practice, the pitch order of a complete work was predetermined by a specific plan (see page 329). Every melody, every harmony was controlled by this design. It will be useful to restate that this procedure is a highly logical practice. Once conceived, the plan exercises a fundamental control over choice of pitches. What Messiaen did was to extend this controlled plan to the areas of rhythm and dynamics. In a totally serialized piece, nearly every aspect of the musical design—melody, harmony, rhythm, and dynamics— is predetermined. A piece that demonstrates this technique is the second of the *Four Etudes on Rhythm*.

There has never been a more abstract approach to composition than total serialization. In fact, composers who adopted this technique have been called "ultrarationalists." And they learned that technique from a man whose most basic and purest musical source is the song of a bird!

Messiaen: Additional Listening

Four Etudes on Rhythm (complete; No. 1 is discussed below)
(1949–50)

Quatuor pour la fin du temps (Quartet for the End of Time; 1941)

Vingt regards sur l'enfant Jésus (Twenty Views of the Child Jesus;
1944)

> *Connections in the Messiaen Discussion*
>
> The classic-romantic continuum.
> Musical style may be a blending of many influences.
> Use of an abstract, mathematical plan.

 Messiaen, *Four Etudes on Rhythm*, No. 1 24d (1949–50)

The theme of this piece, heard in the opening measures, is taken from the tribal music of New Guinea. Among the other musical elements are the occasional bird songs which accompany the theme. Like Stravinsky's *Rite of Spring*, the rhythm seems both primitive and new. As you listen, focus on the other elements, especially anything that sounds like a birdcall.

Listen | Ligeti, *Lux aeterna* 24e (1966)

The text is from the *Agnus Dei* of the Requiem Mass:

Lux aeterna luceat eis, Domine,	Let eternal light shine on them, O Lord,
cum sanctis tuis in aeternum,	with Your saints throughout eternity,
quia pius es.	for You are good.
Requiem aeternam dona eis, Domine,	Grant them eternal rest, O Lord,
et lux perpetua luceat eis.	and let perpetual light shine on them.

Listening Activity

Before we discuss this excerpt, consider the following as they affect you, the listener: How does the work make you experience the passage of time? How would you describe the forward potential? What basic and universal musical impulses do you sense beneath the level of style? (Answer in the space provided below)

passage of time
(place an x in box)

slow ⟵——————————⟶ fast

forward potential
(place x in box)

none ⟵——————————⟶ high

Circle any basic impulses that seem to apply:

song, chant, dance, drama

Listening Activity — Stockhausen, *Momente* (excerpt) [24f]

Consider the same questions as on page 349.

passage of time   slow ⟵——————⟶ fast

[ ]

forward potential   none ⟵——————⟶ high

[ ]

Circle any basic impulses that seem to apply: song, chant, dance, drama

---

GEORGY LIGETI

Among Georgy Ligeti's earliest works are pieces based on the folk music of his native Hungary. He was in his twenties when his country embraced communism, a political philosophy that strongly discouraged the pursuit of experimental music. In general, ultramodern styles were viewed as "Western decadence." So Ligeti was not only unable to experiment, but even more important to a composer, he was denied contact with others who did. In 1956, Ligeti came to the West and sought out composers like Stockhausen. Within a few years, his career as a major composer was in full swing, stimulated by this interaction with other innovators.

The two areas in which Ligeti's music is especially inventive are *texture* and *time*. In some of his compositions, there are no melodies, no short-range rhythms, and no harmonic progressions in the traditional sense, only blocks of dense musical textures drawn out in slowly changing patterns. The effect on the willing listener is to produce a very different state of time-perception—one that is somehow contemporary, meditative, and primal. Perhaps it is these qualities that caused director Stanley Kubrick to use Ligeti's *Atmospheres* and *Lux aeterna* in the movie *2001*.

Despite its very modern sound, *Lux aeterna* is one of Ligeti's more traditional works. At the "outer layer" of the listening experience, we hear very little melody in the traditional sense. For the most part, we respond to long, drawn-out textures that seem to be slowly changing. One of the interesting ways that the textures change is by being "thin" or "thick." The "thinnest" texture is created by the voices singing one pitch; the "thicker" textures result when they sing many pitches close to one another. (You can get some idea of the thick-texture sound by playing six or so adjacent white and black keys on a piano or organ.) Interestingly, these effects are produced by one of the oldest polyphonic techniques, which is hidden inside the dense sound: The piece is a *canon*.

Ligeti: Additional Listening

Volumina (1961–62)
Atmospheres (1961)

KARLHEINZ STOCKHAUSEN

Karlheinz Stockhausen did not come to composition as a major concern until he was in his twenties. Born in Germany, he studied both music and philosophy. Among his varied youthful activities was a stint as a popular pianist. Although he had actively studied the works of Schoenberg, Stravinsky, and Bartók (who, by the 1950s, were all part of the establishment), it was not until his exposure to the newest trends in European music that he made a full commitment to composition. Among the works that most impressed Stockhausen was the *Four Etudes on Rhythm* by Messiaen. In fact, he went to Paris to study with him, and it was from that time on that he began to make his mark as a composer.

Stockhausen has gone through so many stylistic changes in so short a time that there is no simple way to describe his style. It may even be suggested that he doesn't have a style, in the traditional sense. And here we encounter another main current of modern music, especially that composed in recent years: *each piece may take on a style of its own in accordance with some preconceived plan.* This idea is quite different from that underlying the living musical language described in Chapter 4 (see page 105). And since this new stylistic flexibility is one of the basic keys to understanding and responding to certain types of modern music, it will be very useful to examine it from more than one angle.

UNLIMITED STYLISTIC CHOICE

Imagine for a moment that it is the eighteenth century and you are a designer of houses. You have at your fingertips a few basic plans, but their differences amount to only minor variations on a standard model. You probably have a relatively small number of choices as to building materials. Perhaps you usually build with wood, and once in a while you get to try your hand with brick or stone. All in all, both design and materials are fairly restricted by tradition and technology. Now, imagine you are an architect today with unlimited funds (!), and you have a client with no preconceived notions of what style a house should be. Instead, you may consider many possibilities. You must, however, have some idea, purpose, or principle you would like the house to fulfill. For example, you might be interested in flooding a house with light while maintaining a sense of isolation from the world. This idea would then suggest certain materials and shapes. Eventually, guided by the original idea, the various aspects of design and materials would generate their own style.

Now suppose someone decided to describe and label your architectural

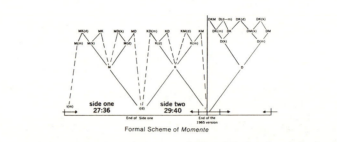

Formal Scheme of *Momente*

style, commenting on the "characteristic use of glass" as a feature of your work. You may, in fact, have been experimenting with glass in a series of houses that look somewhat alike. But then your basic goal changes. You want to design a house that evokes a sense of the past, so you decide to use stone, and an entirely new type of design results. Having no "rules" that tie you to a particular tradition or plan, having unlimited funds and access to a great variety of materials and technologies, you approach each new house with a totally fresh stylistic outlook. No one could describe your style other than to evaluate the way it implements its purpose or principle of design.

In real life, of course, architects do not have unlimited funds and materials. But consider the modern composer. While there are certainly some limits on the implementation of a composer's ideas, *recent musical culture has provided an incredible array of musical resources, languages, and techniques*. If you can imagine the excitement felt by an architect given the kind of freedom described above, you have an idea of how some composers feel about the possibilities in modern music. Not limited by "rules" or traditions, and having what amounts to a nearly unlimited variety of musical styles, each new piece represents the challenge and excitement of hitherto inexperienced realms. And "style" is nothing more than the latest manifestation of some deeper process of exploration.

Stockhausen is a perfect example of the modern composer who moves through various "outer" styles in order to implement some all-important "inner" plan. Considering the sound sources of a few of his works can suggest the diversity of his musical languages. There are works for piano, orchestra, and chorus, as well as for tape (electronic sounds). There is a piece called *Mikrophonie I* for tam-tam (a gong), two microphones, two filters (electronic devices for altering sound), and potentiometers (another electronic device). There is even a piece for unspecified forces. Imagine trying to describe the style of a piece that changes instruments at every performance! One work, *Ensemble*, uses short-wave radios to bring musical sounds of the whole world into one room at the same time. And here one may experience the importance of the plan. By knowing something of its intention and sound source, it is possible to experience something tangible *about* the piece *even before hearing it*.

STOCKHAUSEN, *MOMENTE*

The plan for *Momente* involves a variety of ideas and intentions concerning the experience of time. The title is a key to the work. Stockhausen wishes to create a musical experience of time in which each moment is equal to the next; no single moment of the work is a result of another. Unlike the many goal-directed designs of Western musical culture, for example the sonata-allegro plan, there is no continuity of musical flow toward important highpoints in *Momente*. But if one moment is to be no more important than the next, how can it have a beginning or an end? In one sense, it doesn't. Various sections of the piece can be performed in any order, thus removing the question of goal direction. This type of design is called *open form*. (Conversely, *closed form* denotes a design with a definite beginning and end.) The order of the "moments" is not the only flexible element in this piece. There are many details that are improvised according to a basic plan supplied by the composer. It is part of Stockhausen's intention that the piece can never be exactly duplicated. This aspect, called improvisation in other situations, has been labeled *indeterminacy* in our twentieth-century culture. The plan itself has both dramatic and mathematical characteristics (see opposite page). Reading through it will give you a rough idea of the complexity of Stockhausen's process. Clearly, *Momente* is deeply involved with intellectual principles. The mathematical-scientific flavor of the plan is unmistakable.

Stockhausen: Additional Listening

Mikrophonie I (1961–62)
Stop (London version, 1973)

OPEN FORM   A musical design with no fixed beginning or end. Conversely, *closed form* denotes a design with a definite beginning and end.

INDETERMINACY   A type of improvisation in which the composer specifies an element of chance in the musical process.

TOTAL SERIALISM   A compositional procedure in which many aspects of musical design—including pitch, rhythm, and dynamics—are controlled by a mathematical plan.

COMPOSER AND MUSICAL LANGUAGE—A NEW DEVELOPMENT

Throughout this book we have been following the way composers absorb a living musical language from their culture. You will recall that such people as Bach, Mozart, Beethoven, and Mendelssohn learned their musical language at an early age. Furthermore, this absorption at a basic level was unquestioned and somewhat spontaneous. A good comparison may be found in a child's absorption of speech, also a spontaneous acquisition of skills which stay with the individual through life. In fact, until the late nineteenth century, the musical language absorbed by composers as children remained with them throughout their lives. As they grew older, they enriched this "natural" language without ever questioning its structure. For example, there is nothing in Mozart's mature works that contradicts the basic musical tradition of his childhood. But as we have discovered in Span II, this situation began to change. Already evident in the evolution of the styles of Mussorgsky and Debussy, the new trend is firmly in place with Schoenberg, Messiaen, Ligeti, and Stockhausen. *Rather than continuing to use the musical language absorbed as children, modern composers are expected to invent their own.* Often, these new styles are in total contradiction with the composer's early spontaneous musical habits. Compared to the past, this represents perhaps the most profound change in how the modern composer acquires a musical language. Furthermore, this trend tends to foster more complex, individualized, and less accessible musical idioms* and is a basic reason for the well-known lack of communication between today's "serious" composer and audience.

The Changing Musical Language in Span II

Since the two hundred years in what we call Span II are characterized by increasing stylistic diversity, it becomes more difficult to document the different trends as we get closer to the Modern end of the spectrum. In the Classical era, one musical language prevailed; in the Romantic period, differences between composers' styles became more pronounced. In the twentieth century, stylistic diversity reaches a climax with the fragmentation of tradition into a multitude of musical languages. An entire book would be necessary to trace this complex development. What we can do here is trace one trend that symbolizes a basic thrust in Western music—the decline and the disappearance of the major–minor tonal system along with traditional concepts of melody, harmony, and form. Chronological preci-

*These become more accessible through study and familiarity.

sion is not of importance in this presentation. What we are looking for is a broad understanding of a long-range tendency in the musical culture.

Listen   Sequence 24 (These pieces have already been heard individually.)

Follow the chart on page 356 as you listen. It describes the general aspects of the changing musical language in Span II.

Summary of Basic Trends in Span II

Throughout our discussion of the Classical-Romantic-Modern span, we have found changes in various aspects of the musical language. Concerning these changes, we can note several basic trends:

1. Growing stylistic diversity
2. The exploration and decline of the major–minor tonal system
3. The growth of complex rhythms
4. The exploration and rejection of large-scale forms
5. Development of the large orchestra and new timbres
6. The growing importance of texture and timbre in composition
7. Innovations of genre and form

The following discussion summarizes these basic trends in the musical culture of Span II.

GROWING STYLISTIC DIVERSITY

The basic trend of the musical culture throughout the nineteenth and twentieth centuries is the increasing proliferation of individualized musical languages. As we move forward in time, stylistic contrasts between the music of composers contemporary with one another *increase*.

Listening Sequence 24

Span II

	Classical	Romantic		Modern		
	24a	24b	24c	24d	24e	24f
	Haydn, *Rondo from Sonata in E minor*	Chopin, *Revolutionary Etude*	Debussy, *Chromatic Etude*	Messiaen, *Four Etudes on Rhythm,* No. 1	Ligeti, *Lux aeterna*	Stockhausen, *Momente*
	clear theme, presented in traditional manner, cadences	clear theme	melody exists in fragments rather than as a continuous flow	modern, complex melodic patterns; fragmented melody	no traditional melody	no melody or harmony in traditional sense
	classical spirit of restraint	virtuoso playing				
	strong, regular meter	regular meter	strong meter, but rhythmic complexities create irregular patterns	irregular rhythms and meter	no meter	texture, timbre, rhythm most important musical elements
		importance of texture	higher level of dissonance	still higher level of dissonance	harmony very dissonant, closely related to texture and timbre	
	strong tonality	strong tonality	tonality is present but somewhat vague	tonality is present but in an "expanded" modern idiom	no clear tonality	no clear tonality

FRAGMENTATION AND DISSOLUTION OF MAJOR–MINOR TONAL SYSTEM

INCREASE IN IRREGULAR METER AND COMPLEX RHYTHMS

STEADY INCREASE IN LEVEL OF DISSONANCE

GROWING PROMINENCE OF TIMBRE AND TEXTURE

DISAPPEARANCE OF TRADITIONAL MELODY

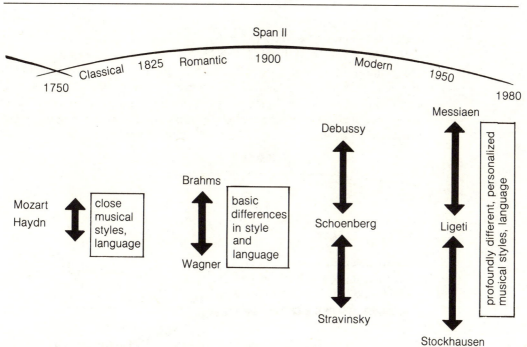

The growing diversity is also reflected in the number of descriptive labels that are used to categorize music. For example, the following is only a partial list:

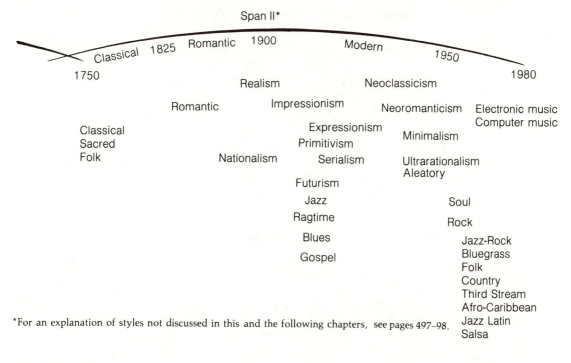

*For an explanation of styles not discussed in this and the following chapters, see pages 497–98.

THE EXPLORATION AND DECLINE OF
THE MAJOR–MINOR TONAL SYSTEM

The major–minor tonal system had been at the foundation of musical culture since the Baroque period. Some composers of the Romantic era explored the limits of this system; many modern "serious" composers have abandoned it entirely. Most twentieth-century popular music, however, has continued to be based on the major–minor tonal system.

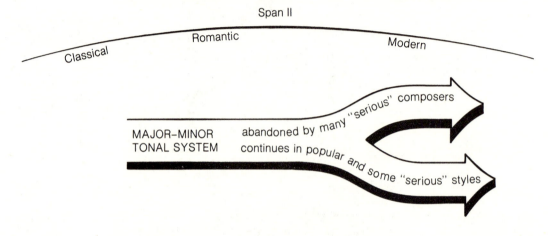

INCREASED USE OF COMPLEX RHYTHMS

As we move toward the twentieth century, rhythms become more irregular and fragmented. The Classical period is firmly rooted in regular meter. In the Romantic era, composers started exploring more complex rhythmic structures, including irregular meters and uneven phrase lengths. In the twentieth century, this trend explodes into a variety of directions, in many of which the traditional rhythmic practices that had dominated European music since 1600 are abandoned. In some cases, not only meter is suppressed, but also the pulse itself. Other rhythms show a primitive insistence on pulse and meter, but in new combinations of metrical groupings. Popular music perpetuates the regularity of rhythm, but with a vital new complexity drawn directly from Afro-American and Latin American musical traditions.

THE EXPLORATION AND REJECTION OF LARGE-SCALE FORMS

After Beethoven's revolutionary use of symphonic form, composers seemed compelled to create large-scale works. This tradition reached a climax with the operas of Richard Wagner. In the twentieth century, there has been a movement away from such grandiose conceptions. Although many long works are still composed, the overall trend is toward brevity.

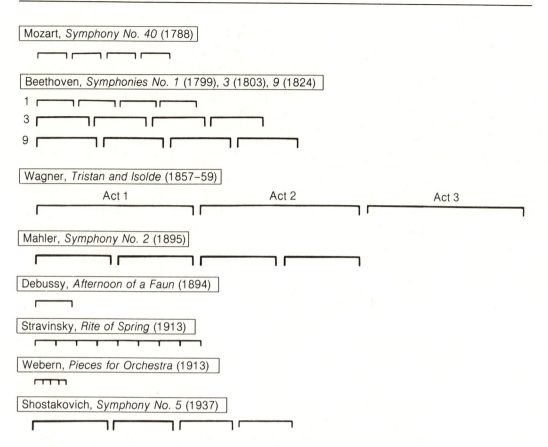

DEVELOPMENT OF THE LARGE ORCHESTRA AND NEW TIMBRES

The orchestra in the Classical era consisted of 30 to 40 players. The Romantic era saw the emergence of the full modern orchestra, which might have as many as 100 instrumentalists. Composers of today have added even more instruments to the full orchestral sound, although, for practical reasons, a great deal of contemporary music is written for small ensembles.

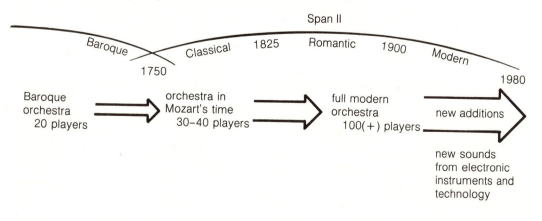

The advent of electronic technology has provided a wholly new type of sound. The synthesizer and advanced recording technology present the composer with endless tone-color possibilities. In the 1970s, composers, musicians, and producers of popular music have helped bring about a virtual revolution in the role of recording technology in the compositional process.

THE GROWING IMPORTANCE OF TEXTURE AND TIMBRE IN COMPOSITION

Approaching the twentieth century, we find that composers increasingly use texture and timbre as *essential* elements in their musical thinking. To illustrate: A symphony by Mozart or Beethoven can be played on the piano (usually by two players) and retain its essence. The themes, harmony, and form—the basic structure of the work—remain intact even when stripped of their orchestral identity. In contrast, works such as Debussy's *La Mer* or Stockhausen's *Momente* rely so heavily on timbre and texture that they cannot be separated from their original sound source.

INNOVATIONS OF GENRE AND FORM

Although important traditions of genre and form continue into our time (the sonata-symphony group, for example), many composers have adopted a radical, innovative approach to these artistic choices. This new freedom has been expressed in various ways: traditional genres and forms are altered or transformed into unique designs (for example, Ligeti's *Lux aeterna*, a canon, is in the tradition of the sacred motet and Mass). Taking this freedom one step further, many composers have abandoned traditional notions of genre and form completely, approaching each work with a totally open mind. Anything is possible. Works like Stockhausen's *Momente* have no recognizable model in the musical culture.

The Changing Society

In Chapter 5, we traced some of the flexible connections between the changing European society and the music of the Medieval, Renaissance, and Baroque eras. Of special interest were general shifts in sensory awareness and intellectual traditions, both of which affect the aesthetic environment in which music is created and heard. This task will be far more difficult for the Classical-Romantic-Modern span. The reason is clear: The social and cultural forces at work in Span II are vastly more complex than those of Span I. Therefore, what we say about Span II must reveal even greater flexibility. However, there are trends that suggest a general context for the many styles that have evolved during this period. Moreover, it is within the last 150 years that the styles, values, and habits of our own musical culture came into being.

The following discussions suggest, in general terms, some of those forces that have shaped the modern world and its music. Perhaps the best way to deal with broad generalizations that encompass such a wide range of human activity is to take them in, one at a time, and at an easy pace.

REVOLUTION AND THE TRANSITION TO MODERN CULTURE

Since the American and French revolutions in the late eighteenth century, there have been a series of political and social upheavals which substantially deprived aristocratic monarchs of their absolute powers. As we know, some of these upheavals resulted in the formation of Western democracies. Now you might think, "What does this have to do with music?" In fact, *these great social and economic shifts affected musical culture at the very deepest level*. First, consider the image of the composer: we have traced the radical changes in the composer's social position in our discussions of Bach, Mozart, and Beethoven. It is during Span II that the composer emerges as an honored, even privileged member of society. No servant could have composed *The Magic Flute, The Ode to Joy* (Beethoven's *Ninth Symphony*), *The Damnation of Faust, Tristan,* or *The Rite of Spring*. These are artistic statements supercharged with personal or political freedom, or both. In the wake of vast political change, the transition of the composer from servant to prophet was accomplished in a matter of decades. Obviously, the self-image of an artist directly affects his or her artistic choices.

Secondly, consider the audience. Fundamental to a living language of music, traditionally speaking, is the existence of cues shared by composer, performer, and audience. The social adjustments in the eighteenth and nineteenth centuries created a new and larger audience for "serious" music, comprised not of the nobility but of the middle classes, and centered not in the courts and salons of the aristocracy, but in the new concert halls. The institution of public concerts came into being during the Classical-Romantic span. The age of revolution led to a democratization of musical culture; this, in turn, seems to have furthered the split between popular and serious musical styles.

THE POPULAR-SERIOUS SPLIT

One of the most fascinating yet least understood phenomena in music is the historic tension between "popular" and "serious" styles. This dichotomy, firmly rooted in the social fabric, has always been an issue in European musical culture in one form or another. It takes on special meaning for us from the nineteenth century on, since the particular version of the popular-serious split with which we are most familiar originated at that time. Several interacting factors that helped reinforce this cultural energy may be suggested:

1. Composers like Beethoven and Wagner became symbols of a new elite group. Suddenly, here were men from ordinary social backgrounds who were revered, almost worshiped, for their extraordinary musical achievements. Artistic elitism, once the province of the aristocracy, was embraced by many members of the middle class. Without the status of noble birth, being connoisseurs of "serious" music became a symbol of their hard-won social position.

2. As previously stated, the social upheavals created a vast new audience for notated music. Inevitably, there were those who took advantage of an uneducated public and marketed some very bad music. The tension between competent, gifted composers and these "quick-buck" opportunists further hardened the notion of what "good" and "serious" music was supposed to be. Thus was born the negative connotation of *commercialism*, a prejudice that still gnaws away at "official" acceptance of many highly crafted modern popular styles.

3. Another factor was the growing perception of "art as religion." Span II has been characterized by a continuing process of *secularization*. In the continuation of a tendency that has been growing since the Renaissance, modern notions of politics, economics, and science have taken over many of the realms once controlled by religious thought. An extreme example was the anti-church stance of the French Revolution, in which a whole society that had functioned under a powerful church influence was suddenly transformed (though briefly) into a society in which church officials were persecuted and even executed. As every society that has tried to outlaw religious activity has discovered, it is deeply ingrained in the habits and consciousness of the people.

    One way religious feeling survives is to be *transformed*. The secularizing process of the nineteenth century produced what one might call a "heightened experience gap." And here is where music steps in. There is no question that in the great symphonic and operatic works of Span II, many listeners experience a solemn, heightened state that could be described as "religious." The "cult of the artist" and the "art as religion" trends that we have discussed may be understood as a kind of secularized religious impulse. And indeed, this notion has been well documented in several composers' own philosophies (Wagner immediately comes to mind).

    Thus, notated music, whether it had a religious subject or not, took on a new solemnity or "seriousness." The idea of an attentive, "serious" mass audience, sitting in a concert hall in a state of heightened intellectual and emotional solemnity, not merely for entertainment but for some "high" spiritual goal, has no precedent in Span I, *except in actual church rites*. To understand the formal concert as a type of secularized ritual in which art has replaced religion as its focus is another cultural strand that has shaped our image of "serious" music.

Herein lies a basic difficulty surrounding musical response in the twentieth century. The notion that the performance of symphonic music was a solemn occasion (and it is), and that audiences were to be quiet, serious, and, more important, were not to move, became our inherited image of how to listen to "serious" music. To a great extent, it works, especially with music designed for formal concerts. But when applied to music not intended to be heard in such a solemn environment, the potential for what one might call "overseriousness" exists. For example, consider the *Branle* dance group from Span I (Renaissance). This music was designed for dancing and not merely for listening. While it is certainly not wrong to listen to it "seriously," without moving, it is also not wrong to tap your foot to it, or even get up and execute your own version of that spirited step. We have, in fact, *two contrasting styles of listening in our culture* (with many shades between): one is to remain motionless, attentive, contemplating the music with solemnity; the other is to move, dance, and otherwise become actively involved with the music on a physical level. If you have always had the habit of moving with the music, it may be a mismatch of traditions for you to sit still through a two-hour concert. The opposite is also true. If your background has taught you that listening to *all* music must be a totally motionless act, you may find it hard to respond to musical styles created specifically as experiences in movement as well as sound. Of course, there is that all-important middle ground: many listeners are able to find a flexible approach, taking a little from each side of the two traditions, changing their habits from piece to piece and place to place. *There is no right or wrong way to listen to music.*

Without question, a sometimes fluid, sometimes polarized continuum of "popular" and "serious" musical values once again became an important part of the aesthetic environment in which music was created and heard.

"*popular*"	"*serious*"
music as	music as
informal experience	solemn art

These are extremes between which some composers shifted back and forth. In fact, we have been documenting a good deal of that back-and-forth movement. For example, Mussorgsky *consciously* sought to shift his musical language toward the popular side. Schoenberg, on the other hand, stated his unequivocal belief in the evolutionary value of "serious" music, and considered popular music to have no place in "advanced" music making. Nonetheless, he sometimes drew on popular impulses (as in the *Gigue*). Leonard Bernstein, the contemporary American composer of *West Side Story*, has received a good deal of criticism for incorporating "popular" elements in his "serious" music. He has consciously experimented with styles that draw from both sides of the continuum. Finally, there are many composers (and listeners) like Messiaen, for whom the entire matter doesn't seem to apply at all. We will pick up this strand in the last chapter.

THE EXPANSION OF THE WORLD VIEW

To a great extent, the music and cultural traits we have been discussing have been a regional European phenomenon. But during Span II, the connections between European culture and the rest of the world multiplied with startling rapidity. These connections had begun to appear, but to a lesser degree, during Span I; but in the late nineteenth and twentieth centuries, cultural interactions became one of the single most important influences in musical life. A few examples will demonstrate this idea:

1. Composers (like Mussorgsky) who were outside the main currents of European music composed in styles that reflected a blend of the traditional with regional styles, which were then reabsorbed into the mainstream.
2. Music from every corner of the world began to pour into Europe through notation and recordings. Composers like Debussy and Messiaen incorporated elements from far-flung traditions into their living language.
3. Ideas and philosophies from the rest of the world reached Europe. Eastern philosophy, especially, influenced many composers, among them Stockhausen.
4. Since its beginnings, notated music had been almost exclusively based in Europe. In the Modern era, America became another important center for the notated tradition. In a real sense, the tradition is now found throughout the entire world.
5. Since World War II, the culture of Third World countries has had an increasingly important influence on the modern scene. The musical consequences of this trend will be discussed in the final chapters.

The impact of this cultural expansion can be brought into sharper focus for us by comparing the musical languages of Mozart and Messiaen. While Mozart's style was a synthesis of relatively few traditions—mainly German and Italian—Messiaen's musical vocabulary is drawn from many corners of the earth. (But remember that not all contemporary composers have chosen to be so all-embracing.)

THE DOMINANCE OF THE SCIENTIFIC VIEW

A basic moving force in the history of Europe and the world has been the steady increase in the influence science has had upon culture. In Span II, and especially in the Modern era, this influence has reached an unprecedented highpoint. It is important to understand that scientific advances not only affect such disciplines as biology and physics and create new technologies like tape recorders, television, and spaceships, but also *influence the way we view the entire spectrum of human activity*. Thus a book on music, like this one, is expected to produce many rational explanations and data for its conclusions. The scientific view, then, suggests that analysis and technical considerations are the determining factors in the understanding of reality—music included.

The "serious" musical culture of Span II has shown a massive reversal in terms of its relationship to scientific thinking. Romanticism encouraged the undefinable, even mystical bond between composer, audience, musical sound, and life. While science was certainly on the rise in the nineteenth century, the Romantics saw not its rational possibilities, but its potential for providing keys to the irrational world of the unattainable. Faust, by the way, is introduced to us as a scientist of sorts, who rejects rationality as a means of understanding life. (Perhaps the most telling example of how the Romantics regarded science may be found in Mary Shelley's novel *Frankenstein*.)

In our time, there has been a rejection of Romantic "irrationality" in "serious" music. Replacing the Romantic view, we find various manifestations of a scientific-rational approach to composing *and listening*. For example, compare Berlioz's programmatic instructions to the audience for the *Fantastic Symphony* (pages 260–63) with the liner notes supplied by Stockhausen for the recording of *Momente* (page 352).

Perhaps the ultimate effect of scientific concerns on modern music is the purposeful preoccupation of many composers with techniques that often lead to rational, mathematical, and abstract musical designs. This in itself is not new, being one of the oldest impulses of musical culture. But in the Modern era, the tendency has clearly reached its apogee. One reason may be the lack of a shared living language. You will recall, the major-minor tonal system was a basic feature of music *throughout* Europe from 1600–1900. When Mozart traveled to Italy, he entered into a neighboring musical zone; despite their slightly different "dialects," Germans and Italians shared a basic musical language. *The Modern era has no such unity.* Among composers and listeners today, *the rational-analytical approach has become one of the few connecting strands that holds the modern musical culture together.*

Rationality as an Influence in the "Serious" Musical Culture of Span II

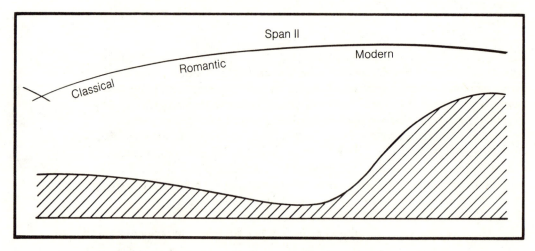

INDUSTRIALIZATION AND TECHNOLOGY

During Span II, humans began their love–hate relationship with the technologies of the modern world. From its beginnings in England, industrialization took on great momentum as it sped through the nineteenth century. Today, the world is clearly divided into those societies that are already "modern" and those about to take the plunge (the Third World). The impact of industrialization and the growth of technology are not always easy to describe. Perhaps they can best be understood by contrasting our world with Mozart's. In the mid-eighteenth century, when Mozart went on his European tours, he traveled by horse-drawn coach across a largely rural landscape, as yet untouched by industrialized society. Great cities were like magnets for the artistically hungry. Separated from one another by days, even weeks of travel, the legendary centers of Paris, Vienna, and Rome were the hubs of an idealistic civilization. The dehumanizing effects of a mechanized society were yet to come. Would Mozart have composed *The Magic Flute* in a machine age? Would Felix Mendelssohn have composed the *Overture to a Midsummer Night's Dream* in 1826 if a railroad ran near his family's private estate in Berlin? (The railroad *did* come to Berlin, in 1838.) The pervasive feeling of innocence and idealism in Classical and early Romantic music would somehow seem a bit out of place in an industrial society. Suppose you were a movie director and had to choose music for a scene showing a sunset over a skyscraper city. Would Mendelssohn's "fairy music" fit the bill? By the same token, consider both Stockhausen's *Momente* [24f] and Blue Öyster Cult's *Godzilla* [25] (heavy rock); how would these pieces sound in Mendelssohn's garden? What effect does industrialization have on the listener? What kind of cultural filter does someone who works on an automobile assembly line bring to Mendelssohn's delicate evocation of fairies in the woods? Clearly, the accumulated experience of modern life affects the aesthetic environment of music in ways that are profound, yet difficult to quantify.

Other effects of our modern age are more tangible. One of the most far-reaching is recording technology. Composers and listeners of today have at their disposal an unimaginable diversity of musical traditions, past and present, drawn from every corner of the world and made available on records and tapes. We are only now beginning to grasp the connections that this electronically communicated web of human musicality sets before our ears and minds.

INFORMATION OVERLOAD AND SENSORY CLUTTER

A geometric increase in the number of things to see, hear, feel, read, know, consider, has paralleled the rise of industrialization and modern technologies. Ours is a vastly more complex and cluttered world than Mozart's was. The college student of today, for example, is expected to absorb many more facts about any given subject than the student of even twenty years ago, but in the same amount of time. How does this overload affect the aesthetic environment? The contemporary composer John Cage reacted by composing a now-famous piece entitled *4'33"*, in which nothing happens other than the performer sitting in front of an open piano for four minutes and thirty-three seconds of total silence. This piece of "anti-art" may be seen as a commentary on the noise and sensory overkill of modern civilization, which deaden our senses and make the perception of music a futile endeavor. In Cage's

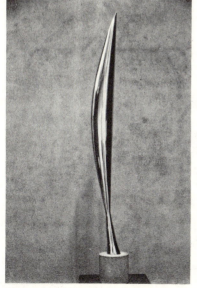

Constantin Brancusi, *Bird in Space* (1928?)

Jackson Pollock, *Ocean Greyness* (1953).

BRONZE (UNIQUE CAST), 54" HIGH. COLLECTION, THE MUSEUM OF MODERN ART, NEW YORK. GIVEN ANONYMOUSLY

OIL ON CANVAS, 57 3 4 x 90 1 8". COLLECTION, THE MUSEUM OF MODERN ART, NEW YORK work, the silence becomes music, rescued for a brief time from the cacophony of sounds, events, ideas, styles, machines, cars, wars, facts, and more, that surround it.

One musical style that seems at home in a world of sensory clutter, and even thrives on its energies, is rock. Perhaps part of the success of rock is its ability to drown out, in both volume and energy, what some consider an already loud and hyped-up environment.

Adding to the overall clutter is the existence of so many musical styles. While a basic purpose of this book is the development of skills that will enable you to listen beyond style, this idea must be tempered with an awareness that hearing too many styles in close proximity can have a negative effect: namely, obscuring the meaning of any single style. It takes a pretty hardy set of ears to listen to Mozart and rock back-to-back. Those who appreciate both usually separate their listening experiences with time, purpose, and mood. Messiaen has an interesting reaction to the stylistic and cultural cacophony of the modern world:

> In dark hours, when my futility is brutally apparent, when all musical languages—classic, exotic, ancient, modern, and ultramodern—seem to me reduced to the meritorious product of patient studies, while nothing behind the notes justifies so much work, what is there left but to rediscover the true forgotten face of music somewhere in the woods, in the fields, in the mountains, by the sea, among the birds?*

Messiaen's response is unique; but it reflects the undeniable fact that our cluttered culture is a powerful shaping force for composers and listeners alike.

SENSE OF TIME

While the experience of time is certainly an elusive matter, it is such an important aspect of music that it is useful to consider it, if only in general terms. Perhaps the easiest aspect to describe is the change that accompanied industrialization; modern society is certainly faster-paced than the late eighteenth century. This shift in time sense can still be experienced by moving between city and country. More difficult to describe is how we perceive the very nature of time. Since the nineteenth century, a variety of discoveries, technologies, and experiences has greatly altered our sense of what time is, among them the following:

*William W. Austin, *Music in the 20th Century* (New York, 1966), p. 395.

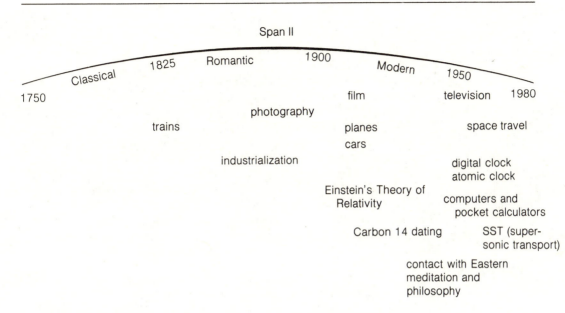

Span II

Classical   1825   Romantic   1900   Modern   1950

1750   film   television   1980

photography

trains   planes   space travel

cars

industrialization   digital clock

atomic clock

Einstein's Theory of Relativity   computers and pocket calculators

Carbon 14 dating   SST (super-sonic transport)

contact with Eastern meditation and philosophy

Photography can "stop" time. Film can "compress," "extend," and "chop it up." Einstein's theory that time is variable and actually goes faster and slower was later proven through experiments. (A clock on the twentieth floor of a building runs infinitesimally faster than one on the ground floor.) Plane travel alters the sense of time in relation to body, distance, and cultural experience. Television, perhaps the ultimate time-altering mechanism, creates its own electronic schedule for millions. In sum, time has become an amazingly flexible experience.

Early nineteenth-century clock.

Salvador Dali, *The Persistence of Memory* **(1931).**

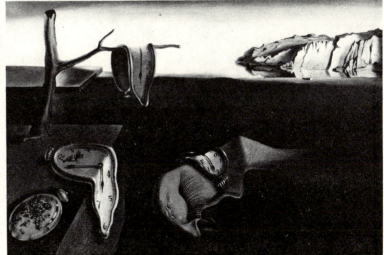

It is no surprise, then, to find composers like Messiaen, Ligeti, and Stockhausen consciously experimenting with how rhythm and other musical elements affect time perception. In fact, *deliberate attempts to control the experience of time are one feature of many twentieth-century styles.* For example, the American composer Elliott Carter has said, "My interest and thinking about musical time were also very much stimulated by the kinds of 'cutting' and continuity you find in the movies . . ." Another time-dominated musical experience is found in Joni Mitchell's song cycle *Hejira* (see pages 433–36).

QUESTIONS—SUMMARY

The following questions summarize some of the basic trends of Spans I and II. You may want to review questions in previous chapters before answering these.

1. Write in approximate dates and names of the historical style periods depicted on the diagram.

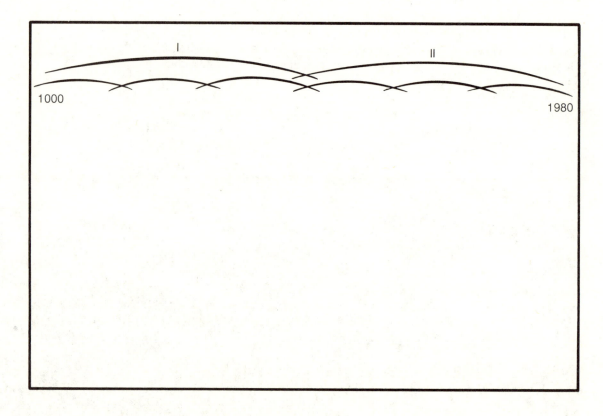

2. Place each of the following composers in his approximate place on
   the diagram on page 370:

Mozart	Ligeti
Stravinsky	Schoenberg
Beethoven	Mendelssohn
Berlioz	Debussy
Ockeghem	Bernstein
Dufay	Wagner
Bach	Mussorgsky
Verdi	Messiaen

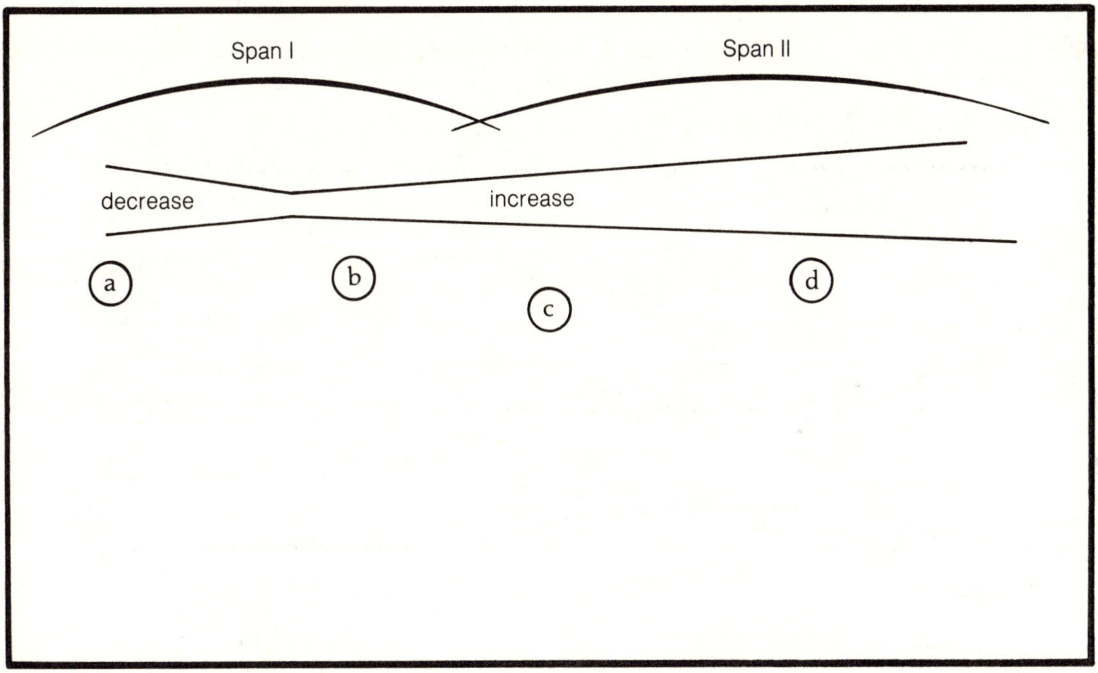

Span I   Span II

decrease   increase

a   b   c   d

(Questions 3 through 9 refer to the diagram above. For each question, cross
out inappropriate answer(s).)

3. The *decrease–increase* configuration could represent the history of
   (major–minor tonal system, polyphony, dissonance).

4. A composer living at which moment in history (represented by
   letters) could *not* have composed a fugue? (a b c d)

5. Composers living in which historical period(s) could have written a symphony? (a b c d)

6. Composers living in which historical period(s) would be likely to include Gregorian chant in their compositions? (a b c d)

7. Composers living at which historical moment(s) would be most likely to consider themselves *artists* and not *servants*? (a b c d)

8. Composers living at which historical moment(s) would be most likely to *specify* the instruments for which they were writing? (a b c d)

9. Composers at which historical moment(s) would be most likely to know about music of the distant past? (a b c d)

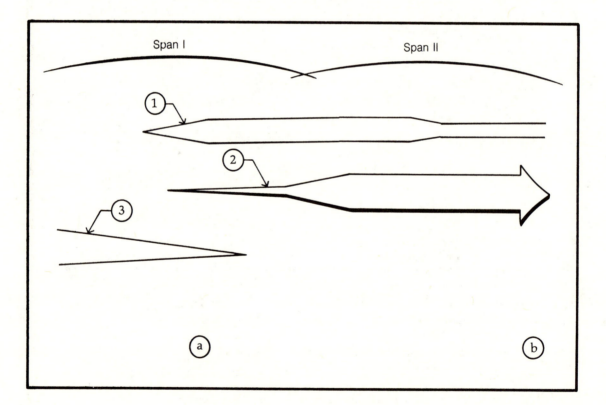

(Questions 10 through 15 refer to the diagram on page 372.)

10. Figure ① represents the historical life of (modal harmony, the major–minor tonal system, sonata-symphony group).

11. Figure ② represents the historical development and continuing existence of (the major–minor tonal system, Gregorian chant, the symphony orchestra).

12. Figure ③ represents (the influence of the Church on musical culture, the decline of polyphony, the decline of dissonance).

13. A composer living at moment ⓐ might compose a (Mass, sonata, string quartet).

14. A composer living at moment ⓑ might compose a (symphony, fugue, Mass).

15. A person living at moment (ⓐ or ⓑ) might know a great deal about Medieval music.

14
American Music

The Importance of National Styles

At various places in this book, we have explored the relationship between music and a particular nation or region. The role of national styles is among the most important yet elusive issues in music's history. Among the connections we have noted are: the English madrigal, a blend of English and Italian traditions (see page 162); opera and what it owes to Italian song —originally an Italian practice, opera evolved many national styles (pages 172–73); the music of Mozart, a synthesis of German and Italian styles (page 220); Viennese lyricism—influences on this style include German and Italian melody, as well as Viennese dance (page 298); the music of Debussy, deeply influenced by his desire to compose according to the French, not German, aesthetic (pages 319–20); the music of Mussorgsky, reflecting his Russian heritage (pages 312–13).

We may summarize some basic ideas that these examples suggest:

1. A living musical language *may* be deeply related to a national or regional heritage.
2. The traditions of different nations or regions often interact, resulting in new styles.
3. This interplay among national or regional styles is one of the basic enriching processes of the world's musical language.
4. This interplay is *extremely flexible* and is often difficult to describe in exact terms; there are pieces, styles, composers, and situations in which the issue of a national style may not be relevant.

American Music: A Living Language

A recent review of an all-American music concert had this to say about the conductor: "No one conducts American music better than Leonard Bern-

stein. He has its inflections, its rhythms, and its spirit in his blood . . ."*
These words echo a theme encountered in many guises throughout this
book: *there is an essential part of musical experience that cannot be separated from culture. Although this quality is difficult to define, it is often a
powerful presence.* The reviewer assumes that he and his readers share the
same cues of a living American musical language. How else could they
understand which inflections, rhythms, and spirit he is referring to? Although there is no consensus as to what constitutes an American style, there
is general agreement that an American music does exist. American culture is
complex. Because of its diversity, many musical styles fall under the category "American." The characteristics, influences, and composers to be discussed in this chapter represent only part of the story.

THE HERITAGE FROM THE BRITISH ISLES

Basic to the American musical heritage are the folk traditions of the British
Isles, brought to this land by English-speaking settlers. The general time-
frame for this transfer of traditions is shown below.

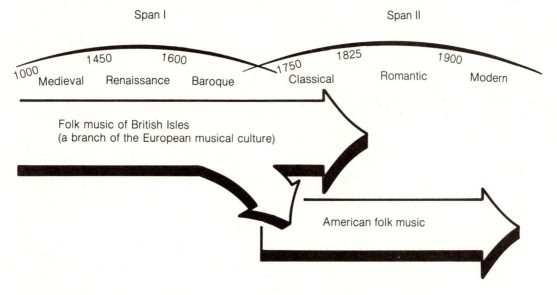

Before tracing these traditions *forward in time,* as they become part of
American music, we may recall that Anglo-Celtic folk traditions have roots
in an ancient past. For example, the story type of the ballad *I Will Give My
Love an Apple* 6a is quite old, as evidenced by its appearance in many
European cultures. The melody was most likely a creation of a Renaissance
minstrel. The sea chantey from the Hebrides 4a may likely reach back to

*Donal Henahan in the *New York Times,* February 6, 1981.

such sea-faring cultures as the Vikings, who populated the northern shores of Europe and beyond during the Middle Ages. The *Ossianic Chant* 7c , also from the Hebrides, is undoubtedly among the oldest music discussed in this book; the melodic formulas used to preserve epic legends may well have been sung for thousands of years.

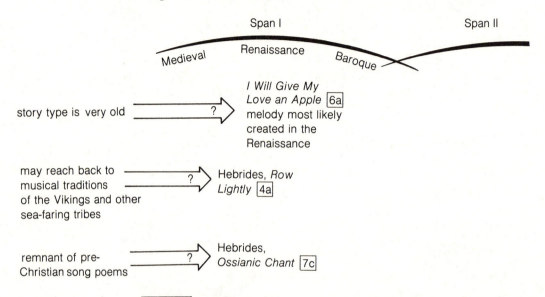

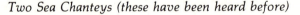

Listen   Listen to the following pieces as a continuous mosaic of musical and cultural connection. In a way, this sequence might be considered symbolic of a total musical culture, meshed with the life-rhythms of the people who made this music. These selections hint at a great human chain. For millenia, similar chains have linked the world's music across distance and time.

Two Sea Chanteys (these have been heard before)

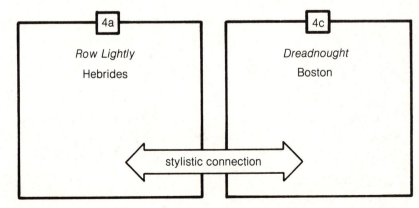

Two Dances (these have been heard before)

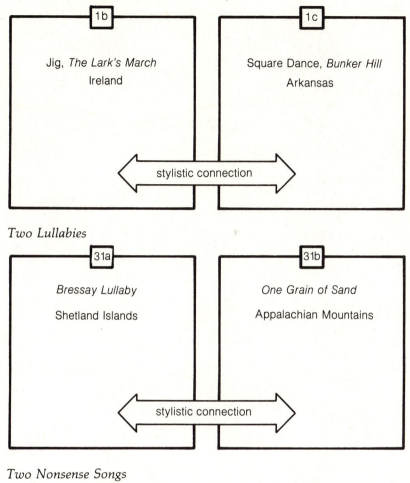

1b	**1c**
Jig, *The Lark's March*	Square Dance, *Bunker Hill*
Ireland	Arkansas

stylistic connection

Two Lullabies

31a	**31b**
Bressay Lullaby	*One Grain of Sand*
Shetland Islands	Appalachian Mountains

stylistic connection

Two Nonsense Songs

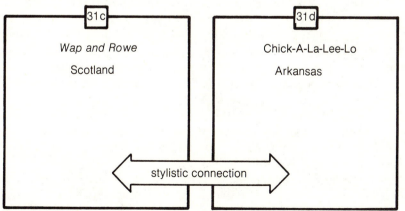

31c	**31d**
Wap and Rowe	Chick-A-La-Lee-Lo
Scotland	Arkansas

stylistic connection

Two Ballads

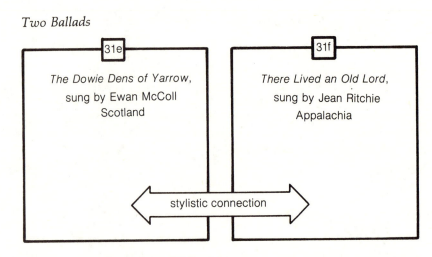

The Dowie Dens of Yarrow,
sung by Ewan McColl
Scotland

There Lived an Old Lord,
sung by Jean Ritchie
Appalachia

stylistic connection

Two Excerpts from Sacred Worship

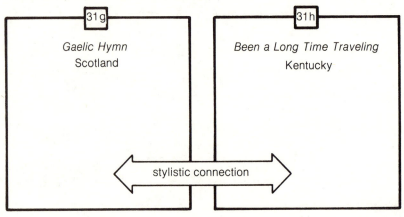

Gaelic Hymn
Scotland

Been a Long Time Traveling
Kentucky

stylistic connection

The sea chanteys have been discussed on pages 112–13. Since the sailing ship was vital for the colonization of America, it seems appropriate to begin by listening to this genre. A wonderful moment of connection between American and English musical traditions is the refrain ". . . with a down, derry, derry, derry, down, down." These playful words were common in English popular songs during the Renaissance. In *Dreadnought* they celebrate a nineteenth-century sailing ship out of Boston.

The dance comparison illustrates that the "pickin'" and "fiddlin'" of American country music is clearly a stylistic descendant of the earlier folk tradition heard in the Irish Jig.

Little need be said about lullabies, other than that they are given life by the same universal impulse the world over. An interesting experience beyond style is to listen to these lullabies while looking at Picture Sequence A.

Wap and Rowe and *Chick-A-La-Lee-Lo* provide a window into an ancient song style in which the rhythmic, playful sound of language is joined with melody in a delightful, inseparable unity. This style, which, by the way, was an important source for the art of poetry, has for the most part died out in modern culture.

The Scottish ballad tells the story of love and warfare among clans of the border region between Scotland and England, most likely a retelling of actual events. The Appalachian ballad presents a somewhat different situation. Although it may sound like a real story, it is actually a variant of a mythical story model found throughout Europe. *El Rey de Francia tres hijas tenía* 5a , of Medieval Spanish origin, is of the same story genre.

The Gaelic hymn was recorded in a rural church in Scotland. This simple, yet powerful vocal style, in which a leader "calls out" to the congregation and they answer, is one of the most universal structures in the world's musical language. This *call-and-response* format may be as old as music itself. The manner in which the leader calls or sings out the words before they are sung is known as *lining* the hymn. You may sense a certain "blues" quality in *Been a Long Time Traveling*, making this piece an interesting forerunner of contemporary American popular music.

Early Sacred Music in America

The colonists who settled in New England had a no-nonsense attitude toward sacred music. Joyful singing of psalms and hymns was central to their daily lives. One of the practices they brought with them was simple monophonic song (like the Gaelic hymn 31g). But leaving Europe at the end of the Renaissance, they also brought with them a polyphonic tradition. However, these people were neither professional musicians nor aristocrats who could afford the elaborate kind of music making found in Europe. Therefore, what came with the colonists was not the complex polyphonic style (for example, Gibbons's *I Am the Resurrection*) found in a wealthy cathedral, but the *familiar* style of congregational hymns and chorales that had made its way into churches throughout Europe. In other words, they brought that part of the European notated tradition which was accessible to most people. To this day, it takes a professionally trained chorus to perform complex polyphony, while hymns and chorales sound fine sung by everyone.

THE SINGING SCHOOLS

During the eighteenth century, a movement to initiate standards of "proper" musical performance and spiritual guidance resulted in the formation of many *singing schools* throughout the colonies. These community activities, which continued into the early nineteenth century, became an important event in the life of the ordinary citizen. As an example, consider the following excerpt from the diary of a New England teenager:

Dec. 12, 1805. Cloudy more moderate. I went to (the) Mill &c. In the evening I went to the Schoolhouse to consult about having a singing school. We agreed to have it twice a week and to have it kept by Thomas Howe. This night was the first.

Dec. 16, 1805. Something pleasant cool wind. I went to Mr. Solo. Stickney's and get 70 pare of upper leather and 60 pares of sole leather to make into shoes.

Dec. 17, 1805. Pleasant. In the evening Sally, Sam and I went to the singing school.

Dec. 19, 1805. Pleasant weather. I made 4 pares of shoes. Sam went to school.

Dec. 20, 1805. Cloudy day, clear and pleasant evening. We had our 3rd sing. meeting.

Dec. 25, 1805. Cold. I made shoes. Samuel closed 11 pares.

Dec. 26, 1805. Warm sun, cold wind. Sam and I went to the singing meeting in the evening. There were about a dozen. We sing out of Kimball's *Essex Harmony*.

Dec. 28, 1805. Dull and cloudy. We finished threshing rye by noon. Mr. Pingrey helped. We had a good crop . . .

Dec. 31, 1805. Very cold. I made 5 shoes and Samuel 4 and we went to Singing School in the evening. There were about 20 of us to sing and 14 or 15 spectators from Old Rowley & Byefield.*

From the singing masters who led these gatherings came America's first composers of notated music.

JEREMIAH INGALLS

Born in Massachusetts, Ingalls (1764–1838) spent most of his life in Vermont. He was a farmer, cooper, and tavern keeper, but his life's passion

*Alan G. Buechner, *The New England Harmony*, Folkways Album FA 3 2377, p. 5 of liner notes.

was for music. Aside from composing, Ingalls played an important role in the notation of the unwritten tradition of New England folk hymns. His *Christian Harmony* was a collection of such folk material along with more "learned" tunes and anthems. Many of these folk hymns were reprinted in Northern and Southern tunebooks during the nineteenth century and became part of the great tradition of American sacred song. Something of Ingall's character is suggested in this account of music making with his children, recorded by an acquaintance:

> His children were musical, and his sons could play clarinet, bassoon, flute and violin; and they would often practice for hours, the old gentleman leading the band with his bass viol. One Sunday they were having an excellent time performing anthems, and after a while the youngsters started a secular piece, the father with composure joining in; from that they went on until they found themselves furiously engaged in a boisterous march, in the midst of which the old gentleman stopped short, exclaiming, "Boys, this won't do!" Put away these corrupt things and take your Bibles.*

JUSTIN MORGAN

Like other colonial composers, Justin Morgan (1747–1798) practiced other trades—he was also a schoolmaster, tavern keeper, and is still known today as the breeder of the famous Morgan horse. Among his compositions is the tiny masterpiece *Amanda* 32b , with its striking dissonances and "open" harmony (chords without the traditional number of tones).

WILLIAM BILLINGS

The best-known of the early American composers was William Billings (1746–1800). He was a self-taught musician with more talent than training. Characteristic of his unshakable confidence in his natural abilities are these words: "For my own part as I don't think myself confin'd to any Rules for Composition laid down by any that went before me . . . I think it best for every Composer to be his own Carver." **Like other composers, Billings was an active publisher of *songbooks*, collections of music for recreational and religious singing. The success of these books enabled Billings to become one of the first Americans to make a living as a composer. The texts of his compositions usually involve two topics—religion and/or patriotism. Billings's circle included two well-known figures of the American Revolution—Paul Revere and Sam Adams. Several of his compositions became marching songs for George Washington's army.

*Ibid., p. 22.
**William Billings, *The New England Psalm Singer, or American Chorister* (Boston, 1770), preface, "Thoughts on Music."

Listen *Northfield,* by Ingalls 32a

> How long dear Savior oh how long
> Shall this bright hour delay?
> Fly swifter round ye wheel of time
> And bring the welcome day.
> > (repeat last two lines)

Listening Activity

For both pieces, indicate the texture in the boxes at right.
For *Amanda,* also circle the words in the text that correspond to dissonant harmony.

Amanda, by Morgan 32b

> Death like an overflowing stream
> Sweeps us away; our life's a dream;
> An empty tale; a morning flow'r,
> Cut down and withered in an hour.

m h p
[ ]

Washington, by Billings 32c

> Lord, when Thou didst ascend on high,
> Ten thousand angels fill'd the sky;
> Those heav'nly guards around Thee wait

m h p
[ ]

m h p
[ ]

> Like chariots that attend Thy state.
> > (repeat last two lines)

m h p
[ ]

THE FUGING PSALM TUNE

Northfield and *Washington* are quite similar in form. Both pieces are organized in the following manner:

Opening phrase(s) in the familiar style

m h p
[•]

A contrapuntal refrain created through imitation

m h p
[•]

A final cadence in the familiar style

m h p
[•]

This is the traditional design of a *fuging psalm tune.* Adopted from England, the fuging tune became the most popular genre used by colonial composers.

THE YANKEE TUNESMITHS

Billings, Ingalls, and Morgan were part of a group that has been dubbed the "Yankee Tunesmiths." The label is a good one. It captures an essential spirit of informality, the foot-tapping rhythms and lively tunes, that make their music so typically American. In contrast with the genteel music that sounded in Europe's courts, castles, and churches, the style of the Yankee Tunesmiths reflects a sturdy populist spirit concerned more with tuneful singing than with elaborate counterpoint and form. In their music, we find some of the qualities that have become part of the musical mainstream of America:

1. *Tuneful melodies*: The melodic style grew from American folk song and dances. These melodies were catchy and quickly learned.
2. *Dancing rhythms*: Lively, strong rhythms that evoke an immediate body response are a dominant element in American musical culture.
3. *An emphasis on vocal harmony*: The music of the Yankee Tunesmiths is filled with "old-fashioned harmony." Glorious, full-bodied harmony, often in a homophonic setting, became another feature of many American styles.

The Essential Relationship between the "Popular" and "Serious" Traditions

The music of the Yankee Tunesmiths will be used as a point of departure in this discussion of an important long-range connection. In previous pages we have examined relationships between certain notated music and the anonymous folk-popular music of its time. In each case, a notated style grew from, or had an integral connection to, a body-based popular musical language. Among these have been:

folk song and popular ⟶ opera
   music drama
folk-popular dance ⟶ suite (example:
   tradition (example: *Jig*)   *Gigue*)
German folk song ⟶ German lieder

These examples, a few among many, suggest a basic truth about our musical culture: *the notated tradition cannot be fully understood without considering its roots in folk-popular traditions. Despite its many unique characteristics, "serious" music has been continuously enriched by the living musical language of anonymous folk cultures.* Some notated styles reflect this connection more than others; many have moved so far away from the source that connections are difficult to hear, and in some cases are no longer a relevant factor.

The music of the Yankee Tunesmiths is a notated style closely related to an oral folk tradition. You will remember that in addition to composing, some colonial musicians also transcribed anonymous sacred hymns and psalms. The following piece is an example of such a transcription:

 The Young Convert, anonymous folk hymn from colonial New England 33a

THE INFLUENCE OF THE NOTATED TRADITION ON THE FOLK-POPULAR MUSICAL LANGUAGE

The Young Convert may be used to consider a basic influence on the musical language of the world.

1. *The Young Convert*, as stated before, is an oral, body-based piece. It was probably improvised without notation.
2. Its musical structure involves both harmony and simple counterpoint derived from the European notated tradition.
3. Thus, *it demonstrates that basic aspects of the European notated tradition became part of the folk-popular musical language.*

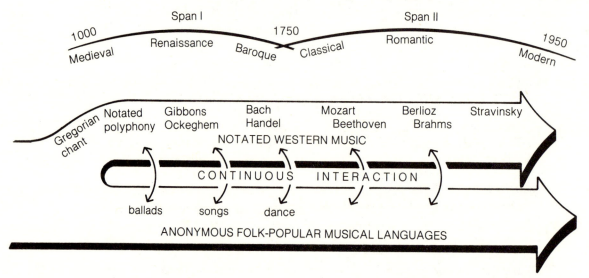

This is true not only of American folk music, but is a worldwide phenomenon. Nearly all the popular music you know today—rock, jazz, soul, etc.—involves basic characteristics (harmony, counterpoint, melodic type, etc.) derived from or influenced by the Western notated tradition.

American Sacred Folk Harmony

We will now trace the sacred hymn tradition of colonial New England into the nineteenth and twentieth centuries. The music of the Yankee Tunesmiths, as well as the anonymous hymns and psalms of rural New England, suddenly lost favor with the New England populace around 1800. The centers of the "Establishment" (New York and Boston, for example) were in the sway of a more aristocratic musical taste based on European culture. The rough-hewn folklike style of the Yankee Tunesmiths was perceived as "crude" and "primitive." Billings, one of America's first professional composers, ended his days in poverty, his music a relic of America's populist revolutionary past. But the music of the Tunesmiths, as well as the anonymous hymns and psalms of the colonial period, made their way southward to become part of rural religious life. Preserved with the help of songbooks, this music became an essential ingredient in a new tradition: *the South became the cradle of a related group of musical styles which eventually included gospel, blues, country, jazz, and rock. Like the notated European tradition, these styles were destined to reshape the living musical language of the world.*

Listen Sequence 33, American Sacred Folk Harmony, and *Walk Around* 3a

This sequence contains a variety of pieces from America's folk-popular sacred tradition. In all of these, vocal harmonies in the familiar style are an essential ingredient.

The Young Convert 33a (already discussed)

I'm On My Journey Home 33b, recorded by the Denson Quartet in 1928 in Atlanta, Georgia. This piece is from the *Sacred Harp* tradition, which developed in the nineteenth-century South. Members of the Denson Family have been performing in this tradition since 1844. Aside from its distinctive style, Sacred Harp music is known for its use of *shape notes* and *fasola* parts. The Southern songbooks (descended from those of the Yankee Tunesmiths) used oddly shaped notes to represent scale tones (see music below). Each tone had its own syllable. Traditionally, Sacred Harp singers began a song by singing a verse with these syllables. The opening of *I'm On My Journey Home* follows this practice.

Opening   "Fasola" singing (syllables representing scale tones)

Verse   Oh, who will come and go with me?
                 I'm on my journey home.
                 I'm bound for Canaan's land to see,
                 I am on my journey home.

An example of shape-notes in a hymn published at the end of the nineteenth century.

Chorus
        Oh, come and go with me,
        Oh, come and go with me,
        Oh, come and go with me,
        I am on my journey home.

(chorus repeats)

The stylistic similarities between this piece and certain types of rock music are quite striking. Among the distinct connections are the "bluesy" vocal style and melodic structure, the modal harmony and strong driving meter. If you were to imagine this piece accompanied by a drum set, and the vocal parts played on electric guitar and bass, you'd have a standard rock sound.

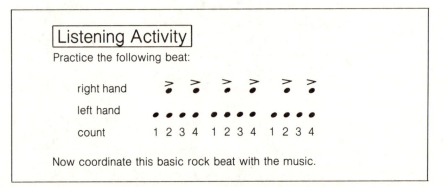

Angel Band 33c . In Southern rural areas, this sacred song was often sung at the bed of a dying person. The sweet, nasal vocal sound is recognizable as a basic trait of today's country music. The traditional religious imagery of *Angel Band* is thousands of years old. A Renaissance vision of these celestial musicians may be found in Picture Sequence B on page 505. For an interesting experience *beyond style*, listen to this sacred song from rural America while looking at that picture from Renaissance Italy, a representation of the same idea from another culture.

Walk Around 3a , The Soul Stirrers (discussed on page 56). Aside from its sacred nature, this piece is influenced by the blues, a genre we consider next.

The Blues

An important genre in the history of American popular music, and, eventually in the musical language of the world, the *blues* is an Afro-American tradition that originated in the South sometime after the Civil War. Its musical roots certainly reach back into the folk traditions of West Africa.

Listen *Yarum Praise Song* 35a , performed by Fra-Fra Tribesmen in Ghana (recorded in 1964).

Paul Oliver, who recorded this music writes:

In 1964, I recorded two songs of a kind called *Yarum*—meaning salt, which in the parched near-desert lands is good to the taste— played by Fra-Fra musicians in the extreme north of Ghana. One played a gourd rattle, throwing it rapidly between his hands to provide a rhythm, while the other bowed a two-string fiddle. They both sang traditional praises for their chief to a rhythmic humming, slightly repetitive accompaniment.*

There are many similarities between this song and the blues, as well as later popular styles:

1. strong, catchy rhythm and meter producing a continuous, dancelike body response
2. the continual repetition of motives
3. improvisation
4. sliding pitches in the vocal line

*Paul Oliver, *The Story of The Blues*, liner notes for Columbia Recording G-30008.

Although this African piece has basic impulses that hint at later American popular music, it obviously is not a blues. The blues genre was to grow from the black experience *in America*, evolving from an interaction between the musical habits of Afro-Americans and the Euro-American traditions they absorbed from nineteenth-century Southern culture. While it is impossible to document precisely, it was this interplay of styles, expressed through the unique experience of Southern blacks, that produced the blues. (This interplay will be discussed in more detail in a later section of this book.)

Listen | *Stone Pony Blues* 35b , Charlie Patton (recording date unknown)

Charlie Patton was born in Mississippi during the 1880s. Since the blues is a living language, it is safe to say that he must have absorbed its essential features at an early age. The style of this piece, then, probably represents something close to the "original blues." Toward the end of the excerpt you will hear some characteristic blues guitar "licks" (short melodic motives) that are recognizable as part of the traditional blues-rock style today.

THE TWELVE-BAR BLUES

Like many genres, the blues has a traditional form that was recreated time and again. The designation *twelve-bar blues* comes from its classic design of three lines of verse, each of four measures. In addition, it often follows a basic harmonic plan. If a guitar or piano is available (or some other instrument that can produce chords), you can create the basic blues progression as follows:

The Classic Twelve-Bar Blues Progression

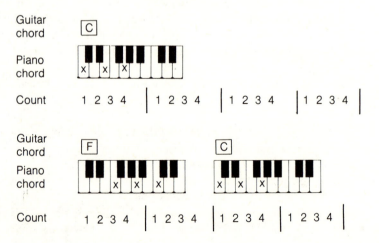

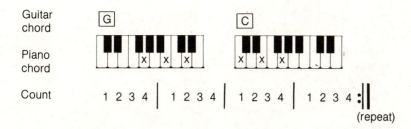

Stone Pony, by the way, doesn't follow this basic model exactly. At certain moments, Charlie Patton adds measures and chords *enhancing the traditional model* with his spontaneous, subtle sense of phrasing.

Listen | *Basin St. Blues* [35c], recorded by Louis Armstrong and his "Hot Five."

This is early jazz, a style we will soon discuss, played by some of its legendary figures led by Louis Armstrong ("Satchmo") on trumpet and Earl ("Fatha") Hines on piano. In this sophisticated, elegant blues, the traditional model is only a brief part of a more complex form:

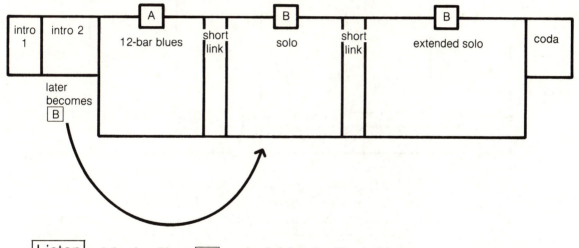

Listen | *Atherdoc Blues* [35d], recorded by the Heath Brothers (1978).

Atherdoc Blues has been discussed on page 226. Cast in an exact twelve-bar blues form, it honors and recreates the classic jazz-blues.

Listen | *Super Blue* [2d], by Freddie Hubbard.

This piece is not a traditional blues. It doesn't follow blues form. But as you might sense from the title and the music, that "blue" feeling, so vital to the existence and history of this genre, is present in a contemporary guise. That *Super Blue* may be considered part of the blues tradition, while not actually conforming to traditional design, amply demonstrates two important principles: 1) flexibility of genre and form; 2) association of a genre with a certain feeling or other elusive quality (in this case, the "blue" feeling).

Listen *Speculation* 36 , by D. Byrd and G. Gryce.

Speculation is contemporary jazz. It is not a blues. Yet heard in sequence with the previous selections, it is possible to hear the influence of the blues on the broader jazz tradition. (A comparison of this piece with a Vivaldi concerto appears on page 190.)

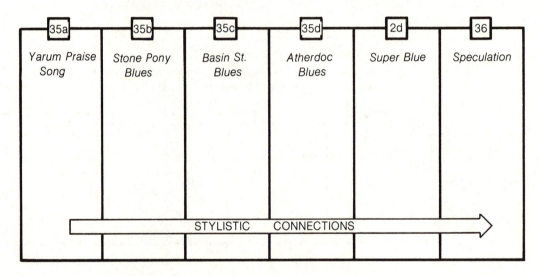

35a	35b	35c	35d	2d	36
Yarum Praise Song	Stone Pony Blues	Basin St. Blues	Atherdoc Blues	Super Blue	Speculation

STYLISTIC CONNECTIONS →

THE BLUES—HISTORICAL IMPORTANCE

The blues was a forerunner of jazz, rock, and soul music. Although it was not the only tradition that influenced these styles, it was, nonetheless, vital to their emergence in the musical culture. Since these later styles have had a tremendous impact on the musical language of the world, the blues, in retrospect, like notated polyphony, represents a crucial development in music history.

Basic Features of Jazz

Centered in turn-of-the-century New Orleans, jazz emerged as a unique living musical language first created by black musicians. It evolved from various traditions (including blues, ragtime,* and Euro-American songs, dances,

*See page 497 for an explanation of ragtime.

marches, etc.) and rapidly became a vital influence on the musical culture. Some of its basic features may be summarized as follows:

1. Improvisation is basic to jazz. Performers spontaneously create new musical details in each performance. However, these improvisations are usually based on preexisting melodies (and harmonies).
2. Traditional jazz is rooted in the *major–minor* tonal system. Some recent jazz styles have explored *modal* and *atonal* harmonic systems.
3. Jazz relies on body-based rhythmic patterns created within a strong, forceful meter. Rhythmic complexity is an essential feature of all jazz styles.
4. Jazz requires a high level of competence. Jazz musicians must have considerable technical ability on their instruments, as well as a highly developed control of melody, harmony, and form.
5. The interplay between soloists and group is basic to jazz structure.
6. The history of jazz is preserved through recordings.
7. The performance of jazz grows from a heightened emotional state which frees, motivates, and shapes each moment of the art.

While a detailed treatment of jazz is beyond the scope of this book, we will soon consider one of its acclaimed masters, Duke Ellington.

Suggested Listening

Span II

Jazz Styles and Musicians*

1875   1900   1925   1950   1975

gospel music   swing   "cool jazz"
ragtime   New Orleans dixieland   bebop   third stream
blues   free jazz
                              Dizzy Gillespie
                         Benny Goodman   Ornette Coleman
                           Duke Ellington   Archie Shepp
                          Louis Armstrong   John Coltrane
                King Oliver   Charlie Parker
        Jelly Roll Morton   Count Basie   Ella Fitzgerald   Chick Corea
        Eubie Blake   John Lewis   Herbie Hancock
    Scott Joplin   Tommy Dorsey   Josef Zawinul
                                                              Chuck Mangione
                                Stan Kenton   Keith Jarrett
                                Thelonious Monk   John McLaughlin
                                Miles Davis
                                Dave Brubeck
                                The Heath Brothers Wayne Shorter
*For definitions of styles not already discussed,   Donald Byrd   Ron Carter
see Appendix IX.   G. G. Gryce

Genre–A Summary

In this study you have encountered several genres which are especially important in musical culture—among these have been the Mass, the symphony (or sonata-symphony group), and the blues. These *are not* the only genres that have influenced music's history; but they demonstrate the vital function that genres fulfill in the connective fabric of musical tradition. The basic ideas of this process are presented below, using the blues, Mass, and symphony as models:

1. A genre may have a traditional form.

Blues	*Mass*	*Symphony*
12-bar blues progression	sections follow Mass text: Kyrie, Gloria, Credo, Sanctus, Agnus Dei	sonata-allegro form and multi-movement plan:

2. The traditional form is often altered, enhanced, and sometimes abandoned:

Blues	*Mass*	*Symphony*
Stone Pony Blues (slightly enhanced) *Basin St. Blues* (expanded) *Super Blue* (abandoned)	With a strict five-section plan, composers found many ways to alter the short-range details of musical structure.	Mozart, *Symphony No. 40* (traditional) Beethoven, *Symphony No. 5* (somewhat altered) Berlioz, *Fantastic Symphony* (fused with a dramatic plan)

3. A genre may be associated with either certain feelings or ideas, or both.

Blues	*Mass*	*Symphony*
a bittersweet, sad quality	religious devotion	a serious artistic statement of many musical elements enclosed in a highly structured form

4. A genre may cross stylistic barriers.

Blues	Mass	Symphony
Stone Pony—folk *Basin St.*—jazz There are blues that are considered rock. There are also blues-influenced pieces in the classical tradition, such as Gershwin's *Concerto in F* and Copland's *Blues*.	in countless musical styles: Medieval, Renaissance, Baroque, Classical, Romantic, Modern, and Folk (to name a few)	in the many styles of the Classical-Romantic-Modern tradition

Afro-American Music

The term *black music,** although often used, really has no precise meaning. If, when using it, we mean music made by people who happen to be black, we encompass the full scope not only of American musical culture, but that of Africa and Latin America as well. There are many musicians in "classical" music (conductors, singers, instrumentalists, composers) who happen to be black. There are musicians who happen to be black in other styles as well (Charley Pride, for example, is a "country" singer; Mongo Santamaria is a "Latin-jazz" musician). But is it really necessary to identify them as black musicians? One of America's great composers, Aaron Copland, is Jewish. He is not known or categorized as a "Jewish composer." By the same token, many composers who happen to be women, no matter how interested they are in womens' rights, do not wish to be known as "women composers," but as *composers* who happen to be women. Clearly, race, sex, religion are not *definitives* that determine musical categories. It is the wonder of our age that a multitude of styles and traditions are available to all of us.

However conscious of this important notion we may be, it is still possible to acknowledge certain styles and traditions that have developed within cultural groups: There are real traditions implied by the words "Anglo-Celtic song and dance," "Russian music," or "Italian song." In this spirit we can acknowledge related musical styles that have grown from various cultural groups which happen to be black. Among these styles are *West African, black gospel, blues, soul,* and *jazz.* Although there are differences among these styles, there are certain basic features that contribute to an Afro-American continuum of musical culture:

1. The creation of a powerful rhythmic environment integrally related to body movement and dance, resulting in a strong *rhythmic bond* between performers and audience. (In West African music and

*See Appendix IX.

gospel music, the notion of an audience may not be relevant, since the community participates in the music.)

2. The use of complex rhythmic structures: for example, *syncopation* and *rhythmic polyphony*.
3. The use of repeated motives in the musical design.
4. The soloist-and-group format.
5. A heightened, complex melodic style closely related to speech rhythms and inflections.
6. A heightened dramatic impulse.

The original source of these traits seems to have been sub-Saharan West Africa, the area from which the majority of slaves brought to America were taken.

THE REUNION OF AFRO-AMERICAN AND AFRICAN MUSICAL TRADITIONS

One of the most fascinating and powerful artistic energies of our time results from the reestablishment of direct connections between long-separated cultural groups and traditions. Various technologies, affecting books, television, and records, have brought all of these connections to our doorstep. At the flick of a switch or the turn of a page, we have before us a previously unimaginable amount of information and experience. The more people deal with this experience, the more connections reveal themselves, ready to reaffirm and enrich the arts (and other human endeavors) with new contact to "lost" sources. Debussy turned to the Middle Ages. The Beatles (and many others) turned to Indian music and philosophy. The following pieces demonstrate the recognition and reaffirmation of African musical and cultural roots by musicians today.

| Listen | *Ponta de areia* [23] , by Milton Nascimento

This piece is from Wayne Shorter's album *Native Dancer*, a group of selections which involve African elements.

| Listening Activity | (The theme of this piece, with its lilting 4-plus-5 meter, has been discussed on pages 52–53. If you haven't read that section, read it now.) The diagram on page 395 provides an outline for the sections of the piece. Add information to the diagram according to the following instructions:

1. Complete letter designations (the first is already done).
2. Indicate sound sources throughout, including voices and instruments. Write in the sound source in the appropriate position that corresponds to its place in the music.

(*continued on next page*)

3. Indicate meter by *yes* or *no*. If there is a meter, you may describe it.
4. Indicate texture on the continuums [m h p].
5. Where suggested, describe musical structure in general terms. Is there a main melody, accompaniment, ostinato motive, etc.? ment, ostinato motive, etc.?

Be sure you understand this format before you begin. It will be useful to hear the piece several times.

A   1:27 (time)

sound sources

texture   m h p   m h p

meter

                                   1:06   :25

                         Describe, in general   Describe, in general
                         terms, the musical   terms, the musical
                         structure.   structure.

sound sources   sound
                                                  sources

texture   m h p   texture   m h p

meter   meter

                                                    2:08

                        Describe, in general terms,
                      the musical structure.

sound sources   What is added here?   Fade
    m h p
texture

meter

(continued on next page)

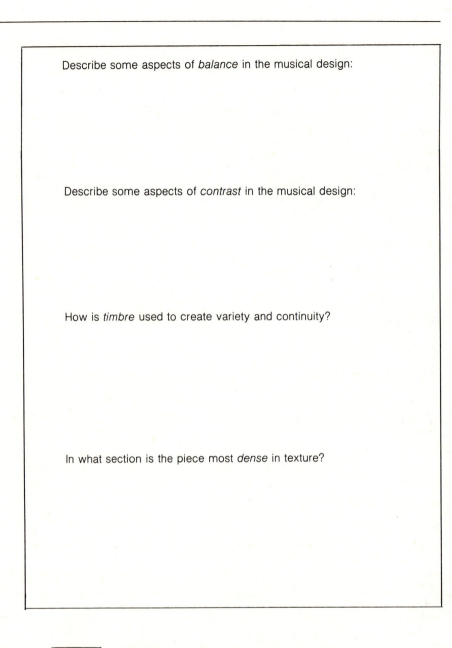

Describe some aspects of *balance* in the musical design:

Describe some aspects of *contrast* in the musical design:

How is *timbre* used to create variety and continuity?

In what section is the piece most *dense* in texture?

 Herbie Hancock, *Watermelon Man* [38]

Herbie Hancock's album *Headhunters*, from which this piece is taken, is one of the best-known fusions of jazz and African traditions. Hancock has been among the most innovative and important keyboard players and composers on the contemporary music scene.

Listening Activity Using the previous analysis as a guide, diagram this piece and describe its design.

1. Listen first for the general design, but don't write anything down.
2. Listen again, adding instruments as you hear them. Some of these sounds may be familiar—use some key words like "flute sound," etc.
3. Divide the piece into general sections.

Don't worry about *exact* answers; the process of listening, describing, and considering the design, even in very general terms, is an end in itself.

THE INTERPLAY OF MUSICAL STYLES IN AMERICA

What happened to the musical traditions of blacks in America's South is difficult to verify in exact terms. Yet a general picture of cultural and musical interplay has emerged: "Inevitably, the two races [southern whites and blacks] exchanged elements of their cultures, and the South over a period of time had developed its own distinct variant of American culture, indebted to interracial exchange."* From this vibrant musical culture, deeply enriched through stylistic interplay, the new traditions came forth:

Interplay of traditions

Blues
African traditions: soloist and group, ostinato rhythms, vocal style
Harmonic progression from major–minor tonal system of the Western notated tradition
British-American folk song

Black Gospel
African rhythmic and vocal style, call-and-response format
Euro-American sacred folk harmony

Jazz
African rhythmic and vocal style, soloist and group
Blues
Western major–minor tonal system, British-American song and dance
Latin-American dance rhythms

As you can see, the creation of these styles was truly indebted to more than one culture. Should, then, the styles even be called Afro-American? Of course. By comparison, consider the madrigal *Since Robin Hood* 13a . Indebted to the Italian tradition, it is certainly as English as any music one can name. The determining factor, in both cases, is a basic cultural orientation that gives the music life. Blues, black gospel, and jazz were fusions of various elements created through the unique collective genius of Afro-American culture. Beyond these origins, each tradition has gone on to include people from many cultural groups. For example, the history of jazz includes many important personalities who happen to be white. Such interactions speak to the ultimate universality of music.

*Charles Hamm, *Yesterdays* (New York, 1979), p. 403.

Italian Lyricism and Afro-American Soul: A Comparison

In Chapter 7 we discussed the importance of that "warm" Mediterranean Italian song and its continuing affects on many musical traditions. That song impulse, rooted in the culture of that region, became one of the most important in European music, and subsequently that of the world. *Soul*, a term that embodies an elusive quality of so much Afro-American music, has also had a worldwide impact. Consider the following comparison:

Italian Lyricism	*Afro-American Soul*

Cultural Context

Both traditions grew from cultures that honored heightened, dramatic song.

Italian lyricism was further nourished by *humanism*, a movement that helped create a cultural environment for the flourishing of Italian opera.	Afro-American soul was nurtured by the collective black experience: slavery, Christianity, urban and rural life.

Melodic Style

Both traditions have a distinct vocal, melodic style. In both traditions, this vocal style has also been imitated by instruments.

In the Baroque, the complex vocal style of Italian opera was transferred to instrumental music.	The heightened, declamatory vocal style of Afro-American melody was transferred to such instruments as trumpet, sax, and guitar. The whole melodic basis of contemporary "popular" music is intertwined with this heritage.

Rhythmic Structure

During the Baroque, the rhythmic complexities of Italian ornamented vocal and instrumental melody were absorbed into European music, and eventually the world's musical language.	The rhythmic complexities of Afro-American music—especially polyrhythms sounding within a strong meter—are now one of the most important influences on the world's musical language.

Genres and Means of Diffusion

(beginning 1600)
Opera and Italian song were disseminated through traveling singers and composers, the existence of opera houses, and the availability of published music.

(beginning 1900)
Blues, popular song, various jazz traditions, and dance have spread through records, radio, television, and sheet music.

This comparison is meant to be a model of musical-cultural interplay. Similar connections underlie all the strands we have been tracing in this book.

Latin Music

Latin Music encompasses many styles that have evolved from various cultures. Related terms, rarely used with any precision, are *Spanish* and *Hispanic* music. In general, all deal with music created by people who either speak Spanish or live in a culture whose roots reflect, in some way, a connection to Spain. In this brief discussion, we will consider a few strands of this broad tradition that have reached America. We will discover that each strand has become intertwined with other traditions, creating new styles, all with Hispanic roots. At this point, it will be useful to review the various pieces of Spanish origin considered in previous pages:

5a   *El Rey de Francia tres hijas tenía*—Although recorded in Greece, this music reflects a far older Spanish heritage.

5d   *Bulerίos*—Flamenco music from Spain.

5e   Rodrigo, *Concierto de Aranjuez* (second movement, excerpt) —Spanish "classical" music from the twentieth century.

13b   *Rίu, rίu, chίu* ⎫   Notated pieces from the Spanish Renais-
13c   *Pase el agoa* ⎭   sance.

Although these pieces reflect a very small part of the Spanish heritage, they do suggest something of a living musical language. In Sequence 5 , you heard some of the musical styles of Spain related to the traditions of the Mediterranean area. Within this general context, it was possible to hear a musical continuum that included ornamented vocal and instrumental melody, and virtuosity on guitar and guitarlike instruments. In the Medieval Spanish music (5a), a Mediterranean-Mideastern scale type was used; the other pieces utilized the diatonic scales common in Europe. The Renaissance works demonstrate a strong dance-derived rhythmic impulse. From the broad musical tradition suggested by this music came the Europeans who colonized parts of North America and all of Central and South America. Their traditions were to be a main strand in the music of the Americas.

Listening Activity

Dividido el corazón 34a 34b and *El Rey de Francia tres hijas tenía* 5a

Dividido el corazón is a sacred song recorded in New Mexico, U.S.A. Compare it to *El Rey de Francia tres hijas tenía*. Describe the stylistic connection.

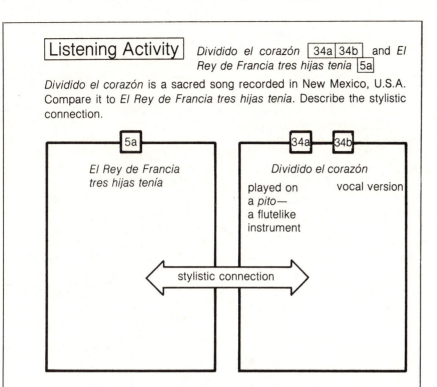

5a

El Rey de Francia tres hijas tenía

34a 34b

Dividido el corazón

played on a *pito*— a flutelike instrument

vocal version

⟵ stylistic connection ⟶

Dividido el corazón*

Al sepulcro va a llorar	Mary goes to the sepulchre to weep
Por su dulce hijo María,	for her beloved son,
A contemplar su dolor	to meditate on his pain
junto de la losa fría.	beside the cold grave.
¡Ay, llora mi soledad!	Ah, my desolate soul weeps!
¡Ay, Jesús del alma mía!	Ah, Jesus, soul of my soul!
¡Ay! ¿quién me acompañará	Ah, who will remain with me
junto de la losa fría?	beside the cold grave?
Mi corazón traspasado	My heart is pierced through
y también el de María	as is the heart of Mary
al dejar a su Jesús,	as she takes leave of her Jesus,
junto de la losa fría.	beside the cold grave.

Describe the form of *Dividido el corazón*:

*Note: only two verses are on the recording.

Listen Sequence 5 and *Thousand Island Park* 37b .

Another connection between American and Spanish music may be heard in *Thousand Island Park*, a contemporary composition by John McLaughlin.

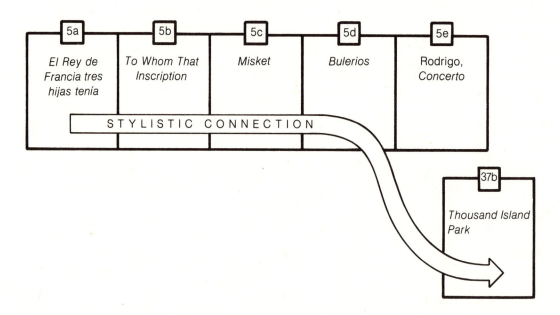

5a	5b	5c	5d	5e
El Rey de Francia tres hijas tenía	To Whom That Inscription	Misket	Bulerios	Rodrigo, Concerto

STYLISTIC CONNECTION

37b

Thousand Island Park

Listening Activity

Describe features of *Thousand Island Park* that connect it to the broader tradition:

| Listening Activity | *Dance of the Ancient Earth* from George Crumb's *Ancient Voices of Children* (1970) $\boxed{39}$. |

Despite its contemporary idiom, the stylistic impulse of the Spanish-Mediterranean culture is quite apparent in this excerpt. What features connect Crumb's work to the broader tradition?

LATIN-AMERICAN MUSIC

The inherited traits of the Mediterranean style are but one aspect of Latin music. In fact, the commonly used term *Latin-American* brings to mind a very different kind of music—a group of styles that have evolved in South America and the Caribbean as a result of stylistic interplay among three basic roots:

1. European music, especially that of Spanish origin or derivation;
2. West African music, notably the vocal style and drumming traditions;
3. Various musics of Amerindians (South and Central America).

From this interaction of styles and cultures, a myriad of related regional traditions grew in Brazil, Argentina, Cuba, Puerto Rico, etc., each with its own distinct blend of the contributing elements. As an example of the many strands that interacted to form these new traditions, consider this description of Cuban music by a scholar of Latin music. Notice the fascinating interplay of style, culture, and history in the account—another documentation of how living musical languages come into being:

Taken as a whole, Cuban music presents a more equal balance of African and Spanish ingredients than that of any other Latin country except Brazilian. Spanish folklore enriched the music of the countryside, of the city, and of the salon. At the same time—aided by an illicit slave trade that continued right through the 19th century—the pure African strain remained stronger in Cuba than anywhere else. Yoruba and Congolese religious cults, and the Abakwá secret society, which is of eastern Nigerian origin, remained powerful almost everywhere. As a result, western African melody and drumming—and even the Yoruba language—were brought cheek by jowl with country music based on Spanish ten-line *decima* verses and southern Spanish melody. The co-existence of European and African rhythmic, melodic, and harmonic procedures led, of course, to their blending, and that blending took place at the most profound level.*

THE INFLUENCE OF LATIN-AMERICAN MUSIC

Latin American traditions have had a deep effect on many American musical styles. Some of the interactions are:

1. *Early Jazz.* One of the centers for early jazz was New Orleans, a city whose unique culture reflects Latin-Caribbean influences. The distinct rhythms of that area, which became an important feature of early jazz, were deeply indebted to Latin dance rhythms.

2. *The Diffusion of Latin-American Dance Genres.* A partial list of Latin-American dances that have entered American musical traditions (as well as the world's) are the *tango, rhumba, mambo,* and *samba.* Like the Viennese *waltz,* these dance genres carried their distinctive rhythms (and other musical features) to many corners of the world.

3. *Contemporary Latin-American Styles.* In recent decades, Latin music has become increasingly visible in the contemporary musical scene. *Salsa,* a Latin style that originated in New York City, is one example of this prominence. Salsa music is a "hot, up-tempo, creative Latin music." The term translates literally as "gravy" or "sauce," but these words only hint at its real qualities. Like the elusive qualities of soul and Viennese lyricism, salsa cannot really be described in words, but only experienced through listening.

   Another important Latin-American style is the *bossa nova,* from Brazil, which combines sophisticated jazz harmony (based squarely in the European notated tradition) with the Latin-Indian-African rhythms of Brazil. The style was further influenced by the Portuguese language, which is the spoken tongue of Brazil.

4. *Crossovers and Blends.* Throughout the twentieth century, various Latin styles have been blended into jazz and other popular traditions. A very partial list includes music of the jazz trumpeter Dizzy Gillespie, the *rock-salsa* style of the group Santana, and the recent album *My Spanish Heart* by Chick Corea.

This brief excursion into Latin-American music only hints at its important role in American musical culture, a historical fact which, for some reason, has remained largely outside most standard evaluations of American music.

*John Storm Roberts, *The Latin Tinge* (Oxford, 1979), p. 4. This excellent book is one of the few studies on this subject.

Perhaps this apparent blindness is coming to an end with the growing recognition that "over the past century, Latin music has been the greatest outside influence on popular musical styles of the United States."* Considering the intriguing history of Latin music—its roots intertwined with African, Indian, and European cultures—it is hoped that this great tradition will receive the interest it so richly deserves.

Suggested Listening

Any recordings by the following:

Ray Barretto—salsa and various crossover styles

Willie Colon—salsa

Mongo Santamaria—fusion of Afro-Latin-jazz

Santana—Latin-rock (early recordings)

Trini Lopez—Mexican and Chicano-influenced popular tunes

Antonio Carlos Jobim and Astrid Gilberto—bossa nova

Chick Corea, *My Spanish Heart*—Contemporary classical-jazz in a Spanish guise

Villa-Lobos, *Bachianas brasileiras No. 5*—Villa-Lobos was a Brazilian composer of international stature. His work represents a fusion of the European notated tradition with nationalistic influences. *Bachianas brasileiras No. 5*, one of his most popular works, combines several interesting influences: Italian lyricism, the harmonic, contrapuntal logic of J. S. Bach, and the song-dance rhythms of Brazilian folk music.

Carlos Chávez, *Sinfonía de Antígona*—an eleven-minute symphony by the contemporary Mexican composer based on the classical Greek drama *Antigone*

Alberto Ginastera, *Estancia*—a ballet suite inspired by scenes of rural Argentina, combining folk-inspired music with avant-garde techniques

Silvestre Revueltas, *Homenaje á García Lorca*—an orchestral composition dedicated to the Spanish poet García Lorca, using Mexican rhythms and folk melodies

Contemporary Popular Song

One of the widest-held misconceptions about contemporary popular songs is something like: "Popular songs have little value because they are simple, repetitive, and trite." Since contemporary popular song, with roots in American musical culture, has become one of the most influential genres in the world history of music, it certainly seems appropriate that this misconception be put in some perspective.

*Ibid., p. vii.

One of the oldest and most important strands in the world's music is the body-based, straightforward message in song. It is found in every culture in many guises. Gregorian chant, for example, may well be considered part of the popular song tradition of the Middle Ages. Songs like *I Will Give My Love an Apple* 6a were the popular songs of the Renaissance. Throughout the ages, song has performed a vital function for society—the celebration and documentation of human experience. Central to most criticism of popular song is its "simplicity." Here, perhaps, is the ultimate irony. While historically the essence of popular song has been its "catchiness," the creation of that elusive magic is far from simple. *While popular songs are sung by everyone, they have always been created by a talented few.* The creation of a great melody, whether by a Mozart, an anonymous Renaissance minstrel, or a contemporary songwriter, is an act of genius. The best cure for this misguided notion might well be an attempt to compose a "simple," "straightforward" tune. Furthermore, all popular songs are not "simple," but may involve various types of musical-lyrical complexity. And when we consider the production of a popular song in a modern recording studio, we are dealing with a high level of craftsmanship designed to make the song "sound simple and catchy" (see "The Role of the Recording Studio," page 423).

A final irony lies in an often-encountered phenomenon—the ability to recognize and appreciate the value of "simplicity" in a distant style (a folk song of another culture, for example), but not the one "right around the corner" (the hit tune on the radio). In recent years, this situation has been changing. There has been an awakening on the part of many observers to the value and importance of contemporary popular song.

| Listen | Karla Bonoff, *Isn't It Always Love* 22

We can hear many of the strands of American music in this tune. If you were to take away the rhythm section—drums, electric guitar, and bass—and listen to the song with a guitar or banjo accompaniment, its basic stylistic source would be revealed: it is in "country-folk" style, a direct descendant of Anglo-Celtic song. The vocal style, especially the background singing, is a modern expression of that broad tradition we have traced under the name *sacred folk harmony*. But what about the rhythm section? That impulse was adopted from Afro-American rhythm and blues. The influence from black music goes even deeper—the bass line, certain of the rhythmic figures, are all stylistic crossovers from black popular music. This example is another demonstration of the continuing stylistic interplay that has created all kinds of American contemporary music.

When Karla Bonoff wrote this tune, did she consciously consider all the influences she was bringing together? Of course not. That many influences can be synthesized into a spontaneous living language is one of the hidden wonders of music.

Some of the Strands in Bonoff's *Isn't It Always Love*

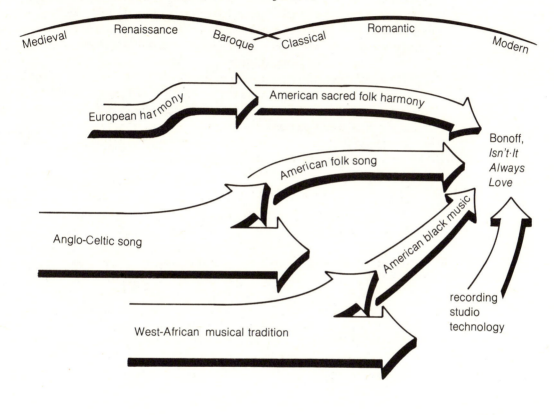

Rock

The people of this country do not have any conception of the evil being done by rock 'n' roll. It is a plague as far-reaching as any plague we have ever had, and now it is becoming international in scope. . . . My complaint is that it just isn't music. It's utter garbage and it should not be confused in any way with anything related to music or verse.*

No style in the history of music has gained a wider audience than rock; and as the quote above suggests, no style has come under such vehement

*A comment by a well-known musician in *The Instrumentalist*, September 1958.

criticism. The "issue" of rock obviously reflects some of the deepest-seated cultural notions about what music is and what function it should fill in society. (These topics are explored in the discussion on pages 459–65.) Whatever one's views on rock, few question its influence. It has become an important stylistic component of the world's musical traditions. Rock encodes, celebrates, and transmits a complex of ideas, feelings, and images that are important to many people. In the 1950s, it unleashed a type of uninhibited dancing and moving into a society that found its character disturbing, and to some extent still does.

These objections reveal the very essence of rock—it is a style rooted in raw emotion and an ecstatic dancing energy. If the listener is willing to accept this basic premise, then responding to "good" and "bad" music within the rock tradition becomes a legitimate process of evaluation. If the listener rejects that basic premise, which is certainly a legitimate response, then rock music will never be a meaningful experience.

| Listen | Blue Öyster Cult, *Godzilla* 25

Blue Öyster Cult is a contemporary group that presents the rock style in its basic guise. Raw, frenetic, purposefully distorted, this music is not meant to sound pretty. The elusive quality we call "energy" is the determining factor in the success of the piece. *Godzilla* is a satire on a type of science fiction movie imported from Japan in the '60s and '70s.

Like some other twentieth-century styles, rock music often has a quality that may be described as "anti-art." This impulse to make fun of what the establishment honors is by no means a recent phenomenon. (See the discussion of Berlioz, "The Romantic Revolutionary," page 266, and of Cage's *4'33"*, page 367.) Furthermore, for the willing listener, rock music seems both to capture and to counter a certain feeling of alienation and despair in our culture.

| Listening Comparison | Compare the end of Stockhausen, *Momente* 24f , with the opening of Blue Öyster Cult, *Godzilla* 25 . It may be suggested that these styles "go together": each seems to capture the spirit of our time. For perspective, play the end of *Momente* with the opening of the Haydn *Rondo* 24a . Your reactions to these juxtapositions are, of course, a flexible matter that cannot be quantified.

STYLISTIC INTERPLAY

As you have heard, Blue Öyster Cult presents rock in its most basic fashion. The rock style, however, has been transformed and incorporated into many musical situations. Consider, for example, Maynard Ferguson's *Birdland* 26 (actually composed by J. Zawinul), in which rock and jazz traditions are fused into a unique style that also incorporates Latin rhythms.

Listen   Maynard Ferguson, *Birdland* 26

Aaron Copland

The very words *American composer* bring to mind the name of Aaron Copland, for among his many achievements has been the creation of a living language that fused European learned techniques with American folk-popular elements. With this language, at once "simple" and sophisticated, he managed to capture that "American spirit" and communicate it to his audience.

Copland, born in Brooklyn, N.Y., in 1900, was the son of Russian-Jewish immigrants. As a young man he went to Paris to study with Nadia Boulanger, a teacher who would guide many prominent young American composers. Why not study in America? At that time, American musical institutions were dominated by the German tradition. Like Debussy, Copland was not interested in imitating Brahms or Wagner. It was only natural that he go to Paris, at that time, a creative mecca for twentieth-century musicians, painters, and writers. It was here that he would forge *his* nationalistic style. As Mussorgsky had done for Russia, as Debussy had for France, so Copland would create an unmistakable American style of "classical" music.

Aaron Copland in 1958.

Copland has experimented with many aspects of American music. In the additional listening suggested below you will find evidence of this exploration. Not all of Copland's works involve an obvious interplay with American folk-popular elements. Like many other composers he explored several areas of musical communication, including the twelve-tone language. The resulting differences in style (when compared to his more nationalist-oriented works) are of greater significance to audiences than to the composer himself. A composer often "tries on a different hat" once in a while, more or less to "see how it fits." However, it is the same personality under that hat, and in all of Copland's work, his compositional craft is abundantly evident.

APPALACHIAN SPRING

Originally a ballet, later reshaped into a concert piece, this work (dating from 1945) unfolds as a series of connected scenes that depict pioneer life in the early nineteenth century. It is set in the mountains of Pennsylvania. *Appalachian Spring* brings together, in one work, many of the connections that we have discussed thus far:

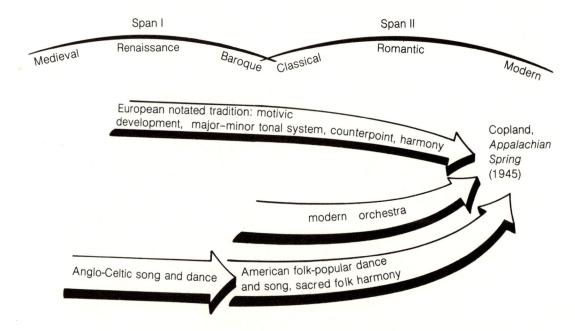

At an even deeper level, *Appalachian Spring* grows from the most profound impulses of human musicality: song, dance, prayer, and drama. The composer himself has provided a description of the dance-drama form.

Listening Activity

Whenever you hear music that seems to be either dancelike, songlike, or prayerlike (hymnlike), write the appropriate word—*dance, song,* or *prayer*—at the right. If you hear more than one simultaneously, indicate them. Also, write in the instrumentation of the beginning of each section (for example, *strings, brass*, etc.). Include any solo instruments if you hear them.

Copland's Description

1. *Very slowly*. Introduction of the characters, one by one, in a suffused light.

2. *Fast*. A sentiment both elated and religious gives the keynote of this scene.

3. *Moderate*. Duo for the Bride and her intended—scene of tenderness and passion.

4. *Quite fast*. The Revivalist and his flock. Folksy feelings—suggestions of square dances and country fiddlers.

5. *Still faster*. Solo dance of the bride—presentiment of motherhood. Extremes of joy and fear and wonder.

(continued on next page)

6. *Very slowly* (at first). Transition scenes reminiscent of the introduction.

7. *Calm and flowing*. Scenes of the daily activity for the bride and her farmer husband. There are five variations on a Shaker Theme. The theme (*The Gift to Be Simple*), sung by a solo clarinet, was taken from a collection of Shaker melodies.

8. *Moderate*—Coda. The Bride takes her place among her neighbors. At the end the couple are left quiet and strong in their new house. Muted strings intone a hushed prayerlike passage. The close is reminiscent of the opening music.

Connections in the Copland Discussion

The ancient unity.
The importance of regional styles.
Nationalism.

Copland: Additional Listening

Music for the Theater (1925; jazz influence)
El Salón México (1936; Latin American influence)
Rodeo (complete) (1942; British-American folk song and dance)
A Lincoln Portrait (1942)
Piano Quartet (1950; twelve-tone influence)

Elliott Carter.

Elliott Carter

Craftsmanship is a quality essential to the art of one of America's most prominent composers, Elliott Carter (b. 1908). His style reflects a careful and thoughtful evolution in which many elements have been synthesized into a consistent, confident living language. Among the influences that have merged in Carter's style are the rhythmic innovations of Stravinsky and Bartók, the twelve-tone language of Schoenberg and his disciples (Carter has not adopted this technique exactly, but has nonetheless been influenced by its general characteristics), and a rhythmic technique from jazz involving the simultaneous use of regular and "free" meters. Carter has had a special interest in rhythmic procedures. One of his innovations—*rhythmic modulation*—involves gradual changes in the tempo of the basic pulse. Carter's rhythmic procedures may be understood as part of the broader twentieth-century trend toward such experimentation (for example, the music of Stravinsky and Messiaen).

Carter's innovations exist within a continuing connection to musical tradition. This is clearly indicated by the genres in which he has chosen to compose: among his major works are three string quartets, the *Variations for Orchestra*, and a *Double Concerto for Harpsichord and Piano*.

DOUBLE CONCERTO FOR HARPSICHORD AND PIANO
Carter's *Double Concerto* (1961) is a carefully planned work of great rhythmic and textural complexity. Economically scored for various contrasting sound sources (see instrumentation below), the piece consists of a fascinating combination of modern, innovative techniques and traditional impulses.

The composer writes:

> The first stage of conception was the *general dramatic plan* [italics added] of a constellation of musical materials and ideas coming into existence, achieving focus and greater differentiation, then finally dissolving again and disintegrating into nothing.*

The composer also describes some of the innovative aspects of this piece:

> The musical ideas are not themes or melodies but rather groupings of sound material out of which textures, linear patterns, and figurations are invented. Each type of music has its own identifying sound and expression, usually combining instrumental color with some "behavioral" pattern that relies on speed, rhythm, and musical intervals. There is no repetition, but a constant invention of new things—some closely related to each other, others remotely. . . . There is a stratification of sound, so much of the time the listener can hear two different kinds of musics, not always of equal prominence, occurring simultaneously. This kind of form and texture could be said to reflect the experience we often have of seeing something in different frames of reference at the same time.**

The *Double Concerto for Harpsichord and Piano* is scored quite differently from the other concertos you have heard. There are two soloists, one playing harpsichord, the other piano, two small orchestral groups and four percussionists playing a variety of instruments. This instrumental array appears on stage in a purposeful plan.

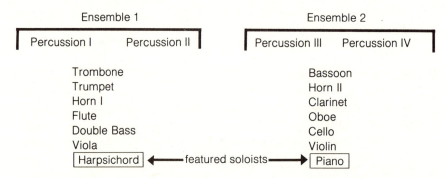

Flawed Words and Stubborn Sounds: A Conversation with Elliott Carter (New York, 1971), pp. 104–5.

**Quoted from the composer's sleeve notes for the Nonesuch recording of this work (71314).

The arrangement and choice of instrumental forces reflects a basic procedure on which this composition is based: *contrast between various sound sources and groups*. This type of organization is related to both the antiphonal effects heard in Gabrieli's *Sanctus* 14 and the interplay between soloist and group in Vivaldi's *Concerto for Oboe and Orchestra* 16 .

Another universal aspect of this work is Carter's attention to balance in the long-range form. Consider the basic form of the work:

Balances in Carter's *Double Concerto*

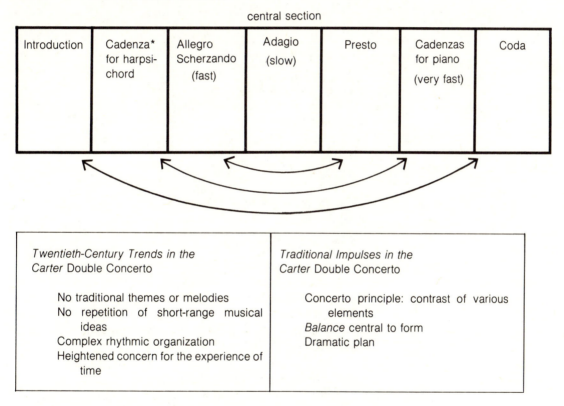

central section

Introduction	Cadenza* for harpsi- chord	Allegro Scherzando (fast)	Adagio (slow)	Presto	Cadenzas for piano (very fast)	Coda

Twentieth-Century Trends in the Carter Double Concerto	Traditional Impulses in the Carter Double Concerto
No traditional themes or melodies No repetition of short-range musical ideas Complex rhythmic organization Heightened concern for the experience of time	Concerto principle: contrast of various elements *Balance* central to form Dramatic plan

You may already have sensed that Elliott Carter's approach to composition leans toward the classical aesthetic, as evidenced by these features of his music: 1) an interplay between tradition and innovation; 2) careful attention to balance and clarity of musical form. Restating one of the basic long-range traditions of musical culture, a strand we have been tracing since twelfth-century organum, Carter describes how he *balances an abstract plan with spontaneous musicality*:

*See page 497.

It is obvious that the real order and meaning of music is the one the listener *hears* with his ears. Whatever occult mathematical orders may exist on paper are not necessarily relevant to this in the least. Now it's true that in writing my own works I sometimes try quasi-"geometric" things in order to cut myself off from habitual ways of thinking about particular technical problems and to place myself in, so to speak, new terrain, which forces me to look around and find new kinds of ideas and solutions I might not have thought of otherwise. Nonetheless, if what I come up with by these methods is unsatisfactory from the point of view of what I think is interesting to *hear*, I throw it out without a second thought.*

Connections in the Carter Discussion
    Balance between intellect and spontaneity.
    The classic-romantic continuum.
    The importance of genre.

Carter: Additional Listening

Quartet No. 2 (1959)
Quartet for Brass (1974)

Duke Ellington

Among the most prolific composers of the twentieth century was Edward Kennedy ("Duke") Ellington. His music, created over a period of more than fifty years, reflects a life-long dedication to craft, innovation, and the search for an art that transcends the limits of style. Born in Washington, D.C., in 1899, his quite proper upbringing included music, good manners, and the teachings of the Bible. By the age of twelve, he began sneaking into local clubs and theaters, where he came into contact with that new type of American music—jazz. Ellington learned his trade by listening and imitating. He soon became a professional musician, caught up in the tremendous popularity of this new American style. During the 1930s, Ellington established himself and his band on both sides of the Atlantic, as exponents of a sophisticated swinging jazz sound. On his first tour of Europe, a London critic reported, "His music has a true Shakespearean universality and as he sounded the gamut, girls wept and young chaps sank to their knees." **As

*Flawed Words, pp. 80–81.
**Derek Jewell, *Duke* (New York, 1977), p. 54.

Duke Ellington.

had the young Mozart some two centuries before, Ellington found acceptance with royalty on a personal basis. He played duets with the Duke of Kent, who was something of a pianist himself, and it was said that he called the Prince of Wales "The Wale," while that noble personage introduced Ellington to his friends as the "Duke of Hot." Not only had Ellington achieved commercial success in those early years, but he was admired and taken seriously by the social elite.

Duke was witty, charming and personable—traits that undoubtedly helped his career—but it was his extraordinary music that ultimately ensured his success. He was, first of all, a brilliant and incredibly quick composer of songs. (He once wrote an entire musical show in a single evening.) Many of his tunes have become "standards"—that is, they have entered into the musical repertory as enduring creations. Among the better known are *Satin Doll, Solitude,* and *Sophisticated Lady*. But of equal importance was his subtle and innovative approach to orchestration. Ellington's basic musical medium was the dance band, comprised of piano, drums, bass, guitar, trumpets, trombones, and saxophones. In his hands, it became a sensitive instrument, capable of producing the most subtle colors and moods. Duke often composed for individual members of his band, creative pieces perfectly suited to a specific player's ability. His devotion to his bands over the years was legendary, and in return, he exacted both loyalty and dedication from the musicians. Ellington could be a hard taskmaster. For example, once a member of the group showed up too drunk to play well. Ellington called upon him to solo again and again, while complimenting him to the audience. Like all great talents of his stature, Ellington was uncompromising about quality. His concern for the band was born of artistic necessity, for his whole creative life was centered around this group. As a painter uses paints, so Duke Ellington used their sound to "paint" his creations. Evidently, color played an interesting role in his aesthetic as a type of musical-visual synthesis of feeling and mood. Many of his works actually have a color in their title, for example, *Mood Indigo*, *Black and Tan Fantasy*, and *Magenta Haze* (compare with the Romantics' quest for the union of sight and sound, page 281 and Messiaen's musical language, page 348).

ELLINGTON'S STYLISTIC EXPLORATIONS

Ellington's career continued at a frenetic pace throughout his life. Increasingly, he experimented with stylistic interplay, merging jazz with "classical" elements in a continuing search for the patterns that unite these traditions. In 1965 he undertook a project that brought together his total musical universe—a series of Sacred Concerts. In these expressions of his religious convictions, performed in churches in the United States and Europe, Ellington sought to transcend stylistic boundaries and to reach the universal impulses that give life to all sacred music.

Such Sweet Thunder (1957), a modern suite,* is an example of Ellington's experimentations in broadening the jazz tradition. The impetus for this piece is the work of William Shakespeare; the circumstance surrounding its creation is another example of a cultural chain. When Ellington's band was invited to play at the Shakespeare Theater in Stratford, Ontario, the plays he saw there became an artistic spark. Subsequently he read and reread each of those plays with Billy Strayhorn, a close musical associate with whom he often composed. (Shared compositional efforts are common in many twentieth-century styles, including jazz and rock.) The title of the suite comes from a line in *A Midsummer Night's Dream*—"I never heard so musical a discord, such sweet thunder." The suite is a series of programmatic portraits of Shakespearean characters.

| Listen | *Such Sweet Thunder*, by Duke Ellington and Billy Strayhorn. |

Among the pieces of the suite are the following:

Such Sweet Thunder: The title piece is actually a twelve-bar blues, and according to Duke is "the sweet and swinging, very convincing story Othello told Desdemona" (from Shakespeare's play *Othello*). The opening theme serves as a bass ostinato for a "sweet" brass sound. Also featured is a solo trumpet improvisation by Ray Nance. The straightforward blues progression is enhanced by subtle chromatic harmonies in the saxophones.

*In Span II, the suite takes on a new identity. It can be a collection of short pieces related in any manner.

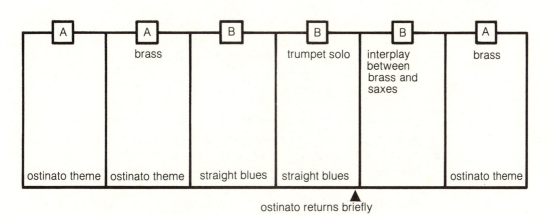

ostinato returns briefly

Although each part of the form can be considered a variation of the twelve-bar blues, A identifies sections that use the ostinato theme, while B identifies the more straightforward blues style.

Lady Macbeth: This "jazz waltz" was meant to evoke the qualities of Lady Macbeth. Duke writes, "Though she was a lady of noble birth, we suspect there was a little ragtime in her soul." Counting "in three" will help bring out the complex syncopations in the instrumental parts. The playful music ends with a tongue-in-cheek foreboding of Lady Macbeth's ultimate plan (the "ominous" chords).

Sonnet in Search of a Moor: After a piano introduction, we hear a delicate dialogue between bass and clarinets meant to characterize Othello.

The Telecasters: This playful selection combines characters represented musically from two Shakespeare plays—the three witches of *Macbeth* and Iago from *Othello*. The witches are portrayed by three trombones; Iago is a baritone saxophone. The use of silence to punctuate the musical flow is typical of Duke's skillful, witty style.

Up and Down, Up and Down: A jazz characterization of Puck, from *A Midsummer Night's Dream*, leading the various pairs of lovers into awkward situations. Clark Terry on trumpet is Puck. The couples include Jimmy Hamilton and Ray Nance (clarinet and violin), Russell Procope and Paul Gonsalves (alto and tenor saxophones), Jonny Hodges and John Sanders (alto saxophone and trombone). At the end of the piece, we hear Puck's famous words (mimicked on the trumpet), "Lord, what fools these mortals be."

The Star-Crossed Lovers: This piece is a characterization of the love between Romeo and Juliet. Quite naturally, it is lyrical. Romeo is portrayed by Jonny Hodges on alto saxophone, Juliet by Paul Gonsalves on tenor saxophone.

Madness in Great Ones: This is a musical representation of Hamlet's madness. The juxtaposition of instrumental timbres and the tense, dissonant polyphony are central to the dramatic effect. Notice, also, the "mindless" repeating trumpet motive at the end. (Compare with the "Fool Scene" from *Boris Godunov*.)

In the program notes to *Such Sweet Thunder*, Ellington states his basic philosophy of music. The following words repeat a basic idea you have just read in the section on Elliott Carter, concerning the *balance between intellect and spontaneity in the musical process*:

In the final analysis, whether it be Shakespeare or jazz, the only thing that counts is the emotional effect on the listener. Somehow, I suspect that if Shakespeare were alive today, he might be a jazz fan himself—he'd appreciate the combination of team spirit and informality, of academic knowledge and humor, of all the elements that go into a great jazz performance. And I am sure he would agree with the simple and axiomatic statement that is so important to all of us—when it sounds good, it *is* good.*

WHAT TO LISTEN FOR IN HIS MUSIC

Ellington made *hundreds* of recordings throughout his career; you will find a wealth of Ellington recordings in most libraries. Before listening to a record, ascertain when it was made. Is it a studio recording or from a live concert? Is it from the early years or later ones? This information provides a helpful context in which to hear the music. Beyond this, listen for:

Use of Instruments. Ellington's art rests firmly in his use of the orchestra. Typically, you will hear expressive solos supported by and interacting with a smooth, "tight" ensemble sound. Like a highly responsive symphony orchestra, an Ellington band plays "as one voice" with incredible precision and unity of feeling. The instrumental colors have a distinct quality that is both extraordinary and unique.

Use of Harmony. Ellington's harmony is remarkable on several levels. Highly dissonant and chromatic chords are smoothly interwoven with deceptive simplicity. Like Debussy's, his harmonies seem to be as much "colors" and "moods" as music, especially in an ensemble texture. We once again find that as Span II proceeds, it becomes impossible to separate *harmony* from *texture*. Many of Ellington's harmonic ideas for ensemble lose their impact when shifted to another sound source.

Duke, p. 125.

Connections in the Ellington Discussion
    Balance between intellect and spontaneity.
    The importance of a cultural chain.
    Stylistic evolution.
    Soloist and group.

Ellington: Additional Listening

Span II

Modern

Black and Tan Fantasy (1927)

Mood Indigo (1930)

Black, Brown and Beige (1943)

The Queen's Suite (1959)

Creole Rhapsody (1931)

Satin Doll (1953)

Second Sacred Concert (1964)

Afro-Eurasian Eclipse (1971)

Solitude (1934)

Latin American Suite (1969)

Third Sacred Concert (1973)

Reminiscing in Tempo (1935)

Stevie Wonder

Steveland Morris (Stevie Wonder) is one of the outstanding composer-poets of our time. With roots in black popular music—soul, rhythm and blues, and gospel—he has explored and created a unique and powerful musical language through fusion with other influences, including synthesizer technology as well as jazz, Latin, and "classical" music. He began his career as a child recording artist singing straightforward pop tunes about boy–girl relationships. As a man, he has enlarged his musical-poetical vision to address those themes that have haunted many great artists through the ages: religious experience, freedom, and the place of humankind in the world.

Stevie Wonder's early career has interesting parallels with Mozart's:

1. *Both were child prodigies.* By the age of thirteen, Stevie Wonder was a recording star for Motown records. He went to school on weekdays and toured on the weekends. Like Mozart, he had early contact with musicians on a professional basis. His natural genius

Stevie Wonder.

was thus enhanced through such activities as performing, composing, and recording.

2. *Both absorbed a living musical language rooted in tradition*. Like many other black popular singers, Stevie absorbed the gospel music of the black church and the closely related *rhythm and blues* style at an early age. Whereas Wolfgang absorbed the melodic tradition of Italian lyricism, Stevie learned the "funky" melody of black soul music (for example, the singing style of Ray Charles and Aretha Franklin). As Mozart had the minuet and trio, Wonder had the blues. Mozart absorbed the reserved, elegant rhythm of European court music; Stevie Wonder absorbed the multilayered, driving rhythms of the street.

3. *Both broke away from a controlling influence to achieve musical maturity*. In Mozart's case, it was his father; in Stevie Wonder's life it was the Motown record company. As we have seen, Leopold Mozart played a vital role in the artistic life of his son; so did Motown in the artistic life of the young Stevie Wonder (or "Little Stevie Wonder," as they named him for commercial reasons). It was with this record company that he produced his early successes—a string of catchy, teen-oriented pop songs. As he reached adulthood, it was inevitable that a talent of his caliber would outgrow the artistic restraints that were placed on him when he was a child. He abandoned the "Little" in front of his name (at least on one album—*The Secret Life of Plants*—his real name appears in a corner after a personal message to his audience), and he renegotiated his contract with Motown so that he would have total artistic control of his output. And thus began a rapid exploration of form, instrumentation, poetry, and subject—in short, a total transformation of his art.

THE ROLE OF THE RECORDING STUDIO

Like Mozart, Stevie Wonder began with a natural and spontaneous musical language. One means through which Mozart explored and expanded his musical language was notation. In the case of Stevie Wonder, a similar function was served by *multitrack recording technology*. This important tool allows the modern musician to experiment with the actual sound materials of the language through various means. A description of the basic procedure by which Stevie Wonder has recorded many of his songs will illustrate this technique of composition.

Multitrack recording technology allows one performer to play many times on a single tape, due to the design of the professional tape machines. Consider the *mono* tape recorder. It has one *track*, a channel for recording:

Now consider the home *stereo* tape machine. It has *two* recording channels:

The stereo machine is really *two* separate systems coordinated to record simultaneously. Now the professional machine used to make the tape that eventually becomes a record has (usually) twenty-four such channels. All of these channels can be recorded separately or in any combination. Stevie Wonder has recorded many songs entirely by himself. For example, he might play the electric piano first, on channel 1:

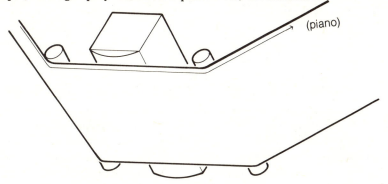

(piano)

He then might add a bass part on an electronic synthesizer, while listening to the piano track:

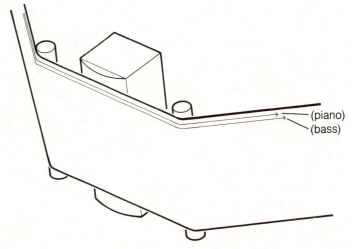

Now, listening to the piano and bass tracks, sounding together, he might add the drums. Drums are usually recorded on four or five separate tracks at the same time, in order to capture the character of each drum in the drum set onto a different track:

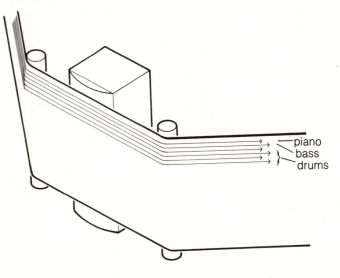

The process continues as he adds voices (often his own, singing several different melodic lines), more synthesizer tracks, etc. If other musicians are playing, any combination may be recorded, either separately or together. But even when all the individual elements have been taped, the piece is far from finished. Now begins another process, all-important for experimentation and expanding the musical language—*mixing*.

All the tracks are run through a *mixing console* or *board*, as it is often called. This allows the composer, often with the help of a recording engineer, to experiment with the balance of all these materials. Each track has its own *module*, a device to control its sound level. The sensitive controls on this module can alter the character of any of the twenty-four tracks in countless ways. Each track can be made "brighter" or "darker"; it can be altered with *echo* or *reverb* (originally, an electronic means of simulating the sound in a large hall, but now considered a special category of effects that cannot be easily described, though they can be heard). The number of ways any given sound can be manipulated is almost infinite. It is not unusual to spend hours on the sound of one or two instruments. The procedure is repeated for all twenty-four tracks.

Now the experimentation begins. These twenty-four tracks may be combined in countless configurations. Although at the beginning of the piece all the instruments are playing, the musician may decide to feature the piano alone, perhaps adding the other instruments one by one. The balance between the instruments is critical. The slightest variation in the sound of any one instrument can completely alter the "feel" of the track.

Recording studio technology provides an out-of-the-body medium (like notation), which allows for experimentation and expansion. When you find something you like, that effect becomes part of your basic language. This process may be likened to orchestration, which deals with subtle manipulations of timbre, texture, and dynamics, but in this case achieved electronically. Mixing is a highly complex procedure requiring years of experience to master. Even the simplest-sounding song may have required long hours in the studio for its "simple" effect. In short, recording-studio technology has become a highly refined and sophisticated art.

SONGS IN THE KEY OF LIFE

Recording technology has been especially important to Stevie Wonder, who happens to be blind. Recording is his "vision"—the tape is the canvas on which he paints the "pictures in his mind." We will consider one of his most ambitious efforts, *Songs in the Key of Life* (1976), a mature, fully developed and stylistically confident work. It is a recorded song cycle dealing with some of the most basic issues of human experience.

Love's in Need of Love Today: The first song sets forth the most important idea of the cycle. Throughout the song there is an interplay between soloist and group. The chorus sings in a sweet, gospel style, providing a solid background for Stevie's improvisations. The song's message may be made even more poignant when you realize the great cultural chain that brought the sacred-harmony style to this musical moment. It stretches back through ghetto street harmonies, to the gospel style of the black church, to the hymn singing of the colonists, and even further, all the way to the hymn traditions of Renaissance Europe. The rhythmic impulse is Afro-American with a touch of Latin (the triangle rhythm). All the elements come together in a style that is part soul, part popular ballad, and all Stevie Wonder. A basic progression is repeated over and over, inviting the listener to sing, move, and feel the message. The semi-sad mood gradually becomes a broad affirmation of the spirit, and initiates an emotional and philosophical journey for the willing participant.

Have a Talk with God, the next song, is slightly faster and a bit (but not much) brighter in mood. Musically, we are being led forward in time, not by sudden contrast, but by a gradual and subtle upturn in tempo and spirit. The song is a straightforward blues, and sets out another important idea of the cycle. Superimposed over the basic blues beat are Latin rhythms and almost surrealistic synthesizer "licks" that create a cluttered, "funky" tension in the music, a tension that sets up a complete contrast of mood and style with the next song.

Village Ghetto Land: Set in a parody style, this song exposes another basic theme of the cycle—the ghetto experience. The "strings" are actually performed by Stevie on synthesizer. The effect of this piece is created by the juxtaposition between the ghetto image and the "refined, classical" style of the accompaniment.

Contusion: An up-tempo, frenetic, electronic, "funky" instrumental, clearly positioned as a contrast to the previous song.

Sir Duke: A straightforward, somewhat jazz-influenced vocal about Duke Ellington's fundamental belief that "It don't mean a thing if it ain't got that swing," and about the joy music brings to life (compare with *The Magic Flute*, page 222).

I Wish: A song built on and about the rhythms of the street. The driving ostinato rhythms with the sudden outbursts by the brass is one of Stevie's trademarks. Syncopated rhythms supply the powerful forward potential of this track. Notice that all the interlocking pieces can be heard, despite the multilayered, dense texture. This suggests that the "mix" is a good one.

Knocks Me Off My Feet: This is the characteristic lyrical style Stevie often uses for love songs. A sweeping, lyrical melody is sung over a jazz-influenced chord progression, in which chromatic harmonies create a forward-moving, goal-directed progression. Toward the end of the song, there is a sudden change of key for the last statement of the melody.

Pastime Paradise: A total change of mood and style. The synthesizer creates a hypnotic, modern background that draws on cues associated with "classical" music. We hear a purposefully repetitive pattern, designed to create the mechanical, hypnotic effect.

Summer Soft: Another contrast of styles. This somewhat impressionistic song evokes images of summer and love through "warm" harmonies and texture.

Ordinary Pain: A bittersweet song in which a slower, lyrical melody is set over a faster, busy bass line, creating the characteristic rhythmic "feel" of the tune. The lilting, dancing effect is not unlike that of certain Viennese rhythms. The song has a contrasting second part—an "answer" to the first, sung by a female counterpart, during which the musical motive of the first part (sung to the words "ordinary pain") is in the background.

Isn't She Lovely: This is one of Stevie Wonder's greatest songs. It celebrates the birth of his daughter. The harmonica solo—formerly the trademark of "Little Stevie Wonder," now singing gloriously as a man—is especially beautiful. We may understand that sounds of the baby laughing and crying have heightened meaning to someone who is sightless.

Joy Inside My Tears: This is a love song of contentment. Stevie Wonder has captured a spirit of deep celebration through the medium of the "ordinary" popular song. Again, the bass line functions as a solid foundation for the rest of the structure, occasionally asserting itself in moments of wonderfully spontaneous music making.

Black Man: A driving, "funky" ostinato rhythm underlies this protest song about prejudice against nonwhite people. This may well be considered in the light of nineteenth-century nationalistic music, which often had political overtones.

Ngiculela—Es Una Historia: Like the previous song, this one is involved with Latin music, evidenced especially in the rhythmic textures and the choice of percussion instruments. Once again, the bass line occasionally asserts itself into the foreground with sliding melodic bits.

If It's Magic: Another complete change in style: A straightforward enough song, but accompanied on a harp. The slow tempo and the message about contemporary life set up the dramatic impact of the last two songs of the cycle.

As: Things "start to come together" in this highpoint of the cycle. The message is that love is an answer to all that has gone before. What begins as a slightly subdued but forward-moving "feel" is slowly transformed into a steady, driving ostinato melody repeated by the background singers with whom Stevie improvises. The gospel sound heard in the opening song returns, bringing with it a sense of balance and unity. As we have observed in Purcell's *Dido and Aeneas* and Bernstein's *West Side Story*, the use of a chorus may hint at the universal. The interplay of the solo and the group merge into one voice—one message.

Another Star: The energy of the previous song flows right into this one; it is really a second ending to the cycle. With a feeling of celebration, Stevie sings an improvised counterpoint to a joyful ostinato sung in the backup voices. This final selection uses Latin rhythms as its basis.

Connections in the Stevie Wonder Discussion

Stylistic evolution.
The absorption of a living musical language.
Musical style may be a blending of many traditions.
Soloist and group.

Joni Mitchell

> I want the full hyphen: folk-rock-country-jazz-classical . . . so finally when you get all the hyphens in, maybe they'll drop them all, and get down to just some American music.*
>
> —Joni Mitchell

Although she is clearly a child of the great American popular tradition, there is no more serious artist on the contemporary scene than the composer-poet Joni Mitchell. Her work, like that of Duke Ellington and Stevie Wonder, transcends the limits imposed by the terms "popular" and "serious." Furthermore, her music-poetry is a remarkable example of the ever-present potential of the ancient unity.

THE INFLUENCE OF BOB DYLAN

Born in Canada, where she lived until early adulthood, Mitchell is a self-taught "natural" musician. She grew up listening to a variety of musical styles—classical, pop, rhythm and blues, country, etc.—heard, for the most part, on radio and records. Singing was only a hobby for the teenage Mitchell, while painting and poetry provided the outlet for her genius. The spark that ignited the artistic synthesis of these elements was provided by the records of Bob Dylan.

> I wrote poetry and painted all my life. I always wanted to play music and dabbled with it, but I never thought of putting them all together. It wasn't until Dylan began to write poetic songs that it occurred to me that you could actually *sing* those poems.**

---

*From an interview with *Rolling Stone*, July 26, 1979.
**Ibid.

It is difficult to describe the impact that Bob Dylan had upon the '60s generation, that youth movement that wrought such profound changes in the course of modern culture. Dylan, in all his scruffy-voiced splendor, was their Orpheus. His disillusioned but visionary, traditional yet revolutionary song-poetry became something of a *rite*: a credo of feelings, ideas, and yearnings expressed with a powerful rhythmic energy. "Any day now, any way now, I shall be released," he sang. And that's exactly how his followers felt when they sang along. A Dylan cult swept through the United States, especially on college campuses. Otherwise "straight" characters suddenly appeared in "Dylan caps," singing with antiestablishment gusto, strumming a guitar, and blowing an out-of-tune harmonica. Such remarkable cultural power was not new to the history of music. The recurrent figure of the musical visionary transcends period and style. Beethoven, Wagner, Hendrix, Dylan, Orpheus, Mitchell, and countless names we will never know in as many languages, all suggest a timeless pattern.

Joni Mitchell was never a follower. If anything, she is something of a musical loner. What, then, did Dylan's example provide? In the first place, Dylan's music was serious poetry. Yet here were important ideas and feelings that could not be separated from their "popular" musical style. In the 1960s, the lines drawn between "popular" and "serious" were even more strictly observed than they are today. For many who had been raised with this perceptual duality, Dylan provided a synthesis. His song-poetry bypassed labels and entered the more universal realm of heightened experience. That it found such immediate and popular resonance only deepened the perception that it was "important." Dylan had, in fact, pulled out a sort of cultural plug, allowing a new stream of musical activity to flow. Many young musicians with "classical" backgrounds entered that stream. Dylan had been more a cultural than a musical model. We have come upon another of those fateful connections between personalities that form a musical culture. What would Berlioz's music have been like had there not been a Beethoven? Would Joni Mitchell have even become a song-poet had there not been a Bob Dylan?

Joni Mitchell pursued a musical course far different from that of Bob Dylan. In Dylan's song-poems the music is purposefully simple, at times hardly more than a hypnotic pattern for presenting the all-important poem. We can rightfully compare it to the repetitive patterns used throughout the ages to support chants and epic poetry (for example, the *Ossianic Chant* from the Hebrides 7c). In Mitchell's music, sophistication of melodic design, intertwined with word, rhythm, harmony, meaning, idea, tension, and release, function at the highest level of creativity. With the appearance of her first album, *Joni Mitchell* (1967), her impact was immediate. This was music hard to categorize: "popular," yes; "folk," yes; but it was more: There was a lean and haunting classicism in these songs. The melodies—

graceful, elegant, strikingly original—were sung to gentle, carefully controlled guitar accompaniments, whose integrated role in the final result was not unlike the "simple" genius of the piano accompaniments to Schubert's songs (*Lied der Mignon*, for example). All of this finely wrought musical craft supported dreamlike, romantic poems, almost childlike in their innocence. It was as if some ancient Anglo-Celtic singer in a modern guise had appeared on the twentieth-century American scene.

JONI MITCHELL'S STYLISTIC JOURNEY

The innocence would not last. The remarkable and profound stylistic changes that this artist would go through are, in a real sense, a reliving of the journey of Western culture from the idealism of the classical-romantic tradition into the "darkness of our age" (see below). Joni Mitchell, whose original artistic vision rested squarely within that idealism, would find, as others have, a totally new energy in the Modern age that has nothing to do with either classicism or romanticism. Whatever "modernism" is, it *seems* to negate the past. Many poets, painters, writers, and composers have expressed a sense of alienation and discontinuity with an idealized past, while at the same time longing for it. The composer Hans Werner Henze expressed this idea in these words about his music:

> Ancient forms appear to me as classical ideals of beauty, no longer attainable, but visible from a great distance, arousing memories like dreams. But the way to them is obscured by the densest darkness of our age; the way to them is the most difficult and most impossible thing. However, to me it seems the only folly worth living for.

We can consider Joni Mitchell's first album as evidence of a musical style still connected to classical ideals of beauty. And even in this "perfect" musical-poetic world, the road to a more "dangerous" realm had been defined (*Song to a Seagull*, for example). You will remember that romanticism lay the groundwork for the image of a personal quest for the infinite— the abandonment of restraints in order that the truth of the world might be known and captured in life and art. What happens when you pursue that idealized quest across the modern landscape? For that is just what Joni Mitchell has done.

Suggested Listening

From the first album, *Joni Mitchell*:

I Came to the City
Michael from the Mountains
Nathan La Franeer
Song to a Seagull

BLUE

Joni Mitchell describes her poetic style as "confessional," a quality we associate with romanticism. Her songs provide a musical commentary on her life, and a far more interesting one than can be provided on these pages. Without spelling out exactly, it is possible to follow her encounters with "what's happening" in our times, encounters that are not always pleasant. The stylistic changes that accompany her various periods of musical activity document in a general way her personal journey. The first important change came with *Blue* (1970). We are quite familiar with this word, having traced the blues genre through a variety of eras and styles. These songs, however, are not blues. The cycle simply adopts the "feeling quality" of that genre without actually using its form and style. The album cover is about as blue in color as one can imagine. Comparing the cover with her previous ones, we have our first inkling that the music will represent a departure in feeling, intent, and style.

While some of the songs on *Blue* are reminiscent of her earlier work, which, for lack of a better way to describe it, might be termed "classical-folk," many of the songs on *Blue* reflect the beginnings of a stylistic fusion with the rhythmic impulse of rock. However, it is a very subdued and original transformation of that impulse; there is no forceful drum track, no blaring lead guitar. Mitchell retains a distinct connection to the classical aesthetic. Restraint and clarity in matters of texture and form are often earmarks of her style. Many of the songs are sung to a small ensemble accompaniment—a sort of miniature rock group. That all-important rhythmic drive of rock is totally transformed in these songs into something quite new: playful yet haunting, dancing yet sad, the background is restrained, yet sets the rhythm free. Like her previous work, the form of each song-poem is clear, but now there is a decisive departure in melodic design and singing style. These aspects are totally integrated; her melodies are born of poetry and actual singing; neither aspect dominates. In *Blue*, she has adopted a new "honesty" in approach to melody and singing style. Comparing it with the first album, you will hear more "flaws." In contrast to the very controlled vocal sound of the earlier songs, we hear a type of singing that is less ideal, more human and "real." At times, the rhythms approach those of speech. The whole poetic-melodic style is bound up in a remarkable unity of expression that is at once "worked out" and "spontaneous."

Two comparisons to composers you have already encountered seem especially relevant at this point. Despite its classical features (clarity of form, texture, and general sense of restraint), the lyrical and melodic style of some songs in *Blue* (especially in *The Last Time I Saw Richard*) leans toward a *realism* not unlike Mussorgsky's in *Boris Godunov*. Secondly, that elusive feeling of total freedom within the boundaries of restraint and the creation of graceful, spontaneous melodies brings Mozart to mind.

Blue, by the way, continues to sell. In contradiction to the notion that "popular" music is a temporary phenomenon, many important records by various artists have gone on to become "classics." Hidden away in the Joni Mitchell bin of record stores in distant places, this quiet masterpiece of twentieth-century art lies in wait for another convert.

FOR THE ROSES

After *Blue*, Joni stopped touring for a year and a half and returned to Canada. Most of the songs in *For the Roses* (1972) were composed during that period, which may have been a time for reflection. *For the Roses* is an album of exploration, both musically and poetically. The opening song, *Banquet*, sets out what has become an all-embracing theme of her work: the juxtaposition of idealism with the flawed yet beautiful modern reality.

> I took my dream down by the sea
> Yankee yachts and lobster pots and sunshine
> And logs and sails
> And Shell oil pails

In *Cold Blue Steel and Sweet Fire*, we hear a modern parallel to Faust's journey to hell (see Berlioz, *Damnation of Faust*, pages 268–76), but this journey goes through the real hell of drugs. Seedy poetic images are accompanied by a strange, metallic music heavy with the timbre of guitars. A saxophone in the background adds a cool, detached comment on this vision of a modern hell that has beckoned to so many searching for "meaning."

Lesson in Survival is one of Joni's first songs to break totally with her previous style. The melody is complex; neither catchy nor tuneful, it leans toward a realistic speech pattern far more concerned with the poetry than anything else. This is not a "sing-along" song. There are moments when the meter disappears, replaced by a free-flowing rhythm. The harmony is non-committal, with no firm tonal home base. In terms of Joni's style, this harmony is experimental. There is more dissonance, less reliance on tonality. It is clearly a stylistic experiment.

Unlike some of her previous albums, *For the Roses* has no stylistic unity. It is, rather, the journey of an artist confronting the chaos of many possibilities. The final song, *Judgment of the Moon and Stars (Ludwig's Tune)*, evokes the image of Beethoven as a model for the artist embarking upon unknown waters.

> You've got to shake your fists at lightning now
> You've got to roar like a forest fire
> You've got to spread your light like blazes
> All across the sky
>
> Strike every chord that you feel
> That broken trees
> And elephant ivories
> Conceal

COURT AND SPARK

Court and Spark (1972) turned out to be one of Joni's happiest albums. Quite tuneful, it represents the closest she has come to a "commercial" sound. The presence of substantial background material gives the record a "slick" effect. One of the songs, *Help Me*, became a "top forty" hit. Among the tunes is one of Joni's most haunting melodies, *The Same Situation*, a modern echo of the Anglo-Celtic song style. Considering the explorations of the previous album, the tameness of *Court and Spark* was something of a surprise. Perhaps she was not ready to explore the unknown musical regions hinted at in *For the Roses*. Also, for Joni, exploring the commercial sound may have been an important detour on her artistic journey. At the very end of *Court and Spark*, as if to say to her audience, "Don't get too comfortable!" there is a total change: *Twisted*, a jazz tune, is radically different from the rest of the album.

THE HISSING OF SUMMER LAWNS

With this album (1975), the exploration takes a radical turn. None of her past efforts depended nearly so much upon other musicians. In this cycle, Joni seems to have experimented with giving up musical control in favor of a group-improvised sound that is jazz-oriented. (Interestingly, though, the most remarkable statement on the album is *Shadows and Light*, performed entirely by Joni.) *The Hissing of Summer Lawns* may be one of her least successful endeavors. Perhaps its real value was to be as a stepping stone. The composer has commented on the process of exploring new musical styles:

> I know that some of these projects are eccentric. I know that there are parts that are experimental, and some of them are half-baked. I certainly have been pushing the limits and—even for myself—not all of my experiments are completely successful. But they lay the groundwork for further developments. Sooner or later some of these will come to fruition.*

HEJIRA

It would be sooner. Her next work, the song cycle *Hejira* (1976), is a modern masterpiece. But wait! Just what is a "masterpiece"? Who determines it? And here we have the very crux of the final chapters of this book: *No one really knows*. In a culture in which there is a multitude of musical styles and, even more important, a vast number of cues that mean different things to different people, the very notion of a masterpiece needs rethinking. When I use the term for a newly created piece, I am following my own instincts, as well as evaluating the reactions of a varied group of listeners to this work. But the statement clearly must be qualified: it is a masterpiece *for*

---

*Rolling Stone, ibid.

Covers of two Joni Mitchell albums: (left) *Hejira* **and (right)** *Ladies of the Canyon*.

some listeners. This lesson is vital for understanding the modern world. *The incredible mix of cues, values, and traditions within our culture have changed the significance of any single person's artistic contribution to society.* There are no Beethovens in our time. The "quest for legitimacy," that motivating cultural force of the nineteenth and twentieth centuries, may well be over. How can a piece, a composer, or a style be granted "official legitimacy" when there is no universally shared value system or set of cues to prompt some semblance of a universal response? Who knows? Certainly not the "experts," who are even less in agreement with each other than with the general public. *Masterpieces have become a very private matter, shared among increasingly separated cultural groups.* Time-honored notions of tradition have been lost to the siren song of change. This, in part, happens to be what *Hejira* is all about.

> The drone of flying engines
> Is a song so wild and blue
> It scrambles time and seasons if it gets through to you
> Then your life becomes a travelogue
> Of picture-postcard-charms
> Amelia, it was just a false alarm
>
> —from the song *Amelia*, in the *Hejira* album

Hejira began as the expression of a personal problem that often arises in a culture in which change has become the norm: running away from a relationship.*

> I was sitting out at the beach at Neil's [Neil Young] place and I was thinking, "I want to travel, I don't know where and I don't know who with." Two friends of mine came to the door and said, "We're driving across the country." I said, "I've been waiting for you; I'm *gone*." So we drove across the country, then we parted ways. It was my car . . . *Hejira* was an obscure word, but it said *exactly* what I wanted. Running away, honorably.**

No simple description can do justice to a multilayered work of art. All we will do here is to hint briefly at the richness of the music through two of the central pieces in the cycle, *Amelia* and *Hejira* (the title song). *Amelia* refers to none other than Amelia Earhart, the famous pilot-explorer who died in 1937. In this song-poem, she and Joni merge in a surrealistic, mythical vision of flight to somewhere. The music creates a hypnotic, "floating" background that never reaches home. At first listening, it seems to have a key center, until you try to sing it. Then you realize that, in fact, it moves back and forth between two keys without ever settling into one. The effect of this harmonic design, coupled with the slow, gently swaying rhythms, may seem to "open up into the sky." Superimposed upon the basic structure are whining, "cool," electric sounds, often dissonant, that haunt the musical background. The musical elements support a carefully balanced poetical structure. In each verse of six lines, the harmonic and rhythmic tension reach a maximum level in the third line, which causes the following three lines to come gently tumbling out in perfect acoustic symmetry.

> A ghost of aviation
> She was swallowed by the sky
> Or by the sea, like me she had a dream to fly
> Like Icarus ascending
> On beautiful foolish arms
> Amelia, it was just a false alarm.
>
> *(fifth verse)*

For the willing listener, *Amelia* evokes a totally contemporary experience of time, prompted and shaped by flight over the vast expanse of the modern world—a source of both confusion and revelation. This journey is

Hejira, literally "running away" in Arabic, refers specifically to Mohammed's flight from religious persecution in Medina to Mecca.
**Rolling Stone*, ibid.

clearly symbolic of Joni Mitchell's personal journey. Just as the harmony never comes home, neither does the song offer any resolution other than the refrain: "Amelia, it was just a false alarm."

The title song, *Hejira*, is certainly one of Mitchell's greatest song-poems. The music is subdued, cool. As Schubert might have suggested a brook running through the Viennese countryside in a piano accompaniment, the background of *Hejira* suggests the whirring of the modern age. It is not exactly "pretty," but as Mussorgsky, another composer somewhat "deromanticized" by reality, might well have commented, "That's the way it sounds." Within this nonidealized musical environment, we are moved from the petty to the universal and back again, without much fanfare.

It is difficult to categorize the musical style of *Hejira*. All of Joni's previous explorations come together in a unified stylistic fabric. The interplay with other musicians, somewhat out of control in the previous work, is now a balanced partnership. Harmonic experiments are now held in check by familiar, secure progressions. There is a balance between the singing and speaking types of melody. Experiments that had sounded tentative and artificial have now been absorbed into a controlled musical language that sounds both crafted and spontaneous. It is a language of synthesis. You might think, having accomplished this, that Joni Mitchell would settle down, but that seems destined not to be. Her next adventure was a collaboration with the great jazz artist, Charles Mingus, who died during the project (*Mingus*, 1979). Joni Mitchell, like our age, is stylistically restless. Many of us await her future works with more than a passing interest. All her explorations seem to have a place when considered and experienced as a whole.

Connections in the Mitchell Discussion

The ancient unity.
The potential interplay between speech and melody.
Accelerated stylistic evolution.
The importance of genre.

QUESTIONS

For the following questions, find any false statement(s) and correct them by changing the word(s) in italics. More than one statement may be false; all the statements may be true.

1. Concerning the importance of national and regional styles in musical culture:

   (a) *Many* musical languages reflect national or regional influences.

(b) It applies to *all* music.

(c) It is a phenomenon that is *easy* to quantify.

(d) It has been one of the *basic enriching* processes of the world music tradition.

2. Important influences on American music include the following traditions (cross out any that don't apply):

(a) West African music

(b) Anglo-Celtic song and dance

(c) Latin music

(d) European notated tradition

(e) European hymn practice

(f) Viennese lyricism

3. The fuging tune

(a) was one of the *popular genres* of early American composers.

(b) follows a *basic model*.

(c) is *strophic*.

(d) opens with a *polyphonic* phrase.

4. Concerning the Yankee Tunesmiths:

(a) Most were *full-time* composers.

(b) Their music reflected *popular traditions* of the day.

(c) They were active around the time of the *American Revolution*.

(d) The influence of their music *ended during the nineteenth century*.

5. Concerning sacred folk harmony:

(a) It has roots in the *European hymn tradition*.

(b) Its basic style is *polyphonic*.

(c) It played a vital role in the music traditions of the *South*.

(d) It may be considered an important root of many *current popular styles*.

6. Concerning the blues:

   (a) It is an *important genre* in American music.

   (b) Its origins are in *Afro-American culture*.

   (c) Its musical design was influenced by the *Western notated tradition*.

   (d) Its influence has been felt *worldwide*.

7. Which of the following were basic influences on early jazz (cross out any that don't apply):

   (a) Western notated tradition

   (b) blues

   (c) ragtime

   (d) Anglo-Celtic song and dance

   (e) the major–minor tonal system

   (f) West African musical traditions

   (g) Afro-American culture

8. Concerning a genre:

   (a) It often has a traditional *form*.

   (b) Its function in musical culture is often one of *continuity*.

   (c) Its use by composers may be described as *inflexible*.

   (d) It is often associated with certain *ideas and feelings*.

9. Concerning Afro-American music:

   (a) It is a *rigid* categorization.

   (b) It has played a *vital role* in the formation of styles throughout the world.

   (c) Among its general rhythmic practices is *rhythmic polyphony*.

   (d) It has absorbed important elements from the *Western notated tradition*.

10. A comparison between Italian lyricism and Afro-American soul demonstrates the following musical ideas:

    (a) That music is *deeply tied to cultural experience*.

(b) That any moment of music is *connected to history*.

(c) That a basic enriching process for the world's music has been the *separation* between vocal and instrumental melodic styles.

(d) That *genres* are a vital link in the world musical language.

11. Concerning Aaron Copland:

(a) He shares a sense of musical purpose with *Mussorgsky*.

(b) His style reflects *one basic* tradition.

(c) His "Appalachian Spring" incorporates elements of *drama*.

(d) The music of "Appalachian Spring" was influenced by American *sacred folk harmony*.

12. Concerning Elliott Carter:

(a) His work reflects the general twentieth-century trend to *experiment with rhythm*.

(b) Among the influences on his style are the *rhythmic practices of jazz*.

(c) His artistic orientation leans toward the *right* side of the classic-romantic continuum.

(d) The design of his "Double Concerto" has certain similarities to the *ostinato* effect in Gabrielli's "Sanctus."

13. Concerning Duke Ellington:

(a) His music shares at least *one* tendency with nineteenth-century Romanticism.

(b) His suite "Such Sweet Thunder" has something in common with *Berlioz's The Damnation of Faust*.

(c) His style *remained unchanged* during his lifetime.

(d) He suggested that a good jazz performer was measured by *spontaneity alone*.

14. Concerning Stevie Wonder:

(a) Like Mozart, he was a *child prodigy*.

(b) Like Mozart, he absorbed a living musical language *at an early age*.

(c) Like Mozart, he *broke away* from a controlling influence to reach musical maturity.

(d) His cycle "Songs in the Key of Life" *does not* use dramatic elements.

15. Concerning Joni Mitchell:

(a) Her artistic orientation has elements of *both classical and romantic* aesthetics.

(b) Her stylistic evolution includes aspects of *realism*.

(c) In this respect, she may be compared to *Mozart*.

(d) Her art reflects a long process of *experimentation and synthesis*.

Toward a World Musical Language

One of the newest aspects of today's musical culture is how much we are learning about some of our oldest musical traditions. In this final chapter we will reach back into the musical past to tie up some additional long-range strands that frame the musical present. We will enter the great fabric of world music through some examples of the traditions of the Amerindians (native Indian people of the Americas). Using these examples as a starting point, we will compare music that comes to us across great distances of time and culture, and beyond traditional barriers of style and perception.

Throughout this final chapter we will concern ourselves with music as a universal art. In doing so, we will once again treat universal impulses like chant, song, dance, and drama as basic musical lifelines. To the ones already considered, a few more universal impulses will be added. Our final task will be to explore the historic roots of bond and tension between so-called "popular" and "serious" styles. In short, we seek to understand our musical traditions within a greater context: the music of the world.

The Balance between Spontaneity and Intellectualization

In this book, we have consistently employed two *related* approaches to suspending cultural filters. As listeners, you have been asked to respond to music as *both*:

spontaneous, body-based traditions; for example, dance, song, chant, drama	←——————————→ information, facts, ideas considered away from the music; in short, an intellectual approach

In many earlier chapters, we've used the idea of continuums to represent related continuities, not separate entities. Thus, you know that we have always been concerned with that flexible middle ground where both sides become one. But it is no secret that in our culture the right side of the continuum above is recognized as the *means for defining truth*. In this chapter we will be concerned with balancing out that emphasis, since any attempt to deal with music as a worldwide language, and even more important, to deal with how we respond to that great and diverse language, must consider and honor other styles of perception. The key word, of course, is *flexibility*, and the key concept is this: *one side of the continuum does not negate the other*. Furthermore, it may be suggested that music's historic role in many cultures has been to "harmonize" passion and intellect, spontaneous and planned, local and cosmic. It is that synthesis we seek.

Amerindian Music and Cultural Filters

As you know, listening beyond style involves a special type of skill. It requires suspending your immediate response to music in order to enter a deeper, more universal realm that unites all musical experience. The inhibiting factors that make listening beyond style difficult are the cultural filters that we have all acquired. These cultural filters can have both a positive and negative effect on listening to music. When we recognize a familiar style, our cultural filter may automatically open up the senses to musical experience; the opposite, of course, is also true. There is no better example of the potentially negative role of cultural filters than attitudes surrounding music of the Amerindians. There is also no better example of how the listener may acquire a cultural filter through habit, and then find it difficult to remove even with conscious effort. The mass media, especially film and television, have conditioned many listeners to think of native American music as "primitive" (in its pejorative sense), through association with fictional stereotypes of Indian life (due largely to the "cowboy movie" genre).

Some would suggest, with the best of intentions, that to describe this stereotype only serves to perpetuate it. I have found, over the years, that some cultural filters are easily bypassed; others, especially those that seem rooted in deep, sometimes hidden social-cultural energies, cannot be moved until they are brought to the surface.

Hidden Basics

We are living in a time when many thoughtful people are trying to redis-cover the universal impulses and patterns that relate our culture (and music) to the rest of the world. For hundreds of years we have consciously empha-sized the differences. Now, in recognition of the increased connections among the world cultures observed in Span II, we are systematically search-ing for the similarities. Essential to this search is the following understand-ing: although a connection may seem basic or simple (for example, two contrasting musical styles that represent a similar dramatic quality), it is nonetheless important. *It may be suggested that we have become so involved with detailed descriptions of stylistic differences that we no longer respond to the most basic and universal similarities.* The basic impulses of music are analogous to the inner, supportive structure in architecture. It is possible to become so fascinated by outside details of building, that these basic supports are disregarded. If the architect does this, the building falls down. To a great extent, the same is true of the composer. Notwithstanding all the stylistic details that creative musicians in any age have used, *the great ones have always crafted those details around deep, universal impulses.* Responding to these impulses without cluttering our perception with stylistic details is a basic skill for listening to music at the deepest level. We can't describe all those impulses; they exist in many guises and combina-tions. Nevertheless, to seek them is to discover what music is about.

Listen   Sequence 30   Consider these selections, focusing on the basic impulses.

Basic Impulses

30a Chippewa healing chant (recorded 1908) — chant

30b Quechua ritual song played on panpipes — song, with subdued dance impulse

30c Same song in a vocal version

30d Plains Apache, *Lullaby* — lullaby

In the next listening sequence, the lullaby of the Plains Apache will be a starting point for entering a universal realm of musical perception. *Focus on the lullaby impulse*. The sequence will include one other lullaby, and two works that have a lullaby-like feeling. The final piece embodies *two* universal impulses that overlap: a lullaby-like hymn (played in strings) and a solo "voice" (the cello) "singing" the universal gesture of mourning.

Listen

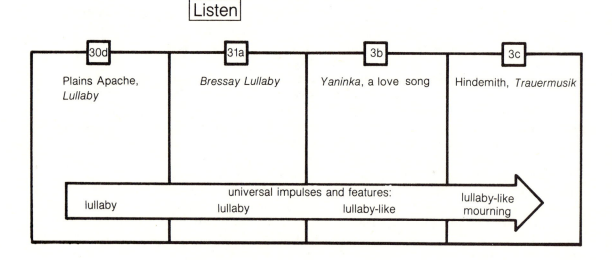

(Two additional pieces which may be perceived as combining a lullaby-like impulse with a gesture of mourning are the finales of Purcell's *Dido and Aeneas* 15 and Bernstein's *West Side Story* 29c .)

In the pieces you've just heard, there are even more basic impulses—those of *song* and *lyricism*. How can the last piece 3c (scored for instruments) be considered a song? As suggested in Chapter 4, the deep channel of human song transfers easily to instruments. Historically, instruments have served as a direct extension of the human voice. When an instrumental melody springs from the composer's song impulse it has a recognizably lyric quality. We have considered some regional types of lyricism such as Italian and Viennese. What is lyricism? It is a word that is used in all the arts; yet it is hard to define exactly. In music it is usually identified with a flowing melody connected to *feeling*. And this universal thread, based in the potential of song for expressing human emotions, runs through the listening sequence above at the deepest level. We can revise the diagram as follows:

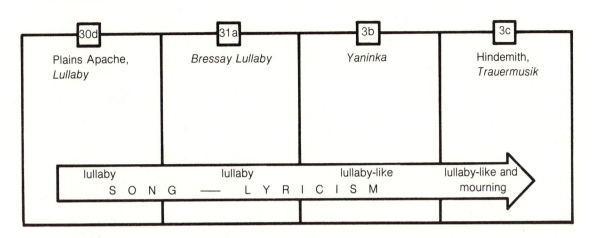

Tracing Lyricism across Stylistic Boundaries

If you can bypass an immediate surface response to style, lyricism is one of the easiest universal qualities to sense in music. To follow it across the barriers of distance, culture, and time, you need only the belief that it springs from the human impulse to express emotion with song (even when instruments are used), and the skill to lower all kinds of cultural filters like "popular," "serious," "refined," "primitive," "art music," "tribal music," etc.

Listen   The following sequences are not intended to be heard all at once. The basic organización of the sequences is a universal strand that knows no boundaries of style and culture—lyricism. However, some of the back-to-back selections reflect *direct* stylistic connections of a more regional nature. These are indicated by the smaller arrows on the diagram below.

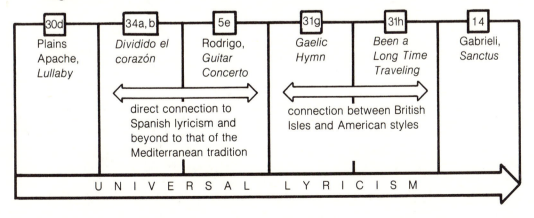

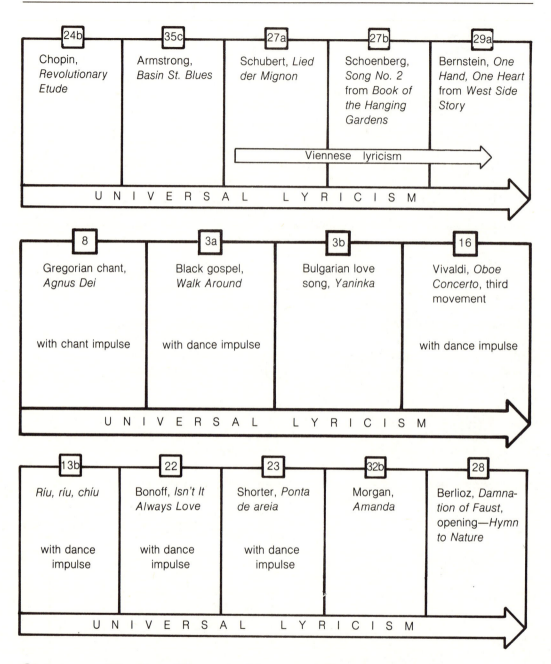

24b	35c	27a	27b	29a
Chopin, *Revolutionary Etude*	Armstrong, *Basin St. Blues*	Schubert, *Lied der Mignon*	Schoenberg, *Song No. 2* from *Book of the Hanging Gardens*	Bernstein, *One Hand, One Heart* from *West Side Story*

Viennese lyricism →

U N I V E R S A L   L Y R I C I S M →

8	3a	3b	16
Gregorian chant, *Agnus Dei*	Black gospel, *Walk Around*	Bulgarian love song, *Yaninka*	Vivaldi, *Oboe Concerto*, third movement
with chant impulse	with dance impulse		with dance impulse

U N I V E R S A L   L Y R I C I S M →

13b	22	23	32b	28
Ríu, ríu, chíu	Bonoff, *Isn't It Always Love*	Shorter, *Ponta de areia*	Morgan, *Amanda*	Berlioz, *Damnation of Faust*, opening—*Hymn to Nature*
with dance impulse	with dance impulse	with dance impulse		

U N I V E R S A L   L Y R I C I S M →

Chippewa Healing Chant in Universal Perspective

The chant *Going 'Round the world* [30a] was sung as part of a ritual for healing the sick. Performed by a Chippewa holy man, it was recorded in 1908 at White Earth, Minnesota. Like many chants, the melody is really a repetitive pattern supporting the text. In this short excerpt, the pattern is heard twice, beginning on a high pitch and gradually working itself downward.

| Ka wita kumi gickaman aki | I am going around the world |
| midwe kumi gickaman aki | I am going through the world |

There is an interesting connection between *Going 'Round the World* and the Vedic chant 7b . Comparing the texts (see also page 116), one finds a type of imagery and reality quite different from that of Western culture. In both chants, the singer reaches a meditative state which allows him to "transcend" the normal boundaries of the physical world (compare the lines "I am going through the world" with "crossing beyond these worlds as desired"). Chant may create a special type of human energy which has been described as "beyond the body." This kind of religious experience, in which the participant enters a trancelike state by chanting, is very ancient and represents an unbroken link with a world tradition that can only be measured in many thousands of years. There has been renewed interest in this style of religious experience in recent times. The sight of a person raised in the West chanting and meditating presents a fascinating cultural image: a return to one of the oldest and purest forms of heightened experience involving music. Understanding chant as one of the basic musical impulses, like dance and song, enables you to sense this impulse in different guises.

Listen The following pieces suggest the transformation of the ancient chant impulse into new styles in Western music.

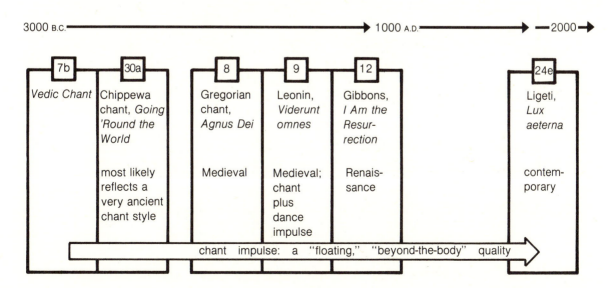

Drama

The notion that drama applies only to a staged play can be misleading. It distracts us from understanding that the impulse to act may take many forms, including dance and song, as well as influence music making in various ways. Among the pieces we have heard in which dramatic elements are important are the following:

Carter, *Double Concerto for Piano and Harpsichord* (read his description, page 414)
Copland, *Appalachian Spring* (read his description, pages 411–12)
Stockhausen, *Momente* 24f (read his description, page 352)
Beethoven, *Symphony No. 5*
Mendelssohn, *Overture to A Midsummer Night's Dream*
Berlioz, *Fantastic Symphony*
Schubert, *Lied der Mignon* 27a
Schoenberg, *Song 2* from *Book of the Hanging Gardens* 27b
anon., *There Lived an Old Lord* 31f
anon., *The Dowie Dens of Yarrow* 31e
anon., *I Will Give My Love an Apple* 6a
anon., *El Rey de Francia tres hijas tenía* 5a
anon., *Ossianic Chant* 7c
Weelkes, *Since Robin Hood* 13a (strong dance impulse)
anon., *Ríu, ríu, chíu* 13b (actual dance)

The following, of course, are either formal music dramas or religious rites, which provide the universal prototype for all drama:

Religious Rites

Chippewa Healing Song 30a
Catholic Mass: Gregorian Chant, *Agnus Dei* 8
          Ockeghem, *Kyrie* 10b
          Gabrieli, *Sanctus* 14
          Bach, *Kyrie* 18
Gaelic Hymn 31g
Been a Long Time Traveling 31h
Ramayana Chant 2a

Secular Music Dramas

Purcell, *Dido and Aeneas* 15
Mozart, *The Magic Flute*

Berlioz, *The Damnation of Faust* 28
Verdi, *Aïda*
Wagner, *Tristan and Isolde* (also something of a "religious rite"—see
    page 305)
Mussorgsky, *Boris Godunov*
Bernstein, *West Side Story* 29

Considering music of the world, *the dramatic impulse is undoubtedly
one of its universal pillars.* Any connections of a dramatic nature are legitimate ground for listening beyond style, for example:

Berlioz,   Bernstein,
Ride to the Abyss 28   *The Rumble* 29b
   from *The Damnation of Faust*   from *West Side Story*

> Similar dramatic purpose and character: both are frenzied moments of
> horror in the drama, expressed through frenetic, tense music. Notice similar
> use of "doom-laden" sounds.
>
>   bell   siren

Purcell,   Bernstein,
Finale of *Dido and Aeneas* 15   Finale of *West Side Story* 29c

>   "summing up"
>   lullaby impulse
>   mourning impulse
>   use of chorus to represent universal voice

Universal Aspects of Musical Form

Going 'Round the World is the last of three songs that make up a longer
healing rite or sacred drama. The musical form of the complete ritual is
familiar: The melody of the first chant is the same as the last.

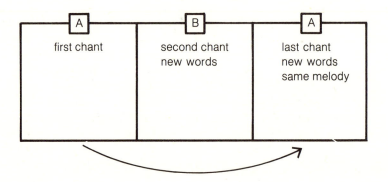

As we've stated before, repetition and contrast occur in every musical style. Embedded in the universal, they have shaped similar musical designs in every corner of the globe. Consider, again, the Renaissance *Branle* dance group 11b :

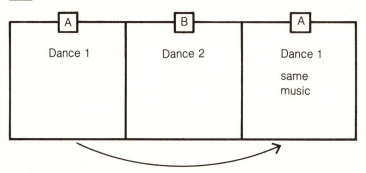

No matter what details may be suggested about this notated music, no matter how involved we become with its harmonies or melodic design, the fact remains that the long-range design of the form is identical to the Chippewa healing ritual. Any similarity of musical form—short- or long-range—may become a legitimate basis for listening beyond style.

Tracing a Sacred Number Plan

Kan Chi Si Pas 30b (Quechua Indians, Peru) is to be the subject of a musical puzzle. Recorded in the twentieth century, its heritage goes back much further. In this discussion, you will be following a set of musical and historical clues to its probable lineage. You will read the clues more or less in the order that I came upon them. The material is presented in this manner for two reasons: First of all, it is more interesting. People who follow such inquiries get caught up not only in the spirit of scholarship, but in the excitement of the chase. Much like the archeologist who finds an untouched tomb, reconstructing a tiny part of an ancient musical consciousness (as best we can) can be a fascinating experience. A second reason is this: In revealing layers of meaning and connection, we will intersect with other strands in the music of the world—the ultimate goal of the hunt.

I chose this particular tune from available recorded music of the South American Indians because I liked it. Without knowing anything about it, I simply found it to be a delightful, playfully haunting melody.

THE QUECHUAS ARE DESCENDANTS OF THE INCAS

The first set of clues is to be found in the background of the Quechua Indians of Peru. There is much interest in this Indian group because they are descended from the Incas, the legendary civilization of the High Andes Mountains. As is well known, the Incas were an Amerindian civilization comparable to other ancient "high civilizations" such as those found in Mesopotamia, Egypt, India, and China. While some scholars disagree, others strongly believe that these civilizations were, in fact, related. One feature they had in common was the place of music in a complex system of mathematically based cosmology—the "sacred science" strand we have been following throughout this book. The intriguing possibility exists that something of Inca music survives today in the Quechua traditions.

PANPIPES—MUSIC AS SACRED SCIENCE

It is very difficult to trace music into the distant past. Since most of the world's music was never notated, we can only suggest connections and make informed guesses. On the other hand, musical instruments survive their users, and tracing the diffusion of instruments throughout the ancient world offers the possibility of more precise information.

Panpipes were known in many parts of the world as far back as 2000 B.C., but flourished and developed to the greatest extent in East Asian and South American Indian societies. We know of their cultural significance from various sources, an important one being ancient Chinese texts, for example:

[The sovereign ordered] . . . show me the symbolic images of the ancients: the sun, moon, stars, mountains, the dragon, the flowery bird . . . and the temple bell, the grass of the water, the flames. . . . Show me all of these spread out in the sacred five colors as they adorn the official robes; . . . let me hear the six pitch-pipes [panpipes] and the five musical tones produced by them. . . . [Let me hear] the eight categories of musical instruments tuned according to the pitch-pipes [panpipes]. They will serve as an examination of the merits and faults of my government. [Let me hear] the odes which are created by the nobles

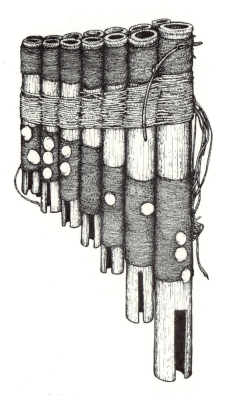

A pre-Incan panpipe discovered in a grave at Ica, Peru.

and the poems created by the people [and examine them as to their] using the [correct] five notes.*

—From the Shu Ching, approximately 600 B.C.

This quote is not an isolated example. Throughout the ancient world, we find evidence that music held a central position in the religious-cultural fabric. Among the commonly held beliefs were the following:

1. Precise numerical measurements of panpipe lengths (or bell dimensions, string lengths, or other instrumental measurements) were related to *all* things, including astronomy, calendar, social order, and history.
2. All these many aspects of life were perceived as part of one great and solemn religious ritual. The correct measurement of tones was considered a fundamental pillar of the universe.
3. Incorrect measurement of tones (produced by a panpipe whose lengths were wrong, for example) could lead to chaos.

Now before you dismiss these ideas as unscientific, remember that our purpose is not to judge, but to capture something of the ancient consciousness

---

*Walter Kaufmann, *Musical References in the Chinese Classics*, Detroit Monographs in Musicology No. 5 (Detroit, 1976), p. 23.

An ancient pot from the Moche culture of Peru, decorated with a depiction of panpipes played in a religious ceremony.

that surrounded music of the past. Such beliefs and the very strict rules they fostered were reality to these societies. A musician might be tempted to experiment on his instrument in private, but to play even one wrong note during a ritual in the emperor's court could be fatal.

In China of 600 B.C., for example, not only were there five sacred tones, colors, planets, etc., but there were also five punishments (far too gruesome to mention) which are enumerated, quite solemnly, in the same text. The "lucky" musician who became the head of music at the emperor's court had the responsibility of keeping things in order. His luck could run out quickly during a period of strife or famine, which, in turn, might be blamed on his inability to maintain the panpipes that "keep the world in tune." Naturally, he would suffer the consequences. Once again, this is not an isolated phenomenon, but appears over and over in different settings and with somewhat different details throughout many ancient cultures. *Sacred musical ritual does not promote experimentation.* The tension that inevitably results when musicians exercising their natural curiosity for new styles, techniques, instruments, etc., collide with an inflexible set of rules has been one of the great continuums in which the music of the world has been forged.

There are several theories about the diffusion of panpipes from East Asia to the Amerindian cultures of South America. Some scholars believe they evolved indigenously in the Americas. My opinion is that they were carried on ancient sea routes.

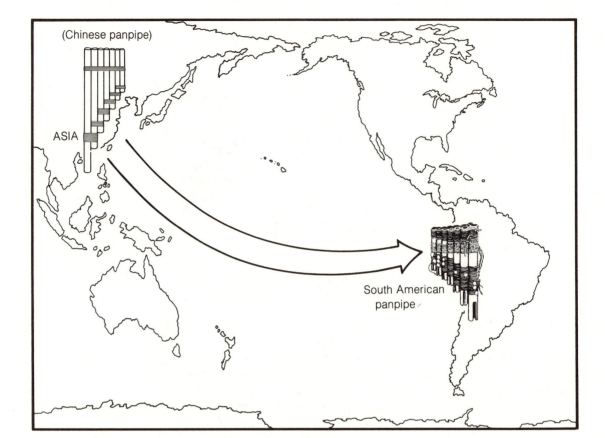

(Chinese panpipe)

ASIA

South American panpipe

QUECHUA MUSIC AFTER SPANISH CONQUEST

The formal music traditions of the Incas were destroyed along with their civilization during the Spanish invasions of the sixteenth century. Since that time, Quechua music has been influenced by other cultures, including Christian liturgical and Spanish folk music. However, a study of Quechua melodies has suggested that they are of two different styles, one reflecting an older tradition that has remained intact. (This music was recorded by the Quechua Indians of Q'eros, a region where modern influences have been minimal.) The melody of *Kan Chi Si Pas* falls into that older style. Other information supports that theory; *Kan Chi Si Pas* is performed only during a specific ritual concerned with domesticated animals, an obvious continuation of an Inca festival. South American Indians, like other cultures converted to Christianity, maintained many features of their original religion. Missionaries found it easier to Christianize a traditional festival than to eradicate it. *Throughout history, seasonal celebrations have survived in one form or another. The repetition of traditional festivals seems related to the cyclic rhythms of world culture*. (See also the discussion of Mendelssohn's *A Midsummer Night's Dream*, page 255, and the background of opera, page 172.) It is likely that music connected to those rituals might also have remained somewhat intact, especially within an isolated group like the Quechuas, who to a great extent have resisted the impact of the outside world.

STRICT RULES SURROUNDING *KAN CHI SI PAS*

With this background in mind, we now focus on the strict traditions that surround the performance of this melody, and find that they are inextricably bound up with number:

1. *Kan Chi Si Pas* is performed only at a festival celebrating three domesticated animals.
2. Only three melodies are ever played on the panpipes, one for each animal. You may have noticed that the form of the melody consists of three phrases, which are then repeated:

3. For the Quechua from Q'eros, *Kan Chi Si Pas* is actually the term for panpipes. Literally, it means "seven years an unmarried woman."
4. The panpipes consist of two rows of seven pipes. The second row is never played. (In other words, it has a ritualistic significance.) Each pipe represents luck in various aspects of life.

Clearly, we are discussing a musical ritual with specific meaning symbolized by musical-numerical configurations involving (so far) three and seven. Let's trace the thread back into Inca ritual to see if there is any connection. The threes are easy enough to find: Inca rites, like those of many ancient cultures, often involved threefold patterns. Among these were three-day fasts, celebrations for three months, singing for three nights, and sacrifices of three (unfortunate) llamas. The sevens are somewhat harder to find, but they do exist. One seven is especially intriguing in light of the meaning of *Kan Chi Si Pas*: In the Inca calendar, the seventh month was especially concerned with woman, because it was the feast of the empress.

The next clue to this musical puzzle eluded me for nearly a year. Even though I had been studying numerical relationships in ancient music systems, it never occurred to me simply to count the number of tones in the melody. Sing along with the vocal version of *Kan Chi Si Pas* and count the tones—each phrase has two groups.

The basic pattern of the melody is this:

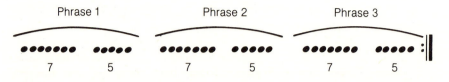

Phrase 1		Phrase 2		Phrase 3	
7	5	7	5	7	5

Besides giving us another "seven" that opens the melody, we also find a repeating pattern of 7 + 5 tones, for a total of 12. (The meter is "in 2" or "in 4.") Lastly, consider in detail the illustration of the panpipe (page 452) recovered from a grave in Ica Peru. Like the Quechua panpipe, it has two rows of seven pipes. Look at the dots on the pipes. There are 12. They are grouped in a pattern of 7 and 5.

The panpipe in the illustration is not from the Inca culture, but from that of the Ica, which predates the Inca by several hundred years. Aspects of Ica culture were absorbed into the later Inca civilization. We have stumbled upon a musical connection that is a thousand years old (and probably older), passed on directly from Ica to Inca to Quechua. *Kan Chi Si Pas* is, in fact, a musical genre involving a traditional instrument, musical form, and basic melodic pattern, and preserved as a sacred correspondence between tone, number, and ritual.

THE SONG IN THE STONE

At the center of the Inca religion, like that of so many other cultures (see picture sequence C, pages 507–10), was the sacred temple. In recent years, scholars have discovered that the positionings of many of these buildings reflect amazingly accurate astronomical measurements. In fact, a whole new field of science—*archeoastronomy*—has arisen. Much of the interest in this field has been focused on Amerindian cultures. At the same time, musicological research suggests that musical measurements may have been used to shape some of the awesome stone monuments of the ancient world. This idea, of course, is not new to these pages. In our discussion of the Medieval era, we found that in some cases, number-dominated musical techniques reflected architectural proportion (see pages 155–57). Therefore, we are dealing not with an isolated phenomenon, but with a long-range connection across culture and time.*

THE NUMBER PLAN AS A WORLDWIDE MUSICAL STRAND

Number plans of all sorts and ranges of complexity inhabit the world of music. No matter what form they take, what their derivation, what other influences they are combined with, the use of numerical plans in music may

*For further reading on "Music, the Sacred Science," see Ernest G. McClain's *The Myth of Invariance: The Origin of the Gods, Mathematics, and Music from the Rg Veda to Plato* (New York: Nicolas Hays, 1976) and *The Pythagorean Plato: Prelude to the Song Itself* (New York: Nicolas Hays, 1978).

be considered part of a world tradition. Our musical culture recognizes such plans in more familiar situations, such as the Medieval isorhythmic motet and Schoenberg's twelve-tone technique, but tends to dismiss it or fails to recognize it in other music.

Listen The following pieces all involve a threefold musical utterance. At the time each was created, both composer and audience understood the significance of this kind of "sacred musical counting."

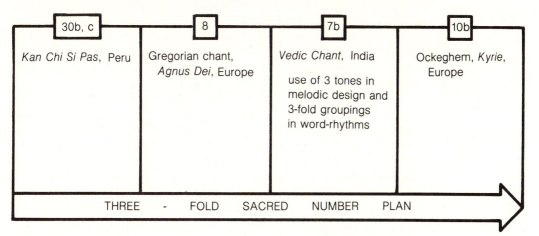

30b, c	8	7b	10b
Kan Chi Si Pas, Peru	Gregorian chant, *Agnus Dei*, Europe	*Vedic Chant*, India use of 3 tones in melodic design and 3-fold groupings in word-rhythms	Ockeghem, *Kyrie*, Europe

THREE - FOLD SACRED NUMBER PLAN

Other examples of a more complex nature abound. The Kutenai Indians of northern Idaho have a long, intricate musical ceremony—the Blanket Ritual—whose long-range form is interwoven with interlocking sets of sacred numbers, including seven and three. Among the most complex of all number-influenced systems is the "sacred-serious" music of India. In this tradition, the rationally derived patterns of rhythm, melody, and form which correspond to religious beliefs have been molded into one of the most sophisticated musical languages in the world.* The oft-held notion that only in Western notated music have number, rationality, and intellectual discipline been a shaping force is very far from the truth. Our complex systems have many counterparts in non-Western cultures. The use of rationally devised number plans, once considered a distinguishing characteristic of Western notated music, is, in fact, *a connecting strand into the greater music of the world*.

The implications of this important connection are many. Bach, for example, one of the last European composers to fashion hidden, musical-mathematical puzzles of specific, sacred intention, was composing with cultural energies that reach back beyond the Medieval world. Perhaps future generations—and perhaps some listeners now—can hear a Bach

*See Appendix X for further listening.

fugue and relate it not only to a European cathedral, but also to an Egyptian pyramid. Not only does Schoenberg's twelve-tone technique have counterparts in mathematically influenced non-Western musical styles, but the twelve-tone scale he used was worked out several thousand years ago as a correspondence between music, calendar, and astronomy. Seven-note scale-types, including our major, minor, and various church modes, can also be traced into that star-conscious past.

Three Great Developments That Have Extended Musical Possibilities

In the very distant past, there was only singing, dancing, and acting. The medium was the human body. A change came with the invention of *instruments*. Instruments became an extension of the body, with which new types of music could be fashioned. The interaction between hands and instruments is, in itself, an expansion of musical possibilities. (Just watch someone fool around on a guitar for the first time!) The next great extender of musical possibilities was *notation*. With notation, new realms of musical art could be explored. Like instruments, notation allowed musicians to consider new musical possibilities *outside the body*. It allowed them to refine those possibilities until they "sounded good." *Notation became the most basic tool of the Western tradition*. The most recent development, functioning in the same way as an extender of musical possibilities, is *recording technology* (see pages 423–25). The impact of recording technology has been an important influence on many types of music in the last ten to fifteen years. Its full impact will only be known in the future.

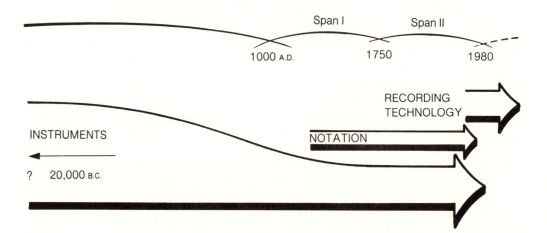

The Cultural Context of Rhythm and Body-Image

Perhaps a basic reason for not responding to music from another cultural group is that its rhythm reflects a different body-image and style of moving. Consider the motionless, meditating Hindu chanter (the *Vedic Chant* 7b, for example). The rhythm of his music is clearly connected to a totally different body-image than most people have in the West. Most Westerners have inherited cues causing them to view this meditative rhythmic style and its associated body-image (motionless, trancelike, beyond-the-body, etc.) with suspicion. Another style that does not sit well with traditional Western cues is rock. Obviously, here is a rhythmic style that purposefully seeks "abandonment" and "loss of control." Rock music thrives on a highly emphasized, unleashed dance impulse. Primal rhythmic movement is rock's basic cultural energy, as anyone who has been at a rock concert is well aware. Body-images and styles of movement associated with "loss of control" and "primal, repetitive rhythms" run against the grain of traditional Western thought. Consider, in stark contrast, the rhythmic style and body-image of the European nobility of past eras. Depicted in the graphic art of that cultural group we find, not unexpectedly, a body-image that is "reserved" and "subdued." Rarely will you find the nobility in motion. Usually they strike noble, stately poses. Clearly, the grace and magic of a Mozart minuet is in no small way a musical transformation of that aristocratic body-image and stately style of moving.

Thus, *different cultures (and cultural groups) honor different types of body-images and ways of moving. These are often encoded in the rhythmic style of their music.* In an early chapter, we discussed the notion of a *rhythmic bond* between performer and audience as an essential part of the musical experience. Now, what happens when listeners from one cultural group hear music in a rhythmic style different from their own? Sometimes, no bond is formed. Listeners and music are "out of sync." And what if the listener has negative cues about the "meaning" of that rhythmic style? The separation between music and listener is then even more severe. This phenomenon reaches far beyond notions of "good" and "bad" music. It reflects the fundamental difficulty of responding to music in a multistylistic culture.*

Popular and Serious

Walk into a large record store and you encounter a reality of our musical culture: the classification system of the records reflects how we perceive the

*For further reading: *Beyond Culture*, by Edward T. Hall (Garden City, N.Y., 1976); Chapter 5, "Rhythm and Body Movement," presents a related scientific view of this matter, not especially oriented to music, however.

music of the world. The music is organized into historical and regional divisions. Those categories, despite many inconsistencies, represent musical styles developed by various cultural groups. In this book, we have traced some of these traditions rather closely, while at the same time establishing many of the deeper connections "between the bins," so to speak. Our final discussion concerns one of the basic divisions in that store, and, to a great extent, in our culture: that of "popular" and "serious" (or "classical"), a strand we have been following throughout this study. (It will be useful to glance back through the sections dealing with this issue: pages 108–9, 361–64.) The task at hand is to explore both the cultural-historical basis for this split and the fading notion that "good" music automatically means "serious" or "classical." Books about music are always playing "catch up with musical reality." We are only following a reality that can be visibly experienced in that record store: more and more people are browsing on both sides of the aisle. And there is a good deal of new music being recorded that does not lend itself to the old classification system. We are in a period when the bond between "popular" and "serious" music (which has always been there) is being strengthened, while the differences (which have been important) are being minimized.

We begin tracing this strand with a description that many will find familiar:

> The new music . . . is noisy and deafens the ear unceasingly. Buffoons and dwarfs who have the appearance of monkeys enter and men and women perform together in a mixed manner . . . This music does not deserve to be discussed and cannot be linked with the music of ancient times. This is the way of modern music.*

THE ANCIENT CULTURAL ROOT

The author of this quote lived in China, sometime around 400 B.C. The quote reflects a basic set of beliefs not limited to the Chinese, but shared by several ancient cultures. The West received its version of this cultural strand directly through Greece and the Judeo-Christian tradition. We choose China as our entry point into this network of beliefs for two reasons:

1. It was referred to in a previous discussion; in other words, we are tracing the places at which the various strands of world music overlap, as continuing proof of their connectedness. For our purposes, the Chinese version is as good as its Greek counterpart (a more direct contact).

2. Virtually no ancient Greek music has survived. Chinese traditions of "sacred-serious" music, on the other hand, have been more durable. There are many recordings of "classical" Chinese music

---

*Kaufmann, pp. 42–43.

which most likely reflect this ancient style. (See Appendix X for listening suggestions.)

The set of beliefs itself juxtaposes haunting perceptions of music as heightened experience with strict notions of *how* music fulfills that goal, *what* its purpose is in doing so, and *who* is the beneficiary of its strict hierarchy of musical values. The following excerpts suggest the essence of these musical-cultural beliefs:

Excerpts from Ancient Chinese Texts

The harmony between heaven and earth is reflected in the harmony of the best in music. The same order that exists between heaven and earth is reflected in the best of ceremony.*

He [Emperor Shun] undertook a journey of inspection . . . he made burnt offerings in honor of heaven and for the spirits of the mountains and rivers. Then the eastern nobles were permitted to appear before him and he corrected their [dating of the] seasons, months, and days [by adjusting the calendar]. He attended to the regulation of the pitch-pipes [*panpipes*].**

In time of confusion, ceremonies are overlooked and disregarded and music is licentious. . . . When this happens the sounds are sad and vulgar, cheerful but unsettled. They [music] are performed carelessly and it is easy to desecrate them. Virtue is forgotten. . . . Desire towards excess arises and the peace of noble harmony is destroyed. The wise *man despises this* attitude.†

If the sentiments are pure and deep, the music is beautiful and clear. . . . Music does not tolerate any pretense or hypocrisy. . . . Music means joy. . . . The superior man is happy to find the right path and the inferior man is happy to obtain things which he wants.††

Together with music come the correct movements of the body; the bowing and tensing, the bending and raising (of the head), the movements and numbers of performers and the tempo, fast and slow.‡

Music has close relations with the ethos of the time. Therefore, those who are aware of sound but do not know the tones are animals. Those who know the tones but not the actual music are ignorant. Only the noble and distinguished persons comprehend music.‡‡

*Ibid., p. 35.
**Ibid., p. 23.
†Ibid., p. 39.
††Ibid., P. 40.
‡Ibid., p. 35.
‡‡Ibid., p. 33.

These quotes have provided a glimpse of a musical tradition tied to its culture at a very deep level. The following ideas summarize the set of cues implied in these and other excerpts from sacred texts of ancient China:

1. Music is strictly divided into "good" and "bad."
2. "Good" music is the controlled, "serious-sacred" style of the priest-nobility class.
3. One of the strict controls of music is the very careful and precise measurements of tones (music as "sacred science").
4. Music mirrors formal court and religious ceremonies.
5. There is a direct relationship between musical style and body movements of the nobility. In this case, the style may be described as "reserved," "controlled," "elegant."
6. Listening to and understanding "good" music distinguishes the nobility from common people.
7. All of these traits were related to a natural order of the universe conceived as a hierarchy from high (heaven) to low (earth).

In many ancient Chinese texts are excerpts like the one on page 460 (the description of "modern music") describing tensions between older and newer styles. There are also attacks on outside influences that corrupt "pure" styles. Before we go any further, it will be vital to understand that this tension is a worldwide and age-old phenomenon. Most cultures evolved special "serious-sacred" musical rites which were carefully preserved. It may be suggested that the more deeply felt music is, the more strictly it may be protected and isolated. There is a universal tendency to say "My music is good; their music is bad!" Our concern in this discussion is with the specific set of cues *we* have inherited that define "good" music.

THE CULTURAL MODEL IN EUROPE
The historian of European culture would need to change very little in the Chinese excerpts quoted above to describe the social-religious framework in the formative era of European notated music. "Serious and sacred" notated music evolved in Europe according to the specific needs of the Church and the nobility. Although there were frequent differences in their musical requirements, and while both often used folk materials as a starting point, each required a style clearly distinguishable from everyday popular music. First, we will consider the Church.

THE CHURCH
The conflict between the Church and "evil" music and dance in early Europe is legendary. A basic thrust of Christianity, and, by extension, of Western culture, has been to subdue and control uninhibited body movement. One practical reason was to break away from older religions whose rites

involved ecstatic dance and seasonal fertility rituals. Many documents survive that ban such activities as dancing in graveyards, a clear remnant of an older religious rite. Various ancient traditions lingered on in different guises into the Renaissance and, in some cases, well beyond. The Church was also concerned about traveling entertainers who sang the ancient songs and chanted old spells, and thus kept pre-Christian traditions alive. As an example of just how long ancient rites held on, listen to the *Ossianic Chant* 7c from the Hebrides (Scotland). Although now considered a folk legend, it is actually a vestige of an older religious tradition (which, by the way, is usually unknown to the person who sings it today). The Church did not look kindly on popular songs and dances, especially those with secular themes. To be a musician outside the Church (or nobility) was to risk being considered a very undesirable character.

THE NOBILITY

Like their Chinese counterparts, the European nobility required music that identified, reflected, and embodied their values. Of special interest to us is their reserved and formal body-image. European aristocratic court ceremonies engendered a rhythmic musical style that we characterize as "elegant," "graceful," "formal." These qualities, along with many others, reflected the distinction between aristocratic music and that of the common people. Thus, through the powerful influence of Church and court, a basic set of related cues that defined "serious" music was woven into the European consciousness. We can represent the extreme positions in the "popular–serious" split by the following continuum:

Extreme Positions of "Popular–Serious" Split in European Culture

profane	sacred
common	aristocratic-noble
low	high
folk	art music
popular	serious
body-based	notation-based
learned by rote	learned from notation
vernacular	cultivated
primitive	evolved
crude, vulgar, cheap	refined, polite, elegant
obvious	subtle
uninhibited movement	controlled movement
spontaneous	planned
for the moment	eternal
improvised, changing	exact, precise
simple	complex

This tension has been crucial to the history of music. In previous discussions, we have concluded that composers were always very conscious of their social status. The lure of a musical career was greatly enhanced by the possibility of social advancement. (Consider Mozart and his father!) From Medieval times right into the twentieth century, to be a "serious" composer has been an honorable profession. In past centuries, people were influenced by the real hierarchy of class distinctions. Everyone was on the way up, and, to be blunt, they often reserved their greatest scorn for those immediately below them. The professional "serious" musician who attained some social status might become the most ardent critic of popular styles.

As we have pointed out before, the tension between the ideas on either side of the "popular–serious" continuum created an active, changing middle ground that continually provided new energy for the musical culture. Some examples below, together with those discussed on pages 361–64, will sum up this idea.

Consider the Bach *Gigue* [19] . This wonderful music would never have come into being if the "popular" folk dance—the jig—had not been transformed and altered by energies from the right side of that continuum. But alternatively, that Bach *Gigue* would not exist had it not been for its popular model. Furthermore, the basic response to this genre, be it a "down-home" jig or a "learned" *Gigue*, is a body-based, spontaneous dance impulse. The notion that Bach didn't move to his music, in his own version of "down-home" spontaneity, is very wrong. And any performance of a Bach dance piece devoid of dance energy is not only boring, but historically inaccurate. Although Bach lived in a time when a learned *Gigue* was considered vastly superior to a common jig, he didn't stop to consider that when he composed. Those cues had become part of an internalized, and in his case, spontaneous language. Never mind where they came from; they were his musical reality. Had Bach been born in the twentieth century to a family in Spain, had his father been a cafe guitarist instead of a church organist, Bach might have become the world's greatest flamenco guitarist. *Each musical genius is born into a world of cues, both musical and cultural. These are profound determinants of the style a genius will take on as his or her living language.*

Opera is a topic that throws the popular–serious continuum into confusion. This genre began as the transformation of popular song and drama into an aristocratic, "learned" style. But throughout its history, it has been continually nourished and sustained by popular influences. For example, consider the music of Verdi. To many native Italians (as well as to many others), a Verdi opera totally transcends the categories of popular and serious. But what happens when Verdi is performed in another country? The perception of his style can slip either way. To some, a Verdi opera is aristocratic nonsense; to others, it is far too popular and obvious. Operas that today might be considered very learned may well have been wildly appealing to many audiences in the past, much in the way movies like *Star*

Wars appeal to mass audiences today. Once again, we find there is tremendous flexibility within the popular–serious continuum, depending upon personal taste and background.

Imagine a listener who doesn't like "classical" music, but is devoted to the music of Stevie Wonder. The harmonic language Stevie wields so effortlessly would never have existed had it not been for the Western notated tradition. Once again, we realize that connections between "popular" and "serious" music are fundamental to both traditions. We are examining a cultural reality that *originated* in strong social notions of "good" and "bad" music. This cultural mechanism created a dynamic back-and-forth continuum that was vital for the development of many of the styles we know today, from Bach to jazz, from Beethoven to rock.

THE POPULAR–SERIOUS CUES OF THE WEST ARE NOT UNIVERSAL

You might think that since the cues we inherited that separate popular and sacred-serious music are so old, they must be universal. They're not. It is only in very recent times that we have begun to consider the music of the whole world with fewer inherited prejudices. And only recently have the lessons of that study given rise to a more accurate understanding that all types of music, from all cultural groups, utilizing all types of cues, have legitimacy and value in their own right. *Thorough study and familiarity with any musical style often reveals unexpected levels of complexity, stated or unstated sets of controls, rules, and nuances.* This applies to all current popular styles, including "country," "soul," "rock," etc. We now understand that high-level musicians from many styles work hard on their craft, refining, developing, and exploring musical possibilities.

Perhaps the most important insights we have recently acquired have to do with rhythm. Our traditional cues concerning rhythm and movement are not universal. Many cultures *do not* equate powerful, emphasized dance and movement with negative values. They have followed cultural streams which honored different cues than our own. For example, the *Ramayana Chant* 2a from Bali, which by our standard set of cues is "primitive" because of its powerful repetitive rhythms, is both sacred and serious to that culture.

One of the great problems in understanding musical response is that *responding to one cue may set off an automatic correspondence with others.* Therefore, if an inherited image of "serious-sacred" music comes from the right side of that continuum, it may take only one cue, like "very emphasized, repeated dance rhythms," to set off all the other cues on that side and thus mask our awareness of other musical features. From another viewpoint, if you have an automatic response to "classical" music as "stuffy" and "without a good beat," with that one superficial cue you are "switching off" some of the greatest music ever created.

It is very important to understand that *cues may still be active long after their social origins have faded.* The truth is, cues become automatic and often separate from their original meaning. As we have seen, the most passionate advocate of Amerindian music may have a hard time bypassing an automatic negative response, absorbed through television and film.

A good way to understand all this is to imagine that some musical motive, considered "cheap" and "vulgar" today, had become part of our "serious" musical traditions but *without negative connotations.* Suppose, for example, that the following melodic motive

served (without the words, of course) as a frequent cadential formula in "serious" symphonies.

Instead of being considered "light," "cheap," or "vulgar," those same notes and rhythm could have become "serious," "epic," "meaningful." Each culture considers as universal its accumulated cues relating music to heightened experience. None of them is. Only music the art, in all its many dialects, can be considered in that light.

Toward a Deeper Understanding of Music as Art

Part of the stress of our time is that cues from different traditions are in conflict. Great strands of music and history are colliding with each other, often propelled onward by the electronic media—television, records, radio, and film.

Let us go back to the "Soul Train" dancers. Many black Americans have retained their roots in West African cultures which honor complex rhythms, not only played, but danced out with a heightened acting impulse. That the highly controlled style of the "Soul Train" dancers seems so free is only a measure of how refined it has become. Thus, if this highly crafted art sets off a few of those "primitive" cues, the nuance, the subtlety, the elegance of the entire performance is lost in misunderstanding.

Our culture allows each of us to follow any musical path we choose. No musical stereotype can be applied to anyone in our time. During the twentieth century, the inherited demarcation between popular and serious styles has become obscured through massive interaction with highly crafted music using many sets of cues. Popular music has lost, to a great degree, its inferior artistic status. More and more listeners are comfortable with both traditions. The ultimate awareness that may dominate post-Modern music will certainly involve abandoning the old "hierarchy habit" of comparing musical styles to one another and labeling them "superior" or "inferior." In that era, which is already upon us, similarities (which have always existed) and not differences (which will always exist) among all musical styles will be the foundation for more universal musical response.

Good music simply means music that moves the listener into a heightened state of being. It can come from any style, place, or time. There is good and bad music, but there are no good or bad styles. Within each style, a group of people share a set of cues. Equipped with these cues they are able to experience and determine what music is very good, what music is ordinary, and what music is just plain bad.

There is a kind of music we may call "art music," or "highly crafted" music. It too may come from any style. Its special features are these: It is created by highly talented musicians; it is often worked upon, manipulated, planned, refined, developed, or otherwise shaped by genius and inspiration. As examples, consider the musics of Aaron Copland, Joni Mitchell, Duke Ellington, Elliott Carter, and Stevie Wonder.

Some years before his death, Duke Ellington was recommended for a Pulitzer Prize special citation. The recommendation was unanimous among the members of the music jury. The Advisory Board of the Pulitzer Prize rejected that recommendation. Perhaps, someday when all the cues fall into place, they will reconsider.

QUESTIONS

For the following questions, find any false statement(s) and correct them by changing the word(s) in italics. More than one statement may be false; all the statements may be true.

1. The idea of "hidden basics" suggests

    (a) letting go of *outer stylistic details*.

    (b) shifting toward more *basic impulses* that often require less description.

(c) that the listener *should not* trust impulses that cannot be defined.

(d) that the listener *need not always* seek details to back up musical response.

2. Which of the following are found in many musical styles throughout the world? (Cross out any that don't apply.)

(a) chant

(b) song

(c) dramatic plan

(d) number plan

(e) dance impulse

(f) Viennese lyricism

(g) leader and group

(h) musical gesture of mourning

(i) repetition and contrast

(j) combination of basic impulses

(k) sacred musical impulse

(l) lullaby impulse

3. The Quechua piece *Kan Chi Si Pas* demonstrates

(a) *a sacred number plan* in musical design.

(b) the importance of *genre* in musical culture.

(c) the importance of *instruments* in the preservation of musical traditions.

(d) the importance of a *cultural chain*.

(e) the importance of *religious ritual* in the history of world music.

4. Recording technology

(a) is similar to the development of *instruments and dance* in its function of extending musical possibilities.

(b) is an *important tool* in some highly crafted musical styles of the twentieth century.

(c) allows for the exploration of *texture and timbre*.

(d) *decreases* the potential for listening beyond style in today's musical culture.

5. Concerning the historic roots between "popular" and "serious" music in Western culture:

(a) These roots extend back *before* European civilization.

(b) They involve the relation between music and *religious ritual*.

(c) They involve the relation between music and the *nobility*.

(d) The cues that define these types *are universal*.

Appendix I
Additional Composers and Listening

The material in Appendix I is designed to serve several purposes:

1. to expand the information in the text with brief surveys of additional composers and their music;
2. to supply a continuing reference section for the interested reader;
3. to provide a list of recommendations for building a record collection. NAWM numbers refer to the *Norton Anthology of Western Music,* a collection of records you will probably find in your college library. Other titles found under *Suggested Listening* are usually available in many commercial recordings. Where I have specified a particular performance under a certain label, it is either because no other recording exists or because the recommended performance is the preferable one.

To facilitate continuity and underscore context, the composers are grouped according to historical span.

Medieval

Leonin (second half of the twelfth century, French)
Virtually nothing is known about Leonin other than his name and some very general evidence that suggests he was connected to the Cathedral of

Notre Dame (Paris) around the time of its building, 1163–1200. Evidently, it was this man who composed the *Magnus liber organi* (Great Book of Organum), a collection intended for liturgical use in the cathedral. These organa comprise the first body of polyphonic music in the Western notated tradition that can be attributed to a specific person. Thus, the name of Leonin occupies a landmark position in the history of music. Leonin's organa were written for two voices (see page 00). The development of this genre into three- and four-voice structures was the work of his successor, Perotin.

Perotin (1183?–1238?, French)
Like his predecessor Leonin, little is known of Perotin. Apparently, he was the next important composer to serve as choirmaster at Notre Dame Cathedral. Perotin revised and enhanced the *Magnus liber* by expanding it to three and four voices. Perotin's organa have a unique sound. As in Leonin's two-voice organa, the chant melody is the musical foundation, its tones stretched out into long drones. These tones may have been played on an organ and sung by several choristers. The upper voices sing short melodic motives which in some performances may have a dancing quality. The resulting texture—the drawn-out, slow-motion chant melody and the faster polyphonic melodies in the upper voices—unites two levels of rhythmic activity in a remarkable way. The effect we hear on records is certainly quite tame compared to how it must have sounded in

470

the enclosed space of the cathedral. This is music that cannot be separated from architecture and religion. If you imagine that you are in that cathedral while you are listening to the music, you may be brought closer to its Medieval aesthetic basis than if you consider it solely in musical terms. Leonin, Perotin, and their anonymous contemporaries have come to be known as the *Notre Dame School*.

Suggested Listening

Leonin and Perotin,
Music of the Gothic Era—The Early Music Consort of London, David Munrow, conductor (DG ARC-2723045)

Adam de la Halle (c. 1250–1300?, French)
Adam de la Halle was both poet and composer. His art reflects a time when poetry and song had not yet been completely separated into different pursuits. In this era, poetry was still often sung. Adam de la Halle was part of the *trouvère* tradition of Northern France. Called *troubadours* in the south of France and *Minnesingers* in Germany, these musician-poets were associated with the aristocracy. Their counterparts in popular culture were the *jongleurs* (or *minstrels*), the "working musicians" of their time. Of low social status, the jongleurs were considered outcasts by the Church. Their varied talents and activities point to the reason for this attitude; not only did they sing and play, they also juggled, acted, danced, chanted spells, and recited (sang) ancient legends and myths. Mixing the old with the new, these popular entertainers provided a musical-cultural connection to pre-Christian times. A fluid relationship existed between low-class minstrel and aristocratic trouvère. A very talented minstrel could, on occasion, rise to the higher status of trouvère. Evidently, Adam de la Halle did just that. Of humble birth, his talent carried him into aristocratic society, an early example of how music could be used for social advancement. Furthermore, minstrels were often employed by trouvères or troubadours as musical collaborators, suggesting that this musical tradition was integrally related to the popular music of the day. Adam de la Halle composed both monophonic songs and polyphonic pieces. In addition, he created music-dramas (the most famous being *Robin et Marion*) which most likely were based in popu-

lar folk tradition. Adam de la Halle and his contemporaries stand at a turning point of European music, as the anonymous lyrical traditions of word and song were being transformed into the learned, notated styles of the trouvères and troubadours.

Suggested Listening

Robins m'aime, (from *Robin et Marion* (NAWM 7)
Motets: *Music of the Gothic Era*—The Early Music Consort of London, David Munrow, conductor (DG ARC-2723045)

Guillaume de Machaut (c. 1300–77, French)
Machaut was one of the most extraordinary creative spirits of the Medieval era. His literary achievements alone would have insured his fame. As a poet he has been compared with Chaucer, Petrarch, Boccaccio, and Dante. Although of humble origins, he enjoyed close contact with royalty throughout his life. He served as secretary to the king of Bohemia, accompanying him on frequent trips across Europe, and was appointed a canon of the Church (a minor church office) by the pope. Machaut was the leading composer of his time, and ultimately became recognized as one of the most important in history.

Most of Machaut's output was secular. Since he was a poet, it is not surprising that his compositions are quite lyrical (a quality that may not be immediately obvious to contemporary ears). A notable example is his *Quant Theseus—Ne quier veoir* (NAWM 20). This is a *double ballade*, a poetry-based genre. It contains two poems (one by Machaut), which are sung at the same time. The form is strophic, and the phrases follow the interlocking design of the poems. There is a marvelous interplay between its linear and harmonic aspects. The Medieval delight in contrapuntal opposition is evident, yet moments of consonant harmony, especially at the ends of phrases, balance out the often dissonant interweaving of the voices.

Machaut's most famous work is the *Messe de Notre Dame* (Notre Dame Mass). Its reputation is twofold: 1) It is the first complete Mass that has been attributed to a single composer (it had been common practice to combine various Mass movements by different composers)—this Mass, therefore, is one of the earliest long-range musical designs of notated polyphony; 2) it is a remarkable work in which melodic lyricism is combined with more esoteric musical qualities like isorhythm, to produce a unified musical experience.

Suggested Listening

Quant Theseus—Ne quier veoir (NAWM 20)
Various motets: *Music of the Gothic Era*—The Early Music Consort of London, David Monrow, conductor (DG ARC-2723045)
Messe de Notre Dame, Agnus Dei (NAWM 21)

Francesco Landini (c. 1325–97, Italian)

Landini was the son of a painter. During his childhood he contracted smallpox and lost his sight, a misfortune that most likely turned him to music. Landini became famous not only as a composer, but as a singer and organist. Like Machaut, he was a poet as well. In a narrative about life in Florence written in 1389, Landini is described as taking part in discussions of philosophy, politics, art, etc. All this activity may be understood as part of early *humanism*, the important cultural basis of all the arts in fourteenth-century Italy (and later, throughout the Renaissance). As one might expect of a poet, Landini's music is quite lyrical, a trait clearly heard in his ballata *Non avrà ma' pietà* (NAWM 19). The ballata was a genre closely related to poetry and dance. This one is "in three." Tapping out the meter along with the music will help you experience the graceful, somewhat syncopated polyphonic style. Landini's musical language was a synthesis of Italian and French practices, once again suggesting the type of cross-fertilization that continually enriched the Western notated tradition.

Suggested Listening

Ballata: *Non avrà ma' pietà* (NAWM 19)

Renaissance

John Dunstable (c. 1390–1453, English)

Although Dunstable's importance was recognized in his own time, very little about his life is known. It seems likely that he was in the service of the Duke of Bedford, and that his activities embraced not only music but mathematics, astronomy, and astrology. For a long time, Dunstable was credited with having introduced the English style of consonant polyphony to the European continent, but this is now considered the accomplishment of several English composers, of whom Dunstable was certainly the greatest. What is most significant is that in Dunstable's music we can hear the beginning of the Renaissance style—smooth-flowing melodies combined with predominantly consonant polyphonic textures. His compositions include isorhythmic motets, sections of the Mass, and secular songs. As has often been suggested in this book, a composer's living language usually has roots in the music of his or her culture. Dunstable's consonant polyphony had been evolving in English music for some time. You can hear this by comparing Dunstable's *Quam pulchra es* (NAWM 25) with the anonymous Medieval *Fulget coelistis* (NAWM 23).

Suggested Listening

Quam pulchra es (NAWM 25)
Motets—Pro Cantione Antique, H. Bläserkreis (DG ARC-2533291)
Sacred and Secular Music—Purcell Consort (Argo 2RG-681)

Guillaume Dufay (c. 1400–74, French)

Like so many early composers, Dufay received his musical training as a choirboy. Among his first compositions was a reworking of a piece by the master musician of the Cathedral of Cambrai, suggesting the importance of models to the absorption of a living musical language. He was strongly influenced by both English and Italian music. Merging with his French heritage, these several influences were molded into a personal style, reflecting the type of rich interplay between regional traditions that was so vital to the evolution of Western notated music. Dufay, whose compositions include both sacred and secular pieces, became one of the most famous composers of his time.

Dufay's works range from "simple" harmonizations of Gregorian chant to elaborately constructed Masses and motets. In his *Conditor alme siderum* (NAWM 26) we hear one of those straightforward harmonizations of a chant melody. (First the chant is presented alone, then with the harmonization.) More than half of all Dufay's works are of this type. They represent a basic source for his art, the musical threads with which he fashioned more complex, esoteric structures. He also wrote many polyphonic *chansons*, revealing his ability to create appealing, catchy melodies. Equally appealing is his isorhythmic motet *Nuper rosarum flores* (NAWM 27), whose flowing lyricism encodes a complex, hidden mathematical structure (see pages 156–57). That Dufay's musical world ranged from the "simple" to the most complex of musical designs is a testament to the full scope of his genius.

(see pages 156–57)

Suggested Listening

Hymn: *Conditor alme siderum* (NAWM 26)
Motet: *Nuper rosarum flores* (NAWM 27)
Missa "Se la face ay pale," on *Music of Guillaume Dufay*—Early Music Consort of London, David Munrow, conductor (Seraphim S-60267)

Johannes Ockeghem (c. 1410–97, Franco-Flemish)

Although he composed in secular genres, it is for his Masses and sacred motets that Ockeghem is best known. For many listeners, these works have a special quality of "vastness and mystery." Their sound is somewhat dark and austere, partly due to his frequent use of the low range of men's voices. Polyphony and harmony in this vocal register can produce a dense, even somber effect, a quality that the composer seems to have cultivated, probably because he himself was a bass.

Ockeghem's polyphony leans towards *linear* organization, in which independence of vocal lines is often at a maximum. In this respect, his is not the typical Renaissance style, which sounds more chordal. An Ockeghem texture may begin with an equal balance between the linear and harmonic, only to become suddenly enmeshed in polyphonic complexity in which our attention shifts to individual lines (the *Kyrie* 10b , for example). Ockeghem's long, intricate, sometimes florid vocal lines are a delight to singers (the good ones, that is!).

Ockeghem's music has little of the "warm" chordal effects that were characteristic of the Italian tradition. Unlike many other Northern composers, he spent little or no time in Italy, and his style represents the more severe, intricate polyphony of the North. But it is not without passion. Ockeghem's works are imbued with a mystical intensity that is almost Medieval in flavor.

Suggested Listening

Johannes Ockeghem—Pomerium Musices, Alexander Blachly, director (Nonesuch H-71336)

Josquin des Prez (c. 1440–1521, Franco-Flemish)

The first mention of Josquin is as an adult singer in the Cathedral at Milan, Italy. However, he was probably born in northern France, and his early musical training was certainly that of a choirboy. It is not surprising that he went to Italy as a young man. Interchange between the Italian and the Northern regions (France, Netherlands, Holland) was a basic source of musical enrichment in the Renaissance.

Josquin was one of the most respected and influential composers of his day. That his work was compared by one observer to the art of Michelangelo suggests an important aspect of this composer's style: in his music, there is clarity, balance, and order, yet it is deeply expressive. The textures are rich, yet each voice can be heard. There is a perfect balance between polyphony and harmony. Although a very imprecise word when applied to music, "purity" seems to evoke something that is central to Josquin's music. His was a "classical" Renaissance style in which beauty found expression through balance and restraint.

Like other great composers of his era, Josquin's output embraced the various genres of the day. His work ranges from deeply religious Mass settings and motets, to playful, secular pieces.

Suggested Listening

Tu solus, qui facis mirabilia (NAWM 29)
Mille regretz (NAWM 45a)
Secular works—Nonesuch Consort, Joshua Rifkin, conductor (Nonesuch 71261)

Tomás Luis de Victoria (1548–1611, Spanish)

Two basic influences on the music of this late Renaissance composer were his religious devotion and Spanish heritage. Victoria received his earliest musical training as a choirboy in the Cathedral of Avila. As a young man he went to Rome to study at a Jesuit college. In Italy, Victoria came under the influence of Palestrina (perhaps as his student). The absorption of certain aspects of Palestrina's style was an important factor in his music. However, Victoria had his own living musical language whose "dialect" was different from that of the great Italian master.

Victoria's life was devoted to the Church. He was ordained a priest, and, after some years in Italy, returned to Spain to live out his days in religious service. Unlike most composers of the time, he wrote no secular music. The scope of his musical world was small, yet within it he created unique masterpieces imbued with radiant religious beauty. Spanish Catholicism is noted for its mystical, ascetic devotion. This cultural strand provided a special ingredient that shaped Victoria's music. As one observer has stated, "In his music there is terror, tenderness, passion, and devotion." One has the feeling that unleashed religious *expression*, rather than strictly musical considerations, are the ultimate source of his art. It would not be wrong to think of him as having a special type of romantic aesthetic (see classical–romantic continuum on page 228), in which artistic power arises from abandonment to religious fervor. By contrast, the music of Palestrina seems to have been shaped by a more classical aesthetic. (Please remember that both composers are Renaissance musicians! These are the applications of the terms in a universal sense.)

Suggested Listening

Four motets—Choral Sant-Jordi de Barcelone; O. Martorelle, conductor (Westminster Gold (ABC) WGS-8277)

William Byrd (1543–1623, English)

Byrd probably received his initial musical training under Thomas Tallis. By age twenty he was already organist and choir director at the Lincoln Cathedral. Early in his career, it seems that Byrd "embarked on a deliberate program of experimentation, both in the kinds of music he wrote and in the composers whose work he looked to." In effect, the composer was imitating various styles and models drawn from his musical world. Out of these, he eventually molded a personal language. Such self-motivated learning is not uncommon in the case of true genius, and Byrd was certainly of that caliber, recognized during his life as one of the leading musicians of his country. Gaining favor with Queen Elizabeth, he was granted, along with Tallis, the exclusive right to print music in England for a period of time. This support in high places was an important factor in Byrd's career.

Byrd's output embraced many genres. On the secular side he composed instrumental works for consorts and keyboard, as well as madrigals, in which he often used English folk songs. The composer's love of that tradition, and its inclusion in his musical language, suggests once again the essential relationship between "popular" and "learned" styles throughout the history of Western music.

Another side of Byrd's character was expressed in his sacred music. A deeply religious man, he adhered to Catholicism during a dangerous period of official persecution. While he also composed for the Anglican Church, music for the Catholic cause occupied a central position in his output. Chief among these works are many motets and three Masses. In the motets, Byrd displayed a wide range of inventiveness and a talent for the dramatic. His Masses, on the other hand, are more restrained and universal in character. Comparisons between Byrd's motets and Masses reveal a shift in aesthetics that can be cautiously considered on the classical–romantic continuum (see page 228). Of special beauty are the concluding sections in the Masses—set to the words "Dona nobis pacem" (give us peace)—which certainly are as eloquent and deeply felt a call for universal compassion as one will ever encounter. Their impact is intensified by that elusive "sense of restraint," a quality that sometimes allows the most profound pathos to be set free.

Suggested Listening

Pavana Lachrymae (NAWM 98b)

Motet: *Laudate pueri dominum* (NAWM 34) This motet is for six voices. You will hear a *fugal* opening in which there are six entries of the initial motive.

Masses—King's College Cambridge Choir, David Willcocks, director (ARGO 5362). The masses are for three, four, and five voices.

Thomas Tallis (c. 1505–85, English)

English music of the Renaissance has a distinct character. Perhaps its most identifiable quality is a rich harmonic sound arising from extremely singable, flowing polyphony. Thomas Tallis, considered one of England's greatest composers, was of this tradition. A church organist, he lived through most of the sixteenth century, a time marked by great upheavals in English religious life. As a musician to the Chapel Royal, he com-

474

posed for both Anglican and Catholic liturgies in accordance with the religion of the monarch in power. His motets in English were for the Anglican service, those in Latin for the Catholic (the same is true of the works of William Byrd).

Among Tallis's works are several remarkable masterpieces. *Spem in alium* is a motet for *forty* separate parts—eight choirs of five voices each, probably composed for the fortieth birthday of Queen Elizabeth I. In the annals of vocal music, there is nothing quite like its massive blocks of harmony, arising from sweeping, lyrical lines. In an age which believed in the Harmony of the Spheres (see page 160), the sound of this motet must have been as close to a "singing sky" as one could imagine. Among Tallis's masterpieces are two sets of Lamentations to the words of the prophet Jeremiah. *Lamentations I* is marked by an intense, somber lyricism. From its opening measures, the tension mounts slowly as one voice interweaves and sometimes clashes with another in a polyphonic web. The tension is released in the quiet, dramatic utterance of the closing on the words, "Jerusalem, Jerusalem," certainly one of the great moments in all of music.

Suggested Listening

Tallis—The Choir of King's College Cambridge, David Willcocks, director (ARGO ZRG 5479)
Motets of Thomas Tallis—The Clerks of Oxenford, David Wulstan, director (Seraphim S-60256)

Orlando Gibbons (1583–1625, English)
The details of Gibbons's early life suggest something that is quite evident in his music—a connection at the deepest level to the great tradition of English church music. As a boy, he sang in the choir at King's College Cambridge, a group which still exists. Even at that early age, he was absorbing a musical language that was sacred in meaning and awesome in polyphonic and harmonic richness. His life was spent as composer, organist, and keyboard player in the service of church and court. His secular works include madrigals, music for consorts, and solo keyboard pieces. These are outnumbered by his compositions for the Anglican Church, which comprise complete services as well as many anthems.

Gibbons lived in a time when the musical culture was in transition between the Renaissance and the Baroque. Accordingly, characteristics of both eras can be found in his style. The polyphonic anthems (for example, *I Am the Resurrection* 12) carry on the older tradition, while other pieces (especially the hymns) clearly point to the coming age. They are more homophonic, in quite regular meter, and often with instrumental accompaniment. His greatest works, however, were the polyphonic ones, making him the last of the great English Renaissance composers.

Suggested Listening

Anthems and Songs of Praise—The Clerkes of Oxenford, David Wulstan, director (Nonesuch H-71374)

Giovanni Pierluigi da Palestrina (c. 1525–94, Italian)
Born in the town of Palestrina, he is perhaps the best known of the late Renaissance composers. Although he composed many secular madrigals, his most significant musical activity was centered in the Roman Catholic Church. The essential spirit of Palestrina's music is that of intense religious devotion expressed through a maximum of artistic restraint, a quality due, in no small part, to the religious climate of the Counter-Reformation.

Musically, Palestrina was a conservative. He rejected many of the innovations and explorations of more "advanced" composers such as Lassus. A notable example of this attitude was his steadfast avoidance of chromatic harmony, whose dramatic, sensual effects were quite in vogue. Palestrina pursued a style in which the complexities of polyphony would not obscure clarity of texture or text. There is a calmness to his rhythms and melodic shapes, a quality rooted in Gregorian chant. In sharp contrast with the more radical approach of many of his contemporaries, Palestrina "captured the essence of the sober, conservative aspect of the Counter-Reformation in a polyphony of utter purity, detached from any secular suggestion." In terms of aesthetics, he may be considered on the classical side of the classical-romantic continuum.

Palestrina's music was to have a lasting effect on the European musical culture. Generations of composers were to study his polyphony as models of traditional counterpoint. A prolific composer, he completed over 100 Masses, 375 motets, 140 madrigals, and many other works.

Suggested Listening

Pope Marcellus Mass, and any of his other Masses, motets and madrigals

Orlando di Lasso (Roland de Lassus) (1532–94, Franco-Flemish)

One of the great composers of the late Renaissance, Orlando di Lasso's life and music demonstrate the interplay among traditions that enriched the Western tradition. Born in a Franco-Flemish province, Lasso supposedly was kidnapped three times as a boy because of the beauty of his voice. By age twelve, he was in musical service to the aristocracy and went to Italy, where he absorbed the Italian tradition into his musical language. He eventually ended up in Germany, where he was employed for the rest of his days. It is not surprising that we find a panorama of European genres in his works: Italian madrigals, French *chansons* (in the Renaissance, similar to the madrigal), German *lieder* (in the Renaissance, also similar to the madrigal). He also composed in the more universal Mass and motet genres.

With Palestrina, Lasso was one of the great masters of the late Renaissance. Unlike his Italian counterpart, however, Lasso was given to more adventurous musical expression. In the motets, for example, he did not hesitate to use the most dramatic means available. In his *Cum essem parvulus* (When I was little; NAWM 33), we hear just such a dramatic rendering: the music of the soprano and alto evokes a childlike quality, while the chorus represents a grown man. At times, Lasso employed a lyricism that is certainly as "romantic" as any in music's history. In comparison to Palestrina, he would be placed somewhat to the right on the classical–romantic continuum. Lasso's style is perhaps best summarized with these words by Donald Grout: "One cannot properly speak of a 'Lasso style'; the man is too versatile for that. Netherlands counterpoint, Italian harmony, Venetian opulence, French vivacity, German gravity, all are to be found in his work."

Suggested Listening

Motet: *Cum essem parvulus* (NAWM 33)

Baroque

Claudio Monteverdi (1567–1643, Italian)

One of the most significant aspects of Claudio Monteverdi's musical art was its fusion to drama. Born in the fading years of the Renaissance, his career paralleled the shift of musical culture to the Baroque, and the development of the new dramatic genre, opera.

Even in Monteverdi's madrigals—an essentially Renaissance genre—there are hints of operatic practice. Melodies and rhythms are closely related to speech and there are clear correspondences with dramatic action. As an example, consider the madrigal *Cruda Amarilli* (NAWM 64), as much a tiny drama as a musical piece. Perhaps the most obvious result of the shift toward the Baroque heard in this piece is the subdued role of polyphony. While the work has a polyphonic texture made of four voices, Monteverdi has crafted the piece so that the dramatic utterance of text and emotion is "up front." In *Ohimè dov'è il mio ben* (NAWM 65), we hear the early Baroque musical language intact. Though called a madrigal, this is actually a duet with accompaniment, for there are two voices accompanied by a continuo background. Compared with the traditional Renaissance style, there is far more dissonance here, heard right from the opening measures. This piece is a beautiful example of that "warm" Italian lyricism rooted in humanistic concern for the text and, even deeper, the expressive melodic traditions of the Mediterranean region. Radiant melodies like these were to influence composers for the next three hundred years, Mozart being a prime example.

Monteverdi is especially known for his operas, considered the first real masterpieces of the genre. The most famous are *Orfeo* and *The Coronation of Poppea* (excerpted in NAWM 70). An interesting aspect of this excerpt is the use of the harpsichord and lute in alternation to supply the chordal background to the *recitative*. Like the Florentine Camerata, Monteverdi espoused a return to the classical ideals of Greek music (see page 173). From this starting point, he sought a style closely connected to words, life rhythms, and emotions. Taking the long-range view of musical culture, we may understand this aspect of his language as simply the regional expression of something more universal: the ever-present capacity to bond music to life, and the potential for melody to be derived from speech patterns and inflections. (See also discussion of Mussorgsky, pages 312–15 and Joni Mitchell, page 431.)

Madrigal: *Cruda Amarillo* (NAWM 64)
Continuo Madrigal: *Ohimè dov'è il mio ben* (NAWM 65)
L'Incoronazione di Poppea (excerpt, NAWM 70)
Orfeo (DGG-ARC 2710015)

Heinrich Schütz (1585–1672, German)

The most important figure in German music before Bach was Heinrich Schütz. Born in the closing years of the Renaissance, he is one of the masters of the early Baroque period. Schütz learned his craft in Italy at the hands of Giovanni Gabrieli, the great Venetian composer especially known for his antiphonal choral pieces (see page 168). Schütz's living musical language was a blend of the German and Italian traditions. Throughout his life, he continued to be affected by the latest musical developments from Italy. His style may be broadly described as combining German "gravity" (evidenced, partly, in textures which often involved polyphonic complexity) and Italian "sweetness" (as in flowing, expressive melodies and motives closely related to the text). The influence of Italian music upon Schütz can be heard by comparing Alessandro Grandi's *O quam tu pulchra es* (O how fair you are, my love; NAWM 82) with the Schütz setting of the same text (NAWM 84). The stylistic connections and differences between these works illustrate the kind of dynamic interplay that is basic to a musical culture.

Magnificat—Rilling, Spandauer Kantorei (Turn-about 34099)
Cantiones sacrae (various recordings)
Symphoniae sacrae—Rilling (Nonesuch 71160, 71196)
O quam tu pulchra es (NAWM 84)

Jean-Baptiste Lully (1632–87, French)

Son of an Italian miller, Lully was brought to France at the age of twelve as a servant. Talented and ambitious, he soon became an accomplished guitarist, violinist, harpsichordist, dancer, and mime. At age twenty, he danced in the same ballet as the fourteen-year-old King Louis XIV and shortly thereafter was named official composer for the royal ballets. In the years that followed, Lully established himself as the most important musical personage in France, through both his talents and shrewd dealings. He forged a successful French operatic style—the *tragédie lyrique* (tragedy in music)—by carefully blending Italian practices with the rhythms and inflections of the French language, another example of how a region evolved its own version of the universal operatic impulse.

An important genre associated with Lully—one that was to become a Baroque staple—was the *French overture*. It is characterized by a slow, serious opening of stately rhythms derived from court ceremony, followed by a faster section built on fugal imitation; finally, the opening returns to balance the form (for example, the Overture to *Armide*, NAWM 73a). The French overture was used not only to open operas, but also as the first movement of various types of instrumental works (the suite, for example). An important source of its rhythmic style was the aristocratic body-image of the French court. That it assumed a life of its own as a musical practice divorced from its original setting speaks to the process of transformation so typical in music's history. By the time Bach wrote French overtures, for example in his *Suite for Flute and Orchestra*, the genre had far distanced itself from its original social setting.

Armide (excerpts, NAWM 73)

Arcangelo Corelli (1653–1713, Italian)

At the center of Corelli's musical world was the violin. It was in Italy during the Baroque that the great tradition of string playing was born. Corelli was among the first to devote himself exclusively to instrumental genres. This is not to say that song played no role in his musical language. As we have discussed before, the transfer of the song impulse to instrumental idioms has been one of the basic mechanisms of musical culture. Corelli transformed that "warm" Italian song tradition from the human voice to the violin, widely considered the instrument that most closely parallels the voice in expressive potential.

If the song impulse is to be mentioned as an important element in Corelli's music, then we must also mention its companion, the dance. The presence of the dance impulse is quite evident in Corelli's trio sonatas, for example his Opus 3, No. 2 in D major (NAWM 91). The name of this genre is misleading, since a trio sonata involves four players: two treble instruments plus the two that make up the continuo.

Corelli also composed some *concerti grossi.* Although his total output was relatively small, his music was quite influential. He was among the first composers to use the sequence (see page 49) as a basic building block in his musical language. This device became a characteristic element in the mature Baroque style of such composers as Vivaldi, Telemann, Handel, and Bach.

Suggested Listening

Trio Sonata, Opus 3, No. 2 (NAWM 91)
Concerti Grossi—Virtuosi di Roma (Angel S-36130); Goberman, Vienna Sinfonia (Odyssey 32360002)

Georg Philipp Telemann (1681–1767, German)
During Telemann's lifetime, his popularity far exceeded that of his contemporary, J. S. Bach. When the position of organist in Leipzig became vacant, it was first offered to Telemann, and only when he refused did it go to the less famous Bach. The reason for Telemann's success was simple enough: While Bach was something of a reactionary who looked back to the great polyphonic traditions of the past, Telemann was more "in fashion." Composing in a popular, straightforward style, Telemann wrote: "To be beneficial one must be readily understood by all, consequently, the first law is to be simple, easy, lucid."

Telemann's art rests on his considerable gift as a melodist. While he wrote many "serious" pieces (motets, cantatas, and Passions), it is certainly for his lighter instrumental music that he is best known. There is no better example of Telemann's genius than his *Water Music*, a sort of extended dance suite with programmatic titles. Designed to delight and amuse, this kind of melodic writing prompted Leopold Mozart to include the music of Telemann in his son's lessons. Telemann, who died only a few years after young Wolfgang's birth, was a very prolific composer, who left hundreds of works in many genres.

Suggested Listening

Water Music—Collegium Musicum of Paris, Roland Douatte, director (Nonesuch H-71109)

Classical

Franz Joseph Haydn (1732–1809, Austrian)
One of the most important and influential composers of the eighteenth century, Franz Joseph Haydn lived through the Classical era from its formative years to its culmination. Haydn's role in the evolution of its musical language was a central one: in his many works, especially the symphonies and string quartets, he helped establish the musical foundation for composers like Mozart and Beethoven. Although the simplistic title of "Father of the Symphony" so often applied to him is far from true, Haydn's contributions to this genre must not be underestimated.

Born to a peasant family, Haydn became one of the most successful composers of his time. Despite his renown, he spent most of his life as a glorified servant in the employ of the aristocracy. Although he was a proud craftsman who knew his own worth, it was not in his nature to question his position in society. In his own words: "I have had converse with emperors, kings, and great princes, and have heard many flattering remarks from them, but I do not wish to live on familiar footing with such persons, and I prefer people of my own class." By all reports, his overriding concern was for one pursuit: composing. Basically self-taught, he patiently explored and refined his skills. Haydn was content with his situation, as evidenced by his description of the long time he served in the court of the Esterházys, a powerful Hungarian family, and of the development of his living language: "My prince was pleased with all my work, I was commended, and as conductor of an orchestra, I could make experiments, observe what strengthened and what weakened an effect and thereupon improve, substitute, omit, and try new things; I was cut off from the world, there was no one around to mislead and harass me, and so I was forced to become an original."

That originality has often been overlooked. Haydn's innovations have, to some extent, been obscured by comparisons with the generation that followed him, especially Beethoven. But in truth, he was one of the first to fashion the symphonic language that was to be so useful to Beethoven, who was, for a short time, his student. For example, in Haydn's later symphonies, the finale takes on its role as the dramatic climax to the long-range sonata-symphony form, a basic plan that was to become essential to most later symphonists.

Haydn's music is best understood from a pre-Beethoven stance. In this context, many of his works may be perceived as strikingly advanced.

Haydn's output was tremendous, reflecting both his long life and constant interest in musical exploration. Since he was born at the end of the Baroque period and survived to see the beginnings of nineteenth-century Romanticism, his works reflect a remarkable continuity of musical evolution, although their basic orientation is always eighteenth-century Classicism.

He composed over a hundred symphonies, which provide a marvelous opportunity to listen at various levels of awareness: 1) Haydn's personal development; 2) the evolution of musical language and practice from the early to the late Classical style; 3) the evolution of the symphony genre; and 4) the many ways a creative genius handles a basic model.

Suggested Listening

Symphony No. 7 (first and second movements, NAWM 111)
Symphony No. 77 (last movement, NAWM 112)
Other symphonies, string quartets, and piano sonatas
Concerto in C for Cello—Du Prés, Barenboim (Angel S-36439)
Oratorios: *The Creation*—Bernstein, New York Philharmonic (Col. M25-773); *The Seasons*—Karajan, Berlin Philharmonic (Ang. S-3792)
Mass: *The Lord Nelson*—Bernstein, N.Y. Phil. (Col. M-35100)

Romantic

Franz Schubert (1797–1828, Austrian)
Schubert's life was the stuff of which romantic legends are made. He lived out his short years in poverty, fighting illness, and without wide recognition of his genius. He never even heard performances of some of his most important works, which were "discovered" years after his death. Schubert's days were totally dedicated to music: "I have come into the world for no purpose but to compose." And compose he did. Schubert was quite a spontaneous creator. He would have had to be, in order to complete his enormous output in only thirty-one years of life: nine symphonies, 22 piano sonatas, many chamber works, numerous short piano pieces, several operas, and over 600 lieder (see pages 290–92).

Schubert's musical style unites qualities of both the Classical and Romantic eras. There is no better illustration of this than the famous *"Unfinished"* Symphony (No. 8), a work of just two movements. (Schubert began a scherzo, but never completed it. It is not known whether he ever conceived of a finale.) The basic outlines of these two movements fit neatly into the sonata-symphony practice of the late Classical era; yet the sometimes dark and turbulent mood of the work suggests to many listeners that romantic quality of "unleashed emotion." The *"Unfinished" Symphony* was never performed during Schubert's lifetime; its first hearing was in Vienna some thirty-seven years after his death.

Suggested Listening

Lied: *Kennst du das Land* (NAWM 129)
Symphony No. 8 ("Unfinished")—Walter, Columbia Symphony (Odyssey 4-30314)
Symphony No. 9 ("The Great")—Walter, Columbia Symphony (Odyssey 4-34620)
Various trios, quartets, quintets, lieder, and piano works

Robert Schumann (1810–56, German)
As a youth, Robert Schumann had two passions—music and literature. He was born to a well-to-do family, the son of a successful publisher and bookseller. Given his intimate involvement with the literary world, it is no wonder that many of Schumann's compositions were deeply influenced by literary associations. In this respect, he fulfilled the nineteenth-century romantic quest for the union of musical sound with the written word.

In his early years, Schumann had difficulty choosing between his two interests. At his mother's request, he even studied law for a time. But Robert was not cut out for such a hard-nosed vocation; high-strung, socially ill-at-ease, prone to weeping, his was the typical nineteenth-century romantic personality. A concert by the legendary violinist Paganini (see page 479) helped him make up his mind. At age twenty, Schumann decided to become a piano virtuoso. He began to study with Friedrich Wieck, and lived at his teacher's home. He fell in love with Wieck's daughter, the young prodigy Clara; and after a terribly troubled period brought about by the elder Wieck's vehement objections, the couple were married. Clara became Robert's greatest supporter, not only playing his music in concerts, but also advising him on artistic matters. She was a strong and determined individual. In addition to having seven children, she had a successful career as a touring concert artist. Utterly devoted to her husband and his music, it was Clara who held their lives together in the tragic years that would follow.

Schumann suffered from a variety of mental and physical disorders which finally led to madness and death at the age of forty-six. For many years, it was believed that insanity ran in his family, but recent scholarship strongly suggests that a case of syphilis, contracted as a young man, was the cause of his many maladies, mental deterioration, and death. In fact, it was probably mercury poisoning (mercury was the standard treatment for venereal disease in those days) that caused permanent loss of finger control in one hand while Schumann was still a student. He was forced to abandon any hope of a piano career and turned to composition and musical criticism instead. In the last fifteen years of his life, the symptoms of the disease gradually worsened, causing hallucinations, loss of speech, and insanity. After an attempted suicide, he was confined to an asylum, where he died a few years later. That he managed, in this short and troubled life, to compose so many masterpieces is a testament to his genius.

Schumann's musical universe was centered at the piano. All his works, even those for orchestra, reflect an essentialy keyboard-oriented musical language. Although his symphonies and piano concerto are widely played, it is in the solo piano music and lieder that Schumann's genius is displayed to the fullest.

His melodies, even those in the piano works, are closely related to song, and his lieder are regarded as a continuation of the Schubert tradition. In addition to his song-based lyricism, Schumann employed a private musical language based in literary and personal allusions. He delighted in these hidden meanings, and though most of this secret layer of meaning remains a mystery, its autobiographical nature gives much of Schumann's music an intense, intimate feeling. In this respect, he is among the most romantic of composers, his music and personal experience being totally inseparable.

Suggested Listening

Lied: *Kennst du das Land* (NAWM 130)
Concerto for Piano and Orchestra—Serkin, Ormandy, Philadelphia Orch. (Col. MS-6688)

Various works for solo piano
Symphony No. 1 ("Spring")—Mehta, Vienna Phil. (London 7039)

Franz Liszt (1811–86, Hungarian)

One of the major figures of nineteenth-century romanticism, Liszt was a radical innovator both as a pianist and as a composer. Born in Hungary, he began his career as a performing virtuoso when he was only eleven. Among the early influences on his art were Berlioz, Chopin, and Paganini.

Berlioz's music provided a model of spectacular Romantic creation, dazzling in scope and effect. Liszt imitated Berlioz's orchestral effects on the piano, a feat which attested both to his pianistic skill and artistic daring. With typical showmanship, he would follow an orchestral performance of Berlioz's *Fantastic Symphony* with his piano version of the *March to the Scaffold* (see page 262) and, according to an account of the time, outdo the orchestra in pure energy. Like Berlioz, Liszt was also preoccupied with program music, and most of his compositions involve extramusical association.

In his approach to the keyboard, Liszt was indebted to Chopin (see page 293). This was true not only in matters of virtuosity, but also in pianistic lyricism and harmonic chromaticism. Throughout his long career, Liszt continued to develop these qualities in often striking and radical ways. Unlike Chopin, who had a subdued streak of classicism in his makeup, Liszt's romanticism was always at full-tilt. No sense of restraint ever held him back, either in music or in life; he always opted for the daring, whether it be a scandalous love affair with a countess, a startling and well-publicized return to religion, or an unexpected harmonic modulation. Chopin's music can sometimes sound tame next to Liszt's most adventurous musical wanderings. Had Chopin lived longer, the musical dialogue between the two men would undoubtedly have been fascinating. As it stands, Chopin and Liszt remain the most important contributors to the Romantic school of pianistic virtuosity. Most great pianists of today still "prove themselves" in the flying scale passages, pounding chords, and singing melodies of these two composers.

Liszt, like many other composers of the Romantic century, was influenced by the legendary Italian violinist Niccolò Paganini (1782–1840). Paganini was an extraordinary virtuoso and showman. Listening to his almost unbelievable feats on the violin, some of his audiences suspected that he was the devil in disguise. (The image of satan disguised as a musician with extraordinary powers has emerged time and again in various cultures. See "Dance of Death," page 511.) It was typical of Liszt's personality that he took up this satanic image in his famous *Mephisto Waltz* for piano solo. At an even deeper level, it was the showmanship of Paganini that most affected Liszt's outlook. If we look to our own time for a performing personality similar to Liszt, the obvious choice would be a flamboyant rock showman like Jimi Hendrix or Mick Jagger. Although Liszt was a thoughtful composer, a dramatic flair for the outrageous was central to his artistic makeup. He was, by the way, the first person to give a solo recital as we know it today. He would stride grandly to the piano, hair hanging down to his shoulders, decked out in decorations and chains, slowly remove his gloves and throw them to the floor. Imagine a pianist today performing Liszt's works in a manner like that! Yet, a really good performance of a Liszt work often evokes a sense of daring and emotional abandonment.

Suggested Listening

Concerto No. 1 for Piano and Orchestra—Watts, Bernstein, N.Y. Phil. (Col. MS-69555)
Various works for piano solo
Symphonic Poem No. 3, Les Preludes—Karajan, Berlin Phil. (DGG 139037)

Peter Ilyich Tchaikovsky (1840–93, Russian)
Peter Ilyich Tchaikovsky, one of the most popular later Romantics, was born in Russia to a middle-class family. He began taking piano lessons at the age of seven and, like Mozart, was keenly sensitive to musical sound. Unlike Mozart, however, his early musical training was quite sketchy.

Highly sensitive and emotionally unstable, Peter Ilyich did not last long as a civil servant, the career for which he had been trained. At the age of twenty-three he entered the Conservatory of St. Petersburg and completed his musical studies in only three years, after which he began a new career as a teacher at the Moscow Conservatory. Tchaikovsky was a troubled personality—at the heart of his instability was his inability to cope with his homosexuality, something one did not openly acknowledge in nineteenth-century Russia.

He married a young woman musician, in a desperate effort to achieve respectability, but the disastrous union lasted only nine weeks. On the brink of an emotional breakdown, and typical of the way Tchaikovsky handled stress, he simply ran away from the marriage.

In that same year (he was thirty-seven) Peter Ilyich embarked on a different type relationship with a woman, more suited to his character. Nadejda von Meck was a wealthy widow who loved music and offered to support Tchaikovsky so that he might devote all his energies to composing. There was one requirement—and a perfect one from the composer's point of view—they were never to meet. And, except for embarrassed exchanges of glances at a few concerts, they never did. Their extensive correspondence has provided us with invaluable insights into Tchaikovsky's musical personality. The "arrangement" lasted fourteen years, at which point Nadejda von Meck abruptly ended it. Rejected without explanation, Peter Ilyich was deeply shaken. At odds with the world, sensitive and frightened, tormented by his sexuality and filled with self-doubt, Tchaikovsky's sad, neurotic life came to a dismal close. He died at fifty-three by drinking contaminated water during a cholera epidemic.

Although Tchaikovsky's music is considered to be deeply Russian in character, he is not a nationalist composer in the same sense as Mussorgsky. As discussed on page 313, nineteenth-century Russian society was divided into two camps: those who wished to imitate Western ways and those who sought an isolated and independent path for Russian art. Mussorgsky belonged to the latter group, but Tchaikovsky was part of the clique that accepted the "academic" genres and traditions of Western Europe. It is not surprising then, that among his important compositions are six symphonies and four concertos (three for piano and one for violin). His symphonic masterpiece is the *Pathétique Symphony* (No. 6). Tchaikovsky never revealed the specific feelings or ideas behind this programmatic work. Intense and tragic in mood, it embodies the essence of Tchaikovsky's art—an unleashed emotionalism, expressed through lyrical melody, supported by his special gift for lush, "sentimental" harmonies and brilliant orchestrations. Because this symphony, especially the last movement, has provided the inspiration for many Hollywood movie scores, many listeners will find the style familiar. Tchaikovsky's music is supercharged with sentimentality and pathos, and it takes its emotional toll of the audience. Herein lies both the magic and "problem" of Tchaikovsky's art: this is music that demands emotional response at the most basic level. For some, this "emotional bath" is deeply rewarding; for others it can be embarrassing.

Suggested Listening

Symphony No. 4 and *No. 6 (Pathétique)*
Ballets: *Swan Lake, The Nutcracker, Sleeping Beauty*
Overture-fantasy: *Romeo and Juliet*
All are on Ormandy (Col. M7X-30830)

Modern

Béla Bartók (1881–1945, Hungarian)
In terms of both audience popularity and critical acclaim, Bartók is one of the most successful composers of the twentieth century. His art combines several strands of the musical culture—among them, Hungarian folk music and the nineteenth-century sonata-symphony ideal. Bartók was born in Hungary, and his nationalist roots go deep. He began his piano studies at the age of five, his early years marked not only by thorough study of the European notated tradition, but by exposure to the varied folk traditions of his native land. A highly accomplished pianist, Bartók's music for that instrument is especially individual, notable for its pounding dissonances and complex rhythms.

Bartók sought to continue, in modern terms, the principles inherent in Beethoven's thematic logic and resulting long-range forms. From Bach, Bartók absorbed the polyphonic ideal. The fugue from his *Music for String Instruments, Percussion, and Celesta* is one of the great examples of this genre. Bartók was also influenced by Debussy's harmonic practices. Although he did not actually adopt the French composer's harmonic style, he often used chords in a similar way—as blocks of pure sound chosen for their individual impact rather than as links in a chain leading towards a goal. Although Bartók's music seems very dissonant, it may be best described in terms of *expanded tonality*. Bartók clung closely to the genres and impulses of the nineteenth century, but found

new ways and new styles (the use of Hungarian folk idioms, for example) to implement that basic tradition. There was quite a "battle" between Schoenberg and Bartók over which course was more valid. In the long run, time has proven that both men found legitimate living languages, once again confirming that the "quest for legitimacy" is too old-fashioned an idea for the twentieth century (see page 308).

Suggested Listening

String Quartet No. 4 (complete; the second movement is on the record set 21)—Juilliard Quartet (Col. D3S-717)
Piano Concerto No. 2—Richter, Maazel, Paris Orch. (Ang. 536801)
Concerto for Orchestra—Szell, Cleveland Orch. (Col. MS 6815)
Music for String Instruments, Percussion and Celesta—Bernstein, N.Y. Phil. (Col. MS 6956)
Various works for solo piano

Sergei Prokofiev (1891–1953, Russian)
By the time he was six, Prokofiev was already an accomplished pianist. Within three years, he was composing an opera. Admitted to the St. Petersburg Conservatory at age thirteen, he soon became the "bad boy" at school, much in the way Debussy had at the Paris Conservatory. At a time when Romantic music still held sway, Prokofiev's percussive, dissonant piano music gave rise to his denunciation as an "extreme leftist." But this was a reaction to his "outward" style. Actually, beneath the surface of his modern harmonic language lie carefully planned structures that often reveal a witty, intelligent transformation of nineteenth-century practice and genres. Time has shown Prokofiev's music to be a sturdy, basically conservative contribution to the modern literature. Among his most important works are sonatas, concertos, and symphonies. His harmonic language, though often dissonant, is tonal, and, like Bartók's, may be described in terms of *expanded tonality*.

Perhaps his most popular work is the *Classical Symphony*, a delightful modern transformation of the late-eighteenth-century classical aesthetic. Said the composer, "It seemed to me that if Haydn had lived in this century, he would have retained his own style of writing while absorbing certain things from newer music. I wanted to write the kind of symphony that would have such a style." An interesting listening comparison, then, is Prokofiev's *Classical Symphony* with one of Haydn's, its historic and aesthetic "parent." Such a comparison reveals not only the continuing validity of the classical aesthetic, but also the connections that shape a musical culture.

Suggested Listening

Symphony No. 5—Bernstein, N.Y. Phil. (Col. MS-7005)

Sonata for Flute and Piano, Op. 94-Rampal, Veyron-Lacroix (Odyssey 4-33905)

Concerto No. 3 in C for Piano, Op. 26—Graffman, Szell (Col. MS 6925)

Peter and the Wolf—Bernstein (Col. MS 7528)

Piano Sonata No. 3—Graffman, Szell (Col. MS 6925)

Piano Sonata No. 7—Richter (Turn. 34359)

Dmitry Shostakovich (1906–75, Russian)

Shostakovich entered the Petrograd Conservatory at the early age of nine. Equally gifted as a composer and pianist, he wrote his *First Symphony* while still a student and gained immediate renown. Nationalism was an important influence in Shostakovich's music and life. Despite many disagreements with Soviet authorities who sought to inhibit his musical creativity by public criticism (see also Ligeti, page 350), Shostakovich found a musical path that satisfied both his artistic vision and criteria established by the government. Combining romantic lyricism, expanded tonality, and his own brand of dissonance, Shostakovich's idiom has been widely imitated, a mark of its success with audiences.

While Shostakovich composed in many genres, it is certainly for his symphonies that he will be best remembered. The *Fifth Symphony* (1937) is one of the relatively few acknowledged twentieth-century masterpieces of the genre. The basic outlines and impulses of this work are quite traditional, but the materials are handled in a new and fresh way. It is a sweeping and lyrical work. The first movement, in a long sonata form, seems rooted in dramatic conflict. Very tense, tragic material vies with the heroic and lyrical in a manner that never seems resolved. As with Beethoven's *Fifth*, the willing listener is left in a state of expectation, even nervousness at the end of the movement. The second movement is a scherzo and trio.

Its playful nature provides a sense of comic relief to the darker character of the first movement. The delightful trio, with its solo violin part, seems half Viennese, half Russian. This is followed by an intense, impassioned slow movement. Here Shostakovich continues the great nineteenth-century romantic tradition of a song-inspired movement which seems to bare the composer's soul. The concluding movement resolves the conflict of the symphony. Heroic in the Beethovenian sense, it brings the work to a triumphant close. The *Fifth Symphony* is certainly modern, but its roots in the Romantic symphonic tradition are unmistakable. Deeply Russian, and composed at a time when most composers had turned away from such emotion-laden styles, it remains a unique, twentieth-century echo of nineteenth-century symphonic grandeur.

Suggested Listening

Symphony No. 1—Bernstein, N.Y. Phil. (Col. M31307)

Symphony No. 5—Bernstein, N.Y. Phil. (Col. MS6115)

Symphony No. 7 ("Leningrad")—Bernstein, N.Y. Phil. (Col. M2S722)

Charles Ives (1874–1954, American)

If ever there was a musical style that could not be fully grasped outside of its cultural context, it is the musical language of Charles Ives. Born in Danbury, Connecticut, Ives was greatly influenced by his father, a bandmaster during the Civil War, who encouraged his son to experiment with music in highly original ways. The young Ives engaged in such activities as playing melodies in two keys at once, composing with the whole-tone scale, and imitating the effects of bells. Experimentation was to become a basic feature of Ives's music, alongside a variety of popular traditions such as hymns, band music, and dance tunes.

Throughout this book we have seen how consistently, though flexibly, music is tied to various cultural criteria which interact with the personality and beliefs of the composer. In the case of Ives, this is especially relevant. In the America of Ives's youth, a deep split existed between "serious" music from Europe and the "home-grown" traditions of American popular music. The prevailing stereotype labeled any man connected with European music as a "sissy," and it was something of a disgrace for an American male in the nineteenth century to be involved with such activity. Ives wrote: "As a boy (I was) partially ashamed of it— an entirely wrong attitude, but it was strong— most boys in American country towns, I think, felt the same. When other boys . . . were out driving grocery carts, or doing chores, or playing ball, I felt all wrong to stay in and play piano. . . . Hasn't music always been too much an emasculated art?" Ives rejected European music as a living language partly because he considered it "unmanly." Typical of his attitude was a comment about Debussy, who Ives felt could have composed better had he "hoed corn or sold newspapers for a living, for in this way he might have gained a deeper vitality and a truer theme to sing at night and of a Sunday." Ives set out to create music that was totally without European conventions— music that would express what he felt were the moral and spiritual values of America. In order to compose freely without having to conform to the dictates of others, he became a successful insurance salesman, and composed at night and on weekends. He was particularly fascinated with a group of American writers, including Emerson and Thoreau, associated with the town of Concord, Massachusetts, and he wrote several essays about them and their work. Ives further celebrated these writers in what became one of the most famous pieces of American twentieth-century music—the *Concord Sonata*.

Ives did not believe that style should be an issue in music. He thought of music as having two aspects: the more important one was "reality or substance;" the less important was "form or manner" (what might be called *style*). In an Ives piece, we hear combinations of musical events that defy simple description. The outward language is often very dissonant, the rhythms complex. Completely on his own, Ives created an innovative modern musical idiom, well in advance of such European composers as Schoenberg or Stravinsky. Woven into this modern, dissonant, multirhythmic language, we often hear American hymn and dance tunes, meant to impart programmatic ideas and associations. Ives considered his literary efforts as important as his music, and he often wrote the texts to his songs. For him, there was no distinction between music, ideas, prose, life.

Ives presents an interesting opportunity to explore the term *romantic* a bit further. At first glance, *Ives is clearly not a nineteenth-century*

romantic; in fact, that was the very musical tradition he rejected. But when we consider his personality and art in more universal terms, a profoundly *romantic aesthetic* emerges. Consider these words that Ives wrote about Emerson, words that might well be applied to Ives himself:

> Though a great poet and prophet, he is greater, possibly, as an invader of the unknown— America's deepest explorer of the spiritual immensities—a seer painting his discoveries in masses and with any color that may lie at hand —cosmic, religious, human, even sensuous; a recorder freely describing the inevitable struggle in the soul's uprise . . ."

These words appear with the opening music of the *Concord Sonata*. Like Berlioz with his *Fantastic Symphony* (see page 260), Ives sought a unified experience of sound, idea, and word. At the short-range level of style, we may call Berlioz a romantic and Ives a modern. At the deeper, more universal level, both may be sensed as having a *romantic aesthetic* expressed in a different outward manner.

Unfortunately, Ives's reputation has rested primarily on stylistic innovations—his *least* important concern. The many-faceted, multilayered collage that was Ives's musical world was meant to be just that—a total world of experience, a fusion of many threads into a cosmic interplay, expressed from an especially American stance. If you are interested in Ives, I strongly suggest you read his writings, as well as some books about his life.*

Suggested Listening

In Flanders Field (NAWM 155)
Central Park in the Dark ⎤ —Bernstein, New York
Unanswered Question ⎦ Phil. (Col. MS-6843)
Symphony No. 4—Ozawa, Boston Symphony (DG 2530784)
Three Places in New England—Ormandy, Philadelphia Orch. (Col. MS-7105)
Sonata No. 2 ("Concord")—Kirkpatrick (Col. MS-7192)

*I especially recommend *Charles Ives and His America* by F. Rossiter (New York, 1975) and *Essays Before a Sonata, The Majority, and Other Writings*, Howard Boatwright, ed. (New York, 1970).

Appendix II · Main Genres Chart

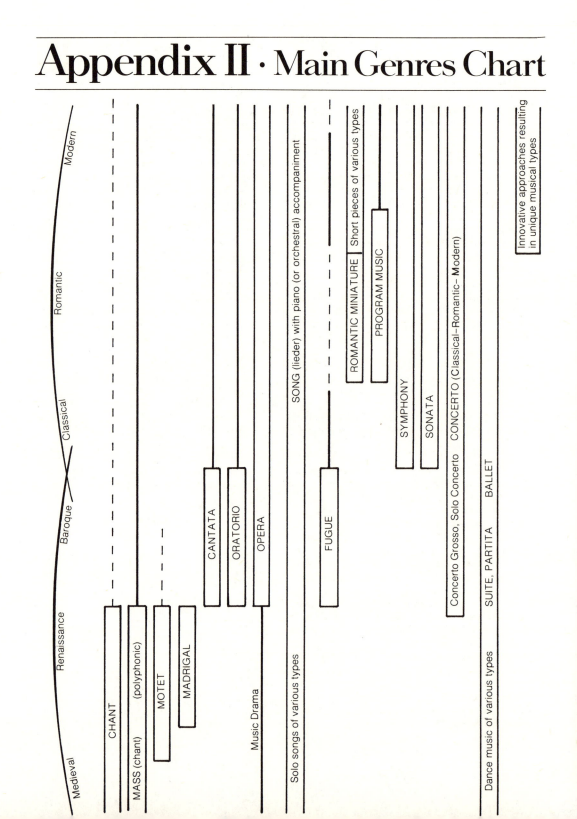

Appendix III

Dynamic and Tempo Markings

Here are some of the Italian words, abbreviations, and symbols commonly used in music to indicate levels of sound and speed to be used within a piece.

piano (p)—soft
mezzo piano (mp)—moderately soft
pianissimo (pp)—very soft
forte (f)—loud
mezzo forte (mf)—moderately loud
fortissimo (ff)—very loud
crescendo (cresc. or ————)—gradually louder
decrescendo or *diminuendo (decresc. dim.* or ————)—gradually softer
sforzando (sf)—sudden accent

grave—slow, solemn
largo—very slow
adagio—slow
lento—slow
andante—toward the slow side, a "walking" pace
andantino—slightly faster than *andante*
moderato—moderately
allegretto—moderately fast
allegro—fast
vivace—fast and lively
presto—very fast
prestissimo—extremely fast
rubato—"robbing" time: taking liberties with the tempo without departing from the basic meter
animato—animated, lively
meno—less
meno mosso—slower (less movement)
più—more
più mosso—faster (more movement)
poco a poco—little by little, gradually

Appendix IV
Notation of Rhythm and
Time Signatures

Notation of Rhythm

Standard notational procedure assigns time values to notes in relationship to the quarter note (♩ or ♪), which is given the value of 1. With this relationship as a reference, other notes have the following relative values:

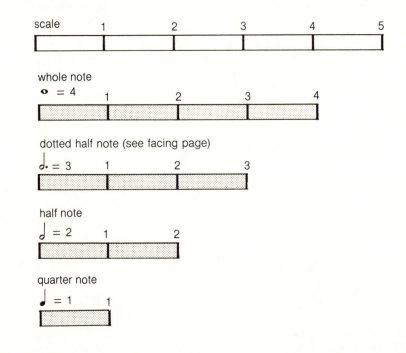

scale 1 2 3 4 5

whole note
○ = 4   1   2   3   4

dotted half note (see facing page)
♩. = 3   1   2   3

half note
♩ = 2   1   2

quarter note
♩ = 1   1

eighth note   sixteenth note

$\flat = \frac{1}{2}$ $\flat = \frac{1}{4}$ etc.

Notes shorter than quarters may be beamed together:

can be written

can be written

can be written

Ties
A tie joins two written notes together into one longer musical sound (the second note is not played).

2 + 1 = 3   4 + 1 = 5 $\frac{1}{2} + \frac{1}{8} = \frac{3}{8}$ etc.

Dots
A dot after a note increases its duration by half its value.

$ = 3$ (same as)

$ = 1\frac{1}{2}$ (same as)

$ = \frac{3}{8}$ etc.

Rests
For each note, there is an equivalent rest indicating a specific period of complete silence.

whole rest = 4   quarter rest = 1

dotted half rest = 3   eighth rest = $\frac{1}{2}$

half rest = 2   sixteenth rest = $\frac{1}{4}$

etc.

Time Signatures

Meter is indicated by *time signatures*. The upper number indicates the number of beats per measure. The lower number indicates the note which is to receive one beat.

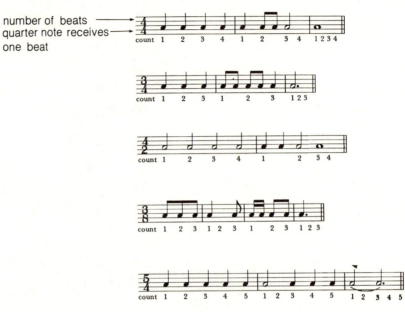

number of beats
quarter note receives one beat

Compound meters involve a "layered" rhythmic structure of faster and slower (or weaker and stronger) pulses. For example:

faster (weaker) pulses

slower (stronger) pulses

Appendix V
Accidentals

Accidentals alter pitch by raising or lowering the notes they modify.

Sharp (♯) raises the pitch a half step.

Flat (♭) lowers the pitch a half step.

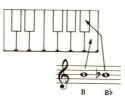

Double sharp (✖) raises the pitch a whole step.

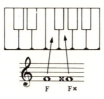

Double flat (𝄫) lowers the pitch a whole step.

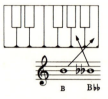

Natural (♮) cancels a sharp or flat of an earlier note.

Appendix VI
Key Signatures and Scales

Key Signatures

A key signature is a configuration of sharps or flats which identify "home base." Key signatures allow a major or minor scale to begin on any pitch. For example:

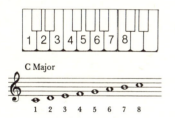

Suppose we wish to begin a major scale on the note D. In order to maintain the same relationship of whole steps and half steps that exist in the C-major scale, both the F and the C would have to be raised a half step to F# and C# . This is accomplished by writing those two sharps immediately after the clef sign. Those two sharps (F and C) are the key signature of D major.

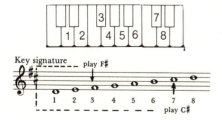

491

A key signature identifies both the major key and its relative minor, which always begins on its sixth degree (notice the use of octave equivalent):

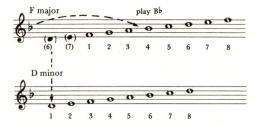

The traditional organization of key signatures is as follows:

Different Forms of Minor Scales

Minor scales may exist in any of three forms: natural, harmonic, and melodic. These reflect the common alterations found in music that conforms to the major–minor tonal system.

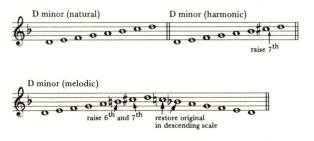

Appendix VII

Intervals and Chords

Intervals

An interval is the distance between two notes (see page 39). We identify intervals by two sets of measurements:

1. *Number of steps*: Each interval is identified by a number according to the scale-steps it contains, for example:

Interval of a   5th   1 2 3 4 5   2nd   1 2   10th   1 2 3 4 5 6 7 8 9 10   3rd   1 2 3

2. *Quality*: Intervals are further measured by *quality*, which fixes their size more precisely. For example:

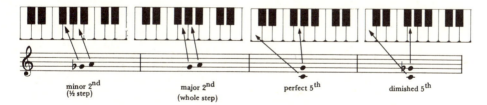

minor 2nd (½ step)   major 2nd (whole step)   perfect 5th   dimished 5th

The most common intervals, arranged according to size, are the following:

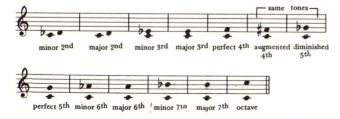

minor 2nd   major 2nd   minor 3rd   major 3rd   perfect 4th   augmented 4th   diminished 5th

perfect 5th   minor 6th   major 6th   minor 7th   major 7th   octave

Triads

The most commonly used chord in traditional Western music is the triad, a three-note group built on intervals of a third:

The individual tones of the triad are called the root, third, and fifth, names derived from the interval of the two upper tones from the lowest:

By far the most commonly used triads are the major and minor, distinguished by the difference of a half step in the third. Notice that the root note gives a triad its basic name:

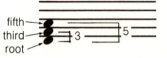

C major   C minor   D major   D minor   Eb major   Eb minor   F♯ major   F♯ minor

Seventh chords

When we add an additional third to a triad, the result is another commonly used chord formation—the seventh chord. Examples of seventh chords:

The three kinds of seventh chords most frequently used are the dominant 7th, the minor 7th, and the major 7th:

F dominant 7   F minor 7   F major 7   G dominant 7   G minor 7   G major 7
(also called
V7)

Appendix VIII

Harmonic Series

The harmonic series, also called the overtone series, reflects a universal principle of nature. As basic to sound as gravity is to motion, it involves many interrelated phenomena, among them the following:

1. A medium produces a musical tone (for example, a string or a column of air) by *vibrating in parts* (see picture on page 71).
2. Although we hear a musical tone as having one pitch, it is actually a combination of a *fundamental tone* with many *partial tones* (called partials or overtones).
3. The most prominent tone we hear—the *fundamental*—is the lowest, and is created by the longest and slowest vibrating part (for example, the full length of the string).
4. The *partials* or *overtones* are less audible and are created by shorter and faster vibrating parts. (See picture on page 71—the partials are created by the shorter lengths of string.)
5. The various parts of the vibrating medium arrange themselves naturally in proportions that can be represented by a *number series*:

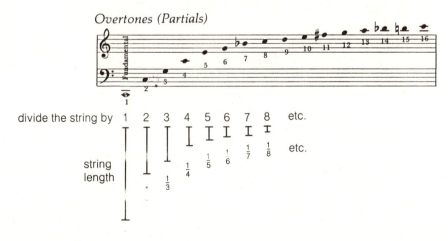

495

6. *Timbre* results from various combinations of overtones, affected by the vibrating medium and the shape and structure of the musical instrument.

The natural laws of acoustics, when experienced through such visual means as a vibrating string, function within recognizable patterns of symmetrical design. For example, the overtone series *is not* generated by *random* divisions of a string (dividing, perhaps, by 2, 3½, 6, 7¼, etc.), but by a *proportionally arranged series* (dividing by 2, 3, 4, 5, 6, 7, etc.). This discovery in ancient times was a key moment in the spiritual and intellectual history of the world. It was thought to be one of the cosmic underpinnings of the universe. The proportional divisions of the string (or sizes of bell, or lengths of pipe, etc.) are but one manifestation of the periodic, symmetrical nature of musical sound "made visible."

Appendix IX

Terms: Assorted and Problematic

CADENZA   A section in a concerto in which the soloist exhibits technical brilliance.

EXPRESSIONISM   An artistic movement during the early decades of the twentieth century, centered in Germany and Austria. Expressionist art exploits extremes of human emotion, especially those of a bizarre nature. It can be considered a continuation of nineteenth-century Romanticism in a dissonant guise. Among those influenced by expressionism were composers Arnold Schoenberg and Alban Berg and painters Wassily Kandinsky (1866–1944) and Paul Klee (1879–1940).

FUTURISM   A movement of the early twentieth century in which machine noises and industrial sounds were used as musical elements. It had a counterpart in the visual arts.

RAGTIME   An early source of jazz, which combined an Afro-American rhythmic approach to Euro-American dances and marches, usually for the keyboard.

NEOROMANTICISM   Literally, "new romanticism": Those twentieth-century styles which are a direct continuation of the nineteenth-century Romantic impulse. The term is not usually applied to atonal styles like expressionism (also a continuation of the nineteenth-century Romantic impulse).

MINIMALISM   Twentieth-century styles in which economy, brevity, and restraint are taken to an extreme. Minimalism is a reaction to the sensory clutter of the Modern era.

ULTRARATIONALISM   Twentieth-century styles which submit to a high level of control from a mathematical or other fixed plan.

ELECTRONIC MUSIC   Music created with synthesizers and usually preserved on tape.

COMPUTER MUSIC   Music created by a computer that has been programmed to compose without direct human participation.

ALEATORY MUSIC   Twentieth-century "serious" music which allows for some type of improvisation. It is also called *chance music*.

BLUEGRASS A type of "country music" associated with the rural mountains of the South. The mainstay of the bluegrass sound is the banjo and guitar. The roots of bluegrass include the melodies of the British Isles.

THIRD STREAM A recent movement to combine jazz with "serious" Euro-American traditions as well as the folk musics of the world.

GOSPEL A style of popular religious singing associated with the South.

DIXIELAND An early type of jazz associated with New Orleans.

BEBOP A jazz style created in the 1940s, characterized by complex melodies and improvisations, and sometimes dissonant harmonies. It was more innovative and complex than the earlier "swing" style. Among its initiators were Dizzy Gillespie and Charlie Parker.

SWING The "big-band sound" of the 1930s. Among the "swing" band leaders were Duke Ellington, Tommy Dorsey, and Benny Goodman.

COOL JAZZ A style which arose in the 1950s out of bebop, characterized by technical virtuosity and a timbre quality, often heard in the saxophone, that was quite "pure" (without too many overtones or vibrato). An example of this style is the music of Stan Getz.

FREE JAZZ A style that takes improvisation to extremes through abandonment of traditional melodic, harmonic, and formal elements.

Problematic Terms

There is a prevalent tendency to think of "textbook terms" as absolutes. They are not. The words we use to describe musical culture, like the culture itself, are often in a state of flux. The following terms involve some type of ambiguity in current usage, suggesting that some additional explanation would be useful.

AFRO-AMERICAN MUSIC The term used in everyday life to describe this tradition is "Black Music." Objections from various sources suggest that this is a tainted term and reflects prejudice. I honor this feeling, but add that I know many black musicians who use the words "Black Music" with a sense of pride. Obviously, most of us involved in this matter have honorable intentions. I invite the reader with another opinion to cross out what I have written and substitute his or her own choice.

TONALITY Limiting the definition of tonality to the harmonic basis of certain music in the Western notated tradition (1600–1900) impedes not only comparisons with other tonal musical traditions (Indian music, for example) but also with the "expanded" tonal sense of many twentieth-century composers. Tonality is a universal feature of many musics. The term "major–minor tonality" seems to me to be more appropriate when describing the characteristics of the Baroque, Classical, and Romantic traditions.

GENRE Throughout this book, I have used this term in a broad sense to mean "type." I have deliberately not excluded musical entities known by such names as "dance." To call a madrigal a "genre" but a gigue a "dance" seems to me more of a habit than a considered decision on how these "types" function within a musical culture. To limit genre to musical models of the Western notated tradition—symphony, Mass, quartet, etc.—inhibits comparisons between popular and serious music. Furthermore, I believe that a broader usage evokes the essential function that models play in all artistic traditions, and furthers basic analogies between music and its sister arts.

Appendix X
World Music: Suggestions for Reading and Listening

Books

Merriam, Alan P. *The Anthropology of Music.* Evanston, Ill.: Northwestern University Press, 1965.

Nettl, Bruno. *Folk and Traditional Music of the Western Continents.* Englewood Cliffs, N.J.: Prentice-Hall, 1965.

Nketia, J. H. Kwabena. *The Music of Africa.* New York: W. W. Norton, 1974.

*Reck, David. *Music of the Whole Earth.* New York: Scribner, 1977.

Sachs, Curt. *The Wellsprings of Music.* The Hague: Nijhoff, 1963.

Wilgus, D. K. *Anglo-American Folksong Scholarship since 1888.* New Brunswick, N.J.: Rutgers University Press, 1959.

Recordings

AFRICA

Music from the Heart of Burundi (Nonesuch H 72057)

Music from Saramaka (Folkways FE 4225)

Music from an Equatorial Microcosm (Folkways FE 4214)

Ewe Music of Ghana (Asch AHM 422)

AMERINDIAN *(Indians of the Americas)*

Anthology of Central and South American Indian Music (Folkways FE 4542)

Indian Music of Mexico (Folkways FE 4413)

The Flutes of the Inca Empire (Arion 91058)

BRITISH-AMERICAN BALLADS

Ballads of Scotland, Ewan MacColl (Folkways FW 8759)

The English and Scottish Popular Ballads, 3 vols. (Folkways FG 3509, FG 3510, FG 3511)

BRITISH ISLES *(general)*

The Chieftains (assorted albums)

Irish Bagpipe Tunes (Folkways FG 3551)

CHINA

Floating Petals . . . Wild Geese . . . The Moon on High: Music of the Chinese Pipa (Nonesuch H 72085)

China: Shantung Folk Music and Traditional Instrumental Pieces (Nonesuch H 72051)

INDIA

Religious Music of India (Folkways FE 4431)

Classical Music of India (Nonesuch H 72014)

The Genius of Ravi Shankar (Columbia CL 2760)

MIDEAST-MEDITERRANEAN

Folk Music of the Mediterranean (Folkways FE 4501)

Arabic Songs and Dances (Folkways FW 8763)

*This excellent book is a perfect choice for an initial introduction to this broad study.

Appendix XV · Picture Sequences

A. Mother and Child

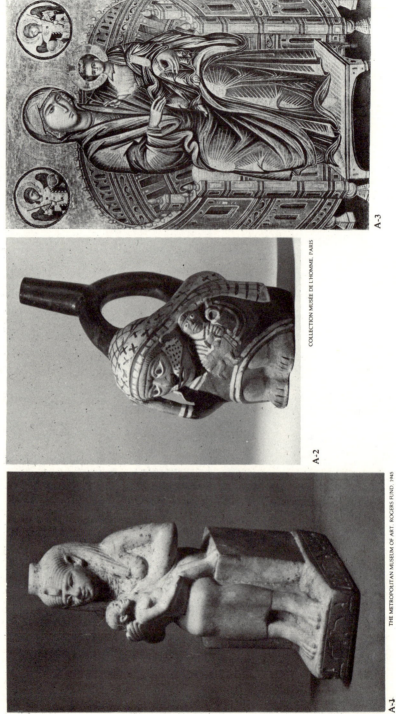

A-3

A-2

A-1

A-1. *Egyptian god Horus on the lap of his mother Isis.* Egypt, c. 600 B.C.

A-2. *Mother and child,* pottery from the Moche culture. Peru, c. 500 A.D.

A-3. *Madonna Enthroned.* Byzantine, thirteenth century.

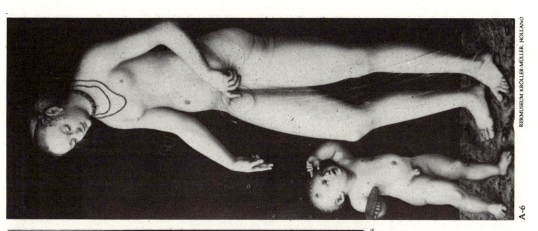

A-6

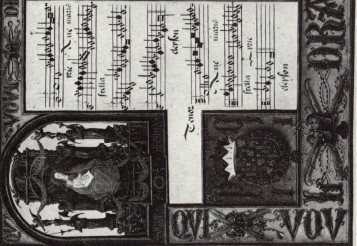

A-5

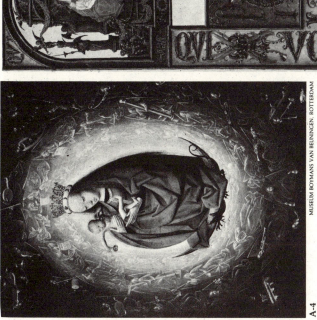

A-4

A-4. *The Glorification of the Virgin,* by Geertjen tot St. Jans. Flemish, fifteenth century. Compare with B-5 and B-7 for motifs from the Harmony of the Spheres. Also notice that the Christ child seems to be dancing and playing music. The religious message—the sound and motion of God's universe—is reflected in sacred music. This "heavenly orchestra" drowns out the forces of evil, portrayed by the squashed serpent.

A-5. Opening page to the Kyrie of the Mass *Ave Maris stella,* by Josquin des Prez.

A-6. *Venus with Amor as a Honey-Thief,* by Lucas Cranach the Elder (1472–1553).

COURTESY OF THE ALEX HILLMAN FAMILY FOUNDATION

A-9

THE METROPOLITAN MUSEUM OF ART. BEQUEST OF
SAMUEL A. LEWISOHN. 1951

IA ORANA MARIA.

A-8

UFFIZI GALLERY

A-7

502

A-7. *Eleonora of Toledo and her Son Giovanni* (1550), by Agnolo Bronzino (1503–72).

A-8. *Ia Orana Maria*, by Paul Gauguin (1848–1903). Gauguin left France to paint in Tahiti. His work may be understood as a reflection of European artists', writers', and musicians' growing fascination with the non-Western world during the nineteenth and twentieth centuries.

A-9. *Mother and Child* (1922), by Pablo Picasso (1881–1973). Like Stravinsky, the Spaniard Picasso worked in different styles during his lifetime. This painting is from his neoclassical period. Compare with Stravinsky's new classicism (page 337) and the discussion of the classical aesthetic (pages 225–27).

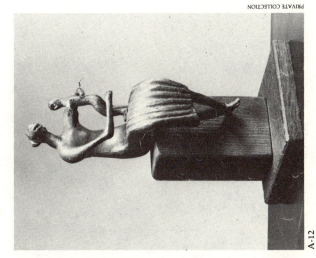

A-12

A-13

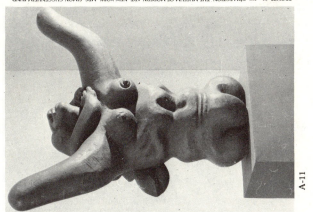

A-11

A-10

A-10. *First Steps* (1943), by Pablo Picasso. Compare with A-9. The use of various "languages" or "styles" by a single artist or composer is typical of the multistylistic modern culture.

A-11. *Mother and Child, II* (1941–45), by Jacques Lipchitz (1891–1973).

A-12. *Mother and Child with Crossed Feet* (1956), by Henry Moore (1898–).

A-13. *Mother and First Born* (1969), by Henry Guerriero (1929–).

503

B. Circle Designs

B-1. "Circle Dance of the Sky." This is a time exposure revealing the circular paths of the stars you would observe looking toward the North Star throughout the night. The turning circles in the sky became a motif in many religious belief systems.

B-2. Round dance with instrumentalist in center, sixth century B.C., Greece. The "dance in the sky" was imitated and celebrated with the round dance on earth.

B-3. Round dance of shepherd girls and the Hindu god Krishna. India, eighteenth century.

B-1

B-2

B-3

B-4

B-5

B-6

B-4. Ramayana Ritual (musical excerpt 2a). Performed in Bali, this Hindu ritual involves chant, song, dance, and drama, all part of the ancient unity.

B-5. Mystic nativity by Sandro Botticelli, 1500, Italy. In this variation of the Harmony of the Spheres, the "dance in the sky" is performed by twelve angels.

B-6. Circular canon: music by Ramos de Pareja, manuscript art work by Gherardo and Monte di Giovanni del Fora, Italy, 1482. In this variation of the Harmony of the Spheres, notated music appears in a circular pattern of cosmological significance.

505

PRIVATE COLLECTION

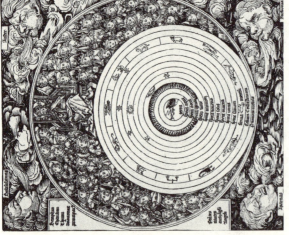

B-8

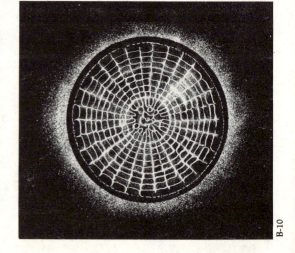

B-10

B-9

OIL ON CANVAS 8'6 1/2" x 12'9 1/2". COLLECTION,
THE MUSEUM OF MODERN ART, NEW YORK. GIFT OF
NELSON A. ROCKEFELLER IN HONOR OF ALFRED H. BARR, JR.

B-7. The Lord as ruler of the cosmic harmony. A woodcut from Schedel, *Buch der Chroniken* (1493). In this representation of the Harmony of the Spheres we see a "complete" rendering of the universe according to Medieval-Renaissance belief.

B-8. *Ring around the Rosie*, by Edward Potthast (nineteenth century). This is the first picture in this sequence without mythical significance, and suggests that the impulse to dance in a circle is innate and universal.

B-9. *Dance* (First Version 1909), by Henri Matisse (1869–1954). Among the qualities that bring this picture to life is the manner in which Matisse has captured the forward potential of dance. This is certainly a picture that has rhythm. Compare with the discussion on page 15 about the perception of forward potential in your imagination.

B-10. Sound waves produced by a vibrating steel disk make this configuration when photographed. The symmetrical patterns are a visible manifestation of the periodicity of musical sound.

C. Pyramid–Ziggurat–Tower Shape

PHOTO BY PAOLO KOCH FROM RAPHO/PHOTO RESEARCHERS, INC., NEW YORK

C-1

C-2

C-3

HIRMER VERLAG MÜNCHEN

C-1. Mount Fuji, Japan. The original inspiration for the stepped pyramids and ziggurats of the ancient world was the mountain, considered sacred throughout human culture as the point where heaven meets earth, and through which divine power flows.

C-2. Stepped pyramid of King Zoser, Egypt, 2750 B.C.

C-3. Ziggurat at Ur, 2100 B.C. Although this sacred structure is from a later period than the stepped pyramid of King Zoser, it is in this region, Mesopotamia, that the earliest ziggurats have been found.

507

C-5

C-4. Amerindian stepped pyramid, Chichen Itza, Mexico, 900 A.D.

C-5. Amerindian stepped pyramid, Palenque, Mexico.

C-6. Amerindian stepped pyramid, Tajin, Mexico. This pyramid, built by the Totonac Indians, has 365 niches in its sides, a structural correspondance with the calendar—one niche for each day of the year. There was also probably a connection between the pyramid and the musical culture of the time: the sacred number "seven" was ritually represented in the number of levels of the pyramid as well as the tubes of the panpipes.

C-4

C-6

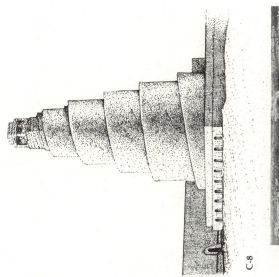

C-8

C-9

C-7

C-7. Machu Picchu, Inca City, around 1400 A.D., Peru. The terraced levels of this mountain city are a variation of the basic stepped-mountain–pyramid theme.

C-8. Great Mosque, Samarra, Iraq, 848 A.D.

C-9. Cathedral at Toulouse, France, 1100 A.D. Another sacred configuration has been added to the design of this tower: the lower part of the cathedral is in the shape of a cross.

509

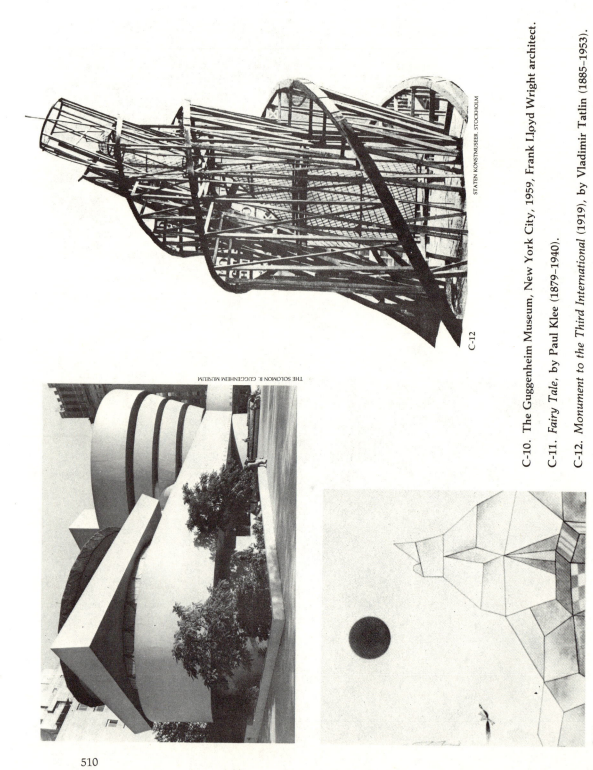

C-12

C-11

C-10. The Guggenheim Museum, New York City, 1959, Frank Lloyd Wright architect.

C-11. *Fairy Tale*, by Paul Klee (1879–1940).

C-12. *Monument to the Third International* (1919), by Vladimir Tatlin (1885–1953).

510

D. Dance of Death

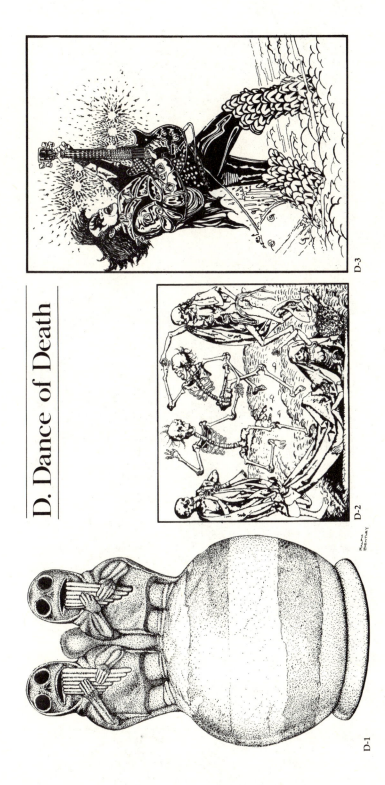

D-1

D-2

D-3

The association of death with music and dance is found throughout the world. This impulse seems rooted at a deep, mythical level of culture. In Europe, the Dance of Death is the counterpart of the Harmony of the Spheres. According to these beliefs, "good" music was the voice of God, while "bad" music was the sound of Satan and death. See also Berlioz, *Damnation of Faust* (pages 268–76.)

D-1. Skeletons playing panpipes, ancient Moche culture (200 B.C.–600 A.D.), Peru. On other pieces of Moche pottery, there are depictions of dancing skeletons playing musical instruments. The Moche traditions were eventually absorbed into the legendary Inca civilization.

D-2. The dance of death was a potent image during the Middle Ages. In time of plague there were outbreaks of frenzied mass dancing, thought to be effective in warding off the disease. (From a woodcut by Schedel, 1493.)

D-3. The contemporary rock group *Kiss* clearly draws on this universal impulse, as do other cult-type groups such as *Blue Oyster Cult*.

511

Index

Page numbers in **boldface** refer to definitions of terms.